BOOMTOWN DA

Best Wishes!

Cal Vance

Boomtown DA

Carol S. Vance

Whitecaps Media
Houston, Texas

www.whitecapsmedia.com

Boomtown DA
© 2010 Carol S. Vance
All rights reserved

ISBN-13: 978-0-9826353-1-5

Printed in the United States of America

Carol Vance may be contacted through the publisher

Let justice run down like water,
And righteousness like a mighty stream.
Amos 5:24

NOT LONG AFTER I started prosecuting, I read a book entitled *Small Town DA* by Robert Travers, a district attorney in upstate Michigan. Although my fifty-year-old paperback is falling apart, Travers' book gave me the inspiration to write *Boomtown DA*.

My most earnest desire is to tell it like it is, to give an honest account of the ongoing challenges faced by the assistant DA down in the trenches and the elected DA in a large city. Although a few names have been changed to protect the parties, each story is true and based on my personal experience. I hope the dedication and splendid work of the great staff that I was blessed to be surrounded by will shine forth through these pages.

It was all a team effort; I was more like a head coach surrounded by excellent assistant coaches and players. And it is to these men and women, as well as to Carolyn, my wonderful wife of fifty-five years who weathered the storm of public life, to whom this book is dedicated.

Carol Vance
Houston, Texas

And what does the LORD require of you?
To act justly
and to love mercy
and to walk humbly with your God.

—Micah 6:8 (NIV)—

TABLE OF CONTENTS

It is the duty of the district attorney in Harris County, Texas (Houston included), to represent the State of Texas in all serious criminal cases. That includes the misdemeanors carrying jail time which are tried in our County Criminal Courts at Law and the felonies tried in our District Courts.

It is the duty of the district attorney not just to convict but to see that justice is done.

CHAPTER ONE

Pounding the Pavement

Work is the curse of the working class.
—Anonymous

THE SUN REFLECTED OFF the blue waters of Corpus Christi Bay. I turned off Ocean Drive in the city of Corpus Christi to make one last run to the Nueces County Courthouse. The day was Friday, June 29, 1979. The previous afternoon, the jury had found Elmer Wayne Henley guilty of six murders. The verdict brought closure to one of the most horrific mass murder cases in our nation's history. Henley was the last of two men to be tried for the brutal torture and murder of twenty-seven teenage boys. This was the last case I would ever prosecute. After twenty-two years in this business I was hanging it up.

Perhaps now the parents of the twenty-seven known victims could find some closure and some peace. Six sets of those parents had driven to Corpus to testify and some of them hung around for the entire trial. "Why?" they asked. That question was never answered. Elmer Wayne was more fortunate than their sons. He got off light. Although he received six life sentences stacked on top of each other, he was spared the death penalty thanks to the recent Supreme Court case that overturned every death sentence in America. Now the death penalty would have to be reinstated one state at a time as state legislatures struggled with the issue and the new limitations by the high court. There would be no death sentences carried out for those on death row throughout the nation. Until legislatures reenacted it, the death penalty was off the table even for someone like Elmer Wayne. At least the Henley case was over, a tragic reminder of man's inhumanity to man.

The previous twenty-two years had gone by fast, eight as an assistant district attorney followed by almost fourteen more as the elected district attorney of Harris County, Texas, the home of Houston, our nation's fourth largest city. After my stop at the courthouse to thank the judge for trying this case out of Harris County, I was driving back to Houston to announce my resignation from the office I loved. Saying good-bye to staff and close friends would be difficult, but the season had come to an end. I was moving into the civil world of litigation and would also handle white collar crimes for a large firm. But no job would ever match the excitement or challenge of being the DA, particularly in Houston, often described as a boomtown and heralded as the nation's fastest growing city (the population doubled during my time in the District Attorney's office, to a county-wide total of almost 2.5 million).

I rolled up to the Nueces County Courthouse to visit with Judge Noah Kennedy, a kind and able judge, who graciously took the Henley case on a change of venue out of Harris County. Walking inside his courtroom, I saw Doug Shaver, our office's chief trial counsel. He was chatting with Lewis Dickson, Jr., as they boxed up evidence to carry back to Houston. The three of us had spent weeks together proving up the twenty-seven murders. Doug and Lewis were stuffing the odorous clothing taken from the victims' bodies into boxes and marking it for a third trial, should one be called for, heaven forbid. The case had already been tried once and reversed due to a ruling by the first judge over in San Antonio. No one wanted to ever try this case again—particularly the distraught parents who had to relive the loss of their sons. The night before, Doug, Lewis, and I had celebrated, not the guilty verdicts, but the fact the case was over once and for all.

"Lewis, that was pretty fair wine you sprung for last night."

"Should be. A '72 Mouton. Nothing is too good for the boss." Lewis said. He had also wasted a scholarly wine lecture on Doug and me the night before; Doug and I would have been just as pleased with a couple of Budweisers.

Lewis' good-natured sarcasm reminded me of his father, Judge Lewis Dickson. When I finished the University of Texas School of Law in 1958, Lewis, Sr., the judge, made a critical call on my behalf to the DA of Harris County, Dan Walton, asking him to grant me an interview. I had been out of law school for several weeks pounding the pavement trying to get on somebody's payroll. I was a twenty-four-year-old unemployed lawyer, who just passed the bar exam. Carolyn and I had two small children to feed, Lynn, age two, and Carroll, only three months. Bills were stacking up and the first note on our new house out on the plains of Westbury was coming due. Times were tough in 1958 in Houston. Oversupplies of oil in the Middle East had wrecked the local economy. Lawyers in Houston, the energy capital of the world, were also in oversupply. I desperately needed to be on someone's payroll.

While the top ten in my UT law class were wined, dined, and told how great they were, a guy like me, who struggled to make the upper half, had to pound the pavement for work. At one point I was so discouraged I considered going into private practice with my close friend, Jimmy Brill. Plan B was that we would share his grandfather's office in the ancient and rundown Houston Chronicle building. If we had just had one solid client, the idea might have floated. Jimmy built a great practice over the years to come, but in 1958 he had few clients and even fewer who bothered to pay. About the time I had thrown in the towel, Judge Dickson's call paid off. District Attorney Walton's secretary called me at home and said Mr. Walton could see me. Just last Thanksgiving, sitting at the UT-Texas A&M game with Jack Rawitscher and Jimmy Brill, Jack, an assistant DA, told me that his job was the most exciting thing he ever experienced. He was a recent hire, but even so he was going to court every day and trying cases each week. With an eye on being a trial lawyer someday, I thought that sounded great—except, Jack said, "the office was flooded with applicants."

The big day came. I put on the uniform of the day, my dark blue suit with the regulation striped tie (or, as we called them back then, a rep tie), and walked into the Harris County Courthouse at 301 San Jacinto Street for the first time. Getting off the elevator on the fifth floor I read the glass door leading into the reception room: "District Attorney Dan Walton." I sat down amidst several fellow citizens. One elderly man had his head covered in bandages. A mother in a flowered dress tried to keep two rambunctious preschoolers under control. Another young lady had a black eye and bandage on her nose. Each person was directed into a side office to meet with a distinguished elderly gentleman wearing a coat and tie. It looked like an emergency room. I wondered, What in the world?

Finally, Mr. Walton's secretary came and ushered me back to the hallowed corner office. I walked in and shook hands with a tall and very serious looking man. Mr. Walton looked holes through me as he sized me up. Then with the deepest and most resonant voice I had ever heard, he asked me to have a seat. If anyone fit Hollywood casting's profile for a district attorney, he did. I sat down and we talked. As our twenty minutes quickly came to an end, Mr. Walton told me he had many applicants and no vacancies but he would keep me in mind. As he ushered me to the door, he caught me off guard.

"One last thing, Mr. Vance. What is your ultimate aim in life? What would you like to end up doing with this new law license?"

Totally taken back but without hesitating I said, "I would like to be a judge someday."

Walking out, I asked myself, Where did that answer come from? I really had not thought that far ahead. No one in our family was a lawyer, and I had no specific ambition. I did know, though, that my dress shirt was damp. I felt I was lucky to have graduated from law school. Me someday being a judge? What a wild response. Well, so much for that interview. I was fortunate to get in the door.

Before leaving town to drive to our new home, still without a shred of grass in a new neighborhood called Westbury a million miles from town, I dropped in on Jimmy. I eyed the office which consisted of one long room, perhaps twelve feet wide and thirty feet long. The walls and floors were dark. Little light came through the single window. I told Jimmy I would think over his gracious offer. I had nowhere else to go. But if some unsuspecting client walked in with a parking ticket, I wouldn't know what to do.

I kept on pursuing employment from one blind alley to another. My father-in-law was a manager for Westinghouse Electric, and he arranged an interview at Baker and Botts with Dillon Anderson. Mr. Anderson was a man of considerable fame. He was most polite and courteous, but not in the long history of that firm had they reached down that low in the class. February was drawing to a close. I did have one promising prospect, being an assistant city attorney in Orange, Texas, on the Louisiana border. I would be paid $300 per month once my probationary period was over. This move would force us to sell our new home and leave our kids' grandparents and longtime friends. Carolyn and I had grown up in Houston. I never thought about going elsewhere.

About a week later, I was inside changing little Carroll's diaper when the phone rang. "Hello. Who is this? Oh, Georgette, Mr. Walton's secretary. Yes ma'am. I certainly *can* stop by and see Mr. Walton. I can be there in a half hour. Oh, an appointment for tomorrow morning at nine? Yes, ma'am, I will be there. Thank you. Thank you, ma'am."

Promptly at 9:00 A.M., I was ushered into the inner offices once again. I sat down in a chair facing Georgette. All of a sudden the door opened and Mr. Walton walked out with two men in dark blue suits following him. "Well, let's go up to the grand jury right now so I can get this whole matter straightened out," Mr. Walton said.

"Oh, Mr. Vance. I'm sorry. I forgot you were here. I hope you still want that job. If so, you can begin March 1. That is next week, I believe. One of our assistants just said he was leaving the office and we have a vacancy. I would like you to join our staff."

"Yes, sir, Mr. Walton. Yes, sir. I will be there. Thank you, sir. Thank you."

"Georgette, you give Mr. Vance the forms to fill out. And take him down to meet Pete Moore. You will start off in the Misdemeanor Section. Mr. Moore will be your boss. He will assign you to one of our county courts."

"Thank you again, Mr. Walton," I said as he sailed down the hall, the two men following. "Yes, sir. I'll try to do a good job." As he took off down the hall I hoped he heard me.

Georgette said, "Mr. Vance, Mr. Moore is out today. You sit down over there, fill out these forms and leave them with me. Then bright and early on March 1 at 8:00 A.M., you report to Mr. Moore. I will show you where his office is on your way out."

Other than our marriage and the arrival of our children, becoming an assistant district attorney was the biggest thing in my life. I had work and a nice salary, $400 a month. I knew this was going to be as good an adventure as any young lawyer could have. I couldn't believe my good fortune. Going to court and trying cases. Mr. Walton, later to become Judge Walton, would always be my hero. I was eternally grateful to this man for this incredible break. Even though I did not see much of Dan in the months ahead, he was a great role model: always did what was right and known for his integrity. He was never one to bend with the wind. I was fortunate to enter into gainful employment and work for such a man of character.

The first of March came. I doffed my white Stetson—we actually wore them in those days—grabbed my new leather briefcase, and headed for downtown. I drove our only car, leaving wife Carolyn and the kids stranded in suburbia. Parking several blocks from the courthouse for 35¢ for the day, I had to wait outside that glass door to the reception room until someone with a key showed up. The man was a look-alike for one of my favorite movie stars, Alan Ladd.

"Don't make me guess. You're the new assistant? Carol who?" Pete Moore asked.

"You're Mr. Moore aren't you? I'm Carol Vance."

"Just call me Pete. We aren't very formal around here. You sure must live right, because you are going to be assigned to the honorable Judge Jimmie

Duncan's court. He chews up new prosecutors and spits them out for break-fast. And I'm not going to mention how he treats defense attorneys. You couldn't have a better judge to break you in."

Pete supervised the Misdemeanor Section's nine assistants. Each of the three criminal county courts had a team of three prosecutors which handled all of the cases that fell in that particular court. These nine assistants, plus boss Pete Moore, would represent the State of Texas in some 10,000 serious misdemeanors which fell in these county courts each year. With about 3,000 cases per court and a little over 250 working days, Judge Duncan's court had to dispose of twelve to fifteen cases per day to break even. Most new pros-ecutors begin their career in county court. Pete was the only seasoned lawyer of the group. The nine of us had somewhere between my no experience and eighteen months' experience. In each court the three-man team consisted of "the chief," a "number two man," and "the mullet." The mullet was assigned to handle anything and everything the first two guys did not want to fool with. The mullet got to try "the dogs," in the courthouse vernacular. Dog cases were next to impossible to win.

Pete was a great boss who became a good friend. He had a steady flow of one-liners and great patience with his cubs. He later became First Assistant (the DA's second-in-command) and after that was elected to the bench, first for a county court at law and later as a career district judge. He was probably the most popular judge on the criminal side of the street. Pete was a hand-some, chain-smoking, former P-51 fighter pilot—he had been an ace in both World War II and the Korean War. Pete was willing to take risks. He made quick decisions. He also backed us up, but sometimes it was after a well-deserved chewing out.

A dark-complected handsome guy walked into the office. Pete said, "That guy standing at the door waiting to feed you to Judge Duncan is named Gus. I can't pronounce his last name. Just go follow him around and do what he says. And if you are lucky, someday I'll assign you to a real lawyer."

Gus Zgourides smiled back and said, dripping with sarcasm, "Thank you, Mr. Moore."

Zgourides ushered me into an office and introduced me to a teenaged-looking fellow by the name of David Gibson.

At this point I asked, "Gus, where is my office?"

Dave broke out laughing. "You're looking at it. Where we stand is not only your office, but my office and Gus's office. Someday we'll get a window, so Pete says." The room was square, about ten feet by ten feet, just enough space for three green steel desks to fit back to back. There were no other chairs except the ones we sat in.

Gus said, "Now, when one of us has to talk to a witness or defense attorney, the other two leave the room. Gives the other two a good excuse to go to the coffee shop. Bring some dimes to work." Among thirty-two assistant district attorneys, only Mr. Walton, First Assistant Gene Brady, and Pete Moore had private offices. That was okay with me; I was eternally grateful to have a desk and a paycheck.

OF THE ASSISTANTS, TWENTY-ONE were assigned to courts. Twelve served up in the three district courts that tried the felony cases while nine of us served in three county criminal courts of law which handled misdemeanors. Our misdemeanors were not traffic tickets—a fellow could get up to two years in jail and a big fine for the offenses we tried. The remainder of the assistants served in specialized places like the grand jury, juvenile court, child support, the complaint desk, and the hot check section. With one appellate lawyer and First Assistant Gene Brady, that rounded out the staff.

That day I reported for duty reminded me of when I reported for duty as a second lieutenant in the Military Police Corps at Camp Gordon. I was handed my carbine and my government issue of clothes and equipment. My first day in the DA's office I was issued three crisp yellow pads, a box of paper clips, two pink telephone notepads, and a small box of No. 2 yellow wooden pencils. A dirty dark green blotter donated by a local bail bondsman covered my green metallic desk. The walls were colored hospital green. No one bothered with the niceties of pictures or diplomas on the wall. I put my framed law license and UT Law diploma back in my empty briefcase. A giant paper calendar, also donated by local bail bondman Sam Alfano, hung on the wall behind my desk. During my unsuccessful interviews at some of Houston's finest and worst firms, I noticed each lawyer had his own office with a mahogany desk sitting on a carpet. Even the most junior of lawyers had a window. We three were jammed up, but I could not have been happier. I had a job and was going to court. I had also noticed the large civil firms were deathly quiet. Here, secretaries yelled across the room, "Gus, it's for you, baby, line 431." Also at the other firms I never saw visitors in the lobby with head injuries or black eyes.

Our nine county court prosecutors shared a single secretary. Pete had a private secretary, but that poor girl had to type up 10,000 formal charges a year. Each one was called an "information," the equivalent of the indictment in a felony case. I learned a single typo in that "information" could get a case thrown out of court.

Gus turned to Dave and me. "Okay, guys. Ten to nine. Vance, don't ever, ever be late to Duncan's court. You're gonna love Duncan." Dave Gibson giggled, grabbed a manila folder with about twenty "files"—one for each case set that morning—and our little trio went up two floors to seek justice. I was shocked at the brevity of each file, at most two pages long: a cover sheet and a one-page police report that usually a radio patrol officer had written. We marched into Jimmie Duncan's court ready to go for whatever that day would bring.

As the wall clock clicked nine, Jimmie Duncan opened a door behind his "bench" and entered the courtroom. None of the judges wore robes in those days. His Honor had on cowboy boots and a string tie under a white shirt and sport coat. The fat bailiff bellowed out, "Please rise. County Criminal Court at Law No. 4 of Harris County will now come to order and is in session, the Honorable Jimmie Duncan presiding. You two men in the back row, shut up. There will be no talking in this court or I will remove you."

Duncan was tall, wiry, and stern. He took the bench with cigar in hand. He slammed down the large gavel, piercing the silence. "This court will come to order. Mr. Zgourides," he said with sarcasm rolling down his tongue, "is that the new mullet you have brought down to my court this morning?"

"Yes, Your Honor."

"Well, boy, come up to this bench so I can meet you."

The judge began to call the docket of twenty-some-odd misdemeanors. Every case on the docket was set for trial that day. The courtroom was packed out with defendants, attorneys, witnesses, and police officers. They all looked nervous. Most smoked. I was surprised the fire alarm did not go off. After the judge called out the names of the cases to see who was going to trial first, most of the defense attorneys surrounded Gus and Dave trying to work out a plea bargain their clients could live with. Defense attorneys usually did not like to go to trial in Judge Duncan's court, or in any court for that matter. Most of the lawyers charged small fees for poor clients. This part of the criminal defense bar survived on volume, and most just eked out a living. Even though each case was set for trial, seldom had the defense attorney or the prosecutor ever interviewed a witness in advance of the court date. Defense attorneys did not seem to be burdened with even a two-page file.

As each case was called, Gus would announce, "The State is ready for trial, Your Honor." The lawyer, now facing a real jury trial, would hustle his client out into the hall and usually give him a good tongue lashing to take the plea bargain the prosecutor offered rather than roll the dice with a jury. Still, some defendants wanted a trial and their day in court.

Once when Gus announced the State ready for trial, Duncan growled, "What says the defendant?"

A bald-headed little lawyer said, "I'm not ready, Your Honor. I need a continuance."

Duncan snapped back, "Yeah, and I need a million dollars. I'm announcing you ready for trial. Mr. Bailiff, get this jury panel seated."

"Your Honor," the lawyer pleaded, "give me five more minutes. I am sure we can work it out."

"Five minutes? Make it three. I don't have all day for you to mealy-mouth around."

In the next case when a police witness did not show, the State could not announce ready. His Honor looked over at me and said in a voice everyone could hear, "You go get the lieutenant in radio patrol on the line and tell him Judge Duncan says if Officer Dingman doesn't get his ass over here in thirty minutes, one of Houston's Finest is going to the slammer. Don't just stand there, boy. Grab that phone!"

After a few minutes Gus reminded the judge I needed to be sworn in as an assistant district attorney. The judge said, "Raise your right hand, boy, and say 'I do' when I ask you these questions." Without looking at a note the judge administered the oath. Now I was official.

When docket call ended, Dave Gibson began trial in a DWI case, the most common kind of case to be tried in county court. David did a great job cross-examining the defendant and made a closing argument that would have made Clarence Darrow proud. I later found out Dave had won the national collegiate debating title during his University of Houston days. The case was a plain vanilla DWI, no wreck, no blood test. Just two officers in the patrol car who said the guy staggered, talked thick-tongued, and weaved across the center line twice in one block. Dave dramatically suggested that had the officers not stopped this fellow, that he probably would have run into a car and wiped out some family.

The jury found the man guilty and gave this oilfield equipment salesman ten days in jail and a $500 fine. I did not think I could ever be as good a prosecutor as Dave Gibson.

"Gus, that Dave Gibson guy is really good," I said.

"Yeah, but don't you go tell him that." I knew I was out of my class.

Daily docket call was akin to the Black Hole of Calcutta. So many people jamming into the little courtroom. So many names of defendants, complainants, witnesses, and lawyers to remember. So many different fact situations to try to get a handle on. Mass confusion reigned. I was like the juggler at the circus trying to keep the balls in the air. Fifteen minutes was max to review a file, talk to the complainant, haggle with the defense attorney, and then get the lawyer and his client up at the bench for the plea of guilty. The object was to dispose of as many cases as possible in order to stay current. Unless we kept up, cases would be set for trial a long way off with witnesses, victims, and police officers either moving out of town or not being able to recall the facts. Staying current was as important as getting a good result.

Also, most of our complaining witnesses—the victims, in other words—were unpredictable and uneducated. Most victims either wanted to have the book thrown at the defendant or wanted us to dismiss the case. They were not easy to extract facts from or deal with. Emotions ran high. Domestic violence offenders and drunk drivers hogged the docket. Usually a guy had beat his wife, his common-law wife, or his live-in. Then, after the little woman filed on him, he would get religion and be nice to her until his case was over. Few women worked in those days. Desperate for love and someone to pay the rent, the woman would come to court pleading for a dismissal. In fairness to the victim, there was no victim assistance of any kind, no day care centers or any other kind of place a woman could seek shelter. The woman and the kids needed to eat, and often the defendant was her meal ticket. The prosecutor was left with two great choices: dump poverty on the family by sending the bully to jail, or dismiss the case and set her up for more beatings. Probation, with its stringent reporting requirements and conditions, was simply not an option in any misdemeanor case in those days.

Each morning when the victims, the eyewitnesses, the defendants, the police officers, the lawyers, and the bondsmen overflowed the courtroom, there was one person who stood in the center of it all: the prosecutor. The judge could enjoy his second and third cups of coffee in the quietness of his chambers, while everyone tried to mob the three prosecutors. Bail bondsmen wanted you to know why their guy was going to be late. Defense attorneys wanted to work out a deal, a plea bargain. Witnesses wanted to know when they were going to take the stand. Police wanted to report in and then go back on duty or to that extra job and be on call. Only the prosecutor could answer these requests.

When we walked in that courtroom we had no idea which of twenty cases would go to trial. All cases were set for trial back in those days. Statistically, over 90 percent would plead guilty, but who they would be we knew not. Only in a "big case" like a negligent homicide would we go to the scene, make diagrams, or interview a key witness. Our objective was, Keep the docket moving. Our enemy was not the clever lawyer on the other side but the lack of time to deal with the multiple cases and personalities. In short, our goal for the morning was to get through docket call. "Docket call is a bitch," most prosecutors observed out loud and with frequency.

Today, following an overhaul of the system, docket calls make more sense. Each new case is set down for a pretrial hearing. Many are disposed of without any trial setting, making it much easier on witnesses and parties alike. Prosecutors can zero in on the 10–20 percent of the cases where the lawyer says he wants a trial. Today's system relieves most of the pressure. Even so, docket call is the toughest time of the day. Docket call makes it nice to finally go to trial and have some order in the courtroom.

The term "plea bargain" sounds terrible. Imagine a justice system of bargaining away rights of the accused and victims alike. Is our justice system on the auction block? In actual practice the system is not as bad as billed. A plea bargain consists of the prosecutor and the defense attorney sitting down and discussing the facts. Each side tries to present the best case possible to the other. The prosecutor usually starts on the high side and after hearing the mitigating factors arrives at a "bottom-line" offer. The defense attorney takes the offer back to his client and has a heart-to-heart talk. If the defendant accepts the offer, the plea of guilty is entered before the judge. Most judges rubber stamp the agreement. The judge knows he does not have the time for both sides to put on evidence in the case and stay current. The judge figures the lawyers for both sides know their case better than anyone, and each are making a compromise in the best interest of that client. If every one of these plea-bargained cases were submitted to a jury, the results would be bizarre. We would need about five times as many courts to handle the volume. Consider, too, that inexperienced jurors are not going to do a better job. They have no framework from which to draw. At least the lawyers know the going community rate for common offenses.

Even so, the old Houston *Press* had a field day publishing stories daily about plea bargains and accusing the State of giving away the store. Another reason defense attorneys engage in plea bargaining is because juries often render outlandish verdicts. Shortly after I started prosecuting, my friend

Jack Rawitscher prosecuted a plain vanilla DWI. There was no wreck and no injury. The defendant was a hard-working man with no record. After hearing the evidence, the six-man jury sentenced the poor fellow to two years in jail. The man had a family and a job. He turned down a plea bargain sentence of three days in jail with credit for two days. Jack asked the jury to send the defendant to jail for ten days and the jury gave the max. The verdict was so shocking that Jack, the judge, the defense attorney, and the client agreed to the setting aside of the verdict to let the poor guy plead for ninety days in jail. Truth is, the outcome by any jury is a dice roll.

My first day on the job, I experienced the unfolding human drama that takes place daily. Nothing we did was covered in any law book or office manual. I saw people get mad at the prosecutor, the defense attorney, and each other. Arguments, moans, and sobs echoed outside the courtroom. The mass of sticky human situations were not resolved that day, either. At the end of docket call Judge Duncan summed it up. "Vance, docket call is a bitch. Let's go get a cup of coffee. Which one of you knuckleheads is buying?"

The second day on the job as I followed Gus up the stairs going to court, Gus said, "I think I'll find some good case for you to try and get you broke in." I assumed he was kidding. Still too frightened to make a decision and take part in the plea bargains, I pretty much stood around and watched Gus and Dave operate. And smooth operators they were. Near the end of docket call, Gus was true to his word. In Dave's presence, Gus handed me a file and said, "Well, here's one Carol can try. Time to put the mullet to work."

"But, Gus …" I protested.

"This is easy. It's a trial to the court. No jury." Gus turned to the judge, "Your Honor, Mr. Vance says he wants to try this next aggravated assault case to the court."

Duncan had a wide grin. "Well, boy, don't just stand there. Call your first witness. The defendant will come forward. And don't forget to read 'The Information' to the defendant, Mr. Vance."

"Judge, could I have ten minutes to talk to the complainant?" I begged.

"I'll give you five."

The defendant, Big John Jordan, was accused of committing the crime of aggravated assault on Timmy McBiff. Specifically, Big John was accused of "stomping one Timothy McBiff with his feet" at the Blue Night Café, a cheap bar out on old Highway 90 close to the Houston Ship Channel. After too much Jack Daniels, the men got into a fight. When McBiff went down on the barroom floor, Big John allegedly kicked McBiff in the ribs, fracturing one of them. Under Texas law a person could beat another person half to death with his fists and the crime was a mere simple assault with no jail time and a maximum fine of $25. But if one kicked another with his feet, the law said this was an aggravated assault, as feet could cause serious bodily injury. The possible punishment for using feet and not fists escalated the punishment to two years in jail and a $500 fine.

I called McBiff to the stand. After stammering through complex questions such as "What is your name?" and "Where do you live?" I finally got the two men in the same bar at the same time and began to ask about the fight. When I asked McBiff what happened in the bar all he kept saying was that "Big John jumped me and kept pounding me with his fists. He was unmerciful."

Gus, who was sitting behind me at the counsel table, nudged me and whispered, "Ask McBiff if Big John kicked him with his feet."

"Gus, I can't ask him a leading question. They could object." At that Gus shrugged his shoulders and gave up.

After I rested my case, the defendant wisely chose not to take the stand. The testimony concluded, Judge Duncan found Big John guilty of only simple assault and gave him the maximum fine, all of $25. Then with dripping sarcasm the judge said, "Mr. Vance, in the future if you try a man for kicking someone with his feet, you might want to ask him if he used his feet for a weapon." From then on I was never shy about asking leading questions.

Later in my first week I was trying a second case to the court. I made an objection to some obviously inadmissible testimony but failed to stand up to do so. Judge Duncan roared, "Boy, I can't hear you when you are sitting down. If you are going to address this court, you had better stand up."

"Yes, sir, Your Honor." I never forgot that lesson, either. Later in life I would see lawyers who, despite having twenty years experience, would not stand up to make an objection. I felt like saying, "You would never get away with that if Jimmie Duncan or I were the judge."

I also learned that if I objected to inadmissible testimony but gave the court the wrong reason for the objection, Judge Duncan would take great delight in overruling me. For many a night thereafter, before I went to bed, I would pull out my old evidence textbook written and taught by the famous Dean McCormick in order to master these nuances. I was glad I didn't sell my evidence book when I finished law school.

These first two days were exciting. I had earned right at $20 a day for those two days. I had a job and was no longer walking the pavement. And Wednesday was yet to come.

CHAPTER TWO

My First Jury Case

Of all the things of a man's soul which he has within him,
justice is the greatest good and injustice the greatest evil.
—Plato in *The Republic*

I EXITED THE NUECES County Courthouse to the smell of the cool salt air, a refreshing start to a hot summer day. I climbed into my sleek blue Oldsmobile, furnished by Harris County, and pointed towards Houston. I was sad I would no longer be prosecuting. By now I had tried somewhere between 200–300 jury cases, most of them as an assistant district attorney.

Trying cases was part of my makeup. I loved to stand before the court, the adrenaline going strong, and announce, "The State of Texas is ready for trial, Your Honor." I loved being the first lawyer to address the jury, the first to make an opening statement, and the last lawyer to make the final argument. I loved my client, the State of Texas. No individual client by my side to have to please. Besides, if I didn't have a case, I dismissed it. I believed it was all about justice, and I was fighting for the right. The courtroom had become a second home.

However, this had not always been the case.

HOW WELL I REMEMBER my first jury trial. No sooner had I returned to the office after Judge Duncan found that guy guilty did I receive new orders from my boss, Pete Moore. Pete grabbed me and said, "Carol, are you ready for this? Tomorrow morning you are to drive out to the Justice of the Peace court in Waller and try your first jury case. The old JP who has been serving for years called and said he wants a prosecutor. Says it's his first jury trial. I just couldn't tell this nice old man that it was your first trial, too. Fact is, I promised him I was sending down one of our best young trial lawyers. I don't have a clue where his court is. You call over there and get the details, and just don't be late. He said he starts up at 9:00 A.M. prompt."

"Sure, Pete. Great," I said with a lump in my throat. "What kind of case is it, anyway? Is there a file I can take home and read? Will the witnesses be there? What do I do to get ready?"

Pete said, "Cool it. It's traffic court. I don't have a clue what the case is about. Just show up. Don't be late and do what's right. Besides, you'll get rich. The county will pay you 4¢ a mile out there and back. Don't forget to keep a record of your mileage and then fill out all the forms. Get them from my secretary."

After a sleepless night, I put on my suit and drove over to old Highway 290, the Hempstead Highway. Back then the 290 superhighway was two lanes with little traffic. Driving northwest I came to my destination, the little town of Waller. I had already calculated I would get paid almost $3.00 for the round trip and my gas would only cost me 80¢. Carolyn sent me off with a large peanut butter and jelly sandwich with a couple of homemade cookies.

Waller consisted of a gas station, a general store, and several grain silos. I took a right on a lonely black asphalt road. A recent norther cleared up the sky. Rains had given way to a clear, cold, sunny day. Tractors were working the black moist soil on both sides of the country road. Spring was coming. Planting time was here. Finally I came to an old farm house with a white wooden sign saying "JP Court." The sign was stuck in the grass on the front lawn. About ten cars littered the front yard as farmers dressed in coveralls headed around the house to the back. I went to the front door and knocked. A short elderly lady came to the door and said, "If you're lookin' for court, you go around back to the barn. We don't allow no court in this house."

"Yes ma'am," I said. It turned out that was the JP's wife. I headed around back and tried to jump a puddle left over from last night's rain. Grey mud oozed out over my left black shoe which I just polished that morning. Cold water dampened my sock. I squished my way over to a big red barn, walked in the huge doorway and stood on the dirt floor.

A kindly man in his seventies walked up and said, "I'm Judge Davis. You must be the young man from the DA's office. Glad you are here, son. I got a mess on my hands. I think it is going to take a jury trial to straighten out the bad blood between these two boys."

Judge Davis continued. "Now son, I'm no lawyer. I've never had a jury trial so you gotta help me out. I don't want you to object to anything or ask me to do anything unless you know you are right. Understand? That will make it easy. I will always rule with you so don't ask me to do anything not proper. You understand?"

"Sure, judge, I understand. I don't object unless I am right." I understood most JPs were not lawyers so I was glad to help out. I felt like saying, "Judge, what if I don't know?" I dropped that idea.

I didn't tell the judge I was brand new. Judge Davis said, "Son, these people involved in this case are my friends and neighbors, but these families feel strongly about all of this. And this fistfight these boys got into made it worse. We better have us a jury to decide all of this. I just can't take sides in this thing. Are you with me, son?"

The old barn was worn down by years of weather and was damp and dark. The John Deere tractor was parked outdoors to make more room to hold court. Judge Davis proudly pointed out six small school desks that had been bolted to a small slab of concrete at the corner of the barn. The six-man jury would sit there. Next to these seats was an old rolltop desk like my grandfather used to have. The judge sat down there and turned his leather swivel chair around to face the witnesses and the spectators. I sat close by with my folding chair pulled up to my counsel table, an old wooden bridge table, which held all I brought with me: my county-issued legal pad. The defendant sat close by on an old pew bench.

The barn was free of cows but not their smell. I started sneezing from the smell of the hay up in the loft. Judge Davis walked around and tapped on the shoulders of the first six farmers he came to and told them to sit in the little elementary school chairs. Five of these good ol' boys were large. Couldn't get their knees under the little desktops. They took off their straw hats and laid them down, the hats covering up the writing area portion of each desk. At this point I made a command decision not to tell the judge that the lawyers were supposed to talk to the jury first about their qualifications and then each side should be able to strike any three from a panel of twelve. The local defense attorney sat there not saying a word. He was a large man, too, and wore a very wide red tie with large yellow flowers painted all over it.

"Boys, let's crank this trial up now. Mr. Vance, you tell us what you want to do next."

"I don't know, Judge. You said I had a witness. Could you ask him to come up here and swear him in?"

A good ol' boy stood up and walked down to the chair the judge pointed to. Like most everyone else, he was dressed for the farm. In fact, the only people with ties on were the judge and me and the plump, middle-aged defense attorney who had been kidding with some of the jurors earlier when I walked in. Turns out he had a little office in Waller and he later told me he did a little bit of everything, including land sales and wills. In a kidding way he told me to take it easy on him because this was his first jury trial in a criminal case.

The man on trial, Ernest Shultze, was charged with having an affray. The judge pulled out a dusty old book and showed me the statute from the 1925 *Texas Statutes*. An "affray" was where two men "voluntarily agree to engage in a fight using their hands or fists." Of course I never heard of this crime. We never had such a case in my two days in county court.

I said, "What is your name?"

"Orville Dexter," he answered.

I didn't have a clue what to ask him next, so I just said, "Well, Mr. Dexter, why don't you just tell us what happened the other night and why you think Mr. Shultze is guilty of the crime called an affray."

"Well, we were over at the monthly auction barn biddin' on cows the first Saturday night of the month, about month before last. I had my eye on buying this pretty, little red heifer. I really wanted that animal. But old Shultze sittin' over there just made me mad as a wet hen. I kept biddin'. He kept goin' higher. Finally I put in a high bid, more than that heifer was worth. I got so mad that I walked up to him and said if you bid one more time over my bid, you and I are going to fist city. I bid, but he bid again. I was standing there beside him and I hit him upside the head. He was a little dizzy but then he started hitting me and we got into a good one. I had a broken finger. We had us what the law says is an affray. I had my lawyer look it up.

"So the sheriff comes up and takes me down to the jail and charges me with a simple assault. So I went down here to Judge Davis' court like a man and paid my $25 fine. So it all seems simple to me. I hit him and paid the fine. After I hit him, he starts the fight, this 'affray' thing. So he is guilty, too. My lawyer looked up that law. Told me even the judge never heard of it before. So he needs to take his medicine and be fined for an affray. Not right for me to pay the only fine. I reckon that tells all I know. I don't have nothin' else to allow."

"All right then. So now you go back in the barn and have a seat," the judge said.

"Judge, I just have one question and it's my turn," the defense lawyer said.

"Okay, just don't be long-winded," the judge replied.

"Now, Dexter, you have told the truth here today. Isn't that right?"

"Yes, sir, I sure have."

"So there is absolutely no doubt in your mind that you walked up to my client Shultze and hit him in the head?"

"Yes, sir."

"And at that time he had never threatened to hit you or raised a hand against you, had he?"

"That's right, Mr. Lawyer, but he sure did cheat me out of that little heifer."

Mr. Durden, the defense lawyer, fingered his wide flowered tie and spit a chaw on the dirt floor. "Judge, that is all the questions I have. The fact is, Judge, that I am not even going to call my client to the stand since this man admitted to have hit my client first while he was just standin' there."

Speaking to the defense attorney and me, the judge said, "You boys wanna say anything to the jury?" We nodded yes. "Mr. Vance, who gets to go first?"

"Judge, the prosecution gets to go first and last. Mr. Durden gets to talk in-between," I said.

"Now Mr. Vance, these jurors need to get on with their plowing, so I think it is enough for you to talk one time. You go on ahead and then Mr. Durden can talk. But don't you boys take long now."

I cleverly went over to the judge's rolltop and picked up the dusty statute book entitled *Vernon's 1925 Texas Statutes*. I read the jury what the law stated. Then I said, "And that, gentlemen, is the law of the great state of Texas that your elected representatives passed just to prevent fights like this from taking place. I don't care what happened out there first. These two men got into a fight. They broke the law. One man has paid his fine and now the other one should, too. Seems pretty simple to me."

For his part, Mr. Durden said in America a man has the right to defend himself and that was all his client did. "The other man not only admitted he hit my client first but he pled guilty to that charge. Now you go find my client not guilty. You would defend yourself if you got hit up on the side of the head. So just go say not guilty."

In half an hour the jury came out from their huddle in the cow pen beyond the barn. The foreman said, "We find the defendant not guilty."

Driving back to the office about noontime, I wondered if I would ever be a trial lawyer. At least the jury stayed out a half hour. I dragged my tired body up to our fifth-floor cubicle. Pete was in our little office talking to Gus and Dave when I walked in.

"Want to tell us about your first jury case, Mr. Vance?" Pete said.

I told the story and apologized for the result. After Pete, Gus, and Dave heard me out, Pete said "You tried that case? Have you ever heard about making a motion to dismiss?" The three broke out in laughter. Dave nearly fell out of his chair.

Pete said, "Carol, we don't try people who are innocent. How come you just didn't dismiss that dog and drive back home?"

"Pete, you told me to go down there to try that case. I really didn't know I could have dismissed it. Particularly since the judge had that jury waiting."

"Well, if the evidence shows someone is innocent, you are supposed to dismiss the case. Don't worry about it. It says something for you that you climbed in that ring and tried that old dog," Pete said.

Gus suggested my education should continue down in the coffee shop. Two assistants named Jon Hughes and Erwin Ernst got on the elevator with us. "Meet our new mullet, fellows. This is Carol Vance, and he just tried his first jury case today," Gus said.

Ernst asked, "Well, did you win?"

"Not exactly," I said.

"Well, I'm sorry," Ernst said. "Even great trial lawyers like me and Jon Hughes lose a case once in a while. Did anybody tell you that our custom in this office is that we always flip coins to see who gets to buy the coffee? The odd man always buys."

We walked into the cafeteria in the basement of the courthouse. Ernst scratched his head and declared it was time to flip. We flipped our nickels. Everyone came up heads. So we had to flip a second time right after Ernst said he was patting his wallet for good luck. Everyone had tails except me. I had to fork over a quarter to pay for five coffees. I had not only lost a case that day but was already burning up my county gas money from my seventy-mile round trip to Waller, Texas. As we sat down for coffee. Gus said, "Let me tell you about the case our mullet decided he would try today."

Driving home that evening, I got to thinking about the trial. Then I thought about Ernst rubbing his head in the coffee shop and how they all came up with heads. Then Ernst scratched his rear and they all had tails; all except me, of course. Sure enough, what Ernst said was true, "A new mullet is born every day."

CHAPTER THREE

Breaking in the Mullet

*What I have learned bears no other fruit
than to make me realize how much I have to learn.*
—Montaigne

I ALLOWED TIME FOR a leisurely drive back to Houston. I would take the coastal route as far as I could. My best summer days had been at the beach. I never tired of seeing the waves roll to shore.

After clearing the downtown Corpus traffic, I drove over the tall causeway and was headed home. Looking over at the bay side, I rolled my window down to breathe the sea air. Two seagulls screeched as they dove into the shallow water. Two mullet jumped, escaping the predators. Another large school of mullet were churning up the water not far from shore. Mullet were limitless, not fit to eat, and usually too large for bait. Good for fertilizer, though. Yes, I knew something about mullet.

HAVING BEGUN MY CAREER as the mullet—that is, the number three man in county court—I understood the drill. I would be the guy everyone dumped the unwanted cases upon until I was promoted to a number two slot. Someday three assistants were going to have to resign from the trial section of the office before this took place. Only then would there be someone lower on the totem pole. But until that day came, I was determined to make the most of the "dog" cases. Eventually, after nine people from the DA's trial group left the office, I would go up to that hallowed ground called District Court, the place where the real gangsters, rapists, and robbers were tried. Whenever I finished my work, I made a practice of sneaking off to district court to watch the big boys work. The prosecutors up there had so much confidence and always seemed to know what to do. The defense attorneys also seemed much better at the job. I never saw myself getting to be as good as those district court prosecutors. It was a good thing I could stay in county court for many months before trying felony cases.

At the time I started in the DA's office, the three county court judges included Bill Miller, the defense attorneys' favorite; Wendell Odom, a real gentleman and right down the middle in his rulings; and rough-rider Jimmie Duncan, the tough guy. Judge Odom later went on to serve on the state's highest criminal court, the Court of Criminal Appeals. Judge Duncan set an all-time record for time on the county court bench (thirty-five years, disposing of some 150,000 cases, a state record) and was unquestionably the bench's most unforgettable character. If Judge Duncan didn't like someone he would leave that person alone. If he liked you, he would ride you hard and jump on you when you goofed. Down in the coffee shop, he liked to tell war stories and talk about stupid things lawyers did. In today's world of political correctness, he would have drawn five formal complaints a day, but not from his friends that he made fun of.

One day during docket call, a black lawyer named Ned Wade told me he resented how the judge was always calling black lawyers "boy," not exactly a term of endearment. As soon as the two of us walked back into Judge Duncan's court after one of our little plea bargain sessions out in the hall, His Honor looked up and said, "Hey, boy, get up here to this bench." Ned looked at me as if to say, "I told you so," and started for the bench. Judge Duncan instantly responded, "Not you. I want that boy, that mullet standing next to you, to come up here right now. You understand me, boy?"

"Yes, sir," I said. I knew who he was talking to.

Judge Duncan kept things stirred up. When I began in his court, women were not eligible to serve on juries in Texas. With three small children at home, I figured the men controlled things and none of them wanted to change all those diapers while "the little woman" was stuck on a murder case. A half century after they obtained their right to vote, women were finally considered fit for jury service. One of the first women I had on one of my juries happened to be very attractive. Right in the middle of trial and seem-ingly without any reason, Judge Duncan said in a loud voice, "You lawyers approach the bench." The two defense attorneys and I gathered at the bench. Judge Duncan said in a quiet whisper, "See that second juror from the end? She's a knockout, isn't she?" We all nodded in agreement. Then with an extra stern voice, the judge said, "You lawyers get back to your seats and move this case along! This jury doesn't have time to listen to you lawyers all day." No one ever went to sleep in Duncan's court.

Jury cases were set Monday through Thursday. Fridays were for pleas of guilty as well as providing time for the lawyers to argue their contested motions before the judge. Often court ended around noon on Fridays. Tradition was that a long lunch hour was our reward for all the pressures of the dockets and the trials during the first four days of the week. Some assistants were known to have a beer or two at lunch on Friday. I never remember anyone having three at lunch. I may not have spent the same long hours at the office as my friends in the law factories, but they led a quieter existence. Trying cases constantly will take it out of you. Only a handful of civil lawyers handling the insurance dockets tried anything like the number of cases we did. After fighting docket calls and being in trial a good part of the week, we deserved our Friday break. Many a day, after being in trial, all I could do when I got home was go take a nap before recovering enough civility and energy to face the kids.

Today the assistants and most defense attorneys have a myriad of opportunities for trial training and legal education. In fact the State Bar requires it. Back then our training sessions were on the job or in the coffee shop, not to mention an occasional hour stopover at a local watering hole on the way home. There, I could sit and listen to trial tales from the likes of Erwin Ernst and Jon Hughes. The best training was on the job, and one learned more from losing a case than winning one. Ernst liked to hold court over a Pearl beer at the "Linoleum Club," the name he gave the DeGeorge Hotel's coffee shop, drawing a sharp contrast to Houston's famed and plush Petroleum Club. Ninfa's on Navigation and the Fan Con bar were other favorite hangouts over the years. We saved The Last Concert, just on the other side of the bayou from downtown, for special occasions.

A prosecutor had to enjoy trying lawsuits or he was going to be miserable. Some assistants never took to trial work and went looking for other ways to practice law. Few of us were born trial lawyers; most of us had to develop our skills from repeatedly getting kicked around the courtroom. Somehow and someday we would climb out of the muck, see the big picture, and discover we really could be a trial lawyer.

As prosecutors, we were always complaining about how the law stacked the cards against us. We were constantly having to overcome "reasonable doubt" and having cases thrown out because the indictment was not quite right.

Years later when I defended some clients from the other side of the table, I realized the enormous advantage the prosecutor has, beginning with the investigative stage. Few defense attorneys had clients with enough money to hire investigators to interview witnesses or pay for elaborate trial exhibits. We had the police at our disposal, not to mention our own investigator assigned to each court. Next, we had the advantage of getting to set the stage in the trial, of being the first and last one to address the jury. We could plan in advance how we would put on our case and not just react to whatever the prosecutor did. In our system, the prosecutor talks to the jury panel first. After the jury is chosen, the prosecutor makes the first opening statement, telling the jury what the evidence will be about. When the jurors are sworn in, it is the prosecutor who puts on his case first. After the defendant puts on his case the prosecutor usually has the last evidence to present in rebuttal. At the end of the trial the closing arguments take place. Again, the prosecutor goes both first and last. Defense counsel has to be sandwiched between. The defense lawyer finds himself in a more reactive, rather than a proactive, mode. It is simply an easier task to prosecute than to defend. Besides, the prosecutor can dismiss a case where the evidence is weak. The defense attorney just has to sit there and grin and bear it.

As I gained experience I also learned much more about human nature and how to make better guesses as to who to leave on the jury. Lawyers speak of "picking jurors," but this is a misnomer. Lawyers do not "pick jurors." They strike off the list the ones they do not want. Each side gets just so many strikes depending on the type of case. Both sides usually look for the jurors believed to be the most sympathetic to their side. The first jurors on the list who have not been struck will make up the trial jury. Although the system is clouded with guesswork, I generally knew which ones the defense would strike, and an experienced defense attorney would know whom I would strike.

In today's moneyed world, the big time lawyers in the really big criminal cases and the high-dollar civil cases might hire jury specialists who will study each prospective juror's every gesture, their hairstyles, the magazines under their arms, and their facial reactions to each question thrown at them. I never had hired a jury specialist until I practiced civil law and there was a few million riding on the outcome. We just went by the seat of our pants back then.

Back in my assistant DA days, as soon as the jury retired to deliberate, the judge would most often bring in another jury and begin another trial. Also in the old days, the jury decided the issue of guilt and the punishment during a single deliberation. Today after a guilty verdict is returned, the court recesses and then goes through a second mini-trial. The lawyers present evidence about how bad or how good the defendant is from past records and sometimes specific deeds. Then the jury goes out to deliberate a second time to assess the punishment within the range permitted by law.

I averaged to try about twenty-five cases a year as an assistant DA. I sat second on many other cases. Two trials in one week was not unusual. Sometimes I prosecuted the case by myself and sometimes an assistant sat beside me, too. That assistant would put on the less important witnesses and run errands, usually to run out into the hallway and talk to a witness waiting to testify. I never kept score on my win-loss record. All of us who tried a lot of cases won some and lost some. In misdemeanor court, juries acquitted perhaps a third to a half of the defendants on trial. In felony court the juries usually found about five out of six persons guilty. The prosecutor who didn't fear taking on a difficult case to prosecute was the one who received the most respect. I learned more lessons from cases that ended in "not guilty" than the cases where the jury went with me. Actually, I did not like looking at the verdict as a win or lose proposition. You did your best to present the evidence and convince the jury, but in most instances it is the facts that determine the outcome, not the skill of the lawyers. Obviously, a good lawyer is worth paying for. A good lawyer can figure out more ways to score points with the jury than a bad lawyer. Even so, the outcome of most cases was predictable and depended much more on the quality of the evidence than the quality of the lawyer.

Not long after I had been assigned to Jimmie Duncan's court, docket call ended without any trials. When that happened I always breathed a sigh of relief. I guess I always had a love-hate relationship about going to trial. Trials were exciting and put the adrenaline rush in overdrive. But quiet days, a little time for lunch, reading files, and returning phone calls were also a relief. On this particular day when the docket folded, Judge Duncan barked, "Boy, come back to my office. We need to talk." I thought to myself, How have I messed up now? I sat down in the judge's office. He said, "Hey, boy, you got anything to do the next two hours you can't get out of?"

"No, Your Honor," I said, clueless about what was coming next.

"A new John Wayne movie just started at the Majestic. It's an order of this court we both go see it." The old Majestic Theatre was in downtown Houston, five short blocks away. Not being one to risk contempt of His Honor, we were soon lost in John Wayne's quest for justice. The judge even paid for the tickets. John Wayne got justice when he rescued the widow and pumped the bad guys with bullets. I wished that all of our cases had such clear delineation as to who was right and who was wrong.

After several months of getting beat up and chewed out as the mullet, I was promoted. Also my $400 a month salary went to $450. We would eat a little better. I moved to Judge Wendell Odom's Court as the number two man. Judge Odom had a quiet nature and operated efficiently and effortlessly. He was the exact opposite of Judge Duncan. He never raised his voice but he still held everyone's feet to the fire. I enjoyed this more peaceful existence, and I still got to try plenty of cases. After several more months passed, a good number of assistants had resigned to go into private practice. At that time I was promoted to be the chief prosecutor in Odom's court. Carolyn particularly appreciated my new $500 monthly salary. Now I headed my own little law office within the DA's office. As chief I could try whatever cases I wanted to and hand off the rest. Not a bad way to make a living. We only had one investigator for the entire misdemeanor division. Being a chief I could call upon him to go out and find a witness or go to a crime scene and take pictures and draw out the measurements of the scene to be used during trial.

By picking which cases I would try, I decided early on that anytime there was a really good lawyer on the other side, I wanted to try the case. I could learn more from a good lawyer, and the trial was usually a more pleasant experience not having to put up with so many phony drama scenes.

I had a good relationship with most of the defense bar and with the leading defense attorneys. We did not have coffee in our offices in those days, so we hit the coffee shop each morning and afternoon when not in trial. And sometimes the judge would take the prosecutor and defense attorney for coffee while the jury was out. I am sure the jury would have been shocked to see the three of us sitting together, talking and laughing. The case was over. There was nothing any of us could do about it, so we turned our attention to sharing war stories. The judges made about $20,000 a year, much more than the prosecutors and more than most defense attorneys, so the judge usually bought the coffee. A poor appointed defense counsel might receive as little as $10 for representing an indigent back in those days.

Many of the guys who hired on to the DA's office were there for the trial experience. I say "guys" because we only had one female lawyer on staff and she worked with the grand jury. I only recall two or three female lawyers who were defense attorneys back in my early days. In fact, back at UT Law we had eight hundred students with only two or three women. Today the females sometimes outnumber the males in the Harris County office. Most of the prosecutors were there to get some experience and then move on down the road. My dear friend Erwin Ernst was constantly asking his fellow assistants, "What are you going to do when you grow up?" He even asked me that when I was the district attorney! All said and done, being an assistant was a dream job in my opinion. Where else could a lawyer try twenty-five cases a year, shoot from the hip, collect war stories to share, and lose cases and still not lose sleep.

After I had been up in district court for a few years trying felonies—including a good number of murder cases—Frank Briscoe was elected District Attorney. Of course I campaigned some for Dan Walton, my boss, but Frank won on his law-and-order plank, promising tougher prosecution. One of Frank's promises was he was going to beef up the county court prosecution by assigning experienced prosecutors to serve as chiefs in the misdemeanor courts. True to his promise, I was one of three sent back down to county court for a six-month assignment.

At first I thought this was a real bummer. As it turned out, I had a great time. Instead of feeling like a novice, I had total confidence. While I never kept score on wins and losses, one day the clerk told me I had run up a dozen guilty verdicts in a row. That is fairly unusual for county court. Juries were giving my DWI defendants sixty- and ninety-day jail sentences for being first offenders. Once again I was serving in Judge Duncan's court. He loved it. Fewer defendants were asking for jury trials. Also, he treated me like a long-lost friend. This time around the judge treated me with great respect: When he said "Hey, boy," it was clearly a term of endearment.

CHAPTER FOUR

Poor Man's Psychiatrist: The Complaint Desk

The highest wisdom consists of distinguishing between good and bad.
—Plato

I SWITCHED FROM COUNTRY music to KTRH in order to get the inter-office report. KTRH kept a full-time reporter at the courthouse. To make his keep the reporter made the rounds and came up with several courtroom stories a day. Back then the majority of all news stories centered around crime, namely the police station and the courthouse. I wanted to see if the media had picked up on my soon-to-be resignation as DA. No, they were silent so maybe my secret was still safe. I wanted to be the first one to tell the staff I was leaving. Actually I had made the decision a couple of months before to accept an offer to be a partner in a growing law firm called Bracewell and Patterson. Today it is called Bracewell and Giuliani and has over four hundred lawyers. Then the firm had eighty-five lawyers and I was to be the twenty-sixth partner. I would be in their litigation group and handle a growing white collar practice along with civil cases of many varieties for corporate clients.

With our oldest child finishing college and four more to go, family finances played a role in my decision. A district attorney does not need to be worried about such things. Besides, after four elected terms I had accomplished every goal I set out to do. With superb help from our staff, we blazed new trails and made monumental changes in the office. Most prosecutors around the country considered ours a model office. As painful as the decision was, it was simply time to turn the page on a new chapter.

Three months previously my friend Bill Wilde, who headed up litigation at Bracewell, called and asked me to come over to his office and meet with him and his younger brother, Carlton, the managing partner of the firm. I had gone to school with Bill since the seventh grade, and Carolyn and I had taught a ninth-grade Sunday school class at First Presbyterian Church with Bill and his wife, Ann.

Enjoying a fancy meal catered by the Houston Club from their corner office overlooking the city, out of the clear blue I said, "I know why you wanted to meet with me. You want to offer me a job." They looked at each other and said that was right, but that it was all just exploratory conversation. As things fell into place I decided to make the move. Nothing is worse than a lame duck DA or lame duck anything. I met with each of the twenty-five partners. Everyone kept the whole process a secret for months. I said I needed to finish trying the Henley case which was set a few weeks off and then I would be finished. Now Henley was over and my resignation in a couple of hours would be my last act. The only person at the office who knew I was resigning was my First Assistant, Johnny Holmes, whom I had given a heads up. He had faithfully served the office for ten years, worked his way up to First Assistant, and would be well-qualified to be the DA himself. I thought he could get appointed, and I knew he could get elected. He would keep the staff in place and run the office right. As it turned out, he did both of those things and went on to serve a record twenty years as Harris County's district attorney.

KTRH had no news from our office as of yet. I pulled over at a small coffee shop facing the highway. After ordering eggs and bacon, the middle-aged waitress said, "You're that DA from Houston, ain't you? Seen your picture in the paper. Up here trying that case involving those poor kids. If I was one of those parents, you wouldn't have to try that case. Shame he didn't get the chair. What's this country coming to, anyway?"

As I walked out to my car, I saw a man grab his wife or girlfriend and shove her into the car. He was yelling at her. I had called the police from my car to arrest more than one drunk driver, but I knew to leave this domestic squabble alone. This incident outside the café brought back memories of my earlier experiences as an assistant DA and those horrible times I had to man something known as "The Complaint Desk."

Cʒ

THE DISTRICT ATTORNEY'S OFFICE always had a section called "The Complaint Desk." During most of my days as an assistant, the complaint desk consisted of an elderly and distinguished white-haired man by the name of W. J. Coulson. He was assisted in his work by the receptionist and by some masterful investigators that no one ever met. He was kind and sympathetic and more of a kindly psychologist than a crime-fighting lawman. He seemed to have the ability to make down-and-out people feel good. He enjoyed giving simple and practical advice. He did not file many charges. He seemed to know that the criminal courthouse was not necessarily the best place to resolve the conflict before him. Although Mr. Coulson loved his work, the rest of the staff who had to sub for him dreaded these temporary assignments.

On every Saturday morning from 8:00 to noon, over the weekday lunch hours, and on days when Mr. Coulson was away, the misdemeanor prosecutors took turns doing his job. The complaint desk was the court of last resort, the place a hurting person went when no one else would listen. Human beings of all shapes and sizes dragged into this office to tell their story to the DA. Many of the down-and-outers believed the DA could right every wrong and fix every problem. Little did they know.

The complaint desk was aptly named. No one came there except to complain. In today's world, multiple assistants and paralegal types have replaced the work that Mr. Coulson did single-handedly for the entire county. In those days the complaint desk handled consumer frauds, wife beatings, runaway children, missing persons, trees growing on another's property, and other strange or bizarre altercations. Today's victims of domestic violence have at their disposal Child Protective Services and victim specialists within the DA's office to assist their needs. Before victim's rights became popular, all the poor people had was Mr. Coulson.

Mr. Coulson's office had no window. He operated in a ten-foot-square room, big enough for one desk, his leather chair, and two straight-back wooden chairs for visitors. The elderly receptionist directed the stream of "complainants" in and out of his office. To avoid claustrophobia and ensure personal safety his door remained open. Often the loud, demanding voices of the complainants invaded the reception area. Not a thing was on the wall or on Mr. Coulson's desk but a yellow pad and two pencils.

Sometimes when the lobby overloaded with complainants, the receptionist wandered into the adjoining misdemeanor section to ask the first warm body for help. One of us, usually a mullet, would lend a hand and interview one or two citizens. Dealing with people who claimed to have been beaten up some days before but who had not even called the police was a challenge. Our basic objective was to listen and get them out the door without filing some charge that would clog up the system. We had enough "dogs" pending trial as it was. Once in a while a case was bad enough to file a charge, but convictions in even these cases were rare.

The first complainant I interviewed was a woman who wanted to file a criminal charge on her husband for adultery. True, Texas did have just such a statute. However, the Texas Court of Criminal Appeals, our last word on criminal law, said that a man could not be convicted of adultery unless the evidence showed he had many acts of intercourse with the same individual. Also, that court demanded strict proof of the multiple acts. Anyone checking Texas law would not be able to find a single case where an adultery conviction was permitted to stand. Even after explaining I could not take a charge, the lady said, "I don't care what you think, young man. I want that man in jail by nightfall!"

I said, "No, under the law we simply have no case. I cannot file one."

She marched out in a huff but not before saying, "Young man, you ought to be fired. I voted for Mr. Walton. He is going to hear about you."

One solution we learned from Mr. Coulson was to tell the complainant we would put our investigator on the case. One day in a conversation I overheard as I passed Mr. Coulson's office, the little lady said, "Sir, you promised me you would put your investigator on my case a year ago and I have yet to see him."

"Little lady," Mr. Coulson said, "you're not supposed to see him. If you ever see him, you call me immediately so I can fire him." Hearing this, the woman calmed down and walked away.

W. J. Coulson was so kind and patient that he had some regulars who came in weekly for their "Mr. Coulson fix." The habitual complainers often went into serious rejection when they saw a young kid like me sitting in Mr. Coulson's chair. Mr. Coulson could hear out the most outlandish claim and still offer encouragement and hope in his soft but authoritative voice. Often at the close of the session he would hand some poor woman a crisp $1 bill. All I could offer were meaningless words when I tried to explain why a criminal charge could not be filed.

Mr. Coulson would authorize a criminal charge if he had some facts to back it up. If a woman came in all beat up and bruised at her husband's hand, he would call Homicide, arrange for her to go have her picture taken and issue a warrant for the man's arrest. In a few months the case would come up in one of the county courts. Our file would consist of a two-sentence report written by Mr. Coulson from a page off his legal pad. Because Mr. Coulson accepted few charges, we knew the facts were aggravated. The problem with these cases was that 90 percent of the time the woman did not show up in court. If she did show up, it was to request the case be dismissed. More than once I forced a "Coulson case" to trial only to have the woman testify she was not sure what happened.

One day a woman approached Mr. Coulson and said a strange man followed her around shooting painful electric rays into her frail body. As Mr. Coulson listened to her extended tale of woe, he carefully joined one paper clip to another, creating a four-foot chain. Finally, Mr. Coulson stood up. The interview was over. He handed the woman the chain and said, "Now little lady, you just clip this little steel chain onto your belt and let it drag the ground. When this man shoots at you again, you won't feel a thing. The electricity will be grounded." She hooked the chain to her belt and left the office smiling.

Something that none of us looked forward to was Saturday duty. In those days the misdemeanor prosecutors took turns manning the Saturday morning complaint desk. Whenever I drew that duty I knew I would be downtown all alone and would have no senior assistants to turn to for help.

My first Saturday in the pit came. I got off the elevator outside our office at 7:45 A.M., fifteen minutes early. When I got to the door, some fifteen people were crowded around wanting to be first in line. A large lady was bleeding from the nose from a family altercation the night before. Fridays were bad. Payday—Friday afternoon—brought with it the means to buy alcohol. This brought about heavy drinking and accompanying violence. Most murders occurred on Friday and Saturday nights. As I opened the door I noticed some of the complainants carried legal papers and documents in their hands. I gasped for air, took the key out of my pocket, and unlocked the door.

"I got here first," one woman said.

"No you didn't. I did."

"That's right, this second woman was first because I got here second."

It was heating up. With a sudden stroke of brilliance I said, "I am not seeing anyone until you line up in the order you came in and then sign up to see me on this piece of paper. And give me my pencil back or I won't be able to write down what any of you are telling me."

It was a long day even though it ended shortly after noon. That morning I was the district attorney, the judge, the jury, and King Solomon, rolled up into one. No one ever felt so helpless.

One two-hundred-and-fifty-pounder in cowboy boots with arms as big as my legs introduced himself. "Son, I'm Buddy Jackson and I want you to get the troopers to arrest my ex-friend Billy Bob. The little S.O.B. ran off with my best girl in my new Ford pickup. I know he's headed for Vegas. He has a brother there and has been talking about it for days. I figure he should be getting into Abilene in a couple of hours. I was told they left Lefty's Bar a little after midnight. You just go file on him for car theft and get that warrant issued quick. I been an auxiliary deputy constable some years back and know all about these things. You stay on this and call me as soon as they have that little so-and-so in jail. Understand? I want to drive up there and see his smiling face behind bars. You understand me, son?"

I told him he had to go over to the Auto Theft Division at HPD since it happened in the city and that we didn't file auto thefts without a police investigation. He said, "You city boys aren't worth shooting. I guess I just have to take care of that little S.O.B. myself. Then you'll sure enough have yourself a case." He stomped out red-faced with his boots pounding the floor.

Later in the day I encountered the only thoughtful and considerate person I saw that entire morning. An elderly black man with white hair and dressed in coat and tie came in and sat down. After saying good morning he plopped down a sheath full of papers on my desk. My first thought was that if I had three days to sort through all of these papers, I still wouldn't understand what his case was about. He said his Uncle Isaiah had died and only left one child, a daughter who could not read or write. Uncle Isaiah owned a forty-acre tract with a small house up in Washington County. "That girl needs to get that land in her name before her no-account neighbor cheats her out of it. Mr. Vance, I just know you can help make this happen."

"Well, I really can't. This is a probate matter. This whole will thing has to go before the judge up in Washington County. How come you thought the DA in Harris County could handle this?" I asked.

"Well, I went to see Deputy Red back home. Do you know Deputy Red? Everybody knows Deputy Red. Deputy Red said that the district attorney down in Houston can get anything done so I should go see him."

The next woman who walked in was in a highly emotional state. She was matronly, heavyset, and wore a dark blue dress with little white prints. She went on and on about how some Catholic priests had raped her at a convention at the Rice Hotel. "When did this all happen?" I asked.

"Oh, I'm not sure. Just call the hotel. They will remember when the priests were there at their convention. By the way, young man, where is Mr. Coulson? I usually come in during the week and he takes care of me."

"He's so tired from handling problems like this all week he just can't make it on Saturday."

"Well, young man, you just tell Mr. Coulson about all of this on Monday and tell him that his friend Emma came to see him. You be sure and tell him what happened to me. He will do something to those priests."

After seeing about thirty folks that morning, I went to the door and locked it. It was about 12:30 P.M. I had not taken a single charge. I do not believe I had helped a single soul that morning except for sending that fellow back to Washington County. Problems ranged from electricity that had been cut off to a neighbor's dog barking all night. One fellow wrote a check to buy a used car, but the car made it only two blocks from the used car lot and stalled. We had no consumer fraud division in those days, and there were no law enforcement people to investigate that problem. The experience taught me there were many helpless people out there that somebody was taking advantage of.

When I got home, Carolyn took off to go to the store. The house was packed with our kids and some unknown neighbor kids. They were squealing and roughhousing. The dog was chasing them and ripped into son Carroll's new trousers. All pandemonium had broken loose, but it was heaven compared to the complaint desk.

CHAPTER FIVE

Murder Cases in District Court

What comes out of a man, that defiles a man. For from within, out of the heart of men, proceed evil thoughts, adulteries, fornications, and murders.
—Mark 7:20–21

THIS TIME THE KTRH reporter gave the hourly news from the police station. Another killing in River City, the newscaster announced. "The victim, Tommy Sanchez, went to bed last night and never woke up. Homicide detectives reported his irate wife emptied a clip into her husband from his .45 automatic as he slept. She told police she was fed up. She said she had filed on him for aggravated assault on two previous occasions. The killing occurred about 3:00 A.M. She reported he came home drunk and threatened to kill her. As soon as he went to sleep she shot him five times. Murder charges have been filed. Bail has been set at $5,000."

What a gulf there was between the glamorous murder plots on television and most of the murder cases we handled. Barroom brawls and domestic squabbles. Wife beatings and wives fighting back. Some Texas jury would give probation to the woman mentioned in the radio story—if they convicted her at all. Truth is, most murder cases are not glamorous whodunits but frustrated lives played out in tragedy.

DURING MY DAYS AS an assistant DA some civil lawyer would approach me at a party and ask, "Tried any juicy cases lately?"

"Yeah, just tried two murder cases this week. Both were jury cases."

The person I was talking to would look at me in awe. "Wow, really? Two murder cases in a week?" What I did not explain was how simple it was to try the typical murder case. Most murder cases were over in a couple of days. In fact there was one less witness than we had in an aggravated assault case, that being the victim. In the average murder case, lawyers on both sides were usually stuck with witnesses who were neither articulate nor winsome. Usually the defense attorney had a field day with all of the inconsistencies and contradictions given by some of my witnesses, who had also been in that bar, six sheets to the wind. In some cases I felt lucky to even have witnesses show up, much less testify. It was amazing to me how many witnesses just happened to be in the bathroom at the time the shots went off. The good news for the State, however, was the fact the defense attorney had to put the defendant on the stand if he was to get an acquittal. Most defendants made atrocious witnesses, and the jury often couldn't wait to unload on the guy. The fun part of a murder prosecution was catching the defendant in a pack of lies. That did not take as much skill as one might think.

On television, highly scientific evidence usually nails the murderer in the face of all odds. In real life, our scientific evidence usually consisted of some little .22 shell recovered from a punctured lung and our medical examiner explaining how the deceased bled to death internally. I even had trouble getting police and expert witness not to use the word "deceased." Nobody connects a "deceased" person with a live human being. Also, I never saw a single murder case like Perry Mason had week after week where he skillfully extracted a confession from the star witness. For six and a half years I tried more murder cases than any other type of crime, probably over fifty but less than a hundred. Additionally, I think I tried ten murder cases during my time as DA. Out of all the murders I tried, only a fraction involved the death penalty. As a practical matter, a defendant had to kill someone while committing a crime or for hire or kill a police officer, before a jury would consider a death sentence. A good number who were convicted of murder received suspended sentences.

Still, during my prosecutorial days I had several death penalty verdicts. But no one I ever tried was actually executed, as the Supreme Court reduced all those on death row awaiting execution to life sentences. The Supreme Court ruled that the laws of all of the states pertaining to capital punishment were constitutionally inadequate. Texas and most states had laws that permitted the death penalty as a possible punishment for murder or rape or kidnapping. No state legislature had ever set out any specific formula in order to justify a death penalty verdict. The Supreme Court ruled that any state that wanted to have their death penalty upheld had to pass a new law where the jury found the individual would probably endanger other lives in the future. I think the majority of the Court really wanted to abolish the death penalty but stopped short due to public outcry. The net effect of the ruling was that the large number of people on death row in Texas and other states had their sentences commuted to life. The death penalty is now only applicable in special kinds of cases like multiple murders, hired killings, police officer victims, and murders committed during a rape, robbery, or kidnapping.

Back in the sixties Houston averaged around 300 murders per year. The number of murders has not increased greatly today, even in the face of Harris County's population explosion. This means the murder rate has decreased substantially over time. I think most juries know a death penalty case from a non-death penalty case. The Supreme Court is trying to weed out or cut down the death penalty even though the Founders would roll over if they read the opinions. I do think the death penalty deters some murders. At least those sent to prison for murder aren't able to kill again. Occasionally someone on death row kills while trying to escape. One recently killed the chaplain who came to minister to him. Besides, back in my day the average life sentence resulted in a defendant serving about twelve years. And some of these defendants got out earlier than that.

Next to barroom shootings, spousal murders came in second. In all these sudden crimes of passion, the preferred weapon was whatever could be found at the time. I tried murder cases where the instrument used was a hammer, an ice pick, an axe, a hatchet, a big butcher knife, a small paring knife, a car, a truck, a switchblade knife, a hunting knife, a large rock, a shovel, a shotgun, a rifle, a piece of lumber, and guns galore consisting of pistols, rifles, and shotguns of all calibers. A very small .22 pistol, which we called a Saturday Night Special, was often the weapon of choice. A barhound could stick that deadly little thing in his belt, put it in his hip pocket or shove it in the top of his boot. Rule was, keep it handy and keep it loaded. Some Houston bars resembled the "OK Corral."

Texas law was also unique in that it had a strange defense to murder no other state had. This defense was called "the paramour statute." If a defendant was male and married, then he had a legal right to kill his wife's lover, or paramour, if he caught them together. When a married man killed another man, often the defendant claimed he had just seen the guy in the company of his wife, no matter where she really might have been. He could testify he reasonably believed they had just had sex even though the victim was fully clothed and alone at the time. If this defense was raised, the jury would be instructed that before they could convict they must believe beyond a reasonable doubt that the killer really did not believe his wife and the deceased had a thing going.

I did my best to convince juries to take these domestic and barroom killings seriously. I was a borderline crusader trying to make the case that human life was valued in Harris County, that those guilty of taking another life would be punished appropriately. Although I convicted plenty of killers for the offense of murder, and a good number drew life or ninety-nine, I didn't scratch the surface. People didn't have any way to know what verdicts juries were handing out because the word never got out to the public at large. After a hard fought case, a miniscule story would appear in the back of section four saying Sam Smith got ninety-nine years for killing John Doe in Big Jim's Kumback Bar on Telephone Road. That was it.

Some murders were bizarre, like the case I tried involving a three-man triangle consisting of Beowulf, Cool Breeze, and Red Rover. Cool Breeze was shot by his longtime companion Beowulf for kissing Red Rover outside a Montrose tea room. Beowulf and Red Rover had been sharing an apartment together for several years at the time of the murder. The paramour defense did not apply since this was an all-male ensemble, and at least no one thought about giving them the right to marry back then. I was convinced the all-male, redneck jury would laugh my case out of court, but they hit Beowulf with ninety-nine years. The police were never sure of the real name of the killer or the victim. The indictment read, "A man better known as Beowulf."

One unique privilege about trying one of these cases was going to the scene. Going into a bar on Telephone Road or out on the old Beaumont Highway was an experience my friends at the silk stocking firms never encountered. I liked to go out there and draw a diagram of the place and take notes. I knew I was doing far more than most defense attorneys (not the really good defense attorneys, of course). My investigator would take pictures to be blown up in order to put meat on the bones. The cases were so short and sweet that I needed something tangible to get the jury's attention.

Fighting my way through smoke-filled dens with guys drinking their way through lunch was a necessity in locating key witnesses. One hot summer day my investigator, Johnny Fox, and I strolled into a local bar, the scene of a Saturday night killing. The bartender, built like an Oiler linebacker, was behind the bar. No need to hire a bouncer here, I thought. Johnny walked up to the man and said, "Do you know Joshua Eckert?"

"What makes you think I would tell you if I did?" came the terse reply.

Johnny pulled back his coat exposing his badge and his large black .45 automatic, always—and I mean always—kept in the cocked position and stuck inside his belt.

"Well, sir, I just thought you might want to talk to this young man here. He is an assistant district attorney. The way I see it is you can talk to this assistant right now or you can go down and talk to the grand jury. In fact I just happen to have a subpoena right here in my right ass pocket."

The bartender said, "Give me a minute, and I'll join you in that far booth over in the corner. I'd appreciate you guys not showin' you're law." Johnny was in hog heaven badging that bartender. That made his day.

After I became DA, I appointed Johnny as my chief investigator. He was a loyal friend, loved his job, and didn't mind making waves. He welcomed any assignment I ever gave him. He hauled me around to airports and to and from speeches when I needed the time to think about what I might say or just needed to catch up on all the office happenings. Johnny made a habit of trying to know everything that was going on in the office.

The most enjoyable part of any murder preparation was during lunch hour over in Houston's Third Ward or Fifth Ward. Claude Langston, my investigator during my days in Judge Sam Davis' Court, knew every backyard barbecue spot in town. Thirty years in the homicide division gave Claude a nose for finding witnesses and good barbecue. Behind many a house on those side streets feeding into Dowling or Holman or Lyons stood an old smoker sitting on packed down dirt in someone's back yard. That cooker would have a side of beef smoking slowly with a smell of mesquite or pecan wood stirring the appetite. Some old black guy who ran the show would have put that slab of beef on the iron grill the evening before and then covered it with bananas and oranges and barbecue sauce to keep it moist. There it would simmer all night. By noon the next day, some of the men in the neighborhood couldn't resist the smell and wandered up to eat. The men, including us, sat on barrels and ate off homemade wooden tables. For a dollar each we got a half pound of beef served on a sheet of wax paper with a couple pieces of light bread and three large slices of onion. Then the whole thing would be drowned in barbecue sauce. Close by was a washtub with chipped block ice covering large orange and red "sodie waters." Claude often said, "You know, even sittin' outside in August in ninety-nine degrees isn't so bad if a man has some good barbecue and a large orange. That's just part of a good homicide case."

Once we got in a friendly conversation, Claude often got someone talking who was willing to tell us how to locate Big Red or Skeeter or someone else with a last name unknown. "Yeah, old Slim is living over that liquor store over on Dowlin' street. Just see'd him yesterday. Now don't you folks go tellin' him how you found out his whereabouts."

My friend and fellow prosecutor Erwin Ernst loved barbecue more than anyone. He knew how to talk to the fellows standing around. Ernst would have been as lost as a goose wearing his clip-on tie and marching into the elegant Houston Club, but in the world of backyard barbecues he was right at home. Ernst's order was, "Give me an in-and-out afloatin' and a lage ange." In the King's English this translated, "Serve me a half pound of barbecue beef. Make half of it from the inside cut and the other half from the burnt outside part. Now take that beef and drown it in barbecue sauce. Then to drink, bring me the largest orange soda pop you have from that tub over there."

HOW I MISSED MY friend Ernst. He had left the DA's office several years earlier. I looked around at that moment and realized I was driving through the town of Rockport, a favorite resort of some of the old Houston families. I saw the sign saying "Courthouse." I took a right. Rockport was a peaceful little place and the town closest to Houston where the Gulf water was blue. This courthouse was way too modern for my tastes. I liked the old stone courthouses. A handful of cars were parked outside, but no one was coming or going.

I wondered how many murder cases had been tried in Rockport. After all, it was the county seat of Aransas County. Maybe they had one a year or one every five years. Harris County assistant DA's must have tried about fifty to a hundred murder cases a year to juries. I wondered how it would be to be the district attorney in such a quiet and peaceful community. Maybe have one assistant, a secretary, and an investigator. Houston was booming, bustling, and bursting at the seams, a true boomtown. Always action. Wouldn't trade it for the world, but sometimes the sheer numbers and size of it all could wear a person down.

Houston was now the nation's fourth largest city, the undisputed energy capital of the world, home to the largest medical center on the planet, and the world headquarters for space travel. "Houston, the Eagle has landed" and "Houston, we have a problem" were household phrases first uttered from outer space. Unfortunately, we were also known as the nation's murder capital. We even had an extra 300,000 illegals who were more law-abiding than most but still added to the crime rate. Boomtown atmosphere brought boomtown crime. The harder we worked to dispose of cases the greater the case load grew.

DELAYS BETWEEN ARREST AND trial increased to the point that career criminals could keep on plying their trade while on bond. More often than not it took two years or more to bring a defendant to trial.

The legislature finally gave us some relief. They created two more district courts, bringing the number from three up to five. Governor Price Daniel appointed Arnold Krichamer as judge of the Criminal District Court No. 4 and former district attorney Sam Davis as judge of Criminal District Court No. 5. The increase accrued nicely to my benefit. To staff the courts six new felony positions were created, causing me to get an early promotion up to district court before I was ready. With less than eighteen months experience I was now trying murder cases. I was assigned as the three man or mullet in Criminal District Court No. 5. Fred Hooey was my chief while the great Erwin Goree Ernst, was our two man.

At that time in mid-1959, our three existing felony courts included Criminal District Court, which presiding Judge Ed Duggan said was the oldest court in Texas; Criminal District Court No. 2, where Judge Langston King, our most senior judge, presided; and Criminal District Court No. 3, with a relatively new judge named Miron Love. Frank Briscoe was chief prosecutor in Duggan's court. He was young and talented and destined to be the next district attorney. Assisting Briscoe in Duggan's court was Jon Hughes who would go on to be a district court judge and then an appellate judge.

In Judge King's court we had Ben Woodall, who also became a district judge. His booming voice could frighten anyone. One day I walked into the library urgently trying to find one of our appellate lawyers to help me out of a legal bind in the middle of trial. I ran into the library and encountered Mr. Woodall. I asked him if he knew where our appellate lawyer was. Mr. Woodall boomed out, "Young man, you have a law degree. You are in the law library. Use it. You young prosecutors need to quit running in here for help!" Woodall was assisted by Conrad Castles, the man Percy Foreman described as his nemesis. Conrad also became a career judge. In District Court 3 where Miron Love presided, the chief prosecutor was Neil McKay, who would later become my first First Assistant and then go on to be a judge. Woodall's right-hand man was Fred Hooey. He became a district judge when the legislature created our sixth criminal district court a few years later. These felony prosecutors were full of talent and experience and overwhelmed most, if not all, of the defense attorneys. I knew one thing: they intimidated me just being around them.

In Court 5, our little family of three prosecutors—Fred Hooey, Erwin Ernst, and me—along with our one investigator, had to grind out a thousand felony cases per year just to stay even.

Fred Hooey was an Abe Lincoln lookalike. He was judicious and intimidating at the same time. Ernst, as the famous author Tommy Thompson wrote, was "a moon-faced man who could make Bob Hope jealous." Fred said Ernst knew more law than anyone in the office. For a long time, Ernst's legal talents were buried under his running one-liners and relentless cross-examination of every assistant who dared enter his office. Ernst later served as chief of the Trial Division when I was DA. After this Ernst became General Counsel to the Texas Prison System, then was elected district attorney of Walker County, and later became the district judge for several counties in the Huntsville area. As I moved a small cardboard box of my belongings into the desk adjoining his, Ernst asked, "Are you ready for district court?"

I knew I would get to try all the "dogs." But at least I would send some really bad guys to prison for bad stuff. As it turned out, DA Walton turned to Fred Hooey to handle most of the major investigations of public officials. These highly secretive assignments took Fred out of the courtroom for weeks at a time; it only left time for Fred to try about four death penalty cases during the year. Ernst and I split the rest of the docket. Ernst in essence became my boss. When I ask him for advice—which was often—he usually said, "Well, you have a law degree don't you? Didn't God give you a mind? What do you think ought to be done?"

Another characteristic of Ernst was that he took no pride in trying big cases. He actually had more fun trying the dogs. He loved the courtroom and trying any kind of case. He had no fear. He could out-talk and out-think anybody. The better the lawyer on the other side, the harder Ernst fought. Ernst let me try whatever cases I wanted. He let me try murder and rape cases from the beginning.

Judge Davis was a good judge. His one fault, however, was that time meant nothing to him. Judge Duggan and Judge King moved through trials like high speed trains; Judge Davis rode a covered wagon. To make up for his pace, Judge Sam kept us down there in court many a night and weekend.

Ernst and I tried one murder case where the verdict came in on a Saturday night at 11:30. Ernst noted we had just enough time for one or two beers before the bars closed.

On my first day in Judge Sam's court, the judge walked in a half hour late. His black muddy cowboy boots stuck out from under his long black robe. Judge Sam may have lived in Houston's finest neighborhood, River Oaks, but his heart was out in the country with his cows at his spread in Montgomery County. Some days the judge was sure to be late. Feeding his cows was a must, and meant a two-hour drive there and back on cold days. Judge Sam also had a habit of excusing the lawyers and the jury for a "fifteen minute" break. We were lucky if he came back in half an hour. Most judges like to quit around 5:00 P.M. Trials take a lot out of anybody, particularly the judge who has to sit and listen to all the lawyer talk. But we never quit on time. Seven or eight o'clock at night was average when we were in trial. Judge Sam was a kind man with gray hair and a dry wit. Ernst nicknamed His Honor, "Judge Sammy Davis, Sr." The nickname stuck although we never used the name to his face. The judge was a humble man who loved to spin true tales from the past. He was pleased that Fred, Ernie, and I were in his court. The judge called Fred "Honest Abe" and he called me "The Strangler" after a few of my early successes in some dog murder cases. He never did know what to call Ernst. The three of us loved Judge Sam.

In those days the assistants prepared the dockets and set the cases for trial in the district courts. The judge and clerk gladly left it up to the prosecutors to decide which cases would be set and when. One or two weeks out of the month the docket was all capital cases, usually murder and rape.

Murder cases occurred for the strangest of reasons. One of my first murder cases arose on Thanksgiving Day during an argument over who was going to get to eat the turkey leg. Another fatal shot was fired over a disagreement as to who won the World Series in 1933, the year I was born (the New York Giants beat the Washington Senators, four games to one). I could always draw a laugh in my civic club speeches when I told my audience to avoid homes and bars because this is where our killings took place. Establishments like the Dew Drop Inn, Bennie's Ice House, and The Flying Frog were venues of choice for one drunk to shoot another drunk with a Saturday Night Special. It was hard to see the little bullet, but often that little bullet was fatal. Killings among blacks in Third Ward, Fifth Ward, and Acres Homes only slightly outpaced the rednecks who haunted the beer joints on Telephone Road, McCarty Street, and Dixie Drive.

The Saturday Night Special, easily stuck in the hip pocket or stuck in a boot, should have been banned by the state of Texas and the federal government. Later as DA I proposed a law that all of the cheap little handguns be outlawed in their entirety. It would have passed, but the consensus was the law would be found in violation of the constitutional right to bear arms. A large segment of our Houston population felt undressed without the little fellow by their side. No self-respecting gun owner would have one of these guns close to their house. They were not good for hunting or target shooting. But in bars they did their job. Brilliant young resident surgeons were always putting gunshot victims back together over at Jefferson Davis, the public hospital. Without Houston's medical schools and abundance of doctors-in-training, no telling what our murder rate would have been.

The first week I was in district court, Ernst and I were enjoying some barbecue over at John's on West Gray, not the fancy Captain John's, but a black barbecue joint where you couldn't spend over a dollar. Ernst said, "How would you like to try a murder case next Monday?" I said yes without thinking or even asking what the case was about.

Ernst handed me the file, all four pages, which included a one-page offense report by the two radio patrolmen who initially made the scene and the two homicide officers, who described their findings in about 100 words or less. There was a two-page autopsy report and a one-page statement from the lone eyewitness. The witness, a fellow customer at the bar, said he saw one man walk up to another at the bar and shoot the victim twice at point-blank range. I had Claude Langston, our investigator, drive me out to the scene that same Friday afternoon to help prepare for next Monday's trial. The case was not complex. The indictment alleged that "Dink Smith had murdered with malice aforethought one Jeeter Johnson, by shooting him with a gun." I knew enough about beer joint killings to know the defense always claimed self-defense or accident. I thought this was a winnable case because with two shots, accident could not be involved. As to self-defense, the other available justification, the deceased was unarmed. The witness said the defendant walked up behind the guy, tapped him on the shoulder, and then fired two shots in him. The more I thought about the case the better I liked my chances to convict this cold-blooded killer.

I came back to the office and had the pistol retrieved from the property room to experiment with it. As a former Military Police lieutenant I understood pistols. It took considerable pressure to pull the trigger on any Saturday Night Special. I decided I would pass the weapon to the jury so they could see a gun like this could not accidentally go off twice.

In this case the decedent never uttered a sound. It was the defendant who walked up to Johnson and said something. When Johnson turned around, Dink put two in his chest. I thought Ernst most generous to pass this case off to me.

All weekend I thought about ways I would negate some phony self-defense claim. I could hardly sleep Sunday. Monday morning Ernst and I went to court. Ernst talked to the defense attorney and reported back that the client was not the least bit interested in taking the fifteen-year plea bargain. Ernst said he wasn't going to plead to anything. We had subpoe-naed six witnesses from the bar. Four showed up. Two said they were in the restroom and did not see anything. The bartender was one of the remaining two witnesses, but of course he was popping a top when the shots were fired. This left the one witness who gave the statement, but that would be enough. The bartender did say that if the two men had been arguing he would have heard it. I would call him and our main guy, who had described the event as "a pure assassination."

"Should I announce ready for trial without these other witnesses showing up?" I asked Ernst.

"Sure. The more witnesses you have the more the contradictions you will have. Among these barroom types, the fewer witnesses the better. Besides, we don't want any resets. This case ain't gonna improve with age," Ernst said.

After the police officers set the stage, I called our star witness, a clean-cut looking man, about forty years old. He even came to court in coat and tie. He spoke slowly and with confidence. How could the jury not believe him, even if he was a friend of the victim? He said Smith walked right past him and up to where Johnson was sitting at the bar. Then Smith said something as he tapped Johnson on the shoulder. At the same time Smith pulled a small gun from his trousers and when Johnson turned around on the stool, Smith fired twice at point-blank range. Jeeter fell to the ground and never said a word. He was dead when the police arrived. On cross-examination, my witness did great. He bombed the defense attorney with the words, "It sure looked like a pure assassination to me."

The defense attorney made a big deal out of the fact that the victim had been in the bar for a minute or less when the defendant walked in and killed him. It appeared the defense lawyer was trying to help the prosecution when he said, "And isn't it true that after Dink walked into the bar, that the only thing he did was to look to see where Jeeter was and then he just walked up to Jeeter and shot him dead?"

"Yes, that's right. He just walked up to Jeeter and shot him dead. Didn't even say hello. Just went straight after poor Jeeter." He also got my witness to say in about three different ways that he had no way of knowing what Dink and Jeeter had been doing prior to either one of them coming into the bar.

What does all that testimony do for the defense? I wondered. I was feeling mighty confident. The testimony just given ruled out self-defense and accident; the only thing left was a cold-blooded assassination. The defense attorney just put the nail in his client's coffin.

I closed our case with the medical examiner, who confirmed not only that the pistol shots caused the death but that the bullets were fired at very close range. At that I turned and whispered to Ernst, "I think we'll get some hard time in this one, Ernie. What do you think?"

"Well, don't go counting your chickens," Ernst said.

Trying to suppress a confident smile, I declared, "Your Honor, the State of Texas rests."

The defense attorney did not ask for the customary recess. "I call Mr. Dink Smith's wife, Lora Lee Smith, to the stand, Your Honor."

As soon as she was asked her name, she broke down crying. The defense attorney handed her a paper cup of water. "Now Mrs. Smith—Lora Lee—I know this is hard on you to come in here today, but try to drink this water and compose yourself. We need to hear what you have to say."

"Okay, I'll try," she said, wiping the tears away. "Oh, I'm so ashamed. I just don't think I can go through all of this." The judge called for a ten minute recess after which the trial resumed.

With tears still flowing, Lora Lee said, "It's all my fault. I had been seeing Mr. Johnson, Jeeter that is, for some time. My husband Dink knew nothing about it. At least until the day he shot Jeeter. He followed me in his pickup truck down to the motel where I met Jeeter. Jeeter and I rented a room. In fact, Jeeter was broke and I paid for the room. After we had sex in that room, Jeeter slipped out the door. I heard his car drive off. Then I went outside to walk to the front desk to pay the clerk. I don't think he saw me come out of the room because he was pulling out of the motel parking lot. I knew immediately that was my husband's truck and that he had to have seen my car parked next to Jeeter's car in front of that motel room. I now know he saw me go into the motel and Jeeter come up a few minutes later. I figured he was following Jeeter but didn't know for sure until he called me from the jail later that afternoon."

"Mrs. Smith, did you ever tell the police or the DA or anyone about this affair you had with Mr. Johnson?" the defense attorney asked.

"Oh, no, sir. The police never talked to me about what happened. Neither did anyone else until you talked to me about all of this when we sat down a few days after it happened."

"And you did have sex with him in that motel room?"

"Yes, sir."

"Are you and your husband living together today as husband and wife?"

"Yes, sir. He forgave me. We are back together. We never did split up. He got out of jail in a couple of days and went back to work. Things were pretty cool between us for some time, but we are finally doing okay, all things considered."

"By the way, you said you paid for this motel room right after Jeeter left. Do you know about what time it was you paid this bill and Jeeter left with your husband following him?"

"Yes, sir. When I paid the $6 for the room and checked out, the clerk had this little clock machine he ran the receipt through. You told me to keep this for the trial so I did. Here it is. See, it says the time and date right here. 12:32 P.M. that same Saturday afternoon my husband got put in jail for all of this."

"Thank you, Lora Lee. The defense will introduce this receipt as Defense Exhibit No. 1 and I have no more questions of this witness."

I turned to Ernie. "Should I ask her any questions?"

"I don't know why. Looks like you just got run over by the 'power mower' statute."

"Power mower" was our sarcastic name for Texas' unique paramour law. Needless to say, any married man on trial for murder could use the defense and often did if he could show the male whom he killed was in the same county with his wife.

Dink Jones was acquitted in short order. He may have set up this killing by knowing that his wife was having this affair and then looked for the opportunity to kill the man. That was known to have happened in cases in the past. Regardless, the law provided Dink with this defense all the same. The motel receipt gave an airtight defense and was unimpeachable. The jury was out about twenty minutes before saying not guilty due to this bizarre Texas law, a holdover from the Wild West days.

After the trial Ernst and I walked a block east down Preston Street to the place Ernst dubbed "The Linoleum Club," his favorite watering hole. Earlier, I had made the mistake of mentioning to him that I drank a little Cutty Sark in my fraternity days at UT. He immediately nicknamed me Cutty Sark. My new nickname stuck, as did all the nicknames Ernst gave to his buddies.

The Linoleum Club was an eating joint in the old, run-down DeGeorge Hotel. The nickname was a takeoff on Houston's plush Petroleum Club, a place where rich oil guys really do drink Cutty Sark. At the Linoleum Club we settled for Pearl beers.

As I was crying in my beer about the trial, Ernst evaluated why I got steamrolled.

I interjected, "But why didn't the defense counsel come forward and tell us about all this good evidence he had?" I asked.

"He didn't want to tip us off or take any chances. He did what you and I would have done. He surprised us. He got an acquittal. In his client's eyes he was also a hero and walked his man."

Years later, as district attorney, I vowed I would get this law repealed. I got my chance while serving on the State Bar Committee that rewrote the Texas Penal Code. When the penal code passed, paramour killings became second-degree murders. The license to kill was finally revoked.

As we walked out of the Linoleum Club, Ernst said, "By the way, Cutty Sark, welcome to district court."

CHAPTER SIX

Drunk Drivers and Tragic Deaths

First you take a drink, then the drink takes a drink, then the drink takes you.
—F. Scott Fitzgerald

ROLLING RIGHT ALONG THROUGH the next little town and ahead of schedule, I spotted a police car almost out of sight next to an abandoned building. Was he taking a little nap or did he have the radar gun in hand? I slowed down. I usually drove too fast. The thing that saved me from several traffic tickets was the fact that every Texas highway patrolman carried around a little book with my name on the front cover and picture inside. I had chaired the Texas Law Enforcement Commission that published a handbook for all peace officers in Texas. The officer would say, "Mr. Vance, you need to slow down. By the way, thanks for writing that little manual we carry around in our patrol cars. I use it every week in making arrests and searches and stuff."

I pulled to a stop at the town's red light. A red Ford pickup trailing a small boat was getting gas at the convenience store. A young man dressed in jeans came out of the store with several six-packs of beer that he tossed in a giant ice cooler. He flipped a "single" to his friend, who made a one-handed catch while holding the gas nozzle. The bay waters this far north still had a bluish cast. A good day for speckled trout and a few cool ones, I thought. But these guys weren't buying four six-packs to take to the house. A case of beer, two people. I could do the math.

DRUNK DRIVERS WERE A huge part of the docket down in county court. We tried about one DWI case a week. The criminal defense attorneys had a better chance for an acquittal when they represented businessmen and housewives for DWI. About half of the DWI defendants were convicted and half were acquitted in the jury cases. Back then, a defendant could refuse to take a blood test or breath test and we couldn't mention that to the jury. Jurors wondered, Where is the blood test or breath test? We could not answer their question.

The penalty for DWI first offenders ranged from three days in jail and a $50 fine, up to two years in jail and a $500 fine. A defendant convicted the second time around faced a felony charge of up to five years in prison. Another related type of case was Murder by Auto where we had to prove someone was killed at the hands of a drunk driver. I dreaded reliving the scene with a surviving parent or spouse. We would not only ask them to testify but also to hang around through the final arguments so the jury might better appreciate the enormity of their loss.

One of my fellow assistants, Jack Rawitscher, tried a case against a man who had no wreck, no injuries, and no blood test. The police stopped the fellow because he was driving very slowly down the Gulf Freeway. He said he thought he was too drunk to drive any faster. The jury convicted him and gave him the maximum punishment of two years in jail. The man was just a regular working guy with no criminal record. The punishment was so absurd that Jack agreed to a new trial so the man could plead for a ninety day sentence. One never knew what a jury in a DWI case was going to do. I tried forty or fifty DWIs to juries. In a good number of these cases the jury hit the defendant with thirty to ninety days. Those kinds of verdicts kept the pleas coming in on DWI cases.

Of our nation's 50,000 to 60,000 annual traffic fatalities, drinking was a major factor in half of them. The use of seat belts and getting tough on drunk drivers work and have saved thousands of lives each year. This is true even though we have many more motorists on the highways driving many more miles. Texas law once said a person was presumed intoxicated if they blew a .15 on the alcohol test. Roughly speaking, a person had to have about seven or eight beers in him or seven or eight ounces of hundred proof whiskey to hit that mark.

Some countries like Sweden and Norway now have a standards of .04, about a two-drink limit. Texans obviously prefer more latitude. Texas has now reduced our standard to .08, roughly four beers or four glasses of wine in the system of an average-sized man. The human body generally burns off one beer or one ounce of whiskey per hour. Nations that imposed harsh mandatory jail sentences saw their fatality rate drop dramatically. The law might not deter some drug addict who will pay any price for a fix, but the tougher laws work miracles in reducing drunk drivers. Besides, law-abiding folks don't want to lose their license or go to jail for drinking. Even most alcoholics know not to run such a risk by being nabbed for DWI.

In most of our DWI cases the officers described individuals who were road-hugging drunk. The highest blood test I ever saw on anyone charged with DWI was a .46. That takes a case of beer or an entire bottle of bourbon in an average-sized individual to reach that level. Most people are dead before that much alcohol is in their blood. What saves many people from dying of too much alcohol is that the heavy drinking causes them to pass out first. Binge drinkers are at a high risk of dying as the intake is so fast it cannot burn off. Alcohol is a poison and too much of it kills.

When I became district attorney I read all the stuff I could get my hands on about the subject and looked worldwide for the best solutions to reducing the many deaths from drunk drivers. What I discovered was a very obvious principle. DWI defendants were usually law-abiding people who were heavily influenced by "risk versus reward" thinking. The Scandinavian philosophy— throw the book at the first offender—worked. Deaths from drunk drivers shrank dramatically as a result of longer mandatory jail sentences, possible confiscation of the auto, and dropping the legally intoxicated standard down to two or three drinks in the system as opposed to five or six. The fishermen I observed down the road would need about eleven beers each over a six-hour fishing trip to hit .10. Thanks to considerable lobbying from Mothers Against Drunk Driving (MADD), other victims' groups, and our office, the legislature tightened the standard.

Most drunk drivers, not all, have a drinking problem. There are many repeat offenders among those charged with drunk driving. Technology that prohibits you from starting your car if you have too much alcohol is an effective way to deal with alcoholics. The main point is that unlike beer joint killings or smoking dope, most drunk drivers are deterred by tough laws.

Trying to combat drunk driving on all fronts, I made many talks on high school campuses and civic clubs on driving and drinking. We distributed literature all over town. Then we got innovative. We produced a movie.

I never heard of any other jurisdiction ever doing this, but I applied for a unique grant from the U.S. Department of Transportation. We received $25,000 to produce a film to warn high school kids and the public about the carnage from driving drunk. Since one of the most famous race car drivers of all time, A. J. Foyt, lived in Houston, I called him to see if he would star in our film. He not only agreed, but he had some great suggestions for the movie. As part of our script, A .J. volunteered his racing team to come out to the large parking area around the Astrodome for the filming. Each driver would drink so much and then drive an obstacle course and be filmed. There were four professional drivers participating. After taking down two ounces of bourbon, the guys drove well. Didn't crash into any pylons and didn't destroy the Astrodome. When they downed two more and waited about thirty minutes for maximum effect, their driving was shaky. They were going fast in and out of these pylons, not usually a problem for pros, but they clipped a few. After eight ounces and getting close to .15 there was not one driver who could sail around this course fast without clipping the pylons. A. J. told the guys they better not flip one of those expensive stock cars. For my part, I quit standing near the track.

To complete the film we added gory scenes from real life. This was easy. We just visited the Ben Taub charity hospital on a Saturday night to catch victims being hauled in on stretchers. In the film, City Chemist Floyd McDonald give the same edifying lecture he gave to jurors about how alcohol messes up the brain and one's ability to make good judgments in tight situations. With numerous copies of the movie, I sent assistant DAs all over the county to schools and civic clubs to educate the public.

We also wanted to evaluate drinking and driving patterns. As part of the same grant money, we enlisted the Houston Police Department and the Texas Department of Public Safety to set up roadblocks at random on freeways on a weekday and then on a Saturday afternoon. The weekday afternoon survey went as expected: some drunk drivers, but in low percentage. Lifestyles in Houston varied. Most of my friends drank a little on Friday or Saturday night. They seldom sat around on the couch getting sloshed during the day; however, Saturday afternoon on the freeways of Houston was a different experience. Our random stops of motorists showed that fully one-fourth of all adult males driving down the Galveston Freeway were legally intoxicated on Saturday afternoon.

Trials of DWIs usually had one thing in common: The defendant would swear he only had two beers. I use the term "he" as I only tried about three women in all of the DWI cases I tried. The defendants often brought their wives and children to court to evoke sympathy from the jury. I do recall one case where a defendant that I was trying for DWI kept walking over to a woman holding a little baby every chance he got. Obviously he wanted to build sympathy from the jury. Since the defense attorney had not mentioned the wife and kid when he was picking the jury, I took a chance. When he finally took the stand, I asked him if that was his wife and child. He said, "No, just a friend."

MY MOST UNUSUAL DRUNK driving case ended up being a murder case and not a DWI. I was still pretty green and new to district court. My boss Fred Hooey was off working on some secret grand jury investigation. The day the case was set for trial Ernst pulled up sick. The two lawyers representing the defendant, a man by the name of Henry James, announced ready for trial. All my witnesses were there so we went to trial. I was up against two talented veteran defense attorneys, Joe Newman and Tom Sanders.

Henry James was charged with killing a lady he had just met the same night by running over her with his car. Henry turned out to be a Warren Beatty lookalike. He was a tall, handsome hairdresser who was separated from his wife. On a hot July night, the thirty-year old Henry made his way to the Dew Drop Inn, a watering hole out on Airline Road. He spotted three women whom he then enticed to come sit at his table. The thirsty strangers were happy to let Henry finance a heavy night of drinking. Henry had an eye on one of the ladies. (By the time the trial came around, Henry was divorced. A pretty young thing, not connected to the case at all, accompanied him to court. I noticed that she hung on to him during the court recesses.)

On that fatal night after quaffing a few drinks between dances, Henry gathered the women and drove to Tomball and back. Tomball was twenty-five miles away. The foursome returned to the Dew Drop Inn, which by then was closed. Henry let the two younger girls out near their car. It was 2:00 A.M. The remaining passenger, Bernice Smith, a thirty-year old woman who had told Henry she was a waitress at a café, remained in his car so he could take her home. Henry and Bernice got into a screaming match when he let the other two girls out of his car to go home. The others offered Bernice a ride, but Bernice stuck with Henry, a regrettable choice.

According to Henry's testimony at the trial, their argument resumed as he drove off. Later, Bernice demanded to get out of the car. Henry stopped. Bernice exited the car door and began to walk down the deserted street. A block later in the 5500 block of Airline Road, Henry's Buick struck Bernice. Henry said this was an accident and would not have happened if she had not suddenly leaped in front of his moving vehicle. "She just jumped out in front of my car, and I hit her," he testified at trial.

Bernice died and was not around to tell her side of the story, but en route to the hospital she told the ambulance driver, "He got mad and hit me." The defense vigorously objected to this testimony as hearsay. It was a close call for the court. When we showed that the dying woman was highly emotional when she made the remark, the judge decided it was a classic *res gestae* statement—meaning it was admissible—and let the testimony go to the jury.

After Henry ran into Bernice, he did not leave the scene. In fact, it was Henry who called the police and the ambulance and gave the police a detailed written statement. I knew I had my hands full trying to prove that Henry's drunken driving caused the death—a felony carrying up to five years. I also knew it would be even harder to prove he intentionally killed her using his car as the weapon, particularly when he reported the incident to the police. Also, Henry was "clean": no previous arrests. He made a pleasant and soft-spoken witness. I thought we would be lucky to get a conviction of any kind.

The first day of trial the veteran defense attorneys seemed confident of getting an acquittal. The HPD accident investigator recalled Henry saying at the scene, "I got mad and bumped her." This was not an admission he intentionally killed her but it was certainly a different version from his statement that "she jumped in front of me." At least we had Henry telling two conflicting stories that night. But why would Henry run over a woman he hardly knew? I knew the jury would be asking that question.

And Bernice was drunk. Her blood test, taken as a routine part of the autopsy, showed .20. That meant she had about ten drinks of whiskey in her plus all of the drinks she had burned off, one for each hour of drinking. The jury knew she was sloshed and not thinking straight.

I put on the investigating officers. They said Henry was intoxicated when he was arrested but not staggering drunk. I laid out the scene and tried to show the positions of the car and Bernice at the time she was hit. Then we took the usual noon recess. Judge Sam always gave us an hour and a half, which gave me a chance to get organized and talk to my next witnesses. Over the noon hour I reviewed the autopsy pictures again. For the first time I noticed a small puncture wound with a blurred semicircle on Bernice's lower back. The semicircle was a couple of inches below the puncture mark. Then it hit me: Henry was driving a Buick. The Buicks of that vintage had a ring the size of a bracelet with a pointed piece of metal in the middle of that ring. A Buick's hood ornament was its trademark. The puncture mark I saw on Bernice's body was in the middle of her back, perhaps the same height as the hood ornament. If I was right in my interpretation, then she had been struck from the rear while walking on the shoulder. Had she leaped in front of Henry's car as he contended, there was no way the arrow in the middle of the ring could be planted in middle of her back.

Could it be the defense attorneys had not examined these autopsy photos? If so, they missed these marks. Maybe they did not realize their client's Buick had a ring with an arrow through it mounted on the hood. Over the recess I asked Dr. Joe Jachimczyk, the Harris County Medical Examiner, to study the photograph, take exact measurements, and draw up a diagram for the jury.

The next morning Dr. Joe told me I was right. He had done the measurements to the millimeter. I told him not to volunteer anything we had done unless the defense attorneys asked him a specific question that called for that information.

As expected, the defense called Henry to the stand as their final witness. He testified as expected: Bernice was walking on the shoulder going the same way as his car. He was driving slow in the right-hand lane. Suddenly, she jumped out to the left in front of the car. He had no time to stop. When they passed the witness, I asked Henry several times if he was certain his car had struck her in the front of her body or the side. Henry kept saying he knew he hit her in the front and perhaps just a little to the side. "Could the car have possibly struck her in the back?" I asked.

Henry said, "There is absolutely no way I struck her in the back." The defense rested. We recessed for the day.

First thing the next morning I called Dr. Joe to the stand. He said that in his opinion Henry's car had to have first struck Bernice in the back. I asked him to walk down the row outside the jury rail pointing out the semicircle and body marks made by a pointed object. He also said it would have been highly improbable a person going the same way as the car could suddenly leap out in front of the car and get hit in the back. I asked the woman clerk, who was within one inch of the same height as the victim, to stand up while Dr. Joe measured how high the marks were on the body. Then he testified the Buick ring would have been the perfect height off the ground to have hit the victim where it did as shown by the autopsy pictures.

Then I called Kenneth Swatzel, always an excellent witness. He was the crime analyst from HPD crime lab. The police had noticed some tire marks on the shoulder close to Bernice's body. Swatzel had made a cast from the tire tracks and showed the jury pictures of the tracks and Henry's tire. The two matched. Now the jury knew Henry's car had swerved off the pavement onto the shoulder, either because he was drunk or wanted to take Bernice out. This also proved Bernice was walking on the shoulder and did not leap in front of Henry's Buick.

The trial ended. Henry had a gallery supporting him, but we could not find a single soul to come forward to testify on behalf of Bernice. The other two girls at the Dew Drop Inn had just met her that night. Henry James' lawyers had called several character witnesses to the stand to say he had an excellent reputation and was very truthful.

During the final summations to the jury, Joe Newman, the defense attorney, argued that Henry simply erred in picking his company that night. "He never intended to harm anyone, certainly not Bernice. Bernice was so rip-roaring drunk that she had to be thinking crazy to just jump out in front of a moving car. This was most unfortunate but she was a barroom drunk just looking for an accident to happen. Henry, on the other hand, has a spotless reputation, holding the same job for years and with no previous arrests. He has several excellent character witnesses vouching for his good reputation." His lawyers kept emphasizing that Henry was a good enough citizen to immediately call the police and that he cooperated with them at every turn. Henry wanted her to live or he would not have called the ambulance, the defense contended.

I had twenty minutes to say the final words on behalf of the State of Texas and Bernice. I don't know what got into me, but I remember getting righteously indignant and pounding my fist on the counsel table and yelling, "She is dead, dead, dead, and nobody cares!" That came out spontaneously. "Yes, it is true we could find not one relative or friend to come in here and say good things about Bernice. What if she is a nobody in this world? What if she does not have a nice, wonderful reputation like this man sitting here? Does that mean this defendant can run his car off the road and hit her in the back at a fast enough speed to kill her? The physical evidence doesn't lie, it shows you what happened. Are you going to give this man a slap on the wrist because he is a somebody and she is a nobody? Just what is a human life worth in this county, anyway? You tell Henry what it is worth. You tell him Bernice may not have made the Social Register, but she has a right to live, a right not to be murdered. You also go tell the next Henry who even *thinks* about such evil they had better think twice. Nobody in this county kills someone and gets away with it. Do justice and let me suggest you give him some extra time for trying to put a snow job on you with a pack of lies. *That* is the real test of his character. Only you can do this. Come out and look him in the eye and give him a long time to think about what he did."

I sat down.

The jury had four options. They could convict for murder with malice (that carried two years to life), murder without malice (two to five years), negligent homicide (up to a year in jail), or aggravated assault (a misdemeanor with a maximum of two years). Some of the assistants watching the trial complimented my closing. They speculated he might be convicted of negligent homicide.

Much to our surprise, in an hour the jury came back and convicted Henry of the offense of murder with malice—the harshest possible conviction. They assessed his punishment at twelve years in the penitentiary. Even the old bailiff was shocked.

Following the trial the defense attorneys, Newman and Sanders, did a very nice thing. They wrote my boss, Dan Walton, a letter praising my trial skills. The newspapers gave the story a page one headline, complete with pictures. Maybe some potential drunk driver would take notice. Even so, in a few weeks few people would recall the case. It was just one in a long line of cases and tragedies played out each week in the courtrooms of Harris County. But I would always remember the woman no one cared about, part of the least, the last, and the left out. This proved to be my watershed case. From then on I followed my gut and argued from the heart, rather than some memorized speech.

CHAPTER SEVEN

The Road to the Corner Office

And it shall be my duty as district attorney not only to prosecute to the limit of the law the perpetrators of crime within this county but to defend with equal vigor the rights and privileges of all its citizens.
—from the *Mr. District Attorney* radio show

How UNLIKELY IT WAS that I should ever become the district attorney of Harris County. I was a political novice. I had never held office or run for office. My only experience in politics was pushing cards for my boss Dan Walton on election day. And he lost. At thirty-two, I was so young. In fact, for the last hundred years no one that young had been elected DA in Harris County. Most lawyers considered me a good trial lawyer, but the office had many good trial lawyers. Others on staff and around town had more trial experience, more prosecution experience, and grey hair. The only people I had ever managed were the two lawyers and investigator who were assigned to my court. The fact that I ended up becoming district attorney was like a dream, a very unlikely dream. I had been on staff seven years before this thought crossed my mind. Although I had a vague idea about being a judge someday, becoming DA was not on my radar screen.

The whole thing started in 1965. I had completed my year of being the president of the Houston Young Lawyers Association, known in those days as the Houston Junior Bar. I was one of the five chief prosecutors in our five criminal district courts, a fun and marvelous job. In the prosecutor's world, I had it made. I was chief of our little three-man law firm with my own investigator at my beck and call. The dependable Ray Montgomery, a good friend and wonderful guy, was the number two man. Big Ray would later be elected DA himself, somewhere up in deep East Texas. Phil Warner was the investigator and a good guy. Phil went to law school at night and became an assistant DA before he went on to be the editor of the Houston *Chronicle*. We had a good thing going. Never a dull moment.

I knew sometime in the future I needed to leave the office to make more money if we were to put five kids through college. But not yet. I had received a couple attractive offers. One offer was with a major oil company in town. The company had suffered a $200,000 loss at the hands of two crooks in a complex oil fraud scheme. The two were indicted, and the case fell in my court. The local head counsel for Texaco's Houston office helped gather facts and witnesses for me to present to the jury. He sat through the entire case as I tried it. None of us were confident the case was a winner, but the jury sent the guys to prison. After the verdict, the Texaco lawyer told me he needed someone for his trial department who was not afraid to make decisions and go to court and mix it up. His trial docket was growing so he offered me a job. Counting the car and fringe benefits, the amount approached double what I was then making. Carolyn and I talked it over. With mixed emotions I turned the job down. My gut reaction was that a corporate career would not be a good fit.

Ernst often asked me, "Cutty Sark, what are you going to do when you grow up?" Ernst opined he still did not know what he was going to do. The thought of leaving the action to get bogged down in the legal paper wars over on the civil side was painful. Then one day about midsummer of 1965, I heard a most interesting rumor. My friend from high school, Jimmy James, was also an assistant DA and considered the chief gossip of the office. Sometimes he missed the mark, but he always had a lot of fun information to spread around. Jimmy came to me and said, "Have you heard the big rumor? Frank Briscoe is going to resign so he can run for Congress."

Jimmy said, "You know what that means don't you? If he runs for that new congressional seat out in our end of town, the law says he will have to resign. That's a scary thought, don't you think? We might get some idiot in here." Jimmy was right. Working for some person with no experience or history in the office would be a bummer. Jimmy, who later went on to become an outstanding district judge and then went on the Court of Appeals, was a person I listened to. He said, "Well, you are pretty well-known. Maybe you ought to make a run."

Jimmy got my attention. I started thinking, "What if?"

I really did not want to see Frank go. I had worked for Dan Walton and wanted Dan to be re-elected. He was a wonderful man and lawyer. But once

Frank came in, I saw that he was a fun guy to work for. I already knew he was an outstanding prosecutor. Frank kept promoting me until I was a chief prosecutor, the best job in the office. The thought of a new boss who was selected by the vagaries of politics was unappealing.

When fall arrived, Jimmy's rumor turned out to be true. Frank played it coy. He had not announced, but he was calling on the town's leaders and making those necessary moves to launch a campaign for Congress. Later the media speculated Frank had the inside track because he was both a proven conservative and a Democrat. In those days, many in Houston never dreamed a Republican could be elected in Harris County. Frank's opponent, who was making his first race, had different ideas. He was a local oilman named George H. W. Bush. Bush won that election and headed to Congress. The rest, as they say, is history.

When Frank tendered his resignation letter in order to run, Governor John Connally would have to appoint the interim to serve until the election was held. I was surprised at Frank's desire to move to Washington to take on a job that would not be as exciting. We figured Frank might possibly run for state attorney general someday, but this Congress thing caught us by surprise.

No one on the staff was pursuing the DA's job. My one-year term as president of the Houston Young Lawyers Association had put me on the map a little bit. But even that election had been a fluke.

When my friend Bass Wallace was president of the HYLA, he asked me if I would put on a mock trial for high school students. I took the project on. I wrote the script and talked Frank Briscoe and Richard "Racehorse" Haynes into being the prosecutor and defense attorney. Next to Percy Foreman, Racehorse Haynes was the most famous criminal defense lawyer in Houston at the time. Judge Ed Duggan presided. The case was a good one for high school kids, similar to one I tried in real life. It was called *State of Texas v. Teddy Bushman*. Good friend Ted Bush played the defendant. This case was perhaps the first major service project the HYLA ever had. It was a lot of work to write the script and organize the trial, but it was a smash hit, complete with front-page coverage. This project led to my election as secretary of the HYLA the next year and president the following year. With all of my real trials, it was ironic that a mock trial was the springboard to my political future.

The biggest miracle of all concerning my appointment and election was the fact that so many friends offered to pitch in and help. A while earlier I had organized a softball league that played at Grady Park behind my house.

The DA's office and the five largest firms in town made up the league. Over the previous two years I had come to know a good number of lawyers with the top firms. All were practicing civil law, of course.

Additionally, as a captain in the JAG Corps Reserve, I was in a unit with about forty enlisted men, all lawyers, and many who would become some of the town's leading practitioners. One of them, Rebby Gregg, nicknamed me "Captain Carol." When we all went off to Army camp every summer, I marched these guys to class as their platoon leader. These friends were quite willing to introduce me to their senior partners and to a few of Houston's corporate leaders.

The fact that finally hit home with me in my thought process was realizing that Governor Connally had to appoint someone. Why not me? I began making the rounds with known politicos, lobbyists, corporate executives, labor union heads, leaders in places like Baytown and Pasadena and fifteen other municipalities. All I knew to say was, "I want to be your next district attorney."

I had Frank's blessing. He loved the office and wanted to see it remain in good hands. Frank was not going to endorse me, but he told many a person I would make a good DA. Frank and the whole staff knew that I wouldn't do anything crazy and fire a bunch of good lawyers as some politicians might. They knew I would keep the staff intact for professional and morale reasons. We all recognized the long tenured prosecutors, who have talent, are the office's most valuable asset.

After being president of the Houston Young Lawyers, I was elected to the board of the Texas Young Lawyers Association. Right after Briscoe said he was resigning, our board met in Midland. This was a watershed moment. My fellow board members and good friends Walter Zivley, Joe Jaworski, and Sonny Sowell, three young and prominent Houston lawyers, stayed up all night telling me who I needed to see and what I needed to do to make the run. I filled up a legal pad with notes. Seems as though they knew everyone in the city with any clout. They also knew all twelve names who were on Governor Connally's steering committee that advised him about Houston appointments. Other than spilling part of my Rusty Nail on my legal pad, that all-night stand came off without a hitch and outlined a strategy for me and my friends to follow. I returned to Houston with more work than I could do. The first goal was to seek the appointment from the governor. If Governor Connally appointed me, I would have the inside track running as the incumbent. Sonny Sowell told me to hire the dean of Harris County politics, Ben

Kaplan, who made his living working with conservative Democrat candidates. I followed Sonny's advice.

The advisors on Governor Connally's Houston committee turned out to be a tremendous help. My law school friend, Bill Barnett, who later became managing partner of Baker and Botts, worked for a well-known trial lawyer named Hugh Patterson. Hugh, Bill, and I had lunch several times. Not only was he on the Connally committee but he had been a roommate of the governor's at the University of Texas. John Singleton, later to become the chief federal judge for the Southern District of Texas, pledged his support, as did Johnny Crooker, Jr., a prominent lawyer whose dad had been district attorney decades before. The non-lawyers on Connally's committee gave me a warm reception and encouraged me to seek the appointment. Lloyd Bentsen, later our distinguished senator from Texas, and Warren Bellows, a friend from church, were among this group.

In Austin, John Connally's right-hand man and executive assistant, Larry Temple, had been my law school classmate. Larry arranged the appointment for me see the governor. Larry also was candid with me about where I stood. He said the governor would have a hard time passing over local attorney John Hill if Hill wanted the job. Hill, who later became Texas Attorney General and was nearly elected governor, had headed Connally's campaign in Harris County. I understood if he wanted the job, it was his.

Whether appointed or not, I decided I was going to run for the office. I felt like I would have a chance to win; and even if I lost at least I would have given it the old college try. Then I could go into the practice of law, putting the DA's office behind me. I had a list of about a hundred key leaders around the county. I called on each one and saw most. The leaders were from all walks of life: Yarborough Democrats and Connally Democrats, minority leaders, business leaders, lawyers, public officials, union leaders, blacks, whites, Hispanics. When I called on black leaders like Hobart Taylor, Barbara Jordan, Judson Robinson, Bill Lawson, and others, I thought I might receive a cool reception. But they all seemed comfortable with me. I think many of the leaders were glad to see someone show up who knew what being DA was all about. I told everyone I called on of my decision that I was going to run for the office whether appointed or not.

Another break was through my friend and fellow assistant DA, Don Keith. For about two years when I lived in Westbury, Don and I rode to work together. Don was the favorite nephew of Everett Collier, the editor in chief of the Houston *Chronicle*. Everett liked me. He was outspoken and told everyone he wanted to see me get the job. I believed if there was a race, I would receive the *Chronicle* endorsement. Also, I had played handball occasionally with Bill Hobby. Along with his mother, Oveta Culp Hobby, Bill owned and operated the Houston *Post*, then the morning newspaper. (Mrs. Hobby had been the nation's second female cabinet member, under President Eisenhower; Bill Hobby later became lieutenant governor of Texas). After a good meeting with those two and their editorial board, I believed the *Post* would either support me or stay neutral.

Outside of Harris County I had some help from strange places. I had come to know Homer Garrison, Jr., the legendary head of the Texas Department of Public Safety. Both he and DeWitt Greer, the respected and long-serving head of the Texas Highway Department, were close friends of my uncle Marvin Vance, who was the longtime pastor of First Methodist Church in Austin. Both of these men contacted the governor on my behalf. Our respected mayor, Louie Welch, and his police chief, Herman Short, wanted an experienced prosecutor in that office, and both told me they put in a good word with Connally. Leon Jaworski, the future Watergate prosecutor and president of the American Bar Association, was a friend and a strong supporter. I had the good fortune of trying a case against him when he took on a court appointment to represent an indigent. He was an incredible trial lawyer.

My friend Dan Arnold, a most active community leader and partner at Vinson and Elkins, took me all over his firm and saw to it I received a nice contribution. Each of the major firms in town contributed $1,000 to my campaign. That was big money in those days. I believed I could run a county-wide and effective campaign for $35,000. I estimated I could raise $20,000 of that without much problem.

Things went better than I ever dreamed. Nevertheless, it took forever before John Connally was available to meet with me. Finally the day came. I arrived in Austin with nervous trepidation. I climbed the tall stone steps of the capitol and found my way to the governor's chambers. After an hour of waiting, I was ushered into this gigantic office for our private meeting. Governor Connally, who may have been the most impressive man I ever met, spoke very warmly and at the same time with great authority. His charisma and winsome way set me at ease. I am sure I was a nervous wreck. Although his secretary warned me our meeting would be brief, he spent close to an hour with me. Even then I thought he would make a great president someday.

Governor Connally said he had been inundated with calls and letters about me. I knew he did not like letter writing campaigns so I never asked anyone to write him. While I had asked key people he knew to call him, many chose to write him anyway, as my blind carbons demonstrated. The governor was very frank. He told me that John Hill had the appointment if he wanted it. The governor told me I was his second choice. He also said he did not know what Hill wanted to do. Everyone knew that John Hill had his political sights set on Austin and ultimately the governorship, and that the DA's job would be just a stepping stone.

I took a calculated risk. I told the governor that I had enough political sense to know that anyone he appointed would probably be elected. I said, "Even so, I am planning to run anyway. I feel like I need to be open about all of this and tell you. My sole desire is to be district attorney. I do not see this as a stepping stone to any other office. I just want to be district attorney, and if I lose, that is all right. At least I will have tried. The plain and simple fact is I love the DA's office and want to be district attorney."

The governor graciously accepted what I said. He said, "If I wanted a job that bad, I would run for it, too. I appreciate the desire and dedication you would bring to that position." Whatever the governor had to do, that was his business and he would have good reason. John Hill was one of the best trial lawyers in the state. And it was a rare and uplifting experience to be in John Connally's presence. I think I would have followed him anywhere.

The *Chronicle* began to speculate as to whether John Hill wanted the job. John was probably the city's best-known plaintiff's lawyer. He was popular. He was young, but he was an old pro compared to me. He knew Harris County politics. He and I later worked together in the trenches for Young Life, the ministry to high school students, where all of our children were involved. John was a good guy. As it turned out, he served the state well as attorney general and later as Chief Justice of the Texas Supreme Court. Indeed, he was one of our most outstanding chief justices as he led the fight for judicial reform and non-partisan elections of judges.

On my return to Houston, Jimmy Brill, my close friend, agreed to be my campaign manager. I put together a lawyers' committee from all over the county. I was ready to leap from the gate when the gun went off.

One day soon the unexpected happened. The office of Secretary of State became vacant. Governor Connally had to appoint a replacement and he chose John Hill. This was a better deal for John as folks from Houston were seldom successful in getting elected to statewide office. I hoped my chances for the appointment had soared.

The local media began to write stories that my appointment was a done deal. They just hadn't informed John Connally yet. I had not heard a word from the Governor's Office. My friend Larry Temple said things looked good. He was too diplomatic to say, "Cool it," but that was what I heard. The problem was that time was getting short. Frank Briscoe was leaving office on the last day of January. January was running out, and my phone was not ringing.

January 31 came. Frank Briscoe would walk out of that office that day, never to return. The staff spent that afternoon joshing Frank and telling him he would hate Congress and all the hot air in D.C. Everyone assumed Frank would be elected, of course, because his opponent was a Republican and not as well-known. Republicans just did not hold office in Texas in those days. Besides, Frank's opponent was from up East. Rumor had it his dad had been a senator somewhere up in New England. Frank, by contrast, had been a well-known and popular district attorney.

That day, January 31, Frank hung around until about 6:00 P.M. He, too, was waiting for the governor to call me. I was beginning to think it would not happen. Frank finished cleaning out his desk. As he headed for home, he handed me the keys to his corner office and the keys to his new dark blue Oldsmobile 98, a beautiful car the county furnished to the DA. I refused to take either set of keys. I thought it bad luck. I headed for home myself as the county switchboards were closing. I picked up a Houston *Chronicle* on the way out. The paper had a story speculating what would happen tomorrow in all of our courts if Harris County had no DA. "Without a duly installed DA, not a single Assistant would have authority to act," the media reported. "Our entire criminal justice system will be shut down."

By the time I got home, Carolyn had a long list of callers wanting to know if I heard from the governor. Friends and media kept calling while I begged them to hang up so I could keep open the only line I had. I kept promising to call everyone later if I did hear something. Around 10:00 P.M. I was very edgy. I grabbed an old rubber ball and went outside to play catch with myself off our brick wall. I was in the fourth inning of an imaginary World Series game when Carolyn opened the door and said, "Some man is on the phone."

"Carol, this is John," the voice on the other end informed me. "John Connally. Sorry for the late call, but I just got back into Austin and wanted to call you myself. I am appointing you as District Attorney of Harris County, effective tomorrow. I just issued a press release to this effect. I know you'll do an excellent job. I'm glad to appoint someone who is as qualified as you are; I don't always have that choice. You have my best wishes."

I felt faint. I managed to eke out, "Thank you, Governor. I'll try to do a good job," or some very original utterance like that.

I simply could not believe it. The whole thing seemed like a dream. How could someone as little known as me ever become the district attorney of Harris County? I told Carolyn the news. The kids were asleep. I did not dare wake them. They were going to have to get up early, put on their best clothes, and march down to the courthouse to be photographed as they watched their dad get sworn in. It was now 11:00 P.M. I started making calls. I woke Leon Jaworski up and asked him to be at the swearing-in and say a few words. I called all of the media—television and radio stations and the press. I called my pastor, Jack Lancaster, to say the prayer. I knew I had to be sworn in as early as possible or else none of the courts could operate. After my swearing-in, I would have to get Judge Duggan to swear in the fifty-five assistants and fifteen investigators so they could legally serve. I would announce my candidacy at the same time. Why not start off with a bang? Lots of work to do. Officeholders today get secretly sworn in and then hold a big public but legally meaningless event later. Not back then. Everyone played it straight. I would be sworn in in a few hours and the whole thing would be as public as I could make it. I was awake most of the night thinking about people to call and things to do.

The next morning the courtroom—the old Criminal District Court—overflowed deep into the halls. The courtroom held about two hundred. My family was on the first couple of rows. No one was more proud of this moment than my mother, "Mama Nell," who always exaggerated my abilities and achievements. My stepfather, R. Lee Chance, was also there. Dad was proud. He always insisted I get the college education he never had. The ceremony went off without a hitch as our five kids, ages one to eleven, sat with Carolyn's parents, Harold and Mae Kongabel. Carolyn was by my side blinking at the flash bulbs and wondering what our quiet little lives had come to. Judge Duggan finally picked up the Bible that had been used to swear in district attorneys through the years and administered the oath. When I said "I do," the judge shook my hand and said, "Congratulations, Mr. District Attorney."

By 10:00 the ceremony was over. The TV people were gathering up their equipment. The crowd had dispersed. Back in my office the kids were asking, "Do we have to go to school today?" Judge Duggan had his own cases to try and for the first time in over three years, I would not be in his court announcing "the State of Texas is ready, Your Honor."

February 1, 1966, one month short of eight years as an assistant, I was the district attorney of Harris County. Young and green, I tried to put on a good front. I announced to the press that morning that Neil McKay would be my First Assistant. I also said that Judy Wayt, who at an earlier time had been Frank's secretary, would be my secretary. Judy was a great help. She had ample copies of the new organization chart that I had given her a few days earlier just in case the appointment came through. My old friend Wells Stewart was re-joining the office as an assistant. My investigator Phil Warner, who just passed the bar, was sworn in as an assistant DA as well.

With the ceremony over, I walked into the first private office I ever had. The office had a private bath, a plush sofa, and big leather chairs. The huge desk was dark wood, not green metal. I sat down. Silence overwhelmed me. I had been so busy trying to get there I had never given a single thought to what this new life would look like. I had also never considered if I was up to all this. Could I lead these close friends who I was used to cutting up with? Would there ever be the time to simply have a cup of coffee with a member of the staff and not talk business? Would I do something dumb and screw up? Would the press always be hanging around like they did with Frank? Judy handed me about fifty pink phone slips. Most were just congratulations and well-wishes, but now I knew the calls would come in much greater numbers than I could handle. God help me.

By now Jimmy James was at the door. He was a chief prosecutor and looking for some direction. "Chief, you know that capital case we are starting next Monday asking the death penalty on that teenage kid who killed the U-tote-M clerk? He doesn't have a record. Not a single arrest we know of. His lawyer called this morning and they want to plead out for life. We might want to do it. He is a nice looking kid and looks about fifteen."

"Well, I want to talk about it when I come up for air. Be sure you check with Juvenile again to see if he is clean. Also I want to know what the widow and parents think. Get on Judy's calendar sometime tomorrow. We need to spend a little time on this one."

Judy handed me the keys to the DA's car, the sleek midnight blue Olds 98. She had me sign some papers showing I would be making $20,000 annually, not to mention have the use of the free luxury car. This was more than a slight boost over my present $10,800 per year. Then she handed me some more phone slips. At the same time, I noticed all four of my private lines to my new office were lit up with that constant bleeping noise. How could I turn them off?

Bob Musslewhite stuck his head in the door. Bob, one of our chiefs, was getting ready to try on a county commissioner charged with a misdemeanor. The offense was minor but could cost the commissioner his elected post. The county judge and the four commissioners composed what is known as the Commissioners Court of Harris County. They ran the county. They decided how many assistants our office would have and how much each would be paid.

"Cutty," Bob said, knowing that our friendship and the informality of the office would not change, "I don't think we can make this case. I will go try it, but it may not be the right thing to do. I can't figure what that runaway grand jury used for evidence when they indicted this guy. Want me to fetch the nolle pad?" Bob was referring to *nolle pros*, the Latin term meaning to dismiss the case.

"Tell you what, Bob. You put together your strongest evidence and tell me piece by piece what it is. I want Jimmy Brough to be here when we talk." Brough was our head legal guru. "You and Brough bring me the closest cases you can find. Let's get together mid-week, and I'll decide. I want to either try this thing or dismiss it soon as possible. I have to go before that Court with our budget proposals by March 1. I don't want this hanging on to us like an albatross when I go. It could look like blackmail. I want the public, the press, and the commissioners to know exactly what our position is on that case."

Then it dawned on me why my salary had doubled. Everyone in the office could go to someone higher in authority to make tough decisions. I recalled Harry Truman's famous quote, "The buck stops here." From that first day I hit the ground running and did not come up for air for a long time.

The first couple of years were not much fun. America was changing, and not for the better. Crime was rising dramatically. Riots spread across the nation's cities and campuses. The TSU riot in Houston was only a year away on the horizon. Protestors burned American flags. The drug trade, previously reserved for the poor and uneducated, filtered into our schools and even into the world of business. LSD made people crazy but they kept on taking it. Police officers were no longer "cops," but "pigs" (and I thought "cop" was bad enough). Disrespect for the law was becoming the rule and not the exception. Fear of the growing number of assaults and thefts ushered in the whole new industry of private security. Jails and prisons were becoming over-crowded. The U.S. Supreme Court had just begun its little social revolution as it radically changed the laws of arrest, search and seizures, and admissibility of evidence at trial. Liberal parole policies and the growing length of time between arrest and trial put more criminals on the street.

To top it off, Texas had just passed a cumbersome and technical new Code of Criminal Procedure which would kick in shortly. Nothing was the same. From where I sat it appeared to me our criminal justice system was in a state of shock. And here I was, a young rookie DA who was the chief law enforcement officer in one of the nation's largest cities. Facing new times and unsolvable problems, I smiled, acted cool, and put on a good act.

At times I longed to be that carefree assistant once again. How uncomplicated my life had been. Although I worked some nights and weekends in Judge Davis' court, most days I left around 5:00 P.M. Ed Duggan worked hard but always recessed by 5:30. The only time I took work home with me was when I was in trial. Trying cases was fun. If I lost one, I never looked back. There would be another one tomorrow or next week. I never fell behind on phone calls. Paperwork was at a minimum. Life was challenging, simple, and fun. In fact, the most fun I had ever had. Now I was already drowning. It was not the tough decisions that bothered me. It was the volume of human confrontations, the little decisions, so many people demanding to see me. That is what sapped my energy.

In addition to my work, I had a campaign to run. From the day I took office until the day I left, I was always running. I made lots of speeches, roughly two hundred per year. Thank goodness for great secretaries. Judy Wayt started with me for several years. Carolyn Hinton took the long haul in the middle, and then Judy returned to finish out with me. Judy and Carolyn were called executive secretaries, but they were a lot more than that. They were administrative assistants, schedulers, reminders of names, and the ones who guarded the door and limited access so I could breathe. They were my second voice in keeping a lot of stuff from reaching my door. They kept me going to the right place at the right time. Both of them instinctively knew which calls I needed to take and who could be referred to the First Assistant or someone else. Assistants, reporters, and well-wishers were always standing over my secretary's desk. I don't know how either one of them accomplished anything considering the traffic in and out of that office. Long before MapQuest, they made me little maps so I would find my way across town. They could always come up with the file I needed. When they gave me a page out of a file to review, they gave me a copy and left the original in the file (I could misplace and lose a filing cabinet, much less a single sheet of paper). If some visitor stayed a minute too long, they rang the buzzer to give me an excuse to end the meeting and say I had to be somewhere else.

Before that first day on the job was over, I announced for office and paid my entire filing fee of $3,000 to run for DA. Within a few days I had drawn four opponents in the Democratic primary. Having a girl's name for a first name and not being well-known to the public, I knew I had a fight on my hands.

My first public appearance was riding in the rodeo parade. I was told nearly a half million would be watching. Every February Houstonians put on their boots and lined Main Street to hear the marching bands and watch drunk cowboys ride into town from many trail rides around the state. A reputable bail bondsman and friend, Sam Alfano, came to me and asked if I would ride in the parade in his antique convertible. Most public officials were riding in new convertibles furnished by local car dealers. Sam said I would be doing him a favor as he wanted to show off his classic 1937 four-door black Cadillac convertible. This awesome car had a straight twelve cylinder engine. Carolyn and our four oldest children, all little tikes, climbed in that beautiful car. We were all uncomfortably attired in strange looking cowboy gear. I splurged twenty bucks at Foley's for my first pair of cowboy boots. When we started down Main Street, on seeing the "District Attorney Carol Vance" sign on the side of the car, many a spectator waived at Carolyn. I over-heard one spectator say, "Oh, we now have a woman DA." Clearly, with a girl's first name I was having an identity problem and would have to campaign harder than ever. I told the kids to wave to the crowd and smile. Years later, many a person would approach me at some function and ask, "Where in the world did that magnificent old black Cadillac come from that you rode in that rodeo parade?"

Each of my four opponents had paid only the $50 down payment on their filing fees. By the final filing deadline, each opponent had to come up with the $2,950 balance. One morning, after six weeks of frantic campaigning, several speeches a week, and many more political events to cover, I awoke to retrieve my morning *Post*. I opened up the newspaper and there on page one was the story, "Vance Alone in DA Race." I could not believe it. I read on. "Carol Vance, the newly appointed District Attorney, will face no opposition in his race for District Attorney. None of the four announced candidates paid the balance of their filing fee by yesterday's deadline. With no Republicans running for this office, Vance will serve as Harris County District Attorney for the next three years."

I ran to tell Carolyn, knee deep in getting kids off to school. The next thing I did was make me a great big old cup of coffee and go in the living

room and just sit there and enjoy it. I bet I did not get to work until 9:30 A.M.
that morning. A happy staff of employees kept dropping by all day to say
how pleased they were.

My predecessor, Frank Briscoe, was not so lucky in his congressional
race. George Bush ran an awesome campaign and won by a good margin to
start his remarkable career. We told Frank, "You sure know how to pick an
opponent." After I became a member of Houston Country Club and took up
tennis with a vengeance, I sometimes played doubles with George Bush. He
was a great tennis enthusiast. Of course he became not only Mr. President
but Mr. Houston as well.

Although I could relax on the campaign trail, I decided to keep attending
the political functions as an investment in the future. I hooked up with my
friend and former chief, Fred Hooey. He was our newest district judge. He
was running for election the first time out and drew an opponent. I would
pick Fred up in my county car and we would talk about how much we
disliked going to political functions. He was a marvelous companion and
hated campaigning more than I did. I even got to return a large portion of
the campaign funds I had received. When I returned $750 of the $1,000 that
Vinson and Elkins had given me, they were shocked. Dan Arnold told me
that was the first time that ever happened. In this election and the next three
to come, I was fortunate to run unopposed and beat the write-in vote.

Politics was never my thing. Being district attorney was. I never had aspi-
rations for some "higher office," although I never convinced either the media
or other politicians of that. Most had me down as wanting to be the state
attorney general. I really didn't. I did not want another job. I did not want
to uproot my five kids to move to Austin or go to Washington. I did not feel
qualified to hold any other elected office, and that was an important consider-
ation. Also, I saw other officials who kept trying to advance up the food chain
without regard for the kind of job it was. I had the job I wanted and I stayed
with it until I went into private practice. During my DA days, I had serious
inquiries about going on the federal bench, being appointed to the Court of
Criminal Appeals or the Supreme Court of Texas, heading up the criminal
division of the Justice Department, and even taking the job as Director of the
Texas Department of Public Safety. I just wanted to be DA.

One historical note needs to be cleared up. Newspapers wrote I was the
youngest DA in Houston's history. Many years later I found out this was
not true. An article written about Houston's early history said a twenty-one
year old man named Peter Gray was elected district attorney back in 1841.

Mr. Gray became the first president of the Houston Bar Association, was later elected state senator, and subsequently elected to represent Texas in Congress. He also formed a law firm known as Gray and Botts, which eventually became the legal giant Baker Botts. I imagine the pages of Houston history contain some highly interesting information about its past district attorneys. I cannot imagine anyone being DA at age twenty-one, but apparently young Peter did a fine job. Houston even named a street after him. Next time you drive down West Gray, think of my really young predecessor.

CHAPTER EIGHT

The Shopping Center Rapist: My First Case as DA

Likewise the men ... being filled with all unrighteousness,
sexual immorality, wickedness, covetousness, maliciousness; full of envy,
murder, strife, [and] deceit ... are haters of God ...
those who practice such things are deserving of death.
—Romans 1:27–32

I WAS DEEP INTO my daydreams of cases in the past as my car approached yet another small Texas town. I slowed down but did not bother to catch the name. A small strip center stood in the middle of town. Outside the mandatory filling station and greasy spoon, there was a small silo and two boarded-up buildings. This "shopping center" had a laundry, a barber shop, and a five-and-dime. I wondered what it would be like to be a small town DA and know everyone in town.

Back in Houston new shopping centers were growing like mushrooms. One was even indoors, a new place called the Galleria. There I could play tennis in one of ten indoor courts at the University Club, choose a movie from the multi-theaters, or stroll by a hundred stores while watching skaters glide on the ice below.

Later, police charting the crimes in the city reported the highest number of crimes was occurring in and around the Galleria. Cars were stolen from the indoor garage. Young kids congregated to sell grass. Beautiful is not necessarily better.

Thinking of the new Galleria brought my memory back to another gigantic shopping mall—Houston's first—a place called Sharpstown. This shopping center was the scene of one of the most heinous crimes I ever handled.

THE DEFENDANT WHO WAS to stand trial in this gruesome murder case was a handsome young man by the name of Jerry Michael Ward. I chose to try the Ward case; it would be my first trial after being appointed DA. Ward was believed to be a serial rapist and kidnapper who brought terror to young women all over the city.

This serial killer's M.O. was to wait in shopping center parking lots and watch for beautiful girls coming to shop. After picking one, he would watch her walk off to shop and then he would park in close proximity and await her return. Armed with a pistol, he would catch her off guard as she entered her car and force her to ride to some pre-selected and secluded spot, probably out in the boondocks. He might kill the victim or release her after the rape. He would drive her car back to the general area, abandon it, and then walk to his own car and drive home.

These crimes occurred between mid-1964 and early 1965, some ten months before I took office. The first abduction involved a twenty-one-year-old secretary who was kidnapped close to a shopping center parking lot by a young white male. The assailant drove her to Galveston where he pistol-whipped her so severely she had to be hospitalized. He did not rape her, and finally let her go. She had no idea who this stranger was.

Later, a pretty airline stewardess was forced from a parking lot into a red Chevrolet Corvair, again by an unknown young white male fitting the same description. He slapped her around and tried to rape her. She put up a hard fight. Her determination to resist probably saved her life, and when a couple walked close by to get into their car, he let her go.

The next crime involved a slight variance as no shopping center was involved. This time another very attractive young woman was kidnapped in broad daylight at 2:00 P.M. in downtown Houston on Pease Street. There were no retail shops in that area. The only witnesses would be motorists on a one-way street, and they could not turn around into oncoming traffic. The abductor, who again fit the description given by the previous victims, carried the young lady off to the empty Astrodome parking lot. There he forced her into the trunk of his car. He drove out to a remote and desolate place adjacent to Addicks Dam in the western part of the county. The assailant raped her and then beat her up. She was battered and bruised, but he did not kill her. Other than the description of an Anglo male who was handsome, strong, well-dressed, and young, the police had no further leads.

HPD's homicide and radio patrol divisions were working overtime trying to solve the cases. Cars with plainclothes cops set out to scour shopping centers and other locations in southwest Houston. A week later an attractive twenty-four-year-old barmaid was forced into a car by a young man fitting the same description outside some apartments in the upscale Tanglewood area. The rapist had to have followed her home. When she got out of her car, he grabbed her and forced her to tell him where she lived. Saying he had a gun inside his pocket, he walked behind her and then followed her to her apartment. Once inside, he raped her, taking her intimate apparel as a souvenir. Although he was rough and forceful, he let his guard down and she escaped out the door. She ran down the apartment complex and found a passerby. Her life was spared; the abductor had fled by the time the police arrived.

The next case occurred at the Joske's department store parking lot across the street from the enclosed Galleria. Again a man, fitting the same description, grabbed an attractive young lady, this time a nineteen-year-old, as she returned to her car. He forced her into his own car and took her out to the remote Barker Reservoir area, not far from the Addicks Dam area. As he began to tear at her clothes she began to cry and told him she was a virgin. She became very emotional and pleaded for mercy. He spared her life, drove her back into town, and dropped her off at a place which would require a long walk back to her car. Distraught, she did not get his license number.

This string of assaults caused police to intensify their efforts. They strongly cautioned all young women to be on the alert, particularly when they got out of their cars in shopping centers in broad daylight. Security in all major shopping centers was beefed up around the city. Plain clothes officers and store detectives still did not who was the parking lot rapist.

Only five days after the Barker Reservoir abduction, a young lady by the name of Joy O'Neal drove out of her driveway to take her mom to work. The date was October 18, 1965, some six months into the saga of the rape-kidnappings. October 18 would have been just another school day for Joy except that her parents had given her permission to miss school that day so she could apply for a part-time job for the upcoming holiday season. Mrs.

O'Neal worked at a large department store at Sharpstown Mall, located on the Southwest Freeway. She planned to introduce Joy to her boss with the hope Joy might get that part-time job.

Joy was a beautiful girl. Her Westbury High School yearbook revealed her kind face and gentle eyes beneath her long blonde hair. She was popular and made excellent grades. She was the pride and joy of her parents' lives. In the words of her father, "She never gave us a moment's trouble. She was the most loving and unselfish daughter a father could have."

That morning Joy climbed into the family's second car, an old green Cadillac. The sun was shining down on one of those marvelous crisp cool fall days. Joy rolled into the parking lot and made her way up to the store's entrance. There she dropped her mother off for work. It was ten minutes to eleven. Her mother went on the job at eleven. As Joy let her mother out in front of the store, she said, "See you in just a minute, Mom." These were the last words any of her family would ever hear her speak. The parking lot was far from being full. Even so, Joy drove back to about the fifteenth row, where she obviously planned to park, in order to meet her mother inside.

When a half hour passed and Joy had not come into the store, Mrs. O'Neal walked outside to scout the parking lot. She went up and down the rows but did not see the car. Then she called the police. So many kids run away from home each day that police are often skeptical when such a call comes in. But in view of recent events and Joy's description, the police jumped into action. When the O'Neal car could not be found in the Sharpstown parking lot or anywhere in the general vicinity, every police car in town was put on orders to keep lookout for Joy and her green Cadillac. The police had the license number and were instructed if there was a handsome young man inside with Joy, that he was dangerous and wanted. Joy's picture was delivered to the local television stations to air throughout the day and on the six o'clock news. The hope was that someone, somewhere, had seen Joy or the Cadillac or her kidnapper before Joy became another victim.

Late that afternoon, a man by the name of Bob Conrad was working his dogs out at his kennel. The kennel was located on fifty acres in a remote area in west Harris County. He was leading the dogs through their exercises amidst the woods and stretches of thicket that game birds called home. Walking behind two bird dogs, he looked down and spotted a shiny object. He bent down and picked it up. It was a woman's compact. This spurred his interest enough to inspect the area. Back in an even thicker, wooded section he found a hair brush and a woman's makeup kit. He kept the items, wondering how they had gotten there. After putting the dogs up and returning home, Bob turned on the news. Joy's picture was on TV. The news told how she was missing and had not been found. Instinctively, Bob called the police. Homicide detectives were out to his house in no time. They took the items he had found to the home of Joy's parents. Before Mrs. O'Neal could grasp the compact out of the officer's hands, she knew it was Joy's.

By now it was dark. The kennel site was soaked from recent downpours. The search had to be put off until daylight as detailed plans were being made by lawmen to comb the property.

At daybreak the following morning, Chief Deputy Sheriff Lloyd Frazier headed up a posse to comb this brush country and woods. His boss, legendary Harris County Sheriff Buster Kern, came out to observe, along with the veteran HPD homicide chief, Captain L.D. Morrison. To avoid the mud, the search team took to horseback. Officers methodically looked behind every bush. Mid-morning, Bob Conrad discovered the body of a young girl. It was Joy O'Neal. Her body lay a half mile from the entrance to the property off Renn Road, a lightly traveled byway. She wore only a blouse. Small wooden tree limbs had been placed in ritual fashion on her abdomen. A rope lay nearby. Three small-caliber gunshot wounds were found in the back of her head. The next day's autopsy confirmed the cause of death was from the three shots. Another bullet grazed her neck, and she had multiple bruises on her face.

Publicity about the discovery was intense. After the news hit the air on Houston's radio and TV stations, citizens began calling information into the police. Houstonians were always willing to pitch in and help. Some calls were bogus or of no use, but some hit pay dirt. Alert citizens had taken notice, and their testimony would be essential. Without all the good information, a good case could never have been built.

The day after Joy was found the police located the O'Neal Cadillac. The perpetrator had obviously driven this car back to the scene but parked at the other end of the mall to avoid suspicion. The car was not there the day Joy was kidnapped, as the police had combed every parking spot for a mile around in search of it. The interior of the Cadillac had been wiped clean. It was the same with the exterior. Not a single print, not even Joy's, was found inside the car. The only thing that was still in the car was Joy's girdle, with her stockings attached.

Back at the kennel property the search for clues continued. Not a single footprint turned up, not even in the fresh mud caused by the recent rains.

Over at the morgue the ME and his team were hard at work. They extracted several small hairs from Joy's clothes and her body. The team was pleased to have found that two of the hairs did not match Joy's hair. They carefully preserved this bit of evidence for whatever future use it may have. Presumably the two identical hairs belonged to the killer. The police needed more breaks than this. Based on the past, this man was still stalking parking lots to feed his insatiable thirst.

Great publicity was given to the case, which prompted more revelations the next day. A woman named Joanne Kelly reported she was driving her catering truck by Sharpstown Mall on the morning of the kidnapping when a young male driver with a woman passenger ran a stop sign and almost hit her. The two were in an old green Cadillac. She looked down at her watch and noticed it was nearly 11:00 A.M.

A man named Alvin Robinson also called the police. He ran a Texaco station close to the mall. He got a good look at a young man who paid him a dollar for gas and drove off in a hurry. He noticed a pretty young blonde in the car but could not see her face well enough to match it up with Joy's picture. This car, too, was a green Cadillac.

Another break came from Robert and Gilbert Lopez. At 11:30 A.M. the day of the murder, the Lopezes were driving along Renn Road. They both observed an old green Cadillac turning off into the very same pasture the dog kennel was located. The 11:30 time was a perfect match for how long it would have taken to drive from Sharpstown to this location.

Next, a Ms. Doris Rodden contacted Homicide. She happened to be standing outside a convenience store only one mile from the pasture where the body was discovered. She too saw a "handsome" young man with a beautiful young female passenger. When shown Joy's picture, she said, "That is her." Finally, a Ms. Anita Topia, who lived in the Renn Road vicinity, reported she had seen an old green Cadillac make a U-turn on Renn Road close to the kennel on the afternoon of the killing. She noticed there was only one person in the car, a man she did not recognize. She looked down at her watch. It was 3:15 P.M. That meant Joy was with her attacker for over three hours in the pasture. Removing her dead body from the car, making sure there were no footprints, placing the little sticks in a pattern on her head, and leaving should not have taken over half an hour at most. That left two and a half hours for the rape, the shooting, and the mental and physical torture.

At this point in the case, the police were discouraged. The witnesses who identified Joy could not yet identify the killer. He was still at large and his identity was unknown. No one had a clue where he lived, what kind of car he drove, or anything else about his identity. With the intense media coverage, he had to be in hiding. Perhaps he had fled across the country and was safely seeking employment in L.A. or Boston or Chicago, bustling metropolises that never heard of the parking lot rapist.

Ten days passed without a break or even an additional clue. On the eleventh day the break came. A courageous young landlady teamed with a dedicated police officer to break the case. One month prior to Joy's death, a young man by the name of Jerry Michael Ward showed up at the apartments managed by a woman named Sally Strump. The apartment complex was on a street called the Old Spanish Trail, or OST, a few miles south of downtown and several miles from Sharpstown. These apartments, although on the lower end of the economic scale, were clean and livable. Miss Strump took pride in her job and only rented to those who looked respectable.

When Ward arrived, she liked his clean-cut appearance. He stood tall in a starched Marine Corps officer's uniform. The shiny gold second lieutenant's bar gleamed from his collar. He looked athletic with handsome features. She was proud to rent to a United States Marine Corps officer and signed him up for a place to live.

Jerry Ward liked Sally. He went out of his way to strike up conversations. After a few days, he expressed a deep concern for her safety. He said, "Sally, in light of all of the things happening to pretty women in this city, you just can't be too careful."

A few days later he dropped by and said, "Sally, I think you need a pistol, just for your own protection." She accepted the weapon and put it out of the way in her closet. She was pleased this new tenant cared.

Strangely enough, during the month Ward lived in Sally's complex, he reported four separate burglaries to the police. He claimed his apartment was broken into each time. Officer J. E. Tucker, a seventeen-year veteran of the HPD, was not a detective but on assignment to the Burglary and Theft Division. He was told to go out and investigate Ward's complaints. He interviewed Ward on each of these four occasions. Tucker became a little suspicious of Ward. Something just did not compute. Tucker couldn't put a finger on it, but he would keep an eye on Ward.

It was during Ward's stay at the OST apartments that Joy's murder occurred. At the time, Officer Tucker noticed that Ward fit the general description of the driver of the green Cadillac. He also fit the description given by the victims in the other kidnappings. At this point Tucker decided he would approach Sally confidentially and get every piece of information that he could about Ward. Sally gladly complied. She told Tucker about the Marine Corps uniform and the gift of the pistol. Next she related a recent incident that made Tucker's hair stand on end. She said, "Two days ago, he came by and knocked on my door. He said he wanted to have his old pistol back but I could have this new pistol which would be easier for me to handle. He told me he had given me the wrong gun by mistake. Of course, I agreed and we exchanged pistols. By the way, he even said, 'Sally, there is a kidnapper at large so you really need a pistol.'"

Tucker checked the dates. The swap came two days after Joy O'Neal was killed.

At this point Tucker asked Sally if he could have the pistol. He did not tell her the reason. He did say the police were looking for someone and may want to do a test. She complied. Tucker called Captain J. E. Morrison directly and told him the story. Morrison, the old Homicide captain with whom I spent a lot of time in my days as an assistant, figured Officer Tucker was on to something.

"Get the gun on down here as soon as you can. I'll have Kenneth Swatzel standing by."

Swatzel was the gun expert. He looked at bullets from a person's body and compared them to bullets fired from a known gun. He could usually tell if there was a match. He was one of the best firearms comparison men in the country.

As soon as Tucker arrived, Swatzel made the comparisons. Peering into the dual microscope, Swatzel studied the bullets from the body with the test bullet just fired into the cotton-filled box at the police station. Then in his quiet way he announced, "This is the pistol."

Police immediately began investigating Ward. The marines had never heard of him. The homicide detectives came to the District Attorney's office where we drafted an airtight search warrant to search for anything and everything in Ward's apartment. By this time it was late at night. We woke up Justice of the Peace Dave Thompson. Dave had been in office for years. He prided himself in always being available to help the police. He signed the warrant. Several detectives and uniformed officers were dispatched to set up on Ward's apartment. It was now 1:00 A.M. and Ward's missing car told them he was not home. Not wanting to surprise him, they patiently waited. Their plan was to catch him with his guard down since he was probably armed and certainly extremely dangerous.

At last, Ward drove up. He had a young woman in his car. He had been out on a date with a girl who lived in the same apartment project. He escorted her to her place and then entered his own apartment for the night. The police gave him time to go to sleep. At 3:00 A.M. they banged on the door. Several officers rushed in as a sleepy Ward opened the door. The police handcuffed Ward and made a thorough search of his apartment. Police recovered a rifle, a large hunting knife, two loaded pistols, and a prolific amount of pornographic material. The next day Ward was formally charged with the murder of Joy O'Neal and held without bail.

Samples of hair were taken from Ward to be compared to the two foreign hairs removed from Joy's body. The city chemist said the hair found on Joy's body looked identical to the known hair belonging to Ward. We had a case. I took it to the Harris County grand jury and they were eager to indict.

DESPITE ALL OF THE leads and the brilliant work done by the police, their chemists and experts, this would be a tough case, built on circumstantial evidence for the most part. There were no eyewitnesses to the murder and no confession. Even though it is difficult in a circumstantial evidence case, we decided that I should go for the death penalty.

I first laid eyes on Ward at a preliminary hearing in Judge Dan Walton's courtroom. (Walton, of course, was the district attorney who had hired me eight years before.) I was taken aback at how handsome and clean-cut Jerry Michael Ward looked. He would not look out of place in a Marine Corps officer's uniform. He also looked at home in his dark blue business suit. He looked like an assistant vice president of a prestigious downtown bank. Out of all of the murder cases I had tried I had never seen anyone accused of murder who looked so unlike a murderer or serial rapist.

By the time the case came to court, we learned that Ward had been born in Chicago in 1944. He was twenty-one at the time of the killing and twenty-two at the time of trial. As a kid he moved often and attended schools in San Antonio, Midland, Denver, and Maryland. His mother had died when he was in elementary school. His father remarried. Ward's stepmother came to the opinion that Ward was strange. Ward's father was a petroleum engineer whose employment kept him on the move. At the time of trial his father was working in Australia. He was the only relative to attend the trial.

Ward attended a college preparatory school called Charlotte Hall in Maryland. There he received military training. The school's commandant remembered him as a kid who did not get into trouble but who had flunked two courses. Ward's grandfather said Ward was a normal kid. Other than wrecking a few cars, Ward never had any trouble with the law. The grandfather also said that his handsome young grandson never dated in high school.

After attending Charlotte Hall, Ward enlisted and served in the navy until he got into serious trouble. In a court martial proceeding, Ward received a sentence of two and a half years for three crimes: assault, larceny, and attempted rape. The military court further ordered that Ward see the prison psychiatrist weekly.

After Ward was arrested for the O'Neal murder, Atlanta police took great interest. They thought he might be the same person who had abducted and killed a pretty young woman from an Atlanta parking lot. This was only a couple of months prior to when the Houston crime series began. The Atlanta victim's body was recovered, and the pattern of that case and our Houston case was the same. There never was enough proof to tie Ward into the Atlanta murder, but Houston police found an interesting handwritten note in Ward's Houston apartment. The only words written were "Jacksonville and Atlanta." A check with Jacksonville police did not produce any similar crimes there.

Shortly before Ward moved to OST, he rented an apartment over on Westheimer, five miles away. This apartment manager said she kicked Ward out of his quarters after he had a nasty altercation with a female tenant. Not long thereafter Ward got into an automobile accident while driving to Galveston. He was injured enough to remain in John Sealy Hospital for several days. After this he leased the apartment from Sally. At that time Ward was employed as a hospital orderly at the Texas Medical Center, a couple of miles away from the OST address.

After Ward's arrest, the police found out that he had rented a red Corvair that had been used in an earlier kidnapping. Homicide ran Ward through one lineup after another. Several victims positively identified Ward as their assailant. Ironically, just two days after the O'Neal murder, Ward put on a self-defense demonstration for two young female tenants at his apartment complex, giving them instructions on how to avoid being raped. One of the girls said she had spent time with Ward alone inside his apartment on several occasions. He was "like a brother to me," she said. He also offered her a pistol that she kept for her protection.

When this young lady predicted the police were going to find the parking lot rapist, Ward said, "No way. Too many men fit that description." After she

Getting ready to run for office. Gittings did this one. Amazingly, I always
ended up unopposed and beat the write-in vote.

The Courthouse Comple. This is where we all worked and held court during the nearly 22 years I was at the DA's office from 1958 to 1979. The top upper left-hand building was the Harris County Courthouse and housed the DA's office, the grand jury rooms, all criminal courts, the sheriff's office and jail, and other county offices. The historic old courthouse (with the dome) was the Civil Courts Building. The modern building in the lower right corner was where the DA's office moved for the last years of my tenure. We took up the whole thing. I got a Federal grant to refurbish this old Post Office building. The other building (lower left) housed the juvenile and family courts. Many of these offices are now housed a block away in the Criminal Justice Center.

(Opposite) The bottom picture shows many of our judges. Most came out of the DA's office. Top row: I.D. McMaster, Joe Guarino, Sam Robertson, Allen Stilley, Bob Burdette, Wendell Odom, Fred Hooey, and Sam Davis. Second row: Jon Hughes, Stilley again, Jimmy James, Phil Warner (an Asst. DA), me (also never a judge), Garth Bates. Third row: Miron Love and Pete Moore. Bottom row: Ed Duggan, Dan Walton, Neil McKay, Lee Duggan, Dan Walton again, and Frank Price. I found this picture in an old scrapbook; someone had done some cutting and pasting which explains the duplicates.

(Top) Most of the felony prosecutors back when Frank Briscoe was DA.
Top row: Jon Hughes, Erwin Ernst, Frank Davis, Howell Stone, Carol Vance,
and Bob Delaney.
Bottom row: Lee Ward, Gus Zgourides, Dan Ryan, Tommy Dunn, Eddie Shaw,
Neil McKay, and Jim Shatto.

L. to R. — Sam Groom, James Brill, Carol Vance, Dee Osborne

HOUSTON JUNIOR BAR ASS'N NAMES OFFICERS
Carol S. Vance will be sworn in on July 1 as the new president of the Houston Junior Bar Ass'n.

FRIENDS AND MENTORS

(Top) I was elected president of the Houston Jr. Bar Association (now the Houston Young Lawyers). This was a big boost to putting me on the map politically speaking, and many friends from this group helped me on my appointment.

(Middle) Golfing with Tommy Dunn (left), who helped train me, and Ted Busch (right). Ted and I served together for over twenty years.

(Bottom) Erwin Ernst was my mentor as we were assigned to the same district court for over two years.

Here I am looking nervous and apprehensive because Judge Ed Duggan just swore me in to be the new District Attorney of Harris County. Frank Briscoe, next to us, resigned to run for Congress against some unknown political novice by the name of George Herbert Walker Bush.

A week after being sworn in, I announced for office and rode in the annual rodeo day parade with the family in this incredible car, a sixteen cylinder, 1937 Cadillac Convertible. With my name "Carol" on the side of the car, people kept yelling "Hi Carol!" to Carolyn. At that point I wondered about my chances to be elected, but the four opponents all dropped out.

VANCE

A.J. Foyt (third from left), multiple Indy champion, brought along his race car drivers who were filmed drinking whiskey and driving. I narrated a film that was shown around the state to high schools and civic clubs on the dangers of drunk driving.

(Middle) HPD's marijuana sniffing dog, Sam, who with his HPD master accompanied me to a couple of high schools to address the students about drugs. Of course the kids were just interested in Sam.

(Bottom) Jimmy Brill, Judge Pete Moore, Richard "Racehorse" Haynes, Dick de Guerin, me, and Frank Briscoe, at a testimonial dinner for Judge Pete. These were all good friends and outstanding lawyers, me notwithstanding. Judge Pete, my first boss, deserved to be recognized.

READY FOR ROUND TWO
From Left, Quebedeaux, Vance and Rep Braun
—Post Photo

(Top) Two of the biggest characters in Texas: Legends Ernie Ernst (left) and Marvinnnnn Zindler (middle) in Mexico trying to get officials to extradite a big drug lord.

(Middle) Representative Rex Braun, County Pollution Chief Walter Quibideaux and I worked hard for tougher laws to prosecute pollutant offenders.

(Bottom left) Ben Barnes, later to become Lt. Gov., speaks at an NDAA convention in Houston. Ben was a tremendous help in my efforts to change bad laws.

(Bottom right) Rusty Hardin (left) left the office to gain more fame as one of the more notable trial attorneys in town, while Ted Busch (right) headed the Trial Bureau under me and then served for years as Johnny Holmes' First Assistant.

U.S. Senator Lloyd Bentsen was a good friend, a neighbor, and represented Texas well in Washington. He helped us get funding for law enforcement projects.

(Right) Gerry Phelps changed her life around more radically than anyone I ever knew. An amazing woman, getting to tell her story alone made the effort to write this book worthwhile.

First-year student, Gerry Charlotte Phelps, 47, sentenced to 35 years in prison for armed robbery and condemned as a "revolutionary," says she found God in the bleak dayroom at Goree.

(Below) Several of our great assistant DAs. Keno Henderson, Sam Dick, Bill Burge, Bert Graham, Tom Henderson, and Frank Price.

heard about Ward's arrest, the disillusioned young lady said she would never trust another man again.

During extensive interrogations Ward made three independent oral admissions that he had committed the murder. He confessed to Sheriff Kern. Then he confessed to Lt. Joe Thorpe of the Sheriff's office. Finally, he admitted the murder to Dr. Red Dwyer, the Harris County psychiatrist. Unfortunately, these confessions would not be admissible in trial. Texas was the only state in the nation that outlawed oral confessions unless that confession led directly to some instrument of the crime. These did not. It did not matter how many Miranda warnings he had received, these oral confessions were useless, thanks to the Texas legislature.

A further twist to frustrate justice was the fact that no matter how helpful it might be for the jury to hear from the several earlier victims, the jurors would be denied that privilege. The only way this evidence could be admissible would be if Ward took the witness stand and denied his guilt. We knew no lawyer would ever let Ward testify. In short, we ended up with a classic circumstantial evidence case. The hair and the bullet comparisons were our strongest evidence linking Ward to the crime. Combining the scientific evidence with the eyewitnesses who could put Ward and Joy together, and Ward in Joy's Cadillac, we had a good case. The time frames worked. Even so, experience taught that death penalties were difficult to come by in circumstantial evidence cases. Jurors much preferred no doubt before they assessed the death penalty.

Of course we wanted the death penalty. The average time for a Texas defendant who got life or ninety-nine years was only twelve years calendar time. Ward's past told me he was likely to repeat. I fully believed that then, and believe it now. Once Ward got out of prison, if he did get life, there was a great likelihood some innocent girl or girls would die at his hands again. Due to Texas law and early releases, getting death for Ward was in the best public interest, no matter how one felt about the death penalty. This would be the only way to insure this smooth talking "marine" would not kill again.

In my eight years thus far in the District Attorney's office, I had never seen a case generate so much public interest. I suppose that was to expected, however, as it had everything to excite the public's attention: murder, serial rapes, a tragic, beautiful victim, a handsome defendant, and a manhunt that had terrified the city.

As a result of all the attention, Ward's defense team moved for a change of venue. At the end of the hearing the judge denied the motion and the case was set for trial in Harris County. Judge Walton noted that he would be quick to change the venue if we had any difficulty in seating a jury.

Back in those days neither side had any rights of pre-trial discovery to speak of. Today the defense is entitled to all tests, access to all physical evidence, and a myriad of other things. In civil cases both sides discover anything and everything to their hearts' desire, leaving little suspense when the case goes before the jury. When Ward was tried, neither side was exposing their hand. Only if evidence had a tendency to negate the guilt of the defendant, did the State have a duty to turn it over. The defense team would not know which tests had been run or the results unless we told them.

As to the results of the analysis and identification of the hairs found on the victim's body, we had a dilemma on our hands. While our case was pending, a new science emerged. This new way to identify hair might be reliable enough to use in court against Ward. The major hurdle was that there was not a single reported case in the U.S. where such evidence had been allowed. An out-of-state judge in one reported case denied its admissibility.

The test was called a "neutron activation analysis." I never understood the nuances of this science. I had made two "F"s in my life and they were both in chemistry. Somehow, the atoms of an individual piece of hair were "bombarded." Then a complex machine would read the numbers and determine the chemical makeup of the hair. Everyone's hair has different chemistry that can be reduced to its elements and measured by mathematical formulas. With this test an expert in this field could opine with greater certainty that a particular hair belonged to a particular person. City Chemist Floyd McDonald told me it would take astronomical odds for two different people to end up with the same result on this kind of test.

The new test would certainly sit better with jurors than a microscopic comparison. In the microscope test the procedure was simple. Put the two hair samples, one known and the other unknown, under a dual microscopic. If the hairs looked alike, the expert could opine the two hairs came from the same person. This science was helpful but not nearly so conclusive as fingerprints or the new neutron activation test.

Floyd McDonald called me to say Texas A&M University had bought one of these expensive nuclear reactors that could bombard hairs. He suggested we make the Jerry Michael Ward case the first case in the United States to use this technology in a criminal trial. He told me the A&M scientists were willing to let him take part in the procedure and train him on the use of the equipment. Then, because he was a chemist working on a PhD and who had read up on the subject, he could say he conducted an examination and express his opinion. Floyd said there were only two places in the country with the capability to run such a test. I gave him the green light but told him to keep the whole process under wraps. I knew it would be a close call whether we could get a new test admitted into evidence. I did not have to tell defense counsel what we were doing unless the test came back negative. I sent someone to the law library to see if there were any reported cases. With no established history of reliability or the use of this test in any court at law, we would obviously face an uphill battle getting the results admitted into evidence.

Floyd and the Texas Aggies ran the test. The results were positive, showing in all mathematical probability it was Ward's hairs that were taken off of Joy's body. Not wanting to risk a reversal I agonized over whether to use the test at trial. Erwin Ernst, the chief in Walton's court and who was trying the case with me, and I talked chemistry. I thought we could get a conviction without the test, but the test would give the jury that greater certainty needed for them to be convinced enough to give the death penalty. Earlier on, we had told the defense attorneys about the dual microscopic test so they knew we would call our chemist to the stand.

THE DAY OF TRIAL came. The defense filed a slew of motions and jury selection began. We questioned each juror one at a time and outside the presence of the other panel members. This took from forty-five minutes to an hour per juror. The State and the defense had fifteen peremptory strikes each. In other words, we could strike fifteen jurors who had otherwise qualified, without having to give any reason of any kind. Counting a good number of jurors who would be excused for other reasons, jury selection would take about three or four weeks. Ernst sat there alone at counsel table most of the time while I went to the office to handle the day's pressing problems and interview our witnesses. Picking a capital jury is a little akin to sitting in a dentist's chair all day. Cat-and-mouse games with each prospective juror. One at a time. Sometimes an hour to question a single juror with constant objections, interruptions, and legal squabbles put before the judge. At last a jury would somehow be seated.

Trying the case was easier and more exciting. After the twelve were sworn, the indictment was read to the jury and the judge said, "and how do you plead?" At that point Jerry Michael Ward uttered the only words he would ever say to the jury, "Not guilty."

The first witness I called was the mother, Mrs. O'Neal, She led the jury through that tragic morning. Of course she broke down. We would recess. She would drink water and start again. It was a painful experience for her when I handed her the beautiful portrait of her daughter. I hated doing that, but the jury had to know a real live human being had died at the hands of the defendant. That one photograph of that beautiful young teenager would drive home to any jury the grief and devastation of such a loss. The O'Neals understood. I never wanted the jury to forget why we were there. I wanted them to see Joy as a person, a live and vivacious teenager with her whole life before her. And we needed that picture not just for the jurors to take back to the jury room during deliberations, but also to hand off to the witnesses to prove that it was that young lady who was seen with the defendant and in the car and near the vicinity.

On cross-examination defense attorney Tom White, trying to plant the notion someone other than his client may be guilty, asked if it was true that Joy went out on frequent dates. Mrs. O'Neal glared down at Tom and said, "Mr. White, she seldom dated. Most weekends she babysat in the evenings so she could earn some extra money." I couldn't tell if the fire in the eyes of two male jurors on the front row were for Tom or his client.

Next Sheriff Buster Kern took the stand. I was never impressed with Buster's administrative skills as sheriff, but Texas could not have had a more dedicated lawman. Buster was a living legend whose strong suit was staying on the trail of a cold case, never letting up until he had his man. He much preferred working on a case to running the Sheriff's office. He was pure country and soft-spoken. The town loved him. Buster was fearless. He was credited for keeping the Mafia out of Houston. Once he personally escorted the mafioso boss of New Orleans, Carlos Marcello, to an awaiting airplane and warned him never to set foot on Harris County soil again. I recall one day crossing the street with Buster at the corner of the courthouse. With no cars in sight a man walked across the light on red. Buster, without identifying himself or showing a badge, lectured the poor man on his disobedience to the law, something Buster could not tolerate.

On the stand I used Buster to put on the aerial photographs that showed the shopping center, its gigantic parking lot, the filing station, the remote roads close to where the body was discovered, and the dense woods the defendant had carefully chosen.

I had been very concerned over introducing the fact that Ward wore a marine uniform when he was not a marine. This act could be considered an extraneous criminal offense—even though most relevant in my book— and thus cause a reversal of the case. I felt safe in asking Buster if he knew whether the defendant had ever been in armed service. He said Ward had not been in the Marine Corps or any armed service to the best of his knowledge. Tom White did not object. Later, our landlady would describe Ward and how he was dressed the day he showed up on her doorstep in Marine Corps dress blues. Some jurors were veterans, and they particularly would be shocked at any man who would fraudulently put on that uniform. They would see Ward as bold and impulsive. We were not going to be able to show any other crimes unless Ward testified.

Detective Paul Nix of Homicide spent most of the second day on the stand. We introduced the bullets he recovered from the morgue. The bullet comparisons were such critical evidence to our case that the defense had to go on the attack. After Tom White made some attempts without serious damage, he tried a new approach. After pointing out the severe damage done to the bullets as they passed through the body, he suggested that with all the evidence down at Homicide that Nix may have received the wrong bullets from the morgue. "Now you weren't present when the autopsy was done and actually see these bullets come from the victim's body, did you Detective Nix?" White asked.

"Yes, sir, I was there. I asked to attend the autopsy and made notes of what I saw. Dr. Bucklin personally handed me these bullets that I initialed right after I saw him take them from the body. These are the bullets, Mr. White. Here are my initials, if you look very closely. And I kept them in my personal possession until I handed them over to our chief firearms examiner, Mr. Kenneth Swatzel. I made notes on that, too, about the time and place, if you want to see them."

Ernst leaned over and whispered to me, "Way to go, Tom. Do you have any more really good questions?"

Next up was firearms expert Kenneth Swatzel who gave his usual scholarly presentation as to how the bullets that came from the body had the same characteristics as the bullets test-fired from the gun that was already in evidence. The jury had heard that this pistol was the same one that Ward had given to his landlady. Although Swatzel could not say positively the bullets from the body came from this gun, he explained the science and told the jury it would be a real long shot for two different pistols to leave the same markings on a bullet. The fact Jerry Michael Ward was in possession of a pistol whose bullets matched those in the body and wanted to get rid of that pistol two days after the killing was not lost on the jury.

Ernst and I took turns calling the various eyewitnesses who either identified Joy or the defendant during that day so we could at least put a man
and woman of similar description in the old green Cadillac close to either
Sharpstown or the killing field. Joanne Kelly was particularly helpful. She
testified that when she saw Ward drive out of the Sharpstown parking lot in
the green Cadillac, he was wearing a white shirt and tie. Tom White asked
her, "You said you were driving your car and the other car came by real fast.
How can you—now months later—be so sure you can identify Jerry Ward
when you only saw him for a fleeting second?"

"Well, he made me mad. I had to drive over the curb to keep from hitting
his right door when he ran that stop sign. I won't forget that face. Besides, I
had a nice long look at him down at the police station at the lineup after he
got arrested."

Ernst leaned over and whispered in my ear again, "Another good question,
Mr. White!"

Dr. Robert Bucklin, the deputy ME, was next. He told the jury that the
gunshots caused the death. He also said the rope burns found on Joy's wrist
showed two things: that she had been tied up, and that she had to have pulled
with all her might on the ropes in an effort to get loose to leave that kind of
indentation in her skin. Bucklin said the large bruise over her eye likely came
from the fist of the assailant. The blow did not come from a sharp instrument, and the blow was delivered with substantial force. He next pointed
out on the chart where the bullets were recovered from the body and that
he handed them over to Detective Nix. After proving the time of death and
showing the diagrams of the body and the wounds, I passed the witness.
Tom White wisely asked few questions of this witness. I then said, "Your
Honor, the State rests."

At this point I was very satisfied with the evidence. Tom White called
for a brief recess and told the judge he would appreciate Dr. Bucklin waiting
around while he conferred with his co-counsel. I went out in the hallway
and noticed Tom having a brief conversation with the good doctor. We all
returned to the courtroom where the judge asked, "Mr. White, would you
like to proceed with your case?"

"Yes, Your Honor. My case will be brief. In fact I only want to call one
witness, Dr. Bucklin. He is outside the courtroom. Could we have the jury
brought in and seated and I will call him to the stand."

When Bucklin sat down to face the jury, Tom got right to the point. "By
the way, doctor, have you ever heard of a test that is called a nuclear activation

analysis? This is a test that allows the positive identification of a hair because of the unique chemical properties of a particular individual's hair?"

"Yes, I am familiar with the test. In fact I have done considerable research about it," Dr. Bucklin said. I held my breath in disbelief. Tom must be trying to show the jury there is this super new test out there that we have not bothered to use.

Tom continued with a fairly scholarly and lengthy discussion with the witness in order to show this was an excellent way to identify hair. Dr. Bucklin agreed with Tom's every hypothesis. Tom was most pleasant and smiled at all of the "good" answers he was receiving. Dr. Bucklin agreed with Tom that the test was very reliable and a much better means of determining a hair's source than a microscopic examination. Finally Tom asked if the test were reliable enough that one could compare two hair samples and say with reasonable certainty that a particular hair did come from a particular individual. Dr. Bucklin said yes.

Tom said, "Dr. Bucklin, I have just one more question and it is an important one. Do you believe as we sit here today that this nuclear activation test is the most accurate test that can be conducted to make a positive identification of a particular hair sample?"

Bucklin thought a minute and said, "Yes, Mr. White, I do. I believe that is a very true statement."

Tom looked over my way. I tried to look surprised. Tom seemed pleased that he had made his point so clearly. With a little smile for the jury, Tom said, "Your Honor, the defense rests." A few jurors looked puzzled. I asked for and received a half hour recess.

When court resumed, I said, "The State of Texas calls the city chemist, Dr. Floyd McDonald, to the stand."

With the exception of our Dr. Joe Jachimczyk, Floyd was the best expert witness I ever called to the stand. The better defense attorneys in Houston left him alone. Floyd could turn complex chemistry into "Ned and the First Reader"—I wish he had taught me chemistry!

When I began to question Floyd my tone of voice indicated that I was going to attack Dr. Bucklin's opinion about the validity of the nuclear test.

"Dr. McDonald, have you ever heard of a new thing in hair comparisons, something called a neutron activation analysis?" Floyd said yes.

I went on with some more innocent sounding questions to get Floyd talking about the test without any objection from the defense. If a lawyer does not object to a particular line of testimony then he often waives the right making otherwise objectionable evidence admissible.

"Well," I said, "this brand new science and this brand new test, is it really a good test or do we really know if this new science works and is more reliable than the microscopic comparison?"

"Well, yes, Mr. Vance, we do know. This is proven chemistry and is certainly a more reliable test."

I feigned surprise and glanced over at Tom, who had the hint of a smile on his face.

"Well, Dr. McDonald," I said, "If this test is that good why wouldn't you run a such a test in as important a murder case as this?"

"Oh, we did run such a test. In fact I did the test myself. I took the hair that had been found on the victim's body and took it up to the nuclear lab at Texas A&M and ran the test while accompanied by two other chemists who were also nuclear scientists."

That brought Tom to his feet. He objected and asked the judge to retire the jury.

Judge Walton said, "Mr. White, you proved up the validity of this test, so the court is going to overrule your objection. Let's continue, gentlemen."

Floyd continued to deliver a twenty minute lecture that anyone could understand. He ended by saying that it would go up against infinitesimal odds that two different people could have the same chemical makeup in their hair. Finally he said, "In my opinion, the two hairs taken off of Joy O'Neal's body belonged to the defendant, Jerry Michael Ward."

A huge *Chronicle* headline the next day read "Judge Admits A-Test in Ward Trial." The story went on about the fact this was the first time this test had ever been admitted in a criminal trial anywhere in the country. When the defense did appeal, the Texas Court of Criminal Appeals never mentioned the test as an unproven science. To the contrary, it noted both State and defense alike presented two experts who said the test was valid. From the time of the Ward case until this day, atomic tests showing the chemical makeup of hair have been accepted in criminal cases tried in the United States.

In fairness to Tom White, he had no reason to believe we had run the nuclear test. Tom had a tough case to defend. I know he felt like he had to do something, he just couldn't sit there. Tom was thinking, "If I can just create a little doubt, I can save my client's life." I am sure Tom did his homework on nuclear activation and believed he might have a way out.

The case was over with the final arguments. Joy's family sat on the front row of the courtroom. Two hours later the jury knocked. They had a verdict. Ward stood at attention in his dark suit and rep tie as the jury announced,

"We find the defendant guilty of murder with malice aforethought and assess his punishment at death."

After the trial Joy's mother paid me the nicest complement I could have received. Speaking of my closing argument, she told the press, "Mr. Vance said it all."

This case still haunts me. It is inconceivable to think of what Ward did. Inconceivable to think of how he approached multiple young ladies with such cold and brutal cunning. I can still see him sitting there at counsel table in coat and tie. Handsome, clean-cut, looking like a nice young man. Had he walked up to me in a marine lieutenant's uniform with a bunch of ribbons, I would have wanted to ask him about the Corps.

Ward's case was affirmed by the Court of Criminal Appeals. But he was never executed. He and every other defendant on death row in America at the time escaped the death penalty. In *Fuerhman v. Georgia* our Supreme Court threw out every death penalty statute in the nation. The court said the states could pass new death penalty statues if they applied the guidelines of that decision. Today, defendants not only have to be convicted of a capital offense, but the jury must also find the defendant is a continuing and dangerous threat to society. With his death penalty commuted to life, Ward was not going to die for his crime.

Ward was shipped off to Huntsville to the Texas Department of Corrections. He became a model prisoner, according to TDC authorities. He knew how to cooperate and get along. Ward had considerable reading and writing skills and became the editor of the prison newspaper, distributed to all of the inmates in the many Texas prisons. That fact alone showed he could have been a success in the free world if he put his mind to that instead of the brutal and bizarre path he chose.

Finally the Texas Board of Pardons and Paroles did what they did best in those days: They paroled Ward after he had served twenty years. At least they kept him there eight years longer than the average lifer. Ward was still young, only in his early forties when released. He settled in Conroe, just north of Houston. After a skirmish with the police there, he moved to Las Vegas, Nevada. One year later in Las Vegas he apparently killed himself with his pistol. I heard that at the time of his suicide he was wanted for another murder, as well as a kidnapping.

Ward's story reminded me of Theodore Dreiser's haunting novel, *An American Tragedy*; the story's tragic theme of the murder of a young girl as a result of twisted thinking rang a bell. Dreiser might well have written about Jerry Michael if he had been around.

CHAPTER NINE

Confronting
the Press

Never pick a fight with anyone who buys ink by the barrel and paper by the ton.
—Anonymous

I STOPPED AT THE next filling station to get a cold Coke. "No, I don't have a bottle to trade in," I said as I gave the man an extra nickel to pay for the bottle as well. Grabbing a Houston *Post* off the stand, I noticed a front-page article about a police shooting. Already that morning KTRH had run three newscasts about crime stories involving the DA's office. I had to read both papers every day and listen to KTRH in the car to keep up with what went on in my own office. In fact, two reporters from the *Post* and *Chronicle* and the KTRH reporter officed one floor below me in the courthouse. All they did was cover the criminal courts building. Television reporters also used the office to call in stories. The courthouse media hung around the courtrooms, the grand jury area, and my office looking for stories. Each reporter needed one good story and perhaps a couple of small ones per day to earn his or her keep. With the old Houston *Press* gone, the *Chronicle* and the *Post* kept good reporters on hand who wrote objectively and accurately whereas the old *Press* delighted in making the police, judges, and the DA's staff look foolish.

THE PRESS TOOK A chunk out of my day during my time as district attorney. Reporters constantly came and went. Most assistants enjoyed getting credit for a well deserved verdict. I know I did. The public attention made most of us feel like our work had significance. I learned quickly to measure my words and talk in sound bites for the TV. Best to cooperate with the press and give a short enough answer than ramble and let them do the editing.

We were careful not to comment on evidence in some forthcoming case, but other than that I left the assistants free to talk to the press, particularly after the case was over. Reporters could cover but one courtroom at a time, so the prosecutor was usually their best source of information to piece together facts enough to write a blurb. I was more than happy to tell a reporter what went on in a trial and furnish him with some dramatic quote from a key witness for a story.

In addition to the city's daily newspapers, we had regional newspapers such as the ones in Pasadena and Baytown. We had a Hispanic newspaper, at least three black newspapers, the network television stations, and the local radio stations. KTRH was the only all-talk station at the time. It takes a lot of doing to fill up twenty-four hours with talk programs, so they were always calling prosecutors for interviews. Assistants and reporters became friends and spent a good deal of time drinking coffee together.

The reporters were an interesting group of people. Some moved on to bigger and better things which had nothing to do with reporting. Others moved up the media ladder. Channel 2's Kay Bailey is now U.S. Senator Kay Bailey Hutchison. Dan Rather was a Channel 11 reporter before he went on to the national scene. Marvin Zindler, who later became perhaps the city's best known local TV personality, first worked for the sheriff (we shared our building with the Sheriff's office). Jessica Savitch became a national news figure. She died early and Hollywood made a movie about her life. Several television reporters who interviewed me on a regular basis became anchormen. These included some of Houston's most familiar household names like Ray Miller, Ron Stone, Dave Ward, and Steve Smith. Also, future national columnist and television personality Cal Thomas was roaming the halls looking for stories for Channel 2 in those days.

I became friends with most of the reporters, particularly the members of the courthouse working press. We did not let the terrible coffee in the courthouse cafeteria ruin our shared time with a fine opportunity to enjoy an interesting story.

The most colorful newspaper reporter in my early days was Margaret Davis. Maggie worked the courthouse for the old Houston *Press*. She was a Rice University graduate, street smart, and could smell a story a mile off. She was one of the reasons the Houston *Press* was referred to as "The Local Scandal Sheet." Maggie often had multiple stories on the front page. The *Press* thought a hometown murder or DWI verdict far more important than some war thousands of miles away. The word was Margaret's husband had been killed by a drunk driver. I don't know. I do know she had a thing about drunk drivers not getting enough punishment. She zapped all of us often for any "tradeouts" in a DWI case where someone was injured. Only the maximum punishment satisfied her. We feared her "poison pen." Heaven help the prosecutor who took a negligent homicide plea on a late Friday afternoon trying to avoid the press. All of the reporters would roast a prosecutor who opted to use that strategy.

The press had a different sense of priorities than the prosecutors. The first death penalty I received for a robbery killing merited only two sentences at the back of section four. At the same time, some petty but unique dispute between two neighbors could make page one. A good example of this was the unforgettable case of Pokey the dog. The story took up most of the front page of the Houston *Press* and half of page one in the other two dailies.

Back when I was the chief prosecutor in Judge Wendell Odom's misdemeanor court, a lady named Beulah worshipped her little dog Pokey. The neighbor, Sadie, had been bitten by Pokey, at least so she said. The bite took a small chunk out of her leg. Sadie demanded that Beulah get Pokey tested for rabies. Beulah refused. Refusal to do that was a crime, so Beulah was charged with a misdemeanor. Beulah and her lawyer asked that Judge Odom hear the case instead of a jury.

The defense to the crime was simple. They claimed Sadie fingered the wrong dog. Sadie countered that she knew Pokey, had seen that dog around for years, and it was indeed Pokey that had bitten her as she reached for her morning paper on her front lawn. Beulah claimed "it couldn't have been little Pokey because I gave Pokey away to a close friend two weeks before Sadie got bit." Beulah proceeded to babble on gratuitously how Pokey was the most lovable dog in the world.

On cross, Beulah could not remember the date she delivered Pokey to her friend, or whether she took the dog to the friend or the friend picked the dog up at her house.

During a recess, Margaret Davis stepped out into the hall to see Beulah and Sadie having a screaming war. Beulah, on spotting Margaret, stopped yelling and grabbed a picture of Pokey from her purse and said, "Miss Davis, do you think you could put the little fella's picture in the paper? The front page if you can. I will show it to him and it will make little Pokey so happy."

After lunch the defense attorney called Beulah's longtime boyfriend, Horace, to the stand as her only other witness. Horace was a meek little man who was as quiet as Beulah was loquacious. He wore a bright plaid sport coat with a grease-stained red tie. He was short and plump. He told the judge he was a "right regular guest at Beulah's house." Horace said he happened to be present on the very day Beulah handed off little Pokey to her friend. "She cried her heart out," he recalled.

Then it was my turn to cross-examine the jolly little man. I said, "Horace, other than your word here today, you don't have one particle of proof she gave that dog away on that particular day in question, now do you?"

The little fellow was silent for several seconds. I had him right where I wanted him. Then he said, "Come to think of it, I do. I keep this little old pocket diary. Here it is in my coat pocket. Let me look at it a minute and just see what is written on that day." At that, he removed an old weather-beaten, small black book. He seemed to take forever to look for the entry. I stood there smiling confidently at the judge.

"Yep. Here it is. Dated October 15, that very day Sadie got bit. I did by golly write it down. Want me to read what I done wrote that day?"

"Yes, sir, I sure do want you to read that to the judge."

I stood close by him to see what he was reading. I could see every word. He began, "That woman finally got rid of that nasty little dog. Maybe I can get some sleep around here at night." Beulah blushed as courtroom spectators broke down laughing. She had just testified she lived alone. Horace's "sleepover" entry turned her face crimson.

I asked to examine the book. There were comments on most pages. The entry in question looked like the real stuff to me.

I said, "Judge, I don't think I have any more questions."

Judge Odom looked down at me and said, "Mr. Vance, I don't think I have any more questions, either. Will the defendant please rise?"

Defense counsel stood up to object. His face was red. He still had evidence to present. I leaned over and said, "You won this sucker. Don't you dare object."

The judge declared, "This court finds the defendant not guilty." Then the judge banged his gavel and walked into his chambers. I knew Judge Odom was having a hard time trying not to break up. Margaret Davis loved every minute. Next day little Pokey took up a big hunk on page one. Beulah marched over to the Houston *Press* photographer who was sitting in the front row and asked if he needed more pictures of Pokey. If so, she would run home and bring them back.

&

MARVIN ZINDLER RANKED RIGHT up there with Margaret Davis as an unforgettable character. The difference was that Marvin was always on a crusade to help the little guy from being swindled by some shady businessman. As a result, I worked with Marvin two different ways. When we opened our Consumer Fraud Section, Marvin was assigned there full-time by Sheriff Kern to work with our assistant DA in charge. Marvin was able to get a story about how our office arrested some bad guy or broke up some scheme just about everyday of the week. He gave me publicity that money couldn't buy and it was all good.

Marvin left this job to join Channel 13, and the rest is a part of Houston history. He did exactly the same thing with Channel 13 as he did in the consumer office. The little guy ran to Marvin when he got cheated. Marvin would work up the case and bring it to our Consumer Fraud Section to file a charge. He would call the reporters to come in and interview him. Marvin loved that and so did the reporters. Zindler was so colorful the vast majority of people were fascinated by him.

When he took the investigative reporter's job at Channel 13, Marvin would still make the case for the little guy and walk the charge over to the courthouse—only this time he would have a TV news crew in tow. There he would interview me saying we would take the case and the crime was serious and the public should watch out for such shenanigans. If I wasn't available he interviewed the Consumer Fraud chief. Marvin spent part of the day in our Consumer Fraud Section and probably brought us more consumer fraud cases than the rest of Harris County law enforcement combined. A crooked businessman had more reason to fear Marvin than the courts. A bad story for a car dealer or discovery of slime in the ice machine could bring a dealership or restaurant to its knees.

Solid reporters like Bill Coulter, George Flynn, Barbara Strong, Nene Foxhall, Tom Kennedy, Gary Taylor, Bob Tutt, and Tom Moran made my job pleasant. Lynn Ashby was one of the better writers, and he wrote a long feature article about my life. It was nearly as good as the one he wrote about my friend, Assistant DA Tommy Dunn. The story was entitled "Who Dunn It." Tommy had tried so many beer joint killings he advised the public to stay out of beer joints.

The local press never took a cheap shot at me. We constantly shared information. I considered the ones who covered the courthouse as friends. I could talk off the record without fear. I both gave out and received information.

The public, the press, and our office were better off because of this. All things said and done, the press was very necessary. If the punishments meted out down at the courthouse were going to deter crime, someone had to get the word out.

CHAPTER TEN

The TSU Riot: A City Gripped in Fear

If I had to choose between justice and disorder on the one hand or injustice and order on the other, I would always choose the latter.
—Goethe

THE BACK ROADS OF Texas were always a delight. Among my favorites were the coastal roads with their diverse waterways, the whitecaps on the Gulf, and the sound of the surf when driving with the windows down. The birds and the lonely marsh grass plains reminded me of the summer days on Bolivar Peninsula at my aunt's beach house. Trips to the beach were our only answer to no air conditioning in those days. I never tired of fishing the back bays or intracoastal canal, or riding the breakers to shore. I liked to ride the Bolivar ferry across the bay to Galveston and watch both the big and little ships, and the porpoises rolling over.

I once bought a deck boat, a big thing some nineteen feet long, underpowered by an outboard engine that would not pull a person of any size on skis. Ernst named it "The Peppermint Park" because of its red and white stripes. I had taken some of the staff out to show it off on a couple of occasions. It would hold fourteen people plus refreshments. I always dreamed someday I would take our two boys on a cruise to Corpus and back, motoring slowly down the intracoastal canal. Our two sons became Eagle Scouts in an Explorer Post that gave them weeks of mountain climbing, whitewater rafting, and canoeing all over the U.S. and all the way to Canada. My idea of fun couldn't compete, but I was always dreaming about some kind of adventure.

I came upon the large highway that would lead to the city of Victoria if I turned left. Victoria brought back memories which now seemed like a strange dream from a distant past. I knew I wanted to forget most everything about that tense trial during some tense days in an otherwise sleepy town. Did the events of 1967 really happen? Did Houston really go through the trauma of a riot in our friendly city?

IT WAS THE SPRING of 1967, my second year in office and one of the first years of the nation's riots. Fires, deaths, protests, and vandalism raged from the East to the West Coast. L.A., Chicago, Detroit, and other cities were left with destroyed neighborhoods, thousands of fires, and even deaths. Some governors called up the National Guard. Mayor Daley of Chicago even put the tanks into action to quell a riot in Chicago.

Nationally known agitators and activists traveled to Houston to stir the pot. Even so, I saw nothing on the horizon to keep me from leaving town for three days to attend a board meeting for the National District Attorneys Association (NDAA). I had just been elected to the board as the board member from Texas. I wanted to talk to other big city DAs who would be at the meeting about riots, organized crime, and all those good things. And I wanted to know the DAs all over the nation. We were always needing help from some other state in order to find a witness, extradite a fugitive, or obtain background information on some known criminal.

The NDAA met in good places. My first board meeting would be at the famous Greenbriar resort nestled in the mountains of West Virginia. Tough duty, but someone had to do it. I left the Greenbriar Hotel phone number with a slew of people, including Mayor Louie Welch and Police Chief Herman Short.

If something broke out, Herman would call me. He would carry the big load on deploying forces, guided by a common-sense mayor and plenty of assistance from our office to process any mass arrests. Up until now it had been all talk and no action, anyway.

Early that morning I climbed aboard the airplane. It would take four different flights to get to those West Virginia hills. All went well, including an unusual experience on the last flight. This was in a four-seater, single engine, top wing airplane. I sat in the co-pilot's seat besides the captain, a little old man dressed in khakis. He even had on an old-fashioned leather aviator's cap. Smiling, he had greeted me at the airport holding up a sign, "Welcome Carol Vance. Flight Service to the Greenbriar."

"Well, young feller, this ceiling is so low today we are gonna have us a pretty good ride. May not see the tops of the mountains, but I haven't failed to find that Greenbriar landing strip yet." Fifteen minutes later, flying down a valley with low cloud cover, he said, "I think we take a right down this valley." I could not see the tops of the mountains on either side of the plane. A few minutes later he put it down on a very short runway. We made it, but by the time I checked in the dinner was over and the guys were in the bar. I wandered up and introduced myself to a few colorful prosecutors exchanging war stories and then headed to bed to be rested up for the 7:00 A.M. board breakfast.

The phone went off in the middle of the night. "Carol, this is Herman. You need to get on back here. Things are heating up on the Texas Southern campus. Joe tells me his informant says we can expect something big at TSU tomorrow night. He's not sure just what. All hell may break loose."

The Joe he referred to was Joe Singleton, the head of police intelligence.

I called the night manager, had him wake the pilot, and made connections to get back to Dodge. So much for my fun trip to the Greenbriar.

En route to Houston, I thought through what lay ahead. When police charged even just a few people at one time, key facts—like which officer did what—often got lost in the shuffle. Often an offense report would read, "Officers arrested four subjects rolling marijuana cigarettes. One subject had a .38 automatic and another a .22 revolver. Subjects admitted to officers having made the buy earlier in the day."

I would pull my hair out. Which officer, which subject, whose gun, who was rolling cigarettes, who said what and when and to whom?

I often found that when such a case went to trial, the wheels came off. The officers could not be expected to recall details two years later without a detailed written account. I could picture hundreds of arrests at the TSU campus becoming a model of confusion. Without a detailed plan to process mass arrests and record the facts, we would get laughed out of court. With that in mind we had already done our homework and were ready for the worst.

Before I left town, I had organized a large team of assistants to go on site of any mass arrests. The idea was simple. The police photographers would simply photograph the arresting officer and the perpetrator along with a blackboard that would have the time, the offense committed, a control number, and at least a sentence or so describing the specific event. As soon as possible, the officer would go back to the station and, armed with the picture, would be able to write up a short offense report. We would use Polaroid cameras and put the suspect's prints on the back of his picture to make a positive identification.

When one charged with rioting asked for a jury trial a year later, the officer could point out to the jury his own picture and that of the accused and describe what happened. When asked the age-old question of, "Officer, how can you be sure this particular defendant did this act many months ago considering all of the arrests you have made since?" the officer could use the picture to show the jury he knew what he was talking about.

As soon as I touched ground in Houston, Chief Investigator Johnny Fox picked me up to go straight to the chief's office. He was always full of news and filled me in. "Better get your toothbrush out of your suitcase and put it in your pocket." Johnny said.

How did we get to this point?

BEGINNING IN THE EARLY sixties, America was being hit by demonstrations and riots. We had the large Watts Riot in L.A., where a large section of town was burned. Most large cities with heavy inner city populations had been hit with or were threatened by riots. A riot needs to be contained from the start. When it gets out of hand many more people join in the riot. It spreads and takes on a life its own. Before long there are not enough police or firemen to bring order out of chaos and control the crowds. Once events escalate out of control the rioters assume the upper hand. Restoring order early is essential. Once things start going south, then all the angry young men in town (or other young men just looking for excitement) will jump into the battle, start fires and break windows, mainly for the thrill. Contain fast. Err on overreacting. If we had multiple deaths and part of our city burned, it could separate the races for years. The people most likely to die in a large riot would be the blacks of the inner city, not the folks over on the affluent west side of town. In L.A. and other cities it was the poor blacks burning their own neighborhoods. Many blacks lost their homes. Housing became a major problem. If a major riot broke out in our city, where would the displaced thousands live? We would be like Beirut or worse, like parts of L.A.

I did not want to see Houston burn on my watch, and the mayor and the chief felt at least as strongly as I did.

To understand the potential danger we faced, one must understand the strong feelings held by the black community. Civil rights and equality of treatment had been slow in coming. Most southern whites were holding on to the relic of segregation. The blacks were pushing for their constitutional rights the Civil War had been fought for. The Constitution made no reference to second-class citizens. While Houston had loosened up considerably, we still did not have a great record when it came to separate water fountains and banning blacks from restaurants and hotels. Martin Luther King, Jr., was leading the black cause with his non-violent protests to secure these rights. He sought change in the most effective way. But King's methodology was not shared by all. Radical organizations and individuals advocated "Burn, baby burn," a slogan of the day that raced across America.

In the midst of these serious racial issues, the Vietnam War was highly unpopular. America was constantly increasing its troop deployment, trying to find some way to exit the conflict, and the cause we were fighting for was being blurred by the demonstrations across the country. The longer the war lasted, the greater the protests. Racial and war issues intertwined. Many blacks who competed in the Olympics for the U.S. during the sixties wore black as a protest to show the world. The radical left looked for dramatic openings to pursue its agenda, which included revolution. Add to all of this the fact that President Kennedy had been assassinated just four years before. Then his brother Bobby, who was the senator from New York and the leading contender for the Democratic nomination for President, was gunned down. And not too long after Senator Kennedy's death Dr. King was killed by an assassin's bullet. Times were changing.

All the while, the young people of our nation (mostly white, self-proclaimed "hippies") were rebelling with their own cultural revolution. Hippies were advocating and practicing public pot smoking, nudity, and profane public language. The growing unrest melded together in a serious attack upon law and order, government, and morality, with the protesters doing whatever they could to bring the establishment to its knees. The social upheaval created a climate where even the burning of a city was a plausible option.

The entire social revolution came upon us quickly. By the summer of 1963, prior to President Kennedy's assassination, there were a thousand demonstrations in over two hundred cities across America. In our nation's capital, a quarter of a million people showed up to march. The police were on edge.

Much of the unrest centered around college campuses. Ted Kennedy, a darling of the liberals himself, was nonetheless booed off the stage and could not proceed with his commencement address at Boston University. *Time* magazine reported 448 colleges and universities were shut down due to demonstrations. Two million students went on strike on 1,100 campuses. Favorite targets for campus disruption were ROTC buildings and the office of that university's president. An underground group called the Weathermen made bombs inside a townhouse in Greenwich Village in lower Manhattan. Somebody's bombs exploded at the courthouse in Cambridge, Maryland. Before all the riots would end in America, our big city DAs would have met with J. Edgar Hoover of the FBI, Mayor Daley of Chicago, and testified before Congress and various state legislatures. All law enforcement could do was to try to be successful in their purely reactive mode.

LEADING UP TO THE TSU riot, Houston was ripe. A few weeks before this night of May 17, 1967, several national leaders had journeyed to Houston to make highly inflammatory speeches. Most all of the city's older and more respected black leaders ignored their rhetoric. The visitors, however, found listening ears on the Texas Southern University campus. TSU was a nearly all-black college. Students at every college in America, black and white, were quick to take on a cause. TSU was located relatively close to downtown Houston in the inner city and in a predominantly black area called Third Ward. The out-of-town agitators had picked a choice spot to get things stirred up.

Houston had not had serious racial trouble since World War I, when a riot occurred near an army camp in Memorial Park, a few miles west of downtown. From that time forward our city had enjoyed peace.

James Forman, a national figure whose call was for "black power," arrived in Houston in 1965 with the purpose of stirring up crowds on and off the TSU campus. He was followed by Franklin Alexander of the socialist "W. E. B. DuBois Clubs," who fired up campus crowds two months before our May 1967 riot.

The final well-known black leader to come to town before the riot was Stokely Carmichael. He was a household name from coast to coast. In April he made impassioned pleas for "action" both on and off the TSU campus. Following Carmichael's arrival, a large group of blacks staged a massive sit-down at the courthouse after a well-publicized march to downtown from TSU. The crowd's purpose was to form a protest in front of the State Attorney General's Houston office. Simultaneously, many TSU students began to boycott classes.

A few nights after Stokely's cry to action, demonstrators trashed the TSU school cafeteria but without significant damage. The demonstrations escalated the press coverage, which although expected and normal, added fuel to the fire. Public attention to promote a cause is one of the primary reasons to have a riot.

By the end of April some TSU students were throwing stones at passing motorists who were innocently driving down Wheeler Street in front of the campus. Some students and agitators demanded the city close off Wheeler for benefit of the students. Wheeler Street was a main artery in that area of town and met the needs of many motorists who needed to get where they were going. The city was not about to be blackmailed into closing this or any other street.

The trouble at TSU did not make sense. The days of the bus stations sit-downs were over. A good part of the leadership in Houston had quietly gone about voluntarily integrating restaurants and places of lodging. The old fountains in the parks saying "White Only" and "Black Only" were gone. Without any publicity, Bob Dundas, vice president of the city's largest department store, Foley's, had quietly integrated the store's popular restaurant. Following Foley's example, the other restaurants in town followed suit.

All of this preceded the Civil Rights Act. With this voluntary reform, out-of-town agitators were hard-pressed to find issues emotional enough to stir up a riot. The best thing they could come up with was the Holmes Road garbage dump. Yes, the dump was a blight and needed strong policing against illegal dumping. And homes in the mainly black area had reason to complain. However, most of the garbage dumps in Houston needed some major assistance, not just this one—this was before pollution laws got tough. Students at TSU could not have cared less about the issue—they just wanted a *cause célèbre*.

The TSU campus, and particularly the Student Union Building, had become the primary soap box to launch inflammatory speeches. As I entered Chief Herman Short's office from the flight from the Greenbriar, Mayor Welch and intelligence chief Joe Singleton told me a good number of students had been hauled off to jail earlier that day for lying down on the roadway at the Holmes Road site. Earlier, Assistant DA Dick DeGuerin had been dispatched to the dump to see if criminal charges could be filed on those tying up the garbage trucks. The news media were giving heavy coverage to Holmes Road. Our office was caught between a rock and a hard place. Our enforcement of a trespassing law could ignite a riot back at TSU, Holmes Road, or almost anywhere else.

Joe Singleton may have been a mere lieutenant, but he was a key part of our discussions and decision making. Joe was receiving information from the

FBI and police departments all over the country. He was surrounded by a handful of bright and experienced officers like Bob Blaylock, who would take a bullet later that night.

Intelligence had informants on the TSU campus and all around the Third Ward area. They knew who was coming to town and where the speeches were to be made. During these troubling days, Joe lived in the chief's office when he wasn't in the field. He talked to the mayor and me daily.

After I arrived at the police station, Joe said the protesters had a busy night planned on campus. Intelligence officers had taken up strategic locations around Wheeler Street and the campus. Numerous squad cars were in the area hidden in inconspicuous spots so as to not arouse suspicion. Chief Short had a contingent force of 300–400 officers standing by at HPD headquarters downtown. Each man had riot gear and was ready to roll. They could be loaded in cars and in action on the nearby campus in minutes.

At 9:00 P.M. Singleton received a call from one of his guys: The students were beginning to form a crowd. At 9:30 Singleton called in to the chief's speaker phone and described how five known leaders were trying to arouse the crowd into action. One kept repeating to the crowd, "They killed a young black child today so what are you going to do about it?" No such child had been killed that day, but Joe said the crowd had believed it.

He added that an older black man approached two of the undercover officers at the scene and said, "Get out of here or you are going to be killed." A few minutes later a student was arrested for carrying a pistol in plain view. From Joe's voice on the speaker phone, I could tell he believed things could break loose any moment.

A city councilman named Bill Elliot, whose hobby was riding with the police, came into the chief's office. He could tell from the police radio traffic something serious was afoot. Bill knew his police department. By now we had some of our top assistants and those on the riot team ready to make the scene. Their task was to make sure the police would follow the procedures we had planned earlier. The police might make whatever arrests they deemed appropriate, but we did not want to accept a criminal charge unless we could prove a case in court. Any acquittal due to insufficient evidence would just play into the demonstrators' hands. Gathering evidence and implementing even a good plan would be a challenge in the darkness.

As trouble escalated, an informal log was kept by an intelligence officer monitoring the police radios. It went as follows:

7:00 P.M.	Intelligence officers take posts on TSU campus.
10:15 P.M.	Crowd growing. 150 persons assembled. Five subjects [later to be known as the TSU Five] approach crowd stating, "They killed a six year old boy out near Scenic Wood School. What are you going to do about it?"
10:20 P.M.	Objects thrown that strike police vehicles.
10:25 P.M.	Subject approaches officers and says you better get out of here before you get killed.
10:30 P.M.	Armed subject arrested on campus with pistol that turns out stolen.
10:40 P.M.	Detective unit struck by thrown brick.
10:45 P.M.	Crowd grows. More inciting statements. Rocks, bricks, and missiles thrown at police vehicles.
10:50 P.M.	Officers move vehicles so their headlights illuminate the Student Union Building.
11:00 P.M.	Sporadic firing from men's dorms begins. Officers see armed students running towards the Student Union Building.
11:30 P.M.	Officer Blaylock is wounded by sniper fire coming from TSU campus.
11:35 P.M.	Police reinforcements arrive at scene as snipers continue to fire from the TSU dormitories.

At this point, bedlam hit, and the log was discontinued.

A little before midnight the crowd swelled. Students and hangers-on were filling up the campus grounds. The noise escalated with shouting and people running here and there. The police mobilized and assembled just off campus and out of sight. Herman Short went to the scene to take charge. He had just arrived when several students began firing their firearms from the windows of the campus dorm in the direction of the officers. Officers took positions behind cars and shelters adjacent to the campus.

Officer Bob Blaylock, Singleton's right-hand man, was hit in his thigh while crouched behind a patrol car. This bullet had to have been fired from the closest student dorm. At this point the police were ordered to advance onto the campus area. Some time had elapsed as it was now 1:00 A.M. As the police made ready to move out, some black leaders, who did not want to see any violence either, convinced the chief to let them go in and talk to the students. The chief gladly gave them this opportunity. Their objective was to get the students to lay down any firearms and march out of the dorms into the open in plain sight. The older men went in and talked their hearts out, I am sure, but their plea fell on deaf ears.

The clock was now pushing 2:00 A.M. A large number of students (and non-students, as we found out later) dashed out of the dorm and began to barricade Wheeler Street. They grabbed some old barrels lying around and doused them with lighter fluid or gasoline. They also set fire to some of the lumber from a construction project close by. Then a group grabbed trash cans and dumped the garbage out on the street.

A separate group, one that looked like they knew what they were doing, had concocted Molotov cocktails, the small homemade bombs consisting of a bottle of gasoline with a rag in the top for a fuse. These would explode seconds after being thrown. They chunked the cocktails at the police, who were far enough away that no one was injured. At that point the chief ordered a hundred officers to advance upon the dorm and take control. Bullets continued to come from the dorm windows, mostly from the second floor.

The chief told his men to fire their guns over the dormitory to make a show of force. If an officer did see someone shooting at them from a specific place the officer could fire back at that spot.

The police advanced. The students kept on firing out of the second floor. Their fire power escalated. Officer Alan Dugger was hit in the face. Then a rookie who had just graduated from the Houston Police Academy was shot and killed as he moved toward the dorm in the first line of police. His name was Louis Kuba, the lone fatality of the riot.

The police began emptying their guns into the dorm as they moved forward. Then the front of the police line reached the outside doors, which were locked. Some police had large axes which made short work of the doors. The police in large number moved through quickly and went upstairs to take control. Only a few minutes elapsed from the time of the first shot until police had control. Officer Kuba was hit between the eyes. He was taken to the emergency room at Ben Taub. He hung on until sunrise and then died.

Officers from the Texas Department of Public Safety and the Harris County Sheriff's Office pulled up to the scene to give assistance, but the riot was over.

The first command the police gave was for all of the students to lie down.

They did. Not another single shot was fired by anyone. Then they searched and handcuffed the students. All of the students in the dorm were placed under arrest. Next came the massive sorting out of just who did what and just what criminal charges would be filed.

Considering the heavy gunfire of the evening, most of the people at the scene said it was a miracle that only one police officer was killed and two were wounded. Students suffered only minor injuries.

The dorm and the street outside were a mess, but it was just broken windows and trash. Not a single building burned up, and there was no mass vandalism, arson, or thefts. For a riot with lots of gunfire, property damage was minimal.

The police arrested 491 people, mostly students. All except for one white man were black; 450 lived on campus. At first only a few cooperated with the police. Later at the jail most students ended up telling what they saw. Ultimately over four hundred students gave brief written statements. Assistant DAs worked the rest of that night and well into the next day sorting through evidence, statements, and police reports in order to assemble files.

The critical pieces of evidence turned out to be the Polaroid pictures showing the arresting officer, the accused, and the little blackboard with the essential information. A jury might acquit, but at least no case would drop through the cracks because of the confusion of the moment and the large number of persons processed.

Because a large number of assistants were still working on some of the cases the next morning, judges rescheduled court dockets. It was a long day and night for all involved, but so far we had gotten off light compared to other cities around the nation.

I could not have been more pleased with the teamwork of police and prosecutors. Except for the five that intelligence labeled instigators, no one else was charged with any felony offense. Some were charged with illegally carrying pistols and some with property damage. For the moment we held off on charging the leaders. Our briefing attorneys hit the books to see what might stand up. We wanted to charge the five leaders with the highest offense in order to deter any future riot.

Our legal challenge was formidable. No one witnessed any of the five leaders shoot anyone or commit any act of violence. One was seen starting a fire in a barrel, and that was about it. It is the district attorney's responsibility to decide what charges will be filed. We did not have a clue as to who shot Officer Kuba or who wounded the two other officers. Bullet comparisons from weapons recovered at the scene turned out inconclusive.

Criticism came fast and furious the next day. The claim, mostly from some black leaders, was the police had overreacted. The mayor had a tougher task than I did. He was meeting with black leaders and other city leaders, explaining the facts and why the riot needed to be shut down as quickly as possible. I was with him during some of these meetings. Mayor Welch took the lead and got his message across. He was not going to stand by and see Houston burn.

Welch asked each of the leaders what he thought might have happened had the police not responded as they did. They all admitted there would likely have been more deaths, injuries, and destruction had prompt and decisive action not been taken. Of course, we will never know what might have happened had the police not brought the matter to closure in an aggressive manner. My philosophy was certainly simple: law and order had to come first. Without law and order no one is going to enjoy any of our precious freedoms anyway.

As it turned out Houston never imposed martial law as so many cities back East had to do. Governor Connally offered to call up the Texas National Guard in Houston, but that was the last thing the mayor wanted. Soldiers in uniform behind barbed wire fences would be a measure of last resort.

After the incident, Welch, Chief Short, and I cast most of the blame on outside agitators. We believed their political objective was not really about civil rights. They wanted another Watts. The outsiders planted the seeds and came back to water them. Then they left town. The local five picked up on this and talked the students into the riot. When the five stirred up the crowd, the students' reaction was predictable.

Unfortunately, the TSU administration did little to help. Their security officers' response was non-existent. Governor Connally publicly scolded the Dean of Students. The chairman of the TSU Board of Regents, a black man, said, "I deplore the violence. Once we find the student agitators who precipitated the violence, we will get rid of them."

Chief Short issued some strongly worded statements. He said neither he nor his men wanted to be out there on a campus that should have policed itself.

My first step was to open a grand jury investigation as we wanted to get the witnesses in front of the grand jury immediately. This was the perfect forum because witnesses who are scared to speak out in public will often tell all in the secrecy of a grand jury room. Also, we could get the witnesses in and out of the grand jury room without press coverage. There were no rules of evidence in the grand jury so we could ask questions to find out who knew what about what was going on. Witnesses could be subpoenaed and then held in contempt if they did not appear or answer questions put to them by the assistant DA.

Police intelligence knew the five men who egged the crowd on. They had hung out together and had participated in other demonstrations for some time. They were around the scene urging the students to a call to action. All were from Houston and four were students. The press dubbed them the TSU Five. But the question was what crime could the five be charged with? None of them were seen pulling any trigger or harming anyone.

Texas had an old law on the books simply called "Riot." Our Court of Criminal Appeals had not written an opinion interpreting this statute for close to fifty years. And the ancient cases did not give us any roadmap. The law was very, very simple. It read that if there was a riot, anyone participating in the riot would be guilty of any offense committed by anyone else who was participating in that same riot. I doubt many people in Texas, including criminal lawyers or prosecutors, even knew this law was on the books. On the other hand, the application of such a law could be subject to criticism. If a hundred people were running around setting garbage cans on fire, should all be guilty of murder if one rioter pulled out a gun and shot someone? Under the way the law was written, the answer was clearly yes.

Joe Moss, a veteran lawyer whom I enticed to return to the office to head our Appellate Section, said the Riot law could be used to charge the five. As the law read, the five could be guilty of murder if they participated in a riot but left the scene before the fatal shot was fired. The law did not require us to prove a conspiracy or anything else. Thus we believed the TSU Five could be found guilty of the murder of Officer Kuba and the assaults with intent to murder officers Blaylock and Dugger. It did not matter that none of the five pulled a trigger or were anywhere to be seen when the trigger was pulled.

I knew going in the use of the law would be highly controversial. In the final analysis it would be up to the jury to convict or acquit. I expected critics to come out of the woodwork crying foul. On the other hand, not to charge the leaders who led the march for the riot would give a free pass to like-minded souls in the future. After all, those students who were involved were stirred up to act by the leaders. This seemingly spontaneous riot was not a spontaneous act. It came as a result of a call to action.

The president of TSU believed the five might return to campus and start more trouble. To prevent this he signed a peace bond to be imposed against each of the TSU Five. He knew he had to keep them off of campus. Justice of the Peace Jack Treadway, a respected magistrate, issued the order.

The NAACP provided counsel to the five at the peace bond hearing. Peace bonds were set in the amount of $10,000 for each of the five men. Four of the five made bond within a day after the hearing. The fifth made bond three days later. The fact they were not in jail was helpful in settling things down. These guys were leaders, and their incarceration might stir up a crowd.

That week I asked the grand jury to launch an investigation. Some fourteen witnesses were called to testify. Some witnesses were going to be important in describing the conduct of the TSU Five. The testimony gave us a better understanding of how the night unfolded. Also it provided a roadmap of how to try the case.

The grand jury indicted the five for Riot, coupled with the offense of murder and the assaults with intent to murder as we had recommended. The outcome would not only hinge upon what the trial jury believed happened but how the trial judge interpreted that seldom-used law.

PUBLIC CRITICISM RAN HOT and heavy against my decision. That was part of the territory. Following the indictments, the five attorneys representing the five defendants filed five separate motions for separate trials. In those days every defendant had an absolute right to be tried separately under Texas law. Not only that, if the defendants agreed on who should be tried first, the trial judge had to go along. It was a common practice for multiple defendants to agree on the order of trial and force the State to try its weakest case first. The lawyers for the TSU Five realized that if the jury acquitted the first defendant, the State might dismiss or reduce charges on the remaining defendants. This trial was big news, and everyone would remember the outcome.

I knew I had to try the case, not something I looked forward to. Nevertheless, even with an acquittal, we could make our statement. Anyone fostering a riot in Houston would know he would have to face up to the full measure of the law. After all, the legislature knew the devastation caused by riots and passed the strongest law imaginable. We would honor it.

The case raised another concern. Students had already marched on the Harris County Courthouse once. A trial on this charge would draw protesters out of the woodwork. The crowds could get out of control. Jurors might be intimidated. Protests would make it difficult to seat a jury in Harris County. Houstonians were saturated with press coverage of that night at

TSU. Feelings ran strong. I did not want a trial in Harris County that might trigger another riot.

The defense attorneys did not want a change of venue; they wanted to try the case in Harris County. The State seldom files a motion for a change of venue. We examined the law and decided we could file such a motion.

The Houston Bar Association volunteered to help. Led by HBA president Harry Patterson, who would later become my law partner at Bracewell and Patterson, the HBA board passed a resolution endorsing a change of venue. At the hearing Harry Patterson testified that a less impassioned jury could be seated outside the greater Houston area.

The case for a change of venue fell in Judge Wendell Odom's court. The judge patiently heard several days of testimony from both sides. He commented with his dry sense of humor that he never had such a problem back in Groveton, the small East Texas town where he grew up. At the end of the day Judge Odom granted our motion. I imagine he thought, Why risk a trial in Houston that could get out of hand? He transferred the trial to Victoria, a convenient, sleepy community two to three hours away by car. Judge Odom made a wise choice.

The case went to veteran District Judge Joe Kelly, a jolly fellow with a serious side for the lawyer who crossed the line. Judge Kelly would keep a tight lid on all court proceedings and particularly any disruptions inside the courtroom or courthouse. I called my friend, Bill Sparks, the district attorney of Victoria, and told him the news, "Hopefully, Bill, the demonstrators won't damage your city too much."

"I don't think I heard that. By the way, Carol, is there anything else I can do for you today?"

The case was set for trial and we found ourselves picking a jury by mid-October 1967, a short time considering all the pre-trial motions. By now the explosive atmosphere of past days had settled down in Houston. Houston's expected long hot summer had passed without incident as, meanwhile, trouble brewed in many major cities across our land.

During this interval I went to the TSU campus twice to address the law students and later a political club. The law student reception started out cool. I challenged them to get involved. "Have any of you ever considered a career in the District Attorney's office where you could be a part of how criminal justice is administered?" By the end they had warmed up. Two came up to say they might seek an interview after they passed the bar.

At the TSU political club, it was cold, not cool. Unlike the law students, they were there to argue. Whoever made the wildest statement drew the most crowd approval. As I walked back to my car by myself on a dark street in the heart of Houston's Third Ward, I took some consolation in the fact that none of my eastern DA friends would have dared go out alone at night in an all-black neighborhood. Our city was not perfect, but intelligent blacks and whites in Houston treated each other with considerable respect.

I moved into a small motel in Victoria for about three weeks. The defense attorneys picked who would go to trial first, but we had the pick of his three cases to try. I chose the assault with intent to murder case involving Officer Blaylock. Blaylock was alive to testify and could say the shot that hit him came from the TSU dorm.

A couple of homicide detectives had suggested to me that Officer Kuba may have been shot by one of the Houston police officers in the melee. The marks on the bullet indicated it could have been a ricochet. Although that was a more unlikely occurrence than not, we never knew for sure. Also, Blaylock could testify that the defendant on trial was not only at the scene but was among the five leaders urging the crowd to take to the streets. Finally, the assault case did not carry the death penalty. Although we would not seek the death penalty, just having it as one of the punishments would have been an inflammatory catalyst for any mob making trouble.

The first day of trial, a group of perhaps fifty Texas Southern followers drove down to Victoria from Houston. The jury selection was boring, of course. After the first day, most if not all of the TSU followers went home and never returned. I was grateful for the change of venue. We had a few folks from out-of-town in the courtroom, but they behaved. Once in a while a spectator would make some emotional response to the testimony being given, but the judge would jump in and keep a reign on the proceedings.

The defense team consisted of old friend Ned Wade and Weldon Berry, two very capable black lawyers who wanted to win their case outright. I know they did not want any radicals from up North making the jury angry at their client. I think they sensed the Victoria jurors would be as fair and open-minded as any.

After jury selection, the testimony commenced, and things went as expected with one major exception. After Officer Blaylock testified he saw the defendant on trial throw a large piece of concrete that hit a police car, I called a TSU campus police officer to the stand to corroborate that fact. I had spoken to this officer in advance and believed he would be a good witness for our side. During cross-examination the guy dropped us in the grease.

When Ned Wade took the campus cop on cross, he said, "Sir, do you have an opinion as to what caused the riot?" I questioned Ned's judgment on that question as I waited for the officer to lower the boom.

"What caused the riot? Well, I do have an opinion. Earlier that evening I was present when the police arrested a student for 'failure to move on.' When they arrested him and cuffed him on such a minor charge in front of a lot of people it wasn't long before things started getting out of hand. I think the way that the Houston police officer handled that arrest was what got the people excited and caused the gunfire and the shootings and all that happened that night."

The TSU campus cop had never told me any of this before, even though I had questioned him at length and demanded he tell me all the facts, both good and bad. He had said he heard the defendants stirring up the crowd. In other words, back at the time, he claimed the TCU Five were responsible and had incited things.

When I got him back on redirect the officer admitted the five guys did stir up the crowd and were a causing factor as well. He also had to agree that Molotov cocktails would take some degree of planning as would the obtaining of firearms and ammo for the occasion. When pushed into a corner he had to agree there had to be preparation by the rioters well in advance of the arrest of the student. Nevertheless, serious damage was done to our case by his testimony.

When the campus officer's testimony ended, the lawyers marched into the judge's chambers to argue the language the judge would put in his written charge to the jury.

The judge's first comment was, "Mr. Vance, don't waste your time arguing your Riot law. I have decided not to charge the jury on the offense of Riot. I just don't believe you can make a case under that law on these facts."

The judge, although bright and respected, was dead wrong. We did have a case the way that law was written. I won't say it would have held up all the way to the Supreme Court, but our research showed many states had similar laws. Without the Riot law, the judge should have thrown out the whole case. We had not put even one of the five men at the scene at the time the shooting occurred.

I expected the judge to end the trial and instruct the jury to find the defendant not guilty. But Judge Kelly said he was submitting the case to the jury on the offense of assault with intent to murder. I thought to myself, How in the world could a jury believe this man was guilty of assault when he was not even there? I fully expected the jury to acquit.

One good practical thing came out of the court's ruling: Things had settled down in Houston. We were picking up no vibes of further trouble. I would have personally been pleased for the whole case to go away. A long sentence would cause more civil unrest.

Unlike other cases, I knew these five guys were spurred on at least in part by ideological goals. They were not criminals. Probation with instructions not to return to the campus would have suited me at this point.

The judge submitted the case to the jury on a regular charge of assault with intent to murder. We returned to the courtroom where final argument took the rest of the day. I had packed my bags and had the dismissal forms already filled out on the other four defendants. I was going to file these as soon as the jury said not guilty. Even if the jury were to find the defendant on trial guilty, I did not see how any conviction of any offense not including the Riot law could withstand the Court of Criminal Appeals on appeal.

The final arguments began with Bill Sparks making the opener. Bill called the outbreak on the TSU campus a "war." Judge Kelly sustained the objection to that characterization, as well as a few others Bill came up with. I will say this for Bill: He didn't hold back.

Ned argued that "this man can't bear a cross for everyone who shot a pistol. The shooter could have been an ex-convict. He could have been a burglar on the campus. We just don't know who he was."

I don't remember what I said. There was nothing logical I could say. I had already accepted the fact the verdict would be a quick not guilty.

The jury retired to deliberate. They had three choices: guilty of the felony assault to murder, guilty of the lesser offense of misdemeanor assault, or not guilty.

We waited and waited all that afternoon. The hours dragged on. The jury retired for the night and we went on into the next day. About every two or three hours the jury reported they were deadlocked. They informed the court on several occasions they could not reach a verdict. Judge Kelly just kept instructing them to keep on deliberating. The questions the jury sent out to the judge in writing made me think they were all over the place. Ned Wade, Bill Sparks, and I drank a little coffee together. Bill and Ned, a great comedy team, took my mind off of just how serious a full-scale riot in Houston would have been.

Finally, when the jury insisted in writing they were hung and could never return a verdict, Judge Kelly declared a mistrial. The jurors walked out of the courtroom. I sensed they did not want to talk and so let them alone. A reporter who got information from one of the jurors reported they were divided into three camps. Two wanted an acquittal, two voted for assault with intent to murder, the most serious charge possible, and eight favored convicting the defendant of the included misdemeanor offense of aggravated assault.

I think Judge Kelly knew what he was doing. I never talked to him about it, of course, but he knew things had quieted down in Houston. I figured that he did not like the Riot law and he had taken me off the hook from proceeding further when he charged us out of court. He probably expected an acquittal as well. As peaceful as Houston had become, he, too, was looking for a way out.

Within a few days I announced we were dismissing all charges in the TSU cases. The local papers editorialized in favor of the decision. Now that things were quiet, it made Mayor Welch happy, too. I am not sure about Chief Short; after all, we did lose one of Houston's Finest that night.

To give a final perspective of how fortunate Houston was, there were 750 riots in the U.S. between 1964 and 1971. The number of people killed exceeded 225, with over 12,000 injured. With 15,000 acts of arson around the nation, many inner city areas were in shambles. The median value of all homes in an inner city without a riot dropped 8 percent, but in the cities with riots the market declined 20 percent. Unemployment also escalated in the rioting cities. The black population took the brunt of the death, destruction, and economic hits.

The TSU Five went their own way. One graduated from Rice University and became a practicing lawyer. Officer Dale Dugger, who had required some three hundred stitches in his face that night, later joined our office's Organized Crime Unit. He finally retired after thirty years service. Blaylock became an investigator for our office and ended up becoming the chief investigator for my successor, Johnny Holmes. The only hero was, of course, Officer Louis Kuba, who paid the supreme price for keeping the peace in our city. And he left a young widow and an unborn child.

Years later on a television show I was asked, "What was the most difficult situation you ever faced as district attorney?"

Without hesitation, I said, "The night of the TSU riot."

THE TSU RIOT PASSED into history; our city was very fortunate. The former TSU Five were quiet. The only blip on the screen was a fellow by the name of Lee Otis Johnson. He tried to stir up crowds. He was an effective speaker and received some publicity. No one seemed to be responding to his message, however.

Officer Blaylock told me the police had assigned one of their own, Officer Williams, to try to befriend Lee Otis and watch his every move. Williams was successful and soon began being used by Lee Otis to chauffeur him around town. They were together wherever Lee Otis went. One day Lee Otis went to a friend's house to obtain a small amount of marijuana. In a minute Lee Otis was back in the car, marijuana in hand. As he climbed inside Lee Otis handed Williams a single marijuana cigarette saying, "Don't let the police catch you with this. You could get twenty years in prison."

Williams said, "Thanks, man. I think I will wait until evening and light up then."

At the first opportunity, Williams turned the cigarette over to the police chemist for testing. It was positive. Lee Otis was indicted, arrested, and put in jail. Lee Otis had been to prison before for burglary and was no stranger to the law. At that time, any gift, sale, or possession of marijuana was a felony that carried a punishment of two years to life imprisonment. A few states had been reducing possession or small amount of marijuana to a misdemeanor, but traditionally it had been a felony.

All of this made the campus police and officials at TSU happy as Lee Otis had long since been kicked off campus and told not to return. Lee Otis was not involved in the TSU riot as he was in jail that night. This arrest came months later after all of Houston had settled down. The arrest and trial and sentence of Lee Otis Johnson became a national news storm that elevated Lee Otis into a hero and me into the goat.

After the indictment the case was set for trial. I knew the case would only take a day to try with two short witnesses. What can one say about the handoff of one cigarette? So I decided to try the case.

The trial began. We obtained a jury with ease. No one on the jury panel seemed to have heard of Lee Otis. After the jury was seated, I put on Williams and the city chemist. There was little cross-examination. The jury was out less than a half hour and found the defendant guilty.

Then we had a short punishment hearing. I called Mayor Welch and Chief Herman Short to the stand to testify that Lee Otis had a bad reputation for not being a peaceable and law-abiding citizen. Not one word was ever mentioned to the jury about the fact Lee Otis liked to make speeches to stir up trouble, nor were his political views, the TSU riot, or anything else brought up.

During my closing argument to the jury, I reminded them that Lee Otis had been to prison before and apparently that did not change his life, so any sentence—even up to the twenty years that Lee Otis mentioned to the undercover officer—would be appropriate.

The jury was out again less than thirty minutes and assessed Lee Otis' punishment at thirty years. I was surprised. I thought they would probably give him somewhere between two and twenty but closer to the lower end.

I could not believe the amount of publicity this thirty-year sentence generated. *Time, Newsweek,* the New York *Times,* the networks, and the press fed on this story for as long as Lee Otis was in jail. I received calls from all over Europe. Thirty years for one cigarette. Texas justice. The DA personally tried this one-marijuana-cigarette case. Those were the themes.

Lee Otis found himself a modern day folk hero. "Free Lee Otis" tee shirts, rallies, peaceful protests, the American Civil Liberties Union, politicians defending and criticizing the verdict. It was all there.

One day the local head of the ACLU asked to meet with me. He was a lawyer, a very reasonable man, so I welcomed his visit.

Over coffee in my office he said the national organization was passing resolutions condemning me and the result of the trial. However, he had gotten hold of the transcript of the trial and had read it over. He said, "Carol, you never mentioned Lee Otis was a troublemaker and you never asked for thirty years. The jury had to give him something between two and ninety-nine under Texas law. Some could criticize you for trying the case, but you are the DA and can choose any case to try you want. I just don't understand this media blitz and controversy."

After I said the whole thing was a mystery to me, he told me that when the national ACLU put their stamp of disapproval on what I had done the local chapter was not involved. I appreciated his coming.

But it was not the ACLU. It was the Eastern press and everyone in America who favored legalization of marijuana that was upset. Texas ultimately reduced possession of a small amount of marijuana to a misdemeanor. I even favored the legislation. But back then we enforced the law. If someone had marijuana in Texas, it was a felony. We did not play God and not prosecute. In this case, Lee Otis asked for a jury and that jury did its duty.

The jury never knew Lee Otis headed up the Students for Non-Violence Coordinating Committee. U.S. Senator McClellan, who headed the Senate committee investigating our nation's riots, blamed the TSU riot on this organization.

Ultimately the case ended up in federal court where Judge Carl Bue (an excellent judge, by the way) reversed the conviction because the trial judge did not grant the motion for a change of venue hearing at the start of trial. Judge Bue cited forty-four newspaper stories about Lee Otis prior to his conviction, not to mention all of the TV coverage.

He said Lee Otis was denied his Fourteenth Amendment right to due process because of the obvious community feelings toward civil rights activists at the time.

I disagreed with his decision because every juror was asked by the defense attorney if they knew anything at all about Lee Otis Johnson. No one on that jury was familiar with him in the least. Even so, I lost no sleep over the decision. At least the East Coast and world media quit calling me every day to ask me the same two questions: Why did I personally try the case, and why wouldn't I free Lee Otis?

One last addendum to the Lee Otis story. During his incarceration Governor Preston Smith came to Houston to make a talk at the University of Houston Student Union. The governor, a fine man of considerable political skills, was a conservative Democrat, a white male, and from West Texas. He was not expecting any problems. Although Governor Smith was not the world's most exciting speaker, he took the podium to address a full house. Throughout his talk people at the back of the large assembly kept yelling "Free Lee Otis! Free Lee Otis! Free Lee Otis!" Even though not much of what the governor said could be heard, he dutifully plowed through his written speech.

After he stepped down, a Houston *Chronicle* reporter asked, "Governor, what did you think of those students who kept shouting 'Free Lee Otis! Free Lee Otis!'?"

"Well," Governor Smith drawled, "I don't know what those good people have against frijoles. I sort of like frijoles myself." The story hit page one in every Texas newspaper.

Ultimately "Free Lee Otis!" not frijoles, became a reality. He was free at last. But not much time expired before someone in the office said, "Did you hear about Lee Otis? He was filed on for burglary."

That was news to me. I didn't ask what court his case fell in or who was prosecuting. A few months later, when reading the morning paper, a story in one of the back sections said a jury had sentenced Lee Otis to seventeen years for burglary. If the national or international press wrote a single word about this event, I was not aware of it. Even a man with a cause shouldn't commit a burglary.

CHAPTER ELEVEN

The Office Overhaul

It was beautiful and simple as all truly great swindles are.
—O. Henry

WHAT COULD I TELL my friends why I was leaving? The staff, friends, and family all knew I loved the job. To a large extent my identity was wrapped up in being DA. I believed if someone ran against me and won, I would go into a blue funk and not come out. People greeted me as "Mister District Attorney." That said it. This office was the focus of my life.

But my priorities were changing. This started three years previously when John Tolson came to town. He had moved to Houston from Dallas where he had been an associate pastor at Highland Park Presbyterian Church. He went on staff at my church, First Pres, to be an outreach minister and to form men's groups. He would be spending time with business and professional men around the city.

Right after John arrived, he called me to have breakfast. I ended up having breakfast once a week with him for a year. He took me through the Gospel of John. Tolson had played baseball and basketball in college, loved sports, and never met a stranger. During his time in Houston John became the chaplain for the Astros, the Oilers, and the Rockets. Guys took to him, including me.

John said we might start a Bible study at the DA's office. I agreed. We had a small group of six to eight who always came, including Ted Poe, Roland Elder, Eldred Hammond, and Tom Henderson. Through John's teaching and influence I discovered my worth in life did not depend on my position or my worldly success. Even attending church every week and being a longtime Elder at First Pres was not the test; it was a relationship with Jesus.

That experience did not make the DA's job less important, but I realized I was not indispensable. I realized being district attorney had been a calling, but callings may come and go in the seasons of life. Three years after Tolson and I began, I felt like I needed to start on another journey. Giving up the thing I knew best and loved would be tough, but I had accomplished all of the things I set out to do as DA. Then the Bracewell opportunity to practice with some old friends presented itself. I was not unmindful of the money factor—partner in a major law firm versus public payroll—and Carolyn and I were facing the cost of college for the five kids. Somewhere between the excitement of a new thing and a dragging reluctance, I made the move.

At Bracewell and Patterson I would have a new challenge. I had never filled out a time sheet. I had never had to deal with a client. I was going to do both civil and criminal work in a day of specialization.

I did not know what the future held but I knew I was going with some darn good lawyers. In the litigation section I would join Bill Wilde, Ken Wynne, and Joe Jaworski, who were old friends, and would also work with Cliff Gunter, Fred Hagans, Chuck King, and finally Ralph McBride, who became one of my closest friends. Four of our little group, including myself, were asked to be Fellows in the American College of Trial Lawyers.

As things turned out I went on to spend twenty-two years there in active practice, the same length of time as in the DA's office. Today the firm is called Bracewell and Giuliani. Coincidentally, I had known Rudy Giuliani back in his U.S. District Attorney days for New York City where he had a great record of fighting organized crime before he became a law partner. One thing I did learn, both at the DA's office and Bracewell, was that *what* one did was no more important than with *whom* they did it.

At least I could leave on a high note, knowing that our office had blazed many a new trail and accomplished some significant things over the past fourteen years. For starters, we created a full-service DA's office for the public good with many new services and we were giving our assistants more training and higher salaries.

The very first thing we did was to create the Special Crimes Bureau to handle the complex white collar crime cases. Through the years we added other specialty divisions: Major Frauds, Organized Crime, and Consumer Frauds. Then we started a Pollution Prosecution Section, a unit to deal with Career Criminals, and a Victim Witness group. We added annex courts around the county. And perhaps the most revolutionary innovation of all was our Intake Division, staffed 24/7.

Additionally, we had stepped up all of our public education efforts. We had also done significant work with others to start the National College of District Attorneys, and even joined with my British and Canadian friends to start the International Prosecutors Association. All of this was done by teams formed from a great staff and good friends.

To those interested in how the prosecutors' office is structured and the public services it performs, this chapter will be informative. For the action readers, skip it or try not to go to sleep. What we did in the Harris County DA's office was to develop the modern day office for big cities in Texas and to some extent around the nation. Improving our capacity to reduce crime, fight organized crime, pollution, consumer fraud, complex white collar crimes, the screening of cases, and offering services to victims and witnesses were all new things. If we did not do another thing, we changed the landscape for the better for the public good. Here is how all of this began.

My many additions of new sections and services for the DA's office did not start by any brilliant master plan. It came about from seeing critical needs that had to be met in order to fight crime and better serve the public. The genesis for Special Crime grew out of a single case.

Not long after my first trial as DA, the Jerry Michael Ward case, I was confronted with the largest swindle I had ever heard of in Harris County. Police departments were not equipped to deal with white collar crimes like this one. The sheriff or police would have thrown up their hands if my complainant had walked in and asked them to investigate something this sophisticated.

Neither the police nor the Sheriff's office had anyone who was trained to undertake an investigation of a complex business fraud. As a result, the only place to go with any white collar crime was the DA's office. In spite of a growing number of cases, we did not have a single assistant who was not already working full-time in one of the courts or other departments.

The typical burglary, robbery, hot check, or theft case involves only a few witnesses. These crimes were typically tried in a day or so with a handful of exhibits and no more than three to five witnesses.

The crimes of violence had even fewer witnesses and exhibits. That is the reason why three prosecutors assigned to a single court could dispose of eight hundred to a thousand felony cases per year. By contrast, a single white collar investigation could tie up a couple of assistant district attorneys, financial investigators, and paralegal types for two or three months to put a case together and to seek an indictment. Then for the trial, we are usually talking weeks, not days. Long and tedious organization, massive amounts of preparation, including devising beautiful charts and graphs, were necessary to convey to a jury of laypeople just how this crook made off with a small fortune.

The Feds and the FBI handle these cases routinely, although each of these complex business crimes is a time drainer. Problem is, more often than not, neither the FBI nor the U.S. Attorney can take the case because there is no federal crime involved. Stealing in Texas is always a crime against the State, but the percentage is small for those cases that violate federal laws. Unfortunately, few DAs had the staff resources necessary to prosecute them.

One day, not long after I became DA, a former law school classmate came to see me. He was a major shareholder in a large title company. His company had been taken for several million dollars in a clever scam. The scam put a cloud on the title to a good number of office buildings around town, and the title company was obligated to cover the loss. He was mad as a wet hen, thanks to an ingenious scheme by a fellow named Buddy Goldsmith.

Goldsmith was a commercial real estate guy. He bought old buildings, fixed them up, got tenants in, and then sold them for a profit. Even though Goldsmith had all his buildings mortgaged to the hilt so he could make larger profits, he needed money in a desperate way to feed his gambling habit. His solution was to go forge "releases" (documents that declared the first mortgage was paid in full) on the buildings that he owned, one at a time of course, and get several hundred thousand dollars out of a new lender. The new lender would engage a title company that would check the records and find the building had no lien as the mortgage had been paid off. Of course the problem was, Goldsmith now owed on two mortgages, and the minute he could not pay both, the creditor would be on his back and his world would collapse around him.

My friend's title company discovered the problem when the lender went to foreclose and get their money from the title company. Even though Buddy's crime had been discovered, he had not been arrested. No criminal case had been put together. Not even a shred of evidence was handy to use for a grand jury indictment.

When my law school buddy came to me, every lawyer we had was up to his neck with his own docket. All of the assistants except those in Grand Jury or Appellate Section were assigned to courts full-time. Here I was, the DA—overrun with the constant decision-making this job required—but I had not a single prosecutor available to pick up this ball and run with it. I promised we would do our duty and see justice done.

Me and my big mouth.

White collar cases come in every variety and size. The Goldsmith case was relatively simple, but someone still had to gather and organize bank records, deeds, mortgages, closing statements, and the like, not to mention follow the money trail through multiple financial institutions. Businesses and banks do not turn over evidence without a subpoena due to privacy laws. So the job required fishing around through grand jury subpoena power for the pertinent stuff. Witnesses would have to testify before the grand jury as well as deliver a multitude of paper for us to go through and decide what was relevant for trial. In the Goldsmith case we needed to find out where the money ended up, the names of witnesses, produce charts and graphs, get handwriting experts, and prove the big gambling losses in Vegas, which involved out-of-state witnesses. None of this took a legal Einstein, but it took time.

Buddy had an insatiable gambling habit. His weakness was the dice table in Vegas. Buddy was broke. He also owed a couple of casinos a goodly amount of cash. The Vegas guys with mob connections had paid a call on him. Although they acted like gentlemen, the conversation made him nervous. The mob controlled most of the gambling. Many a person indebted to the mob has been reduced to some bones in the desert, according my friends in the Las Vegas DA's office.

Now if this were a civil case it would be simple. File suit. Demand documents. Demand the other side answer interrogatories asking the hard questions. This cuts through the chase. The civil judge holds you in contempt if you ignore reasonable discovery requests.

But in a criminal investigation, the DA puts this stuff together the hard way, one grand jury subpoena at a time, followed by going through a ton of records to find the needle in the haystack. Sometimes the financial institutions receiving the subpoena balked. Then we would have to send an investigator to serve a high ranking officer in that bank. After the banker cooled his heels sitting outside the grand jury room there would be a quicker compliance next time around.

I assigned Chief Investigator Johnny Fox to do much of the leg work. He was an old-time lawman, not a white collar expert. But he was a bird dog and not shy. Back then we had no specialists to paint Goldsmith into his corner, just me and Johnny Fox.

After the indictment, the case fell in a specific court. The burden then fell to the chief of that court to prepare the case for trial. A few months later, I tried the case. Goldmsith pleaded insanity for a defense, with his two expert psychiatrists saying he was crazy about gambling to the extent he did not know right from wrong (knowing right from wrong was the test for insanity in Texas).

The good doctors testified Buddy Goldsmith went "totally out of his mind at the dice tables, yelling and screaming and carrying on." Then, with straight faces, those good doctors told the trial jury that Goldsmith did not know right from wrong because he did not know what he was doing.

When Goldsmith took the stand I asked him, "Now, when you were yelling and screaming at the dice table, this was not when any crime was committed, was it?"

He finally admitted it was not.

"So when you sat down at your office and forged this release, did you yell and scream and carry on and shake up the whole building?"

He finally said no.

"Now when you went down to the county clerk's office and paid the fee and handed over the release to the clerk to be recorded, did you yell and scream at the top of your voice?"

"Well, no."

"Now Mr. Goldsmith, when was that crime committed, when you were living it up in Vegas, or in that clerk's office filing that forged instrument?"

He rambled on for fifteen minutes without answering the question. By this time I noticed one juror shaking his head and another looking at the ceiling. They found him guilty and gave him eight years.

After the trial I took my story to each member of the Harris County Commissioners Court, the governing body of our county. Not only did they oversee our office's budget, they also oversaw the county's roads (among many other duties).

I told them, "It is sort of like you had to leave all your supervisory duties and go out to one of your roads and drive one of your tractors all day to get the job done. You would hire another driver right quick, wouldn't you? Now we are going to get a lot more of these complex white collar crimes as Houston grows and we need a small group to deal specifically with this work load. We can't run from it. I don't want to tell businessmen I just don't have the man power."

They understood and came to my rescue. The Commissioners Court authorized enough money for me to hire three lawyers for a Special Crimes Section and capped off my request with a very high salary for the top guy, who would make just a few dollars less than the First Assistant.

I knew exactly where to go to get the man for this job. I called on my dear friend and former First Assistant, Sam Robertson, to come to the rescue. Sam was a lawyer's lawyer. He loved the office and no case was too tough. He gladly left his administrative job running the Harris County Legal Defense

Office to get back in action where he belonged. We hired two persons with great experience in financial investigations to fill the other two positions authorized by our Commissioners Court. Then I also assigned Assistant DA Ted Hirtz, our Harvard grad, to fill out the foursome that constituted our new Special Crimes Section.

So, Mr. Goldsmith: Thank you, sir. You were the spark that led to the beginning of the reorganization of the DA's office. Today, the Special Crimes Bureau has evolved from this humble beginning to perhaps some forty lawyers, investigators, and financial specialists.

The next time some guy called me to tell me how he lost his shirt to some clever operator in some complex white collar fraud, I simply said, "You call Mr. Sam Robertson. He will take care of it."

Incidentally, Sam went on from this job to be my First Assistant after Neil McKay was appointed judge. Sam later was appointed a district court judge, elected several times, and then served multiple terms on the Court of Civil Appeals. Bob Bennett and then Johnny Holmes followed as the next chiefs of Special Crimes. That position has always been occupied by some of our best lawyers. Through Special Crimes flows the public corruption investigations, the consumer fraud schemes, the organized crime conspiracies, and, of course, the plain old "pen and paper stuff" like that generated by Mr. Goldsmith.

NOT LONG AFTER WE kicked off Special Crimes, Congress passed the Safe Streets Act which authorized two billion federal dollars to go to state and local law enforcement agencies. This act was also known as the Law Enforcement Assistance Act, or LEAA.

Texas, the third most populous state, would be allocated over $100,000,000. The money was to be used to enable local governments to find innovative ways to fight crime as well as beef up law enforcement initiatives that had proved effective. The sixties brought a spiraling crime rate which paralleled the growth of the hippies, demonstrators, rioters, and all those new groups who had little respect for law or authority. Drug use and the resultant trafficking in narcotics naturally followed. Drugs, rebellion, and crime have proved to be inseparable bedfellows for a half century now. People cried out for law and order so Congress threw money at the problem by way of the LEAA. The good news was that these federal grants would primarily be administered at the state level, without interference from Washington.

With Texas in control of its share of the crime money, Governor John

Connally established a nine member board to oversee the giving out of the $100,000,000 due Texas. He appointed me to the board, along with other Texas leaders including Wilson Speir (head of the Texas Department of Public Safety), Judge Truman Roberts of the Texas Court of Criminal Appeals, Dr. George Beto (head of the Texas Prison System), and Arleigh Templeton (president of Sam Houston State University, a college with an emphasis on criminal justice). A few years later, the legendary district attorney of Dallas, Henry Wade, was appointed to the group.

In most states, history showed that most of the dollars went to the police, and most of those police dollars went towards buying patrol cars and radios. The cars would be worthless in three or four years from the heavy driving and from drunks throwing up in the back seat. In Texas, our council believed it a high priority to beef up the courts and the prosecutors' offices. How will these dollars deter crime? Will this grant deter crime? That was our sole test as we considered and approved grant requests.

My first grant for the Harris County DA's office was to fund a new Organized Crime Division. This was the first grant of its type in Texas or the nation. There were many different types of organized crime groups operating in the nation: theft rings, swindles, stolen property, gambling, prostitution, white slavery, kidnapping rings, loan sharking, and killings for hire, not to mention the importation and sale of drugs. Houston was fortunate not to have the Mafia in our midst, but we had our share of other organized groups making a living off of crime.

Gangs presented a real problem. Not only did they participate in organized criminal activity, but the gangs fought each other, causing innocent victims to die from drive-by shootings and other carnage.

One day, Bob Bennett, Warren White, and Mike Hinton came into my office to discuss a new idea. All three were brilliant, talented, and fearless. These three were always looking for a challenge. Warren and Mike both served at different times as my administrative assistant. Bob and I had worked together under Frank Briscoe and were longtime friends. Today Bob and Mike are two of the best defense attorneys in Harris County. Warren came to the office after clerking for Judge Jack Onion, the chief judge of the Texas Criminal Court of Appeals. He later pursued a distinguished career with the U.S. Attorney's office.

Bob explained their plan. Our office would have its own Organized Crime Division. The three wanted to be the first ones to staff the unit. Their idea for this grant was that the money would provide for investigators and special equipment. They would work very closely with all of the local police agencies and establish a Harris County Organized Crime Group with specialized representatives from each of the eighteen or so police departments in the county, as well as the Sheriff's office, the Texas Rangers, and the Department of Public Safety (DPS). We would invite the FBI and other Feds to join with us to bust up rackets and drug trafficking.

"Bob, I have been all over this country and talked to every DA of every big city. I have never heard of such a thing in a DA's office—an Organized Crime Division," I told him.

"Well, that's probably why we need to do it," he drawled.

Hinton spoke up. "Chief, you can get money for anything. No one ever turns you down. The three of us could staff it. We will be accountable. We ought to be under Sam Robertson and be a unit set up under Special Crimes. We could concentrate on these theft rings, graft, and corruption, and any group organized to outsmart the law and make money in crime." The three guys sold me on what I still think was a brilliant idea. With our grant, we would take the leadership position in the county and use officers from various agencies as needed.

The grant I applied for was approved by our state committee. HPD liked the concept enough to assign two full-time detectives to report to us and work under our direction. Sam Nuchia, later to become Houston's chief of police, spent a lot of time working with this group. Bob Blaylock of HPD Intelligence and TSU fame was assigned full-time to work with us even though he was on the HPD payroll. He later joined our staff as an investigator under Johnny Holmes and ultimately became the chief investigator in the DA's office.

At the same time we also organized and staffed a Major Fraud Division headed up first by Henry Oncken. Henry went on to be First Assistant under Holmes, then a district judge and then U.S. Attorney. Next Ross Rommel headed the division prior to going with Andrews Kurth, a leading firm where he headed their large litigation section. We had some fine legal talent in Special Crimes.

Houston was undoubtedly the largest city in America without a Mafia presence. Some of my DA friends around the country found that hard to believe, but no one found any evidence the mob was operating any criminal enterprise in Houston. The sentiment in our city was very anti-organized crime. Although we did not have the Mafia, we had our share of "organized crime." We had the Dixie Mafia and the Texas Mafia and maybe fifteen other gangs.

Our Organized Crime team figured innovative ways to catch crooks. One illustrative example was the "retail store" we set up in the middle of a warehouse district. Working mostly with HPD Burglary and Theft, we let the word out that this store would buy anything, pay good prices, no questions asked. Burglars were always desperate for an outlet to turn stolen goods into hard cash.

With undercover police manning the counter at the shop, every transaction was filmed and recorded. Cameras took pictures. We got the conversations on tape. We filmed the thieves coming and going, getting license numbers on every vehicle that came onto the lot. Much information was gathered from checking the registrations. Some were driving stolen cars, but those arrests would have to wait.

Finally the day came when we decided to pull the trigger. On that day the police rounded the crooks up with simultaneous arrests. Sealed indictments had been returned, and police had the warrants of arrest in hand. High bails were set. The cases were processed rapidly. With the films and recordings (which defense counsel reviewed), most defendants pled guilty to stiff sentences. Those defendants requesting trials fell prey to juries who delighted in handing out maximum sentences to those they saw on film selling the widow's sterling silver service. Juries like to know that a defendant will spend his time "making little rocks out of big rocks" as my friend Judge Lee Duggan would say, for busting into someone's home.

Our Organized Crime Unit was aggressive. Bob Bennett got word one day that a Mafia character from Chicago was inside our city limits and out at the Texas Medical Center.

Bob subpoenaed the mob boss's medical records to make sure his visit was legitimate. Sure enough, he was undergoing an operation by the famed Dr. Michael DeBakey. Before he got on his private jet to return to Chicago he also received a visit from our chief of police. I suspect he got the message Houston did not want him in town.

When he arrived in Chicago friends were waiting to give him a private party. At the close of this festive occasion, all but one of the guests left, according to our Chicago police contacts. That guest put a bullet in the back of the crime underboss's head, undoubtedly for some reason not related to Houston.

In another instance the group got word some mobsters had come to Houston and were out at a location on the Katy Freeway, where they were playing poker. Bob's team hit them all with a grand jury subpoena.

When they were hauled down to the grand jury they all took the Fifth. They would methodically pull out a little card they carried next to their driver's license and read it to the grand jury. "I refuse to testify on the grounds that anything I say might tend to incriminate me." I am sure it would. But we were not looking to make a case. We were just sending a message, "Don't let the sun go down on you in Houston."

The DA of the Bronx—whom I knew from the National District Attorneys Association (NDAA)—reported that the Bronx had 13,000 arsons in a single year. Many of these were mob-originated. The *modus operandi* was to over-insure many of the older and run-down buildings and then burn them to the ground to collect the insurance money. Making a half million to two million per fire, the profits were not chicken feed. The insurance companies were intimidated by the mob from using due diligence to question the appraisals. Because proving arson is difficult, this was a real profit center for the mob. Few were indicted and fewer were convicted. Houston, which has more people than the Bronx, had three hundred arsons in the same year, not 13,000.

Reasons like these mandated we keep organized crime out of Houston or else see our city dramatically changed. We were never concerned the mob was going to sue us alleging their civil rights were violated. We would have loved that with civil discovery and depositions available to us. Texas juries would have a field day pouring them out of court.

Our Organized Crime Unit not only supported local police but initiated a good number of investigations on their own. There was the time that Warren White wired a dope dealer in order to collect evidence against some corrupt cops, a rare thing in Houston. A drug dealer reported that two narcs busted him and then took his money and his heroin. They told the dope dealer to leave town and not come back.

Word got out on the street that some cops were shaking down some of those arrested on drug charges and confiscating a large hunk of the money as well as a share of the drugs. Warren made a deal with the drug seller, who set up a meeting with the officers where the conversations were taped.

The chief of police and head of the Narcotics Division could not believe this was happening, until one day they were invited over to my office to hear the tapes. Since Warren would be a key witness for the prosecution, we referred the matter over to the local U.S. Attorney, who indicted seven officers and sent them to prison.

Our Organized Crime Division served multiple purposes and it became my firm belief that every large DA's office needs such a unit.

The next large grant we received went to our one-lawyer-one-secretary Consumer Fraud Section, also under our Special Crimes umbrella.

We added more lawyers and investigators and went after unscrupulous businessmen and con artists. Bob Leonard, the district attorney of Flint, Michigan, started the first Consumer Fraud Division in the country. At an NDAA meeting I attended, he told me all about his project. The NDAA was a good place to go for new ideas and to see what worked.

Our newly beefed-up Consumer Fraud Division went after big time land scandals as well as the little lady who bought a car with a busted block.

They worked a large number of cases in which Marvin Zindler was the driving force. When I first met Marvin, he was a young deputy at the Sheriff's Department who dogged down fugitives from the law. He then talked Sheriff Buster Kern into forming a one-man consumer fraud detail in the Sheriff's office so he could go after those taking advantage of the poor and helpless. He became a one-man crime-fighting machine, busting up frauds.

After we formed our Consumer Fraud Division Marvin talked Sheriff Kern into assigning him full-time with our Consumer Fraud Division. While working with us Marvin made at least one case a day, and you could rest assured that case would be on the evening news. Marvin would go after the unusual types of swindlers or con artists and then call the media. There was no case too big or too small for Marvin. Marvin got our office a ton of great publicity.

He later became an on-air television fixture on Channel 13, our ABC station. He had a field day for decades in his investigations of everything from serious frauds to finding slime in the ice machine at local eateries. "Slime in the ice machine!" became one of Marvin's many signature lines that he would deliver in his over-the-top, exaggerated manner.

During his many years at Channel 13, I could not tell the difference between what Marvin did when he was assigned to our office and when he was a full-time reporter. He busted up consumer frauds and it all made the news. But this time around Marvin made a lot more money and was his own boss. Also he had a cameraman to boss around. Marvin was reportedly the most popular and highest paid TV personality in town. Marvin did more to draw attention to the problem of little people getting ripped off than anyone I know. He was the heart and soul of finally getting some justice in cases that would otherwise be neglected. I can still hear him signing off on Channel 13, "Marrrrrvinnn Zindler, Eyewitness News!"

One of our very talented lawyers in Consumer Fraud was asked to work for the NDAA to help start consumer fraud offices around the country. Bob Susman went into many states and cities as a full-time expert to show others how to begin an operational office. Bob later ended up being a partner of Mike Hinton and went on to head the white collar section at Locke Liddell, a large national firm. The NDAA was encouraging all large jurisdictions to cover these kinds of prosecutions. Bob was their trail blazer.

THANKS TO ANOTHER LARGE grant from the LEAA funds we overhauled all of our office's administrative staff, filing systems, employment and supervision, hiring and firing of administrative staff, and developed a paper flow that made sense to keep up with some 60,000 serious crimes coming into our office annually, a major task in and of itself.

The grant permitted me to hire an administrative assistant to keep up with the public side of the office: all the speech requests, the going out to schools by assistants to talk to the kids about crime, and gave us the ability to generate numerous publications making it easier on the public to get help with many multifarious problems involving different types of crime. Jane Joplin was an excellent writer and editor as our office cranked out hundreds of thousands of booklets for high school and middle school kids to educate them about the consequences for shoplifting, marijuana usage, drunk driving, and other crimes. In fact, we were running a publishing company with free pamphlets assisting citizens filing charges on consumer frauds, hot checks, and crimes against businesses; advice on getting child support, on juvenile crimes, pollution complaints; on the rights of victims and witnesses; warnings about drunk driving; laws for political candidates; grand jury manuals; and handbooks for law enforcement officials, including a little red pamphlet telling police how to handle riots and civil disturbances. The press was fascinated with this one and called it "Vance's Little Red Riot Book."

When Jane left, Marc Wiegand, a former UT tennis star and my doubles partner on occasion, took this position. Marc had been an administrative assistant to Attorney General John Hill. John told me he had a guy on his staff who could whip me in tennis. He was right, Marc and I became good friends on the court so I was able to hire him. Marc later followed me to Bracewell and Patterson where he became a longtime partner.

Through LEAA we received funding for police radios for our DA cars. By now we had about forty cars on the road. The one thing we did not have was our own radio station. We had to share a back channel with the Sheriff's office where they were mainly looking for rabid dogs and trespassers.

Johnny Holmes, who headed Organized Crime after Bennett left the office, had a working knowledge of electronics and technology. Johnny volunteered to write up an application to the Federal Communications Commission for a separate channel on the air just for our office. After he filed the application, I kept bugging him about the status of our application.

"Oh, those bureaucrats won't tell you a damn thing. We pay them good money to get the job done and they sit around on their rears. All I can do is keep calling them," Johnny said.

After months passed, Johnny came into my office one morning with a big smile on his face.

"Well, Chief, we are on the air."

I said, "No kidding? So you got the license?"

"No; there is no license. I just climbed a three hundred foot tower last night and planted our aerial on top of that thing. And it works. We're on the air."

Many months later the license came through, and we were legal. I guess the statute of limitations has expired and I can tell that story. Holmes was a "go to" guy, a former commercial pilot, a computer expert, roofer, carpenter, and as thorough and practical a lawyer as we had on staff.

One of our best new sections was the Career Criminal Prosecution Unit. Every rookie cop knows that a relatively small number of career criminals accounted for an unprecedented number of crimes, particularly burglaries and robberies.

Career criminals practice playing the system. When caught, they are smart enough to have plenty of money on hand to get out on bail. But now they not only have to keep committing crimes to live it up on but they need some additional big bucks to pay the bondsman. So back to work. And more homes and small businesses are ripped off. We had a revolving jail door that needed to be shut.

Our new Career Criminal Section began operation with several experienced prosecutors whose sole job was three-fold: (1) identify this type of criminal when his case entered the system, (2) make certain the bail was set as high as possible, and (3) make certain these cases received a high-priority, early setting, and would be tried as soon as possible. Each day one of these criminals stayed out on the street, homes and businesses were vulnerable.

The tracking system combined with speedy trials cut down on robberies and burglaries. When I left office, future DA Chuck Rosenthal and two others were working the Career Criminal Unit.

Our office lobbied long and hard to get the Texas law changed so that drug money or cars used in the sale of drugs could be confiscated and used for law enforcement purposes.

After the law passed, we once took in a fancy Cadillac coupe which became our "cool car" in police parlance. A cool car was one that did not smell of police. Usually, it was a beat up old car or a fancy Cadillac or Lincoln Continental such as pimps and drug dealers drove. When a boat, car, or airplane was used to smuggle drugs around the county, we latched onto it. If we proved the car was used in some way in some crime, the judge would turn over the title to us after a simple hearing in court.

Of course we did not confiscate daddy's Cadillac or the old man's Ford if his kid was caught with a marijuana cigarette. But we did enjoy taking the car keys from the drug dealers as well as relieving them of whatever cash they had on their person. Drug dealers and pimps often had a thick roll of hundreds in their pockets. We accumulated lots of money that under the new law could be used for law enforcement purposes as determined by the DA. We spread the money around some if we thought it was a high priority cause.

One of our best additions to the office was the creation of the first Victim Witness Unit in Texas and the second in the nation. Victims were often neglected and got lost trying to find their way around the criminal justice system. The same principle holds true for witnesses. Some guy sees a robbery in progress and is subpoenaed to come to court. The case gets reset three times, so he now goes home after losing yet another day's pay.

Our Victim Witness Unit worked with victims and witnesses to make their lives easier and minimize the hardship. We kept the victims abreast of what was going on and also took them into our confidence about plea bargains. Once in a while a witness or victim was in danger from a defendant so we helped with security issues as well. Some victims were entitled to restitution, but someone needed to carefully calculate the amount and how it could be paid in order for the judge to include the payments as part of the terms of probation. Most victims did not know what rights they had. This unit was there to assist.

Suzanne McDaniel kicked off our Victim Witness office. She blazed a new trail, continues to be a legend in Texas on victims' rights, and now works for state Attorney General Greg Abbott dealing with these same issues. A short time back Suzanne and I were asked to come to Commissioners Court along with DA Chuck Rosenthal and his head of Victim Witness to receive special recognition for the twenty-five years of exemplary service of this unit.

Pollution along our ship channel, the nation's second largest port, was a major problem. I went to Austin numerous times to get tougher laws to prosecute corporations and individuals who were polluting our water and air. Although I fought for these changes, Dr. Walter Quibedeaux was our voice in the wilderness urging more effective laws to deter polluters.

Walter headed the anti-pollution office for Harris County. With much assistance from the liberal side of the Democratic Party, namely Congressman Bob Eckhart, State Senator Chet Brooks, and State Representative Rex Braun, things began to happen.

When I took office in 1966, corporations could not be held criminally responsible for anything except for one little pollution statute that provided a maximum fine of $100 in JP court. It did just about that much good, too.

Our concern was over illegal liquid discharges in the ship channel, and those more noxious odors discharged into the air we breathed. Pollution was particularly severe throughout Pasadena, Baytown, and the ship channel where most of our refineries are located. When I drove out to Pasadena or Baytown to make a speech, the smell from the refineries was mild. Coming home later that night, however, the stench and chemical odors were overwhelming, even in my air-conditioned car. While some companies were good citizens and spent a fortune on lowering pollution levels, others just kept on polluting.

Dr. Quibedeaux worked tirelessly and vigilantly for effective laws. Walter and I went to Austin several times to testify for new legislation. Finally it passed. When it did pass, the Commissioners Court gave us funding to begin our Pollution Prosecution Section. We did not turn the world upside down, but we kept the pressure on. Now Walter could make surprise visits to plants and take samples and gather evidence. Before long, most of the problem refineries cleaned up their act.

Another high priority of mine was to get higher salaries for our lawyers. The DA's office is only as good as its lawyers. Over half of our lawyers were bailing out before three years was up. Few were staying on for long terms such as ten or fifteen years. When I left the office after nearly twenty-two years, only one lawyer—Rose Marie Kennedy—in an office of a hundred and sixty assistants had seniority on me. Commissioners Court controlled our budget 100 percent. They decided how many assistants we could hire and the salary for each position.

To correct this problem I began a campaign for higher salaries. I first solicited help from the business community and the Houston Bar Association. The bar association took a firm stand and had their president, George Barrow, appear before our county commissioners in support of higher salaries. The newspapers began to write favorable editorials. Ultimately the campaign succeeded.

I promised the Commissioners Court and the public that I would prohibit any and all outside practice of law if we got a pay boost. The strategy worked. We got the increase and assistants started staying with the office longer. Now as I look back I see very talented assistants like Bert Graham, Ted Wilson, and others who stayed with the office for nearly forty years, something not likely to have happened in generations past.

Along the same lines of attracting legal talent, we began an aggressive recruiting program. We established a hiring committee to interview and rank applicants and make recommendations to me as to who to hire.

I went out to the TSU Law School to recruit blacks and to UT and UH to try to land Law Review types.

The minority recruiting was a challenge as the more outstanding graduates could go wherever they pleased. We just did not pay enough to compete in many instances. All I could do was go on campus and present the public service side and talk about how exciting it was to be a prosecutor. These efforts did produce some results. When I became DA we had no black lawyers and only one woman and one Hispanic. When I left office, we had about fifteen women, ten black lawyers, and five Hispanics. Some went on the bench after showing they were good and competent prosecutors. Among firsts were Jim Muldrow, the first black County Criminal Court at Law judge in Harris County and Nick Berrera, the first Hispanic on a county court bench. John Kyles was the second black judge to be a criminal district judge.

After we started our hiring committee, I usually rubber stamped their recommendations. Rarely did I hire someone on my own. One exception was Mike McSpadden.

He was licensed to practice in Oklahoma but not Texas. He was doing land work for Phillips Petroleum. We met through a mutual friend who said to me, "I know a guy who can whip up on you in tennis." (As has already been seen, this was a sure way to get my interest.) I took the challenge and sure enough, Mike won. We played more tennis and became friends. Mike had been a Big Eight singles and doubles champ at the University of Oklahoma. He was well-liked, and I could see he had potential as a trial lawyer. I talked him into taking the Texas Bar. When he passed he came on board. He became one of our best prosecutors and later one of our best district judges. Mike is now the most senior district judge for criminal cases in Harris County.

I never stopped recruiting. I would meet with students when I went to the University of Texas Law School to speak at a seminar. I met with minority students and women students, who were rapidly increasing in numbers.

When I taught a Criminal Law class at night at the University of Houston Law Center, two of my students were Ted Poe and Larry Urquhart. Both aced all the quizzes and the final exams and ended up at the top of their class. I pleaded with them to come to work for us. Larry went on to head up our Appellate Division, considered the most intellectual assignment in the office. Ted blazed trails as an outstanding prosecutor, then a very respected district judge known for his creative punishments, and now is serving his second term in Congress.

Perhaps our most important innovation and resulting contribution to criminal justice in Harris County was the establishment of our Intake Division. This was huge. With this new division and revolutionary system for tracking cases, we were able to keep up with and prioritize cases moving through the system. Also we nearly eliminated the problem of defendants getting lost in jail. We speeded up trials and the filing process and the grand jury process. Again it was an LEAA grant that funded the coordinators for the criminal courts, the necessary clerks, and the prosecutors who screened every criminal case the police or public brought in the door.

Under the new system the judges appointed lawyers for indigents within forty-eight hours after arrest. We cut a month out of the time it took to get a case before a grand jury. The biggest advantage to the new system was that police officers could no longer walk into a justice of the peace court and file any kind of felony or serious misdemeanor they wanted to. Now they had to go to one central place—our Intake Division—have a conversation with an assistant DA and show him that the evidence in the case was worthy of a charge being filed. The screening of the charges reduced the dismissal rate. We could now keep up accurately with who was in jail and the status at any given time of every pending case.

From the first year I began prosecuting, I was shocked about how much time it took to get a case to trial. I was a believer in that old adage, "Justice delayed is justice denied."

Felony cases took roughly two years to bring to trial. After a charge was filed, a case would take several weeks just to get through a useless procedure called an examining trial. Witnesses might be subpoenaed two times just to show up in JP court to say the accused did not have permission to steal their car. We did away with the long-standing practice of examining trials and took the felony cases to the grand jury within a couple of weeks.

At the time I was bemoaning our non-system, Judge Miron Love, our senior judge, was also dreaming of how we could modernize the way we did things. When I approached Judge Love to talk about revamping the system, I found a comrade-in-arms. Judge Love wanted a more radical reform than I did. He wanted to see all of the felonies and misdemeanor charges filed directly with the district and county courts and do away with the step of going through the justices of the peace.

At that time I was most fortunate to have Roland Dahlin as chief of our Operations Bureau, which ran the administrative side of the office. He had a big job keeping up with about three hundred employees, the salaries, the word processing systems, the budget, and many other administrative tasks. Roland was a capable lawyer who during his UT days had been president of the student body.

Judge Love became head of our county task force of which Roland, the district clerk, and the new county computer expert were key team members. After a year of long tedious meetings (coward that I was, I quit attending after the first two meetings), the group came up with a plan which was implemented through some big bucks from another grant of the LEAA. The intake system was formed and would be kept open seven days a week, twenty-four hours a day, the only one like it in the nation.

Some JPs, defense attorneys, and bail bondsmen yelled and screamed, but the system was excellent. Many jurisdictions throughout the country have come to study our system and then copied it.

Our Intake Division's beginnings were humble indeed. While the first floor of the courthouse was being remodeled so that all of the clerks and prosecutors could have a place to operate, HPD offered us a fairly small office over in the HPD headquarters a few blocks from the courthouse.

Johnny Holmes volunteered to be our guinea pig who would run this operation along with one other clerk. Every charge filed in Harris County was going to come through these two individuals. The poor clerk typed up every charge. Johnny screened every case. The room HPD gave us did not provide much space to operate. It was shabby looking to boot.

Johnny went to the hardware store, bought a gallon of white paint and a paint brush and painted that room himself. Then he proceeded to live in that office night and day. We couldn't figure out when he slept. With our volume of approximately 20,000 felonies per year and 40,000 misdemeanors, Johnny had to make decisions around the clock. Perhaps two hundred cases a day went through intake. That was an ultimate example of hard work and dedication. Vintage Holmes.

Holmes also achieved another goal. He got the respect and acceptance of the police officers that the new intake office was a great benefit, not a hassle. Even a layperson should not want to file a charge and run the risk of a lawsuit if the evidence was insufficient to take the charge. The police now had good counsel when they filed a case. Later we developed a system of having one of our chief prosecutors in district court man the Intake Division over the weekends. This provided heavyweight assistance over the high-crime hours on Friday and Saturday nights.

We paid the chiefs well for this service. This made it possible for the top lawyers in the office to stay with us for more years. A good career chief prosecutor who can mentor the younger ones and try big-time cases is as valuable an asset as a district attorney can have.

After Johnny got the police and everyone else used to the system, Roland Dahlin took over its daily operation. Dahlin later accepted a position setting up and running the Public Defender's Office for the United States District Courts in the Southern District of Texas. After thirty years of service in that office, Roland recently retired.

Jim Larkin stepped in and was the architect of the modern day Intake Division. When Jim began, Intake was still over in the crowded offices of HPD. Under his leadership it was moved to its current huge quarters, taking up most of the first floor in the Harris County Courthouse. He served there until retirement.

For all those years, Jim was the "go-to guy" for all law enforcement agencies in the county who had any question about whether a criminal charge should be filed or not. Perhaps the most critical decisions made in our office was whether we filed a charge. With his laid-back ways and dry sense of humor, Jim kept what could be a highly emotional place on an even keel. And not much got by him. Jim refined the system that is now such a part of criminal justice in Harris County.

To keep officers from driving thirty miles away from the remote cities in the county like Baytown, Katy, Spring, Humble, and Tomball, Jim set up a fax system (faxes were new then). Officers faxed the reports, we took the charge and faxed them a copy right back.

The final and newest innovation to speed up trials was the establishment of something called "Annex Courts." Existing law said we could have two judges sitting at the same time on one bench.

Thus, without creating a new court with its high cost of deputy sheriffs, a host of clerks, probation officers, and the like, we were able to have judges available to try the overflow from each day's docket. Our annex courts were staffed by retired judges.

Obviously one court can only try one case at a time. A capital murder trial might tie up a court a month. But with annex courts to take the overflow, the State could keep on announcing "Ready" each morning and have that case sent over to an annex court, rather than the defendant getting an automatic reset. Reality was that when the State announced ready and the defendant knew he had to face a jury that morning, he usually chose to plead guilty. The free ride was over. More repeat offenders were off the streets. Trials could proceed while witnesses' memories were still intact. Delayed justice is often no justice. Annex courts helped close the gap.

One last thing I did before I left was to put a new and different emphasis on civil rights investigations and prosecution. In the past we had simply let these cases go through the grand jury system and be handled by whichever grand jury assistant was available. We had no specialists to do the investigation or prosecute the case.

Civil rights violations law is an art form of its own. What I did was to assign our three Trial Division chiefs—some of the very best in the office—to investigate and try any civil rights violations.

One of the first such cases was the highly publicized case of Joe Campos Torres. Torres drowned while swimming across Buffalo Bayou in the shadow of the courthouse while in custody of Houston Police Department officers. The case brought about many civil rights protests, was controversial, and needed high priority treatment.

Bert Graham, one our most senior guys, did our investigation, tried the officers, and got a guilty verdict for negligent homicide. Bert was disappointed he did not get a manslaughter conviction, but convictions in these cases are difficult. Some of the most outspoken public officials kept a close eye on the case and praised Bert for his efforts. Holmes, when he became DA, turned this civil rights investigation effort into a full-time and separate division of the office. It is well staffed today and acts as a very positive force against police or other official misconduct.

As MY CAR ROARED toward Houston, I felt good about the innovative changes. Every milestone we achieved was a team effort. I will always believe

I was blessed to have had the best staff of any district attorney in this nation. I also credit the Harris County Commissioners Court for their progressive attitude in making all of this possible, as well as the LEAA funding, and a most responsive Harris County judiciary. I could think of no other thing I could do to improve the office except still higher salaries. So maybe it was time to move on.

CHAPTER TWELVE

The World's Greatest Living Trial Lawyer

Be not deceived; God is not mocked:
for whatsoever a man soweth, that shall he also reap.
—Galatians 6:7 (KJV)

THE LITTLE CAFÉ WAS almost deserted. An older woman sat at the counter sipping her coffee. She had on the same kind of big black shoes with the sturdy heels my mother's generation favored, a solid black dress, and an out-of-place huge white hat that would have kept the sun out no matter where it was in the sky.

I ordered a cup myself, "Yeah, cream and sugar. Never learned to drink it black."

The only other two customers, two men in long sleeve khaki shirts, approached the counter to pay their bill. One had on a thin, dark maroon necktie, the kind of tie that goes with everything so you only need one. His tie was pulled down loose with the top shirt button unbuttoned so he could breathe. He went for his wallet and discovered he had no money. He said, "Fred, just plumb out of money right now. You got a buck?"

The friend gave an "Oh, not again" look and reminded me of myself and the hundreds of times I went to lunch with my friend Erwin Goree Ernst.

ERWIN ERNST WAS THE first guy I got assigned to work with in district court. He was the king of office characters. If his wallet wasn't empty, you could bet your automobile it only contained a single wrinkled dollar bill. Ernst drove his red pickup truck to work. His pretty wife, Virginia, would issue Erwin his dollar when he left the house. At least that was his story.

"I only got a dollar. Maw Maw wouldn't give me any more. See, only one old dollar in that billfold. At least that's my story and I'm sticking to it."

I recalled the first time Ernst and I went for a beer. We had had a long day in court where everything seemed to go wrong.

Ernst, trying to cheer me up, said, "Cutty Sark, you did such a good job crossing that last dude, I'd like to buy you a beer."

Ernst and I grabbed our coats and left the courthouse, headed for the old, run-down DeGeorge Hotel, home of the "Linoleum Club." I remember it was a cold and windy day, matching my mood.

The Linoleum Club's ambience consisted of linoleum floors, winos, and old men sitting around in rusting chrome chairs. We stepped over a couple of street people in the doorway and made our way in from the cold. We sat down at a table. The guy at the table next to us pulled a bottle of Thunderbird wine out of a torn overcoat pocket and took a swig. We were the only ones there in coat and tie. The waitress took our order for a couple of 20¢ Pearls. Premium beer cost a quarter.

She returned with the two bottles of Pearl, saying, "That will be 40¢, please." I looked over at Ernst. He looked back at me. He made no move for his wallet.

Finally, I said, "Ernst, would you pay the lady? You're gonna buy. Remember, you said you were going to buy me a beer."

"Cutty Sark, I never said that."

"Yes, you did."

"No, I didn't. I remember what I said. I said I *wanted* to buy you a beer. I never said I *would* buy you a beer. I spent the only dollar Maw Maw give me on the barbecue at lunch. Remember, you saw me hand that waitress my dollar bill. Maw Maw won't give me more'n a dollar."

Then Ernie pulled out his thin, weather-beaten wallet and emptied it to show how broke he was. Only two items were in that billfold: his driver's license and a picture of himself when he was an eighteen-year-old private first class in World War II.

I pulled out a dollar bill and paid the lady.

Ernst said, "Well, Cutty Sark, tip her more than a nickel. She's been nice to us. Give her a dime and she can give you two quarters. Then maybe with those two quarters you can buy me another beer; that is, if you feel like it and aren't mad. You will still have another dime to tip the nice lady. See this picture that fell out on the table? That's me. I was a PFC in the Big War. Never made corporal. Certainly you'd want to buy the old veteran just one more beer."

Well-known author Tommy Thompson in his bestseller *Blood and Money* described Ernst like this: "DA Vance summoned his top prosecutor, a legendary Assistant DA named Erwin 'Ernie' Ernst. Ernst was a romantic, stocky, loquacious, philosophical lawyer with a common sense voice from the cracker barrel. He was on intimate terms with Roman poets and Greek philosophers. He had prosecuted hundreds of murderers and sent many to the electric chair. He was a practical joker and favorite of the courthouse and a fellow around whom anecdotes hung like ornaments from a Christmas tree." Thanks, Tommy. That is a better description than I could come up with.

To me Ernst was a cross between Jonathan Winters and Will Rogers. After I became DA he was promoted to be the first chief of our Trial Bureau, which housed most of the lawyers on staff. Then one day he came in and said he was quitting to move up North. When I asked "Where up North?" he answered, "Eighty miles due north to a place called Huntsville. I'll get to teach at Sam (Sam Houston State University), and also your friend Dr. Beto (the prison chief) wants me be to be his first general counsel for the Texas Prison System. Maybe you better call him and tell him the truth about me. He might change his mind. Besides, I want to be close to my famous twenty-acre Armadillo Ranch so my two cows won't go so hungry. Lord, they eat a lot of grass."

I think my friend Dr. Beto—the former head and modern day father of the Texas Prison System—wanted Ernst around for company as well as his legal skills. Moving to Huntsville would also allow Ernst to go out to his old shack and listen to the rain come down on his tin roof while he nursed a cold Pearl.

Erwin Goree Ernst was a friend, mentor, and an excellent trial lawyer. He had tried as many cases as anyone in the office. I can still hear his final words to the jury. "Be not deceived; God is not mocked: for whatsoever a man soweth, that shall he also reap." More often than not, the juries applied that passage when Ernst tried a murder case.

Ernst described himself as "the world's greatest living trial lawyer." He enjoyed putting the lowly on a pedestal and bringing down the proud. He had a wonderful sense of justice and did his job with compassion. He loved black people and was more at home eating barbecue with his hands in Fifth Ward than a gourmet meal at some fancy restaurant. In fact, the only times I ever went to high-end restaurants with Ernie were because some defense attorney was buying lunch. When that would happen—and it was not often—Ernst would say, "I've got a live one."

Ernie had a round sort of face and a ruddy complexion. He constantly cross-examined whoever was in his presence, and the conversation would be humorous and serious at the same time. He wore frayed white dress shirts with one of his three or four narrow ties, all of which had been Christmas presents (and two of them were clip-ons). Unless he was talking to a jury, his tie was pulled down from his collar. He dressed just like an upscale school janitor or my famous Criminal Law professor, George Stumberg.

Ernst had no use for any prosecutor trying to rack up wins against some poor defendant. He was always fair. He never took advantage of a stupid lawyer, and he made sure the clients of the smart lawyers got what they deserved. Ernst's biggest weakness in court was battling it out with an incompetent lawyer. He was at his best and most relaxed when he faced a Percy Foreman or Richard Haynes. Foreman once told me, "Ernst had the best sidebar remarks of any lawyer in Texas, including me." That was the only time I ever heard Percy put someone else ahead of him. Ernst's life was one big sidebar remark. That was why he was the most sought after to have lunch or drink a beer with.

Ernst and I would usually go to lunch with our investigator Claude Langston in order to travel free in Claude's county car. One day Ernst said, "Claude, let's use that free county gas and go eat at John's Barbecue. Could you be ready to go by 11:30?"

Claude would answer, "Well, you know me, boss, I'm always hungry."

"Claude, objection! Non-responsive answer. I never asked you if you were hungry. I asked you if you could be ready to go eat at 11:30. I'll try again. Could you be ready to go eat at 11:30?"

Ernst might talk country, but he used grammar and logic like a surgeon used a knife, never afraid to make a correction.

Ernst loved the courtroom. I didn't like to object unless the question and answer would hurt me. Ernst loved to object just to make the other lawyer follow the law and to throw him off stride. He particularly favored technical objections where the opposing counsel forgot to lay the required but obscure predicate. Trying cases with Ernst for two years was worth the fact he made me think about every sentence I uttered. Say it right, or he would get you on cross.

Ernst was a brilliant lawyer who had forgotten more law than most of the staff knew. But he would play the law close to the line at times and get in trouble.

One day I was sitting in my office, meeting with a couple of assistants. My always calm secretary, Carolyn Hinton, broke in and said, "Sheriff Buster Kern is on the phone and said he needs to speak with you right now. I think it's serious."

"Buster, what's going on?"

"Well, your friend Mr. Erwin Ernst is in my office and we are having a nice visit."

"That's nice, Buster, but why are you calling to tell me that?" I said, showing a touch of impatience.

"Well, your Mr. Erwin Ernst has been ordered to jail by Judge Walton. When the poor bailiff panicked and called me personally, I said, 'Bring him to my office.' Now Ernst is welcome to stay in my office, even overnight, but I can't let him leave the jail or my own office or the judge will put *me* in jail. I believe he is your responsibility so you need to go get this thing straightened out."

It seems that Ernst was trying a case before Judge Dan Walton, our old boss. Every time the judge overruled one of Ernie's objections during the trial, Ernst would say, "Note my exception." Defense attorneys have to use these magic words in order to preserve their right to appeal any erroneous ruling by the judge. However, the State of Texas had no right back then to appeal any ruling of the court. Therefore, prosecutors had no reason to ever say, "Note my exception." Only Ernst would do this and obviously did it to show his dislike for the court's ruling.

Finally, Judge Walton had enough. He told Ernst to never say "Note my exception" in his court ever again. But five minutes later when Ernst got overruled, he said, "Note my exception."

This time the judge said, "Mr. Ernst, you have insulted the gravamen of this court." (Gravamen is a legal term referring to something's essence.)

Judge Walton continued. "I have told you time and time again not to say 'Note my exception.' If you do this one more time, you will be in contempt of this court and headed for jail. Do I make myself clear?"

"Yes, Your Honor. Very clear, and note my exception to the ruling of the court."

The judge then ordered Ernst to jail and told the bailiff to deliver him to the sheriff.

After I got off the phone with Sheriff Kern I hustled down to His Honor's chambers and made a deal with Judge Walton. The judge said Ernst had to apologize and promise never to do this again—and mean it; then and only then would he not put him in jail for contempt.

Judge Walton and Erwin Ernst were two of the strongest willed people I knew. I had little hope of getting either to back down. I took another approach with Ernst. I went back down to the Sheriff's office and said, "Ernie, if you don't comply with Judge Walton's request, I am calling Maw Maw right this minute and am going to tell her the story and get her to drive down to the courthouse and bring your toothbrush."

Ernst said, "Cutty Sark, that ain't no fair calling Maw Maw. She didn't have nothing to do with this, and this might worry her. I wouldn't do that to you. I guess I will go along, but Cutty Sark, please note my exception."

From that day forward Judge Walton was known as "The Gravaman," thanks to Ernst. Even fellow judges, who liked and respected the judge, often referred to him as "The Gravaman," but never to his face, of course. Judge Walton was a pretty serious guy.

One day Ernst blessed me with a new nickname, "Utah Carl," and from that name he often referred to me as "Our Beloved Carl."

The genesis of my change in nicknames happened one day when Ernst was in First Assistant Neil McKay's office. Neil was bombarding Ernst with one East Texas story after another, as only Neil could do. The telephone rang. Some citizen was desperately trying to reach me by phone so the receptionist put the poor fellow through to First Assistant McKay.

Ernst overheard Neil tell the poor fellow, "Oh, so you went to high school with old Carl Vance did you?"

As McKay knew, no one ever called me Carl.

I happened to be in Salt Lake City addressing the Utah Prosecutor's Association.

"Well, your good friend Carl can't come to the phone right now. He's out in Utah making a speech to the Utah district attorneys."

From then on Ernst called me "Utah Carl." Every time an assistant DA became a new father, Ernst would go bum a cigar from the new daddy and ask, "How is little Carl?" When he wanted something, Ernst would call me "my beloved Carl."

Thanks to his nicknames, some on my irreverent staff called me Cutty or Cutty Sark or The Sark; while others from that time on preferred Utah, Utah Carl, Our Beloved Carl, Our Beloved; or simply, "Chief." For a staff that always did everything I ever asked of them, they showed no respect in how they addressed me, thanks to my dear friend Ernst.

Ernst gave out nicknames like the parking meter lady gives out tickets. When he and I served together in Judge Sam Davis' court, Ernst nicknamed the judge, "Judge Sammy Davis, Sr." He had nicknames for all the judges, too many to mention and some not suitable for framing.

No one was immune from Erwin's epithets. Assistant DA Jimmy James, who went on to be one of our finest district judges, was called "Fun and Games" or "the Fat Fluff." One day shortly after Don Lambright's son was born, Don told Ernie he had named his son "Ernst." Since Don had given Ernst that honor, Ernst began to call Lambright "Spot." Ernst explained that if Don could name his son after Ernst, then Ernst could name Don after his dog.

Ted Busch was a career prosecutor who replaced Ernst as chief of the Trial Bureau. Ted later served as First Assistant under my successor, Johnny Holmes. Ted served the office for over thirty years and was one of the most popular assistants in the history of the office. In spite of his popularity, he had a reputation for being stubborn, so Ernst named him "Steelhead."

Sam Robertson became "Sambo." After Sam went on the bench, Ernst called him Judge Sambo. One young assistant asked me one day if Sambo was his real name. With a straight face I said, "Yes, but he doesn't like to be called by that."

My good friend Wells Stewart, who later pursued a career as a district judge, had an interest in some drilling properties. When Ernst found that out he became "Oil Wells."

Allen Stilley headed up our Grand Jury Division and later went on to be a district judge and then an appellate judge. Stilley had a reputation for being tighter with a dollar than anyone in the office—and that said a lot! He could even out-fumble Ernst down in the coffee shop. Sometimes he would borrow a penny from several people to come up with enough money to buy a cup of coffee. Rumor was Stilley owned some pretty good tracts of land here and there and had a considerable net worth, but one would ever know that. Ernst nicknamed Stilley "Deadbeat Twilley."

Ray Montgomery, one of our solid chief prosecutors and now a DA up in East Texas, had a strong opinion on every subject. Ernst named Ray, a very large man, "The Biggest Bigot." Everyone called him "The Biggest" for short.

My chief when I was assigned to Judge King's Court was Tommy Dunn. Tommy was a good lawyer and good friend. He was a confirmed bachelor who lived in a very messy apartment. Ernst said he was too set in his ways, so he gave Tommy the name "Fuddy Duddy." "Terrible Tommy" was the second nickname Ernst gave to Dunn. Dunn ultimately proved Ernst wrong as he abandoned his fuddy ways and married a lovely lady. They live in a lovely home, much neater than Tommy's previous apartments. Tommy proved that people can indeed change.

Ernst's names stuck, and even today people can't seem to shuck them.

On occasion Ernst would get wound up in a closing argument and make a statement that would sound outrageous on paper but would be a powerful statement to the jury. Only Ernst could say the most outlandish things to make a point and get away with it.

One day Jimmy James burst into my office one day and said, "Do you know what that crazy fool Ernst did?" Ernst and James were close friends, but one would never know this by the way they put each other down.

"No, what did he do now?"

"I just heard his closing argument in that capital case he's trying. He told the jury, 'In the name of Jesus Christ, Carol Vance, and my little boy, give this man the death penalty.' Can you believe that?"

"Knowing Ernst, yes, I can believe that. What did the jury do?"

"They gave him the death penalty."

Later that day I walked into Ernst's office, "Ernie, far be it from me to tell you how to try a lawsuit; but did you ask that jury to give that defendant the death penalty 'in the name of Jesus Christ, Carol Vance, and my little boy'?"

"Yes, Carl, I believe I did say that."

"Ernie, that just really sounds in poor taste."

"Okay, boss. Next time I'll put your name first."

In one particularly brutal murder case, Ernst told the jury, "If you don't give the death penalty in this case, the dead of World War II will rise up from their graves."

After the jury gave the death penalty, the defense attorneys appealed. In writing about Ernst's argument, the Court of Criminal Appeals opinion read, "The prosecutor's reference to the dead of World War II was highly improper and not based on any testimony in the record. However, the argument on its face is so ridiculous that no jury would ever be persuaded by such an absurd appeal. Thus, since the error could have no impact on the verdict, this court invokes the harmless error doctrine and affirms the conviction and sentence."

The problem with the court's opinion was that those appellate judges were not there that day. I heard Ernst make that argument a couple of other times, and it was very moving. The high court underestimated Ernst's ability to make a point. He may have poked fun at people constantly, but amidst all the fun, Ernst was a serious advocate most defense attorneys wanted to avoid.

He maintained an outrageous bulletin board as tribute not so much to his victories and defeats as to his ongoing sense of humor. Dead bodies from murder cases, strippers, and pictures of staff with ribald captions shocked all who walked into his office. Our rule against nailing anything to the county's walls other than one's degree or law license was waived in Ernst's case.

After twenty years in the Harris County District Attorney's office, with his retirement fully vested, Ernst went on to pursue four separate and different careers. He was an excellent General Counsel to the Texas Prison System and got that office started. He held a position as Professor of Criminal Justice at Sam Houston University in Huntsville. Governor Dolph Briscoe later talked Ernst into accepting the appointment as District Attorney for Walker County; he ran for DA at the next election and won. During his four-year term, he was appointed the district judge for Walker County and two surrounding counties. He was elected three times as judge and then became a "Retarded Judge," as he called himself. As a "retarded (retired) judge," Ernst, now over eighty, still has an office in the Walker County Courthouse and sits on occasion when an old veteran is needed on the bench.

In my active practice days, seldom did a month go by without some lawyer from my firm coming by to say, "I had a hearing up in East Texas before a real character, a judge by the name of Erwin Ernst. He said, 'Say hi to Utah Carl for me.'"

With all his accomplishments I will always know that Ernst's highest and best use came over the lunch hour in the DA's office. At noon every day Ernst would drag out his sack lunch as assistants lined up to get a seat on the floor to see him holding court. His office would hold about ten assistants at most.

As a brown bagger paused at the open door, he would ask Ernst, "May I approach the bench?"

Ernst would grant permission until there was no place for anyone to sit. Then he would pull out his long green switchblade knife from his desk drawer. The knife had been a murder weapon in one of our old murder cases. As he stuck the long rusty blade into a giant jalapeño, he would pull some cold barbecue ribs from his brown paper sack. Often when I strolled past Ernst's office to go make some "important speech" across town, I longed to be on that floor laughing until my stomach hurt. Ernst would verbally destroy one poor assistant after another to the delight of all with his verbal skills. Maybe Ernst was indeed, as he liked to call himself, "The World's Greatest Living Trial Lawyer."

Not long ago I called Ernst up in Huntsville to tell him our friend Ted Busch had died. Maw Maw answered the phone. It was mid-afternoon and a hundred degrees out. Ernst, well into his eighties and still a character, was out mowing his own yard—with one of those mowers you still have to push.

CHAPTER THIRTEEN

Police Officer Down

> *Duty, Honor, Country.*
> — General Douglas MacArthur

As I TURNED INLAND from the coastal plains, a Texas highway patrolman pulled a pickup to the side of the road. Just another traffic stop, probably, but no officer ever really knows what danger might await the most routine stop, even in broad daylight with cars coming and going. There are wanted criminals out there running for their lives who will gun down a police officer to avoid capture, trial, and spending most of the rest of their days in state prison.

One dark evening in an isolated area not far from downtown Houston, one of Houston's Finest made such a stop. It would be his last.

THE EVENING WAS WARM and pleasant for a winter night. Officer Louis Sander was working traffic on his three-wheeler. He had parked just off the asphalt street in an isolated area on Houston's East Side. He did not want to be seen by any speeding motorist. The lonely site was less than two miles from downtown Houston in an old warehouse district where most workers had left for home after working hours. The area of town was full of train tracks, vacant lots, and scattered debris. There were no residences, no restaurants, and little pedestrian movement except for the occasional street person seeking safe haven in one of the vacant lots.

Officer Sander had a partner, Officer Brown, who was stationed a block away. Brown had been passing the time of day with a Detective Lewis, not a police detective but a railroad man looking for vandals and thieves among the railroad cars left on the side tracks running through the area. Sander and Brown purposely stayed close for self-protection in this lonesome part of our bustling city.

Suddenly a pickup truck ran a stop sign close to where Brown and Lewis were standing. Brown took chase to arrest the violator, thus he was out of Sander's sight at the time Sander made his final arrest.

As Brown pulled the driver over to write him up, he heard a single gunshot nearby. A few seconds later five shots followed in rapid succession. The shots came from the area where his partner was last seen. Brown and Lewis, who also heard the shots, rushed to Sander's side.

Rounding the corner Brown saw his partner's body lying on the pavement. He was shot through the chest. Brown called an ambulance, which arrived quickly. Before they could get him to the hospital, however, Officer Sander was dead.

Just before Brown and Lewis rushed up to where they saw Sander on the pavement they had seen a bronze Pontiac speeding away. The Pontiac had a red and white license plate on the back bumper. They could not make out the license numbers or the state. They did not see the driver or how many people were in the bronze car.

Quickly officers out of the homicide, radio patrol, and traffic divisions mobilized into action. The first priority to find that bronze Pontiac with the red and white plates, hopefully with the driver. Policemen from all over Harris County and the Sheriff's office joined the massive search. They divided into units that combed the county's parking lots, shopping centers, and any likely place where a car might be abandoned.

I was on the phone the next morning with homicide chief, Captain L.D. Morrison, who said we were looking for the proverbial needle in a haystack. No sooner had we hung up, than I got a call from a homicide detective saying the car had been found. This car, a perfect fit by its description, was found in a multi-story parking lot in downtown Houston. There was a fresh crease on a fender consistent with that of a passing bullet. Veteran lawmen knew this was the car, but at that time this was the only clue that might lead to finding the killer.

After weeks of a long and tedious investigation filled with excellent police work combined with exceptional breaks, a case was made and two brothers were arrested. One was charged with the murder of Officer Sander. When the case ultimately was presented to the jury, the witnesses told the sordid story.

The trial began Monday, October 2, 1967, in the 180th District Court, Judge Fred Hooey presiding. Judge Hooey, an excellent judge and friend, would keep the trial moving. Assistant DA Bob Musslewhite, the chief in

Hooey's court, would sit second chair while I took the lead in trying the case. With a most unique circumstantial evidence case, we began to weave a web the defendant could not escape. We had neither confession nor witnesses to the murder. Instead, it was like solving a jigsaw puzzle, piecing together witnesses, phone calls, cab rides, motel stays, bar sightings, and coincidences to paint the defendant, Kenneth Hinkle, into a corner. Before it was over, a car theft, a kidnapping, and a robbery would be added along with a dramatic final arrest. Two experienced criminal lawyers, Ralph Chambers and Bill Amaimo, represented Hinkle.

The first witnesses were Sander's partner and the railroad detective. They described the Pontiac and the color of the license plates. Next, a homicide detective laid out the scene with photos and diagrams. Dr. Jachimczyk, our Medical Examiner, testified Officer Sander's death was caused by a single gunshot to the heart.

Don Small of Little Rock was our first fact witness. He was a pleasant young man working his way through school by parking cars in a downtown Little Rock parking lot. He told the jury that prior to the murder of Officer Sander, he watched an elderly man, a Mr. Beight, whose car he tended to daily, drive into the parking lot on his way to work.

As was their custom, Beight drove up and handed his keys to Don so Don could park his car, a bronze Pontiac. The two men exchanged greetings. Beight walked off the lot to make his way to work across the street.

I showed Small the pictures of Beight's bronze Pontiac and asked him if he ever saw a single dent or crease of any kind on that car before. Small said no and added that he was most familiar with the condition of the car. Mr. Beight used to brag about the fact his car had not a single ding. Sometimes when Beight retrieved his car in the afternoon, he and Don would jointly look the car over to make sure it was still in perfect shape.

On this particular day Small said he would never forget what had happened that same afternoon. Mr. Beight left work to retrieve his car to go home, but his car was missing. Small and Beight were both dumbfounded. Small had not left the lot all day and never saw anyone drive off in Beight's car. Small had to fill out all kinds of forms to explain the loss of the car. The jury was able to know the exact day the car was taken. This was two weeks before the murder.

When Mr. Beight himself took the stand, he identified the Pontiac found by the Houston police as his own. Looking at the picture of the car, he said he was certain that "new crease" was not on his car when he dropped it off that day.

Just to make sure the jury got it, my next witness was a records clerk from the Arkansas Highway Department. His testimony established that Mr. Beight did indeed own the bronze Pontiac with the same license plates and motor number as the one found in the downtown Houston garage.

Next, we called an elderly couple to the stand, a Mr. and Mrs. Sartin, also residents of Little Rock. These two had been through hell and back. Even so, they had to relive the horror on the witness stand. The jury had to feel their agony.

They both identified the defendant, Kenneth Hinkle, and his brother William as the two men who terrorized them in their home a few days before the Houston murder.

The Sartins had lived in their lovely house in an upscale subdivision in Little Rock for many years. This couple, both in their seventies, were having a pleasant breakfast in the breakfast room near the back door. Not expecting visitors, they both were surprised to hear a very loud knock at the door.

Mr. Sartin got up, walked to the door, and opened it part way to look out. Two strange men were outside. One grabbed the door and pushed it open so the two could force their way in. The Sartins' door was shoved back with so much force it knocked Mr. Sartin to the ground. Before he could move, one of the men shoved a sawed-off shotgun in his stomach and said, "You S.O.B., you make a move and you're a dead man."

"Do you see either of those men in the courtroom today, Mr. Sartin?" I asked.

"Yes. One was Kenneth Hinkle. He is seated there at that table next to his lawyers."

Sartin told how the intruders first bound both of the Sartins' hands tightly with copper wire. Next they applied adhesive tape across their mouths in such a way the Sartins were both gasping for breath. The Hinkle brothers demanded to know where the Sartins kept their home safe. When neither of the Sartins would say where the safe was, the Hinkles delivered a series of severe blows to the bodies and the faces of the elderly couple.

Then Kenneth Hinkle said, "I'll blow your heart out if you don't lead me to your safe," At that Mr. Sartin gave the invaders directions to the safe.

The Hinkles had the right tools necessary to make short work of opening up the safe. From where Mrs. Sartin was bound on the floor, she could see William Hinkle lift her finest jewelry and mink stole out of the safe. Her estimate of the value was $50,000.

After cleaning out the safe, Kenneth Hinkle pulled out his pistol and shot the lock off of their liquor cabinet nearby.

Kenneth told William, "I got us some pretty good stuff for the road." Mr. Sartin later noticed Kenneth Hinkle carrying away a bottle of his best twenty-five-year-old, single malt Scotch whisky.

The Hinkles fled with the fur, the jewelry, and the Scotch while the hog-tied Sartins writhed in pain on the floor.

Mrs. Sartin was particularly emotional, weeping throughout her testimony. Judge Hooey gave multiple recesses so she could get her composure.

After the robbers fled, the Sartins finally got loose and called the police. Because the Hinkles had a long record and were familiar to Little Rock police, their photos were among those of well-known area robbers the detectives brought for the Sartins to view. The Sartins were going through the gallery of pictures without a clue who these people were until they came across the Hinkle brothers. "That is them. You mean they are brothers?" Mrs. Sartin said to the police. She had no doubt—she would never forget those faces.

Detective Evans of the Little Rock Police Department next took the stand to tell the jury how the Sartin house was in shambles. The safe was ripped out, drawers and household items were disarranged and scattered about. Amidst the disorder, Evans had the presence of mind to do a thorough examination of the house. He knew a shot had been fired somewhere inside the home; the Sartins heard the gun discharge one time.

When he got to the liquor cabinet he noticed an unobtrusive little hole in the outside of the cabinet. The hole was fresh and round like a bullet may have entered it. He took all kinds of measurements, had pictures made, and very carefully extracted the little bullet lodged deep within the cabinet. Dutifully, he initialed and tagged the bullet. Little did he dream that bullet would someday be the critical evidence to prove one of the Hinkles was the murderer of a fellow officer in a faraway city. Out of all of the evidence and circumstances we would show, this bullet was the most essential. It was a great example of the hard work and professional thoroughness that provided the necessary links to prove our case.

Our focus next turned from Arkansas to Texas. We called a string of witnesses who saw Kenneth Hinkle in and around Houston and Galveston close to the time of the killing.

Patrolman Brown put the murder of his partner close to 9:30 P.M. We were able to prove the exact minute of the shooting because Officer Brown had started writing up his traffic ticket at 9:29 P.M., just seconds before he heard the shot.

Officer E.M. Dobbs took the stand next. He was part of the expansive dragnet for the car. One of his assignments was to go inside an almost abandoned downtown parking garage. He was the officer who discovered a bronze Pontiac with Arkansas plates. The police thoroughly tested the car for prints. There were none. Every part of the car had been wiped clean. Though a setback, the fact the car was wiped down gave the police the added clue that the killer was covering his tracks and not a stranger to avoiding arrest; he must have a record somewhere. HPD contacted law enforcement agencies in Arkansas with information about the car, in hopes that something might turn up there.

Back in Little Rock, once the Sartins identified the Hinkles as their robbers police sent the pictures of the brothers to HPD as possible suspects in the killing of the Houston police officer. Now the many HPD detectives and officers working on the case could show the pictures to potential witnesses in their effort find out if the Hinkles were the killers.

Homicide and radio patrol detectives systematically combed the area near where the car had been found. They questioned bartenders, waiters, and waitresses in the cheap dives that lined that side of town.

The police also figured whoever abandoned the car had to be picked up by an accomplice or by a cab in order to make a getaway. They reviewed every cabbie's log from cab company records, and then interviewed every cab driver who had made a call in that general area.

Police fortunately found one cabbie who picked up a middle-aged man at a dive on Congress Avenue, not far from the parking lot. Congress Avenue was the last street on the north end of town and home of rundown buildings, bars, and street people. Beer and wine were cheap, as the many bottles strewn on the pavement attested.

Records from the phone company for a pay phone outside the bar proved that the phone was used to call the cab company just shortly after the time of the murder.

When the police showed the cabbie the picture of Kenneth Hinkle, he did not hesitate. "That's the man I picked up at that bar on Congress that night," he testified. He testified he never saw the other Hinkle brother.

The time of the pickup lined up with the time it would take for Kenneth Hinkle to drive downtown, park the car, and walk the few blocks to this particular bar.

The cabbie explained he drove Kenneth Hinkle to another bar out on Broadway Street, a location close to the ship channel and several miles away. It was also an area with cheap bars and low-priced rooms for rent.

The more the defense attorneys bore down on the cabbie, the more the jury was convinced the man knew what he was talking about.

After homicide detectives found Kenneth Hinkle had been dropped off at the bar out on Broadway, two miles from where the Pontiac was found, they combed the area for any other witnesses who saw the defendant the night of the murder. A few doors down from this bar was a shabby looking motel. That owner recognized Hinkle's picture, checked his records and told police he was certain he rented a room to Kenneth Hinkle the night of the murder. He made a good witness as well, and we introduced his motel records showing the date. He told the jury Hinkle paid cash, used a different name, and went out of his way to avoid conversation.

Detective Paul Nix, who led the investigation for Homicide, took the stand next. Paul was an old friend as he handled some fifteen or more murder cases I had tried in my assistant DA days. Nix was a young guy, a real professional, articulate and well prepared.

After showing the jury the maps and diagrams and leading the jury through the trail of the Hinkles, Nix told how he and fellow homicide officers combed through thousands of telephone records at the Southwestern Bell headquarters. These records revealed several calls made to brother William Hinkle's home in Beaumont, Texas, some ninety miles away. The calls were made from phone booths either close to bars where Kenneth Hinkle caught his cab or close to where the Pontiac was found. This evidence helped prove brother William was in Beaumont and could not have committed the murder. My worst scenario was for the jury to have a reasonable doubt about which Hinkle pulled the trigger that killed Officer Sander.

The first long distance call to Beaumont to the home of William Hinkle was at 9:08 P.M., about twenty minutes before Officer Sander was shot. This would leave time for Kenneth Hinkle to drive to where the officer was murdered and come back downtown, dump the car, and then call his brother again at 11:02 P.M., the time of the second call. The second long distance call was made from a pay phone a block away from the Congress Street bar where the first cabbie picked up Kenneth Hinkle, and a short distance from where the car was abandoned. This call also went to brother William's home in Beaumont. Minutes after this a third call was placed to William Hinkle's home from the pay phone from inside this same bar. Each call was short and consistent with a plea for help or advice.

Homicide surmised Kenneth was calling his brother to come rescue him and the brother wanted time to think about the situation. Or perhaps the brother was out and the wife had told him to call back later.

The next phase of our case moved to Galveston, the island city some fifty miles from Houston and eighty miles and a ferry ride from Beaumont. The police discovered that on January 11, ten days before the murder but after the Sartin attack in Little Rock, Kenneth Hinkle had checked into a Galveston motel.

I called the young bellman who was working his way through college and on duty when he saw Kenneth Hinkle checking in the night of January 11. He identified the picture of the bronze 1964 Pontiac Catalina with red and white Arkansas plates.

Attorney Ralph Chambers charged after this witness with an intense cross-examination. After establishing the bellman helped hundred of guests with their luggage in a single month's time, Chambers said, "How in the world can you possibly remember Kenneth Hinkle?"

"Well, sir, I can't forget him. You see, we were standing outside the motel close to the car and just talking. Then all of a sudden a small pistol fell from this man's pocket. It landed at Mr. Hinkle's feet. I had never seen a pistol that small. Just fell on the ground from his pocket or his belt, I don't know which.

"Then he quickly reached down and picked the pistol up and put it back in his pocket like it was a nothing deal. He didn't say a word about it. I was sure not going to say anything. In fact I was scared and made sure I got a good look at him. I won't ever forget his face. I looked his car over good, too, after he walked away. It had red and white Arkansas license plates and was a bronze Pontiac. I should have written down the license number, but I didn't think about it at the time. I'll never forget what he looked like."

The testimony was a windfall. Had I tried to show the pistol incident on direct examination, possession of a pistol would have been an extraneous offense that could get us a mistrial. Of course, I told the witness if he ever had a chance to tell that story in answer to the defense counsel's questioning then, by all means, jump in and do it.

Ralph had opened the door when he asked how this witness could remember Kenneth Hinkle. Our witness told him. Now the jury knew this defendant was not only in Galveston, but armed and dangerous and probably carried the pistol to avoid trouble or commit a crime. Obviously Hinkle never told Ralph Chambers about the pistol incident or Ralph would never have come close to that trap. Defendants often avoid telling their lawyer the truth and then suffer severe consequences.

On redirect I asked the bellman if he got a second chance to see Hinkle. "Oh, yes. Later that night Mr. Hinkle called for me at the front desk and asked me to go buy him some whiskey. Fact is he gave me fifteen bucks and told me to go buy this expensive Scotch called Chivas Regal. Folks at our motel seldom drink Scotch, certainly not anything like what this bottle cost. When I came back he gave me a $5 tip. That was about as much as I made all day."

Once HPD discovered Kenneth's Galveston journey, they combed every bar, liquor store, gas station, and hotel on the island. Good old-fashioned police work.

One of the first people to recall Hinkle was a barmaid, a good ol' German gal named Pearl Shultze. Pearl was a middle-aged lady who had waited on Kenneth Hinkle for three days straight.

"He plopped down at the bar and asked me what kind of Scotch I had on hand. I told him, 'You must be from out-of-state cause we don't do mixed drinks in Texas. It's beer or wine only.' He didn't know we just don't go and serve up the hard stuff in Texas."

When Chambers pressed in hard on her ability to know that the person she waited on was really Kenneth Hinkle, she torpedoed him.

"Oh, you want to know how I remember him? He had one of the classiest women's diamond bracelets I ever seen. Big ol' jewel right in the middle of it. Pulls it out of his pocket and says, 'Honey, I bet you never seen anything like this before.' I said, 'No, don't reckon I have.' That was some diamond. I remember that man."

The discovery of Pearl Schultze sent Homicide into every jewelry store and hockshop on Galveston Island. At a reputable jewelry store downtown, the police scored.

The owner told the jury how Kenneth Hinkle tried to sell him a large standalone teardrop diamond. Hinkle had asked him, "What would you give me in a quick sale? I need some money to make a down payment on a car."

The jewelry store owner told him, "Sir, I don't do diamonds from someone who walks in off the street."

He continued his story. "Then he said to me, 'Can you give me an idea of what this is worth?' I told him, 'Sir, I am not in this business to appraise diamonds for free.' Then he just walks out. Never said another word. But that was one impressive diamond. I would liked to have bought it off of him. But I couldn't risk it being stolen."

The canvass of the motels of Galveston County unearthed a second motel clerk. This young man testified Kenneth Hinkle checked into his motel on January 19 under the name A. R. Johnson. The witness also saw the bronze Pontiac and noticed the Arkansas plates.

When Homicide scoured every Galveston filling station, one detective came across a man who changed the oil in the Pontiac. This witness had posted the usual oil change mileage sticker on the inside of the door of the car. When I introduced the sticker into evidence, he said, "Yep, that's my sticker, and those are my initials."

The information on the sticker conclusively proved it was the same car with the same license number that was recovered in the garage close to where Kenneth Hinkle made the long distance calls to his brother in Beaumont. This attendant also recognized Kenneth Hinkle as the man who drove in. He had plenty of time to look him over during the one-hour oil change.

Homicide hit a home run in coming up with a barmaid who saw Kenneth on the night of the murder, January 21. Bertha Mae Dallas was a heavyset woman of about fifty years of age. She wore a simple blue dress, no frills. She was country and proud of it.

After she identified Kenneth Hinkle as her customer that night, defense lawyer Bill Amaimo went after her. "Now Bertha Mae, you wait on many strangers each night, don't you?"

"Most nights I do. Some nights are pretty quiet."

"And this was months ago, and by now you have had thousands of customers come and go. Isn't that right?"

"Yes, sir."

"So you can't possibly remember what all those people looked like, including this man here, Kenneth Hinkle. Isn't that right?"

"Sir, I'll never forget that man. My girlfriend Paula come into the bar for a beer, so I introduces her to this guy, that very one sitting there next to you right now, and he gets real chummy with her, you know what I mean? He starts hittin' up on her to go out with him later on. She was taken with him, that I could see.

"I was standing by their table serving him a beer when he said to her, 'I gotta run an errand and will be right back in a few minutes. Will you wait for me?' She said yes. He leaves but he doesn't come back. She waits and waits. I guess at least two hours went by, probably close to midnight before he walks back in.

"Although my girlfriend had been waitin' forever for this guy, when he does finally return, Mr. Big Time there never says a word to her. He goes over to the pay phone and makes a call. Then he asks me for six beers and wants me to put them in a sack. He pays me and walks out without saying a word to Paula, who is still sittin' over there waitin'. That man treated her like dirt."

My last Galveston witness was the manager of a motel. He saw Kenneth Hinkle right after he left the bar where Bertha Mae worked. Hinkle checked in his motel a little after midnight. The manager also pointed out that he did not see Hinkle arrive by car so he assumed he came by cab (this was the only cab driver the police could not find). Kenneth Hinkle only stayed at this motel for little more than an hour and then checked out at 1:30 A.M. according to the motel records we introduced. The manager remembered that a man and woman drove up around that time. Kenneth Hinkle then paid the manager in cash, climbed into the waiting car, and left.

The time sequences fit like a glove with the times of a telephone calls Kenneth Hinkle made earlier to Beaumont and the time it took for his brother to drive over to Galveston from Beaumont to pick Kenneth up.

The trail of evidence proved conclusively that after the theft of the Pontiac and Sartin robbery in Little Rock, the brothers drove back to Texas. Kenneth dropped his brother off at his home in Beaumont, then went to Galveston for several days, then went to Houston and killed the officer. To avoid arrest he abandoned the Pontiac, spent the night in Houston, then went back to Galveston where his brother and wife picked him up. We had all the evidence except the cab ride to Galveston.

Kenneth Swatzel, next to take the stand, was one of my favorite expert witnesses and a real pro when it came to identification of guns and bullets. Swatzel, scholarly and mild-mannered, had an affidavit face. I never saw a lawyer trip him up.

Like a seasoned professor, he explained how the crease marks left on the car abandoned downtown were consistent with the marks a bullet would make. With no sign of rust or weathering, and not even dust residue, Swatzel said the marks had to have been made less than twenty-four hours before the car was found. The crease went in a straight line across the body of the car, consistent with the shooter standing up.

Swatzel next educated the jury on how an expert could compare two bullets and determine whether the bullets came from the same weapon. With blowups of the bullet taken from Officer Sander's body and the one dug out of the Sartin liquor cabinet back in Little Rock, Swatzel matched up the markings and grooves of the two bullets. The defense attorneys knew better than to cross-examine him. He said he believed to a near certainty the two bullets were fired from the same pistol. He made it clear that he could not be 100 percent certain. If his conclusion was correct, one of the Hinkles had to have fired the fatal bullet that killed Officer Sander.

Now my goal took a new direction. We needed to prove to the jury beyond a reasonable doubt that it was Kenneth Hinkle and not his brother who killed Officer Sander.

We knew Kenneth Hinkle's brother, William, had the absolute right to take the Fifth Amendment and refuse to testify. Both brothers were under indictment in Arkansas and awaiting trial there. That being the case, William's wife became an important witness for the State.

Although we could not have forced his wife to testify against William under Texas law, there was no rule to keep William's wife from testifying against Kenneth. Even so, she was nervous and begged not to go on the stand. She was emotional and scared. I knew her testimony would be unpredictable. We also believed the defense would exercise their right to ask her leading questions and solicit testimony not otherwise available to them as they were not about to call Kenneth Hinkle to the stand.

Mrs. Hinkle warily stepped up to the clerk and took the oath. She was plain looking, shy, and would not look anyone in the eye. She began by describing how her husband William came and went from their Beaumont residence as he pleased. He seldom told her where he was going or what he was going to do.

On January 12, nine days before the murder, she said Kenneth and William had been gone for some days to some destination unknown. When she returned home after grocery shopping that day, Kenneth and William were standing in the front yard talking. There were no hellos or hugs or mention of what they had been up to during the previous week. She usually didn't pay much attention to their cars, but she noticed William came back in a new looking Pontiac and not the car he drove off in. I had to drag it out of her that the car looked like the bronze Pontiac in the picture I put before her.

She said she did not know where the car had come from. She did not think it had been her place to ask. She also had not noticed the Arkansas plates.

She said "the brothers didn't hang around the yard long. When my husband Bill got ready to leave, he didn't tell me where he was goin'. Just says, 'Guess I'll hit the road now.' That's about all he ever says when he takes off. Oh, Kenneth was driving when he backed the Pontiac out the driveway." She also made it clear to the jury that Kenneth Hinkle was in Houston and brother William was in Beaumont the night of the shooting.

Norman Zigrossi, an FBI agent out of the New Orleans office, was our next to last witness. He said the New Orleans FBI office received a call from a confidential informant (CI). The CI said Kenneth Hinkle was a dangerous criminal and was wanted in Houston and that he had just seen this Hinkle fellow down in the French Quarter living it up.

The CI further told the FBI man that Hinkle left the French Quarter to take a room out on Interstate 10 a few miles away. He then gave the agent the name of the motel. Incidentally, 1-10 connects New Orleans to Beaumont and then on to Houston if one drives west.

That afternoon Zigrossi took his partner and several New Orleans policemen to the motel. Finding Kenneth's room empty, they watched and waited. Sometime after dark a man fitting Kenneth's description unlocked the door to the room. They found out from the manager the room was rented under an assumed name. From the manager's description they figured Hinkle rented that room. When the occupant, presumably Hinkle, returned, he entered and turned out the lights. It was close to midnight. The police gave him time to go to sleep so they could surprise him. Then they borrowed a motel key to enter the room. Discovering the night latch was on, the officers knocked down the door and stormed the room. Hinkle woke up with two revolvers in his face. He chose not to go for his own gun. As it turned out, he had two pistols, a .38 under the pillow, and a .32 revolver handy under the bed. Police also found a tear gas gun and a large stash of ammunition for all three weapons.

Zigrossi made a good witness in communicating what a tough and dangerous guy Hinkle was. With guns stuck in his face Hinkle had the audacity to make "belligerent" remarks. Zigrossi was a pretty tough looking character himself. In perfect New Orleans dialect, he said, "I stuck a pistol up Kenneth's chest while my partner cuffed him."

The defense attorneys yelled and screamed to the judge that we were introducing an extraneous offense and they demanded a mistrial. The judge overruled their objection. Acts that occur during flight are admissible. Fleeing from an arrest is relevant to guilt.

The search of Hinkle's room turned up three brown cotton work gloves. Two gloves were brand new and a matched pair. The third was a single left-handed glove. This turned out to be a perfect companion to the right-handed glove, which was the only item found in the abandoned Pontiac. Who could explain why Hinkle, who worked so hard to wipe the prints clean, would carry a worthless mate to a glove left in the getaway car from a murder. No crime is perfect.

Hinkle had less than $100 in his wallet. No diamonds or anything else from the Sartin home were found. Drinking expensive Scotch, hanging out in bars, and financing hotel rooms had eaten into his bankroll. If Hinkle

received ten cents on the dollar in hocking the $50,000 worth of stolen prop-
erty from the Sartins, the proceeds wouldn't keep up his lifestyle long.

We closed our case by calling Mrs. Louis Sander. Her gentle words
conveyed to the jury the enormity of her loss. I hated making her relive those
hours, but she was more than willing. Perhaps it would bring a little more
"closure" as she got the trial behind her and saw a little justice done.

She recalled last seeing Louis standing at the doorway of their modest
home. He looked so handsome in his uniform. He gave her a kiss on the
cheek and said, "Love you and see you later." Then he ventured into the night
for another routine tour of duty. And that is what policemen do, night after
night, day after day, trying to keep the peace.

The courtroom was packed for the final arguments. Bob Musslewhite
opened for our side and meticulously laid out our case.

Both defense attorneys addressed the jury. Ralph Chambers' theme song
was, "The State of Texas proved a great case showing the Hinkle brothers
committed a robbery in Arkansas, but to say Kenneth Hinkle killed a police
officer is so circumstantial that you would be guessing that poor man into
the penitentiary. Send him back to Arkansas and let them give him a long
sentence; that is a done deal for the State of Arkansas. He will be in prison
for a long time. But not for murder in Texas. The State has given you just a
hodgepodge of circumstances proving nothing."

After I made my closing, I went to my office to catch up on stuff and await
the verdict. I expected a long wait, but in less than an hour the phone rang.
The jury had a verdict.

I was worried. Often a short deliberation means an acquittal. I needn't
have been.

The jury walked in smiling and the foreman read the verdict, "We find the
defendant, Kenneth Hinkle, guilty of the offense of murder and assess his
punishment in prison at ninety-nine years and a day." (The jurors had apparently believed the common myth that adding a single day to a long sentence
would prevent any defendant from ever being paroled. Not true, just an old
wives' tale.)

Regardless, Hinkle wouldn't ever be getting out. What Ralph Chambers
had said was true: Arkansas planned to try both Hinkles with their airtight
case, so the brothers should be locked up for good.

Sometime after the trial, Chambers was interviewed by a writer for
Master Detective magazine. "In all my years of practice I have never seen a

prosecutor present a better prepared circumstantial evidence case than Carol Vance," he told the magazine.

His statement was accurate, but not due to me. Houston Homicide, aided by radio patrol, had looked under every rock. They ran down witnesses against all odds. The evidence accounted for just about every move Kenneth Hinkle made in the days surrounding the murder. Their dogged determination left no holes and no questions. I have seen Houston Homicide consistently do fine work on many occasions, but I had never witnessed an investigation as thorough or complete as this. A job well done for a fallen comrade.

CHAPTER FOURTEEN

Grand Juries and the John Hill Case

Do not be wise in your own eyes; Fear the Lord and depart from evil.
—Proverbs 3:7

As I MOVED NORTH through Wharton, their courthouse looked deserted except for two old codgers in faded coveralls whittling in the shade of a large oak. I love to look at the Texas courthouses in small towns so I drove around the block. As I did I was able to count ten men and two women who obviously came out of the courthouse together. They were reasonably well-dressed and exchanging greetings and waving to each other as they departed.

This had to be a Wharton grand jury on its way home after several hours of hearing cases. Probably they met once a month and maybe this morning had considered ten to twenty felony cases occurring in their judicial district.

Back in Harris County we had four separate grand juries going at the same time. Each sat three times a week. Each grand jury heard about fifty or sixty cases each time they met, probably over four hundred cases per week. Grand juries are very much a part of the criminal justice system in Texas, even though most laypeople do not understand just what it is that grand juries do.

Watching this grand jury walk out of the courthouse reminded me of the notorious John Hill case. Before the case concluded it would be considered by three different Harris County grand juries. Then, following a mistrial and before Dr. Hill could be tried again, he was assassinated by a paid killer. Solving Hill's murder case involved even more grand juries as we sought justice for those responsible.

What goes on behind grand jury doors is, by law, secret. The grand jury has two basic functions. The first duty is to investigate crime and the second and main function is to determine whether the evidence shows probable cause of guilt. If it does, the grand jury is supposed to indict. If it does not, the grand jury is supposed to return a "no bill" which releases the accused from the charge, if any, that he was under.

Unless one waives the right to have a grand jury consider his case, that person cannot be tried for a felony offense. When the grand jury indicts, a formal accusation is drawn up called an indictment. It is supposed to tell the accused just what he is accused of. This is called a true bill.

Although twelve persons make up a grand jury, the grand jury can meet with as few as a quorum of nine. The vote for a true bill does not have to be unanimous like it does with a trial jury. But whether there are nine, ten, eleven, or twelve grand jurors in attendance, at least nine have to vote yes in order to bring a defendant to trial in a felony. In the serious misdemeanor cases, the district attorney decides whether the evidence is sufficient to swear out a "complaint and information," the legal equivalent of an indictment.

DR. JOHN HILL'S CASE was one of the most controversial in Houston's history. Author Tommy Thompson wrote a bestseller about it called *Blood and Money* which sold four million copies. I found his book accurate and comprehensive. When someone used to ask me, "Did John Hill do it?" I always advised the person to read *Blood and Money* and then tell me what he thought. The book covered the waterfront and recited the known important facts. This chapter is more like a summary of the case, but the Hill case is a great illustration how the grand jury system works in practice.

One thing that made the Hill case unique is that it was a murder case based upon intentional neglect. Cases of that kind occur but are rare. Most murder cases have two elements: an intent to kill, followed by the actual act of killing. An accidental discharge of a pistol killing someone is not enough. The intent to kill must be proved.

The Hill case was one that was based upon intentional neglect, which can be grounds for murder if the defendant had a duty to look after someone and *intentionally* failed to do so, knowing that the failure to respond was likely to cause death. The accusation against Dr. Hill was that he was a doctor who had undertaken to treat his wife for her illness and that he intentionally neglected to get her treated, knowing that without treatment death was likely. I don't think anyone who knew the facts at all would disagree that she died when she could have been saved. The question had more to do with Dr. Hill's involvement in this lack of care which caused her death.

This is not an easy law to explain to a trial jury. The court's charge to the jury is most important. Every word is dynamite. The wording can vary. These are difficult cases for the State to prove beyond a reasonable doubt.

For example, a doctor tells a husband his wife has a life-threatening case of pneumonia and may die if she is not cared for properly. The husband thereafter up and leaves town. The wife is too weak to call for help and dies from lack of medical treatment or basic care. That husband could be guilty of murder. The jury of course must be convinced beyond a reasonable doubt.

A clearer case of intentional neglect might be where a nurse attending a spastic walks off, leaving her patient in a wheelchair close to a cliff. The spastic releases the brake and rolls down into a deep gorge and dies. The nurse might very well be convicted of murder.

In the words of the Hill indictment the State had to prove beyond a reasonable doubt that "Hill was a doctor and husband of Joan Hill and that she was sick and in a helpless condition, which was known to Dr. Hill, and further that the life of Joan Hill was in danger if she did not promptly receive proper medical attention and treatment. Further with these facts known to Dr. Hill, that Dr. Hill intentionally neglected her knowing death could be likely." We did not know exactly how the court would charge the jury, but it would be in the ballpark with the principles just stated.

The grand jury had to believe there was "probable cause" that Hill did those things in order to vote a true bill for murder. Now the crime of negligent homicide, a misdemeanor carrying up to a year in jail, is easier to prove. To have negligent homicide the jury would have had to believe Hill was negligent and his negligence caused her death.

The facts in the Hill case are complex. Dr. Hill was one of Houston's most in-demand plastic surgeons. He was married to the socially prominent and beautiful Joan Robinson Hill. Joan was a regular on the society pages and known for both her fashionable style and her equestrian skills, for which she had won several world championships.

During John and Joan's marriage, Joan became ill. After several days, she died. A few suspected she was poisoned, but only circumstances and not scientific evidence suggested that could have been the case. There was considerable evidence, including medical opinions, that she would have recovered with proper medical treatment. Dr. Hill had definitely undertaken to treat her but did not do so very well by anyone's standards. He did not take her to another doctor nor did he call one to come out to the home.

No one in our office had ever prosecuted a homicide under this theory. There were a good number of cases in England and the U.S. down through the centuries on the interpretation of this law. For example, one case from 1893 involved a niece who was taking care of her aged aunt. The aunt was infirm and unable to care for herself. The niece was using the aunt's money for living expenses but failed to even feed her aunt, much less call the doctor when she was aware her aunt was very ill. The conviction was affirmed by the appellate court on the basis the niece undertook the care and then intentionally neglected the aunt knowing death was likely. In another case a parent left her two-year-old locked inside a car for four hours in 130-degree heat, causing the child's death. The appellate court upheld the conviction after the jury convicted the mother for murder.

There are differences in how a trial judge might instruct the jury on the law. How the judge words his charge to the jury could determine the outcome.

At the conclusion of any future trial on the John Hill matter, the judge would give the jury written instructions explaining the law. If any juror believed there was a reasonable doubt about any of the essential elements that constituted the crime, then that juror should vote not guilty. We knew getting twelve jurors to jump through all of those hoops would be a formidable task. The State would call its expert witnesses testifying that in their opinion—not as a fact—Dr. Hill did these things. The defense would probably call at least as many medical experts who would say that the facts were not all that apparent she was in mortal danger.

Ash Robinson, the wealthy father of Joan Hill, made no secret of his dislike for his son-in-law. He expressed his belief to many that Dr. Hill had caused his daughter's death. He hired lawyers to brief the law and to advise him about what action could be taken against his son-in-law. Ash wanted to see John indicted. I know, as I met with Mr. Robinson a couple of times, the same as I would meet with family members of any victim.

This being a very close call by the nature of the allegation, the grand jury would play the major role in determining whether a murder indictment should be returned. After all, if a DA doesn't have the kind of case that will convince the grand jury the defendant is probably guilty, then he is unlikely to convince all twelve of the trial jurors the defendant is guilty beyond a reasonable doubt. As DA, I liked having a grand jury make the call on close cases such as this.

Grand jurors are just people, regular citizens. Some jurisdictions choose their grand jurors by random selection like a trial jury. Texas does not. In Texas the district judge who will impanel a new grand jury first summons three to five grand jury commissioners. The judge usually picks commissioners whose judgment he trusts. Hopefully the commissioners will then choose intelligent people to serve who have no axes to grind. We need grand jurors with enough sense to follow the law.

The commissioners meet in private to discuss possible candidates and then ultimately come up with a list of fifteen to twenty names. From that list the judge calls those people to come down to the courthouse. He then grills them on their qualifications and chooses the twelve who are legally qualified and that the judge believes should serve. The judge then appoints one of that number to be foreperson and preside at all of the sessions. Most commissioners will select a well-rounded group reflecting the demographics of the county.

When a case is submitted to a grand jury to be voted on, at least nine of the twelve must agree there is "probable cause" of guilt in order to return an indictment. *Probable cause* is a legal term with many definitions. I used to tell grand jurors on orientation day that if the evidence convinces them the person is probably guilty, then that is probable cause, so return the indictment. If not, vote for a no bill. I would also say if the assistant DA tells you we cannot make a case, I hope you will believe him or her and return a no bill.

The DA in a big city assigns his assistants to present the cases to the grand jury; in a small town the DA usually will do this himself. Most cases are obvious, like a burglar caught in a building or a thief arrested in a stolen car. With these cases, little discussion on the law or facts is necessary. In a beer joint shooting where some witnesses say the dead man was coming at the shooter with a knife while others say he was not, the grand jury needs to be a Solomon. Contrary to popular opinion, the DA is not trying to get an indictment in every case.

Although the DA is usually the only party to have close access to the grand jury, the grand jury can hear from anybody. The DA is the one who puts the case together, gathers the witnesses, compiles the facts, and summarizes the case before the grand jury.

The grand jury is perfectly free to decide they want more evidence or want to call witnesses. The grand jury does not have to follow the DA's advice and vice versa. If the grand jury gives us a case we can't make, we will have to dismiss it. Grand juries and the DA need to work closely together. That does not mean the grand jury must accept the DA's conclusions about the facts. And a good DA and a good grand jury share the same common goal: to determine probable cause of guilt.

Should one grand jury refuse to indict and the DA thinks they made a bad decision, he can present the same case to a second or third grand jury.

Grand jury proceedings are secret and grand jury testimony cannot be disclosed unless in a court of law. An example would be where the DA or defense attorney uses a witness's grand jury testimony to impeach that witness during the trial.

It is not uncommon for one grand jury to do some work on a case and then end their service, leaving a continuing investigation and decision to a future grand jury. In fact, the Hill case went to three different grand juries with the last two taking formal votes. Our office did not present enough evidence for the first grand jury to take a vote. Their term expired so the investigation was picked up by the second grand jury.

The foreman of that second grand jury was my dear friend and pastor, Dr. Jack Lancaster. Jack had been senior pastor at First Presbyterian Church for decades. I was an Elder in the church and knew him well. He was as fair-minded and conscientious a person as anyone could be. I was glad his grand jury was the one to consider this case as I knew he would try to do the right thing. Our friendship would have nothing to do with his decision. He would vote his convictions.

The fact the DA knows some of the grand jurors was never a factor insofar as I knew. I always knew a good number of the grand jurors. Judges had a habit of picking community leaders who were well-known. During my time in office I worked with over one hundred fifty grand juries consisting of about two thousand individuals in total. Never did I ask any grand jury to do anything except follow the law. Did all of the grand juries always agree with our staff's recommendations in all cases? Of course not. There will always be close calls where reasonable people differ, like umpires behind the plate. Grand jurors hear the law explained and are presented the facts and then vote on the matter the best they can.

Serving on a grand jury takes a great deal of time. In Harris County the grand jury would work three days a week starting around 8:30 A.M. and quit between noon and 6:00 P.M., depending on the agenda. The sheer number of cases handled is staggering. In 1979, my last year as DA, the sixteen grand juries indicted over 20,000 people. Perhaps another 2,000 were no billed. Each grand jury averaged about 1,200 cases during their three-month term. We had six assistants assigned to the grand jury section who presented most of these cases.

The grand jury system is a good one. It offers protection from indictments being returned with little or no evidence. Grand jurors, trial juries, and prosecutors make mistakes. That is why they built the courthouse. There is never any guarantee the system will always produce a just result. Humans just aren't perfect. Although most all who serve as assistant DAs or on grand juries are honest and conscientious, everyone is subject to error and imperfect judgment calls.

WHEN DR. LANCASTER'S GRAND jury was impaneled, Assistant District Attorney I. D. McMaster presented several witnesses on the Hill matter. After all the evidence we knew of at that time was given to the grand jurors, they took a vote. Less than nine voted for a true bill which made the matter come out a no bill. To this good day I don't know what that grand jury thought. I never talked to Jack about the case. Being DA and a friend, I could have asked him anything I wanted to, and I am sure he would have told me; but there was no reason to do that. I knew he and his colleagues had called it like they saw it. I was not going to second guess them in a case where reasonable minds could differ. To tell the truth, I was glad a group of grand jurors had to make the decision and not me.

Months passed and new grand juries were impaneled. One grand jury ended up with a member by the name of Cecil Haden. He was a very close friend of Ash Robinson, Joan's father. There was no question that Haden, like Ash, wanted to see Dr. Hill indicted for murder. Even so, the other grand jurors did not know the parties or the facts. It would still take eight others on that grand jury to vote an indictment.

By this time Ash had hired the most famous forensic pathologist in the land, Dr. Milton Helpern of New York. This took a court order authorizing an exhumation of his daughter's remains, which Ash's lawyers obtained. Dr. Helpern performed the new autopsy and opined that Joan Hill's death was due to neglect by her physician husband.

Our ME, Dr. Jachimczyk, would never have worked for a family member and taken an advocate's side in a case. He would simply have done an autopsy or medical analysis and reported the findings. Dr. Helpern's report, however, quoted liberally from sworn statements of witnesses. The bottom line of the Helpern report was that Dr. Hill caused his wife's death through neglect. There was some new evidence presented to this third grand jury. They took a vote, and the 10–2 tally resulted in a true bill. Dr. Hill had finally been indicted for murder.

Of course our office had the authority to walk into court and dismiss the case if we believed the case should not be tried. Indictments are dismissed by

district attorneys all the time. Missing witnesses, new evidence, a disagreement with the grand jury decision—there is no legal limitation. Therefore,
Ernst and I had one last serious discussion prior to the decision as to whether
to go forward and try Dr. Hill for murder. I. D. McMaster, who headed our
grand jury division, and Erwin Ernst came into the office and gave me the
following summary:

By 1969 John Hill's marriage to Joan Robinson Hill was going down
in flames. He had openly lived with another woman, Ann Kurth, during
the marriage. Even the week before Joan died—and with guests staying at
the house—Hill did not bother to come home two of the nights. He made
an ironclad promise to Ann Kurth that he would marry her. There was, of
course, a slight problem with that promise: He was still married to Joan.
Complicating the issue was the fact that John had signed a crazy agreement
that Ash Robinson had prepared giving Joan everything should he ever seek
and obtain a divorce. The agreement would give Joan all of the interest in
their River Oaks home. His interest in this home was about all John had at
the time. There was no question that John had a good motive to get out of the
marriage any way he could except by divorce.

The next circumstance Ernst discussed with me was the fact John brought
some éclairs for Joan to eat while she was ill. This was just days before she
died. Joan had houseguests at the time who believed this was strange; he
had never brought her éclairs before. The guests said John made certain Joan
received a particular éclair to eat. The guests recalled that Joan was insis-
tent about trading éclairs with John one evening. He refused, so Joan ate her
éclair. It was strange conduct, certainly, but we had no proof the pastry was
poisonous.

The main evidence in our case would be the fact that Joan was really sick
and John did nothing about it until it was too late. Even though she was
in a terrible state—obvious to all who saw her—John did not take her to
the hospital until his mother-in-law insisted. In fact, the mother-in-law went
along. Instead of taking her to the famous Methodist Hospital where John
practiced and knew the doctors and their specialties, he drove her our to
Sharpstown General, a small hospital, much further away from their home
and not nearly as equipped as his own Methodist Hospital. Even the emergency room at Sharpstown was no match for Methodist. In fact, one of her
physicians at Sharpstown wanted to move her to Methodist, but she was too
far gone. John's decision not to go to Methodist was out of the ballpark in the
opinion of every doctor with whom I spoke.

Right before he finally did drive Joan to Sharpstown, Hill was on plenty of notice she was in terrible shape. That last morning he saw her lying in the bed "in her own poop," according to the maid. Another witness said Joan had thrown up in bed as well. Hill just told the maid to clean it up.

He saw his wife so sick she could hardly move. All she wanted to do was stay in bed. She had trouble just getting out of bed and making it down the stairs to the car. Joan was extremely weak, unable to eat, and probably dehydrated. This wasn't your average female, either. This woman could go out and ride her five-time world champion horse for three or four hours at a time. She was in great shape before she ate the éclairs and became ill. Her husband ignored her until the last when it was too late.

The facts of that last day, March 19, 1969, were damning. With Joan sick to her stomach, going to the bathroom in bed, Dr. Hill left her side to go to an elementary school to play his tuba for a group of school children he probably did not know. He put that ahead of his wife's life-threatening situation.

As he finished at the school and went to his car, lover Ann Kurth was waiting for him. He had promised to have breakfast with her that morning. She was very upset she had not seen him in the last few days. By the time of trial Ann had turned on John and was willing to testify against him. But that morning she was trying to put the pressure on John to live up to his promise to her to divorce Joan. She threatened to walk out on him if he did not get with it.

Finally, after an hour or so, the lovers parted. Did he go home and see about his wife? No, he went to Sharpstown Hospital to perform a minor operation. In doing so he ignored all the warnings from the maid, his mother-in-law, and the houseguests about Joan's dire condition. By the time he got home, Joan was in her last stages of life. And after picking the wrong hospital, John, according to the mother-in-law, drove there excruciatingly slowly. Mother-in-law kept looking at her watch and told John to quit poking around. John took forty-five minutes to make it to a place that should have been no more than a twenty or twenty-five minute drive.

He explained to his mother-in-law that the doctors would be waiting to treat her at Sharpstown. Not so. No one was waiting. He had to spend time checking her in like a regular patient. And then the doctor John chose to treat her had never before seen her professionally. She had shaken hands with him once at a party, he said. Here this poor doctor is trying to save a dying, sick patient without any medical history or a clue of what was wrong.

Later that evening she needed some special treatment, but Dr. Hill had left Sharpstown Hospital. He went home where he became engrossed in his classical music in his famed music room.

The Sharpstown doctors finally reached Dr. Hill at home at 9:15 P.M. But it was not until almost two hours later at 11:00 P.M. before John returned to Sharpstown to be by his dying wife's bedside. He remained there until she breathed her last breath. It was 1:30 A.M. when this athletic thirty-eight year old died. John also had been told that shortly after her arrival at the hospital, her blood pressure registered a near deathly level of 60/40. It was obvious to all that John, a doctor, waited until she was in critical condition to make a move.

As if things weren't strange enough, the next part of this circus is really bizarre. Since she hadn't been in the hospital for twenty-four hours before she died, Texas law required the hospital notify the Harris County Medical Examiner's Office about her death. This is so the Medical Examiner can do an autopsy to determine the cause of death.

All hospitals know that is the law.

Sharpstown Hospital did not follow the law. They did not notify anyone. Somehow a pathologist at Sharpstown was chosen to do an autopsy on her body. This was probably engineered by Dr. Hill. It was hard to believe Sharpstown would take it on themselves to perform an autopsy without Dr. Hill's consent.

The body was then ordered to be transported to Settegast-Kopf, an upscale funeral home on Kirby Drive. Clearly Dr. Hill ordered that transfer, as only a husband can say where to take his wife's body for preparation for burial. The funeral home embalmer drained all the blood out of her body and flushed it down the sink, leaving no blood for cultures or to put under the microscope to see what disease killed her.

At this point, Ash Robinson gets wind of these happenings and calls Assistant DA I. D. McMaster who is alarmed and immediately calls Dr. Joe Jachimczyk, the Harris County Medical Examiner, to go by the funeral home and check out the body. Dr. Joe not only does that but orders all samples taken from her body to be held for his later examination.

We end up with three people doing three autopsies, the last two being probably the two most famous medical examiners in the country, but they had to work under limited circumstances. The blood and other parts needed for critical tests were missing. All three came up with different causes of death, undoubtedly due to the evidence that was lost thanks to Joan's husband.

A few weeks after Joan's death John married Ann Kurth as planned. This marriage turns out to be very brief and stormy. They break up and Ann volunteers to come forward to tell all concerning Dr. Hill. Her brief union with John was violent, if one is to believe her.

Then Ernst said, "Well that is it, but that's quite a bit. I'll try the case. I don't know what a jury will do."

"Well Ernie, give it your best shot. I think he deserves a trial." I was just glad Ernie was trying the case and not me.

Dr. Hill had hired the colorful and talented Richard "Racehorse" Haynes to represent him. Richard was considered one of the best criminal defense attorneys in town, if not in Texas. Not long into the investigation and before the indictment was returned, Racehorse made a bold move and asked that the grand jury permit John to come in and tell his side of the story. Haynes knew that under Texas law he could not accompany his client inside the grand jury room and that Hill would be subject to the cross-examination of Erwin Ernst, the brilliant and unflappable prosecutor.

Nevertheless, I thought this a smart move on the part of Haynes. If Hill could convince even four not to indict him, he was home free, Ash's friend Cecil Haden notwithstanding. Some years later, when I was in private practice, I threw a client in front of a grand jury. He had been charged with murder but after he told his story, the grand jury indicted him for negligent homicide, a misdemeanor. He was acquitted at the trial. I did this again in another case. A school teacher was charged with a felony assault on a child. She went into the grand jury with a felony and came out with a misdemeanor. At the trial she was found not guilty even of the misdemeanor. Both parties in my opinion were innocent, and the grand jury gave major relief in each case. It is risky and dangerous business putting a client before a grand jury. The lawyer can't even go into the room, but I believe Haynes did the smart thing even if an indictment ensued. Ernst told me he thought Hill had made a good witness. Nonetheless, the grand jury true billed him. John Hill would stand trial for murder. I was told the vote was 10–2.

THE CASE RECEIVED AN unprecedented amount of publicity. The courtroom was packed out. Judge Fred Hooey saved a couple of rows for the media. No cameras were allowed back in those days so sketch artists were drawing away. The jury was selected and testimony began.

Early in the trial Ernst called Ann Kurth to the stand. What he heard he never expected.

Ann told the jury that one dark night after she married him, John Hill drove her out to the stables where Joan had kept her horses. While there, Ann said that Hill took out a hypodermic needle and forcibly tried to inject her with something. She also said the doctor confessed to injecting Joan Hill with a needle the same way. John Hill, she said, admitted to her that he killed his wife!

Ann Kurth had not ever told this story before. Because she had injected new crimes into the case, Racehorse moved immediately for a mistrial. Judge Hooey, a most conservative and thoughtful judge, was stunned by the testimony. He overruled Haynes' motion at first, but after further reflection he said he was declaring a mistrial. The next morning, February 27, 1971, the Houston *Post*'s page one headline story began, "Ann Kurth, the State's bombshell witness, had blown the trial right out of court."

One of the worst things that can happen to the prosecution is to put on a witness who tries to lay it on too thick and gives the jury the sense that his or her testimony cannot be believed. In this case, the bombshell exploded and blew us right out of court. Ernst was particularly shocked because he had spent a great deal of time going over the testimony with Ann Kurth prior to trial.

My personal opinion was that our case was doomed after the mistrial, but I withheld making any decision. I wanted to let some time go by and see what developed next.

Not many months later, Ernst decided to take another job. He would be a part-time professor at Sam Houston State University in Huntsville, close to his beloved Armadillo Ranch, and work as counsel to the Texas Department of Corrections, which was also headquartered in Huntsville.

With the trial over and John and Ann now divorced, John began going with a lady named Connie Loesby. Connie was well-liked and respected by those who knew her. The two loved music and both were talented musicians. In short order they were engaged and then married. Connie moved in with John in his River Oaks home.

John was not out of the legal woods entirely. His case was to be retried, beginning in November 1972. Before the trial, John decided to take his bride to Las Vegas for a medical convention. They stopped off in San Francisco for a little honeymoon as part of their trip.

John Hill had no idea that a hired killer and a female companion had also tried to follow him to Vegas to kill him. When the gunman and his girlfriend arrived in Vegas they checked at the convention hotel to see if Hill was in attendance at the medical meeting. He was not, having gone to San Francisco, so the killer and girlfriend left. Their original plan was to kill John in Vegas and make it look like a robbery-murder. The killer left town but not without an alternative plan.

After attending the medical meeting, John and Connie flew back to Houston. It was September 24, 1972. After arriving at the airport they caught a cab to return to their home in River Oaks. When they arrived at the house, Connie went inside while John paid the cabbie.

As Hill stepped inside the door of his home he was confronted by a stranger with pistol in hand, lying in wait. He fired at John at close range. The lone gunman had earlier forced his way in and terrorized John and Joan's twelve-year-old son, Robert, and John's mother, Myra Hill, who was babysitting. He took them hostage to await the doctor's arrival. John tried to grab the assailant's revolver at the same time he was shot. He died in a matter of minutes.

The shooter escaped.

Ultimately the pistol was found in some bushes not far from the Hill home. Lab work showed this pistol was the murder weapon. Houston homicide detectives Jerry Carpenter and J.A. Gamino had been assigned to the case. They were talented and determined and did some amazing police work that resulted in solving the case.

First, they traced the ownership of the pistol back to a medical doctor in a small East Texas town. The detectives paid a visit to the physician, who told them a bizarre story. He had owned the pistol for some time, but a prostitute stole the pistol when she left his house after a routine house call. This happened several years back, he said.

"You don't remember her name do you?" Jerry Carpenter asked.

"Yes, as a matter of fact I do. Her name is Marcia McKittrick."

In checking with the Dallas vice squad and homicide officers, Gamino and Carpenter had their second big break. Dallas vice was familiar with Marcia and knew that she had run for a long time with a man named Bobby Vandiver. Vandiver would be "armed, dangerous, and reckless" they said, as "both Bobby and Marcia had lived outside the law for years." Marcia plied her trade hustling tricks, while Bobby, an ex-con, added to his police record living on the edge.

Carpenter and Gamino focused in on Marcia's past. Another monumental break: They discovered Marcia had close ties to a former madam by the name of Lilla Paulus. Marcia had even lived with Lilla at one time. Lilla

Paulus was well-known to Houston Vice. Carpenter learned that Lilla was connected with some houses of prostitution in Galveston. Further, the officers discovered Lilla Paulus had a long-term friendship with none other than Ash Robinson, Joan Hill's father. Now it was all beginning to make sense. Ash Robinson made no secret he was out to try to have John Hill indicted. Perhaps, after the mistrial, Ash Robinson wasn't going to rely on the justice system to get justice.

After the hit on Hill, Bobby and Marcia took off west and didn't stop driving until they hit California.

Even though the two were waiting for things to cool down and trying to avoid capture, crazy Bobby found time to pull a bank robbery in L.A. Next, he and Marcia drove back to Dallas and settled down there for a season.

Marcia and Bobby had not been in Dallas long when Bobby told an acquaintance that he had shot and killed a man in Houston. The acquaintance turned out to be a part-time informant for the Dallas police. Dallas PD called Carpenter and Gamino, who drove to Dallas, found Bobby, and arrested him. They charged him with the murder of Dr. Hill.

After Bobby was arrested he was positively identified in a lineup by both John Hill's mother and his son Robert. Confronted with eyewitnesses and the identification of the gun which could be placed in his girlfriend's hand and found near the victim's house, Bobby confessed. He implicated Lilla Paulus. Then Carpenter and Gamino went to Bob Bennett in our Organized Crime Unit to fill him in.

Bob assured Marcia that our office would cut a good deal for her if she told all and was willing to testify in court. Marcia agreed.

She confessed that it was her friend, Lilla Paulus, who asked her if she knew a good hit man. Marcia then told Lilla that her boyfriend Bobby Vandiver could handle the job for her. "He was a cool guy and willing to do anything for money."

Now we had the hit man, the go-between prostitute, and the former madam who paid the hit man. But Bennett would not be satisfied unless he could indict and convict Ash Robinson himself, the man he understood had ordered the killing and paid the money.

As details unfolded, we learned that Lilla worked out a financial arrangement with Bobby Vandiver to assassinate Dr. Hill. Lilla, Marcia, and Vandiver had met, and it was Lilla who supplied Bobby with the details about John Hill's life, where he lived, where he worked, and his habits. Lilla learned Dr. Hill would be attending the medical convention in Las Vegas and would return on a particular day. Apparently she knew the flight number, enabling Vandiver to be inside the house holding Hill's mother and son hostage when the doctor walked through the door.

After the murder, Bobby used Dr. Hill's phone to call Marcia to pick him up. She did and they drove straight to Lilla's house where Lilla handed Bobby $5,000 cash in Marcia's presence. Bobby in turn handed a $1,500 "finder's fee" to Marcia. Bobby and Marcia were not inside Lilla's house more than two minutes before they left for California.

It did not take the investigation team long to learn that Ash Robinson and Lilla Paulus, the madam, had enjoyed a close relationship for many years. When police discovered that it was Ash's close friend Lilla Paulus who set up the assassination, Homicide believed Ash paid for the killing. To have any chance of getting to Lilla and hopefully to Ash, we had to make a deal with Bobby Vandiver so he would testify.

Bennett did just that. Vandiver would cooperate. Bobby had to tell all to the grand jury and then testify at trial.

We didn't like deals like this, of course, but our choices were limited. We could send Vandiver and Marcia to prison and let Lilla and Ash go. That would have been the easy thing to do. We had them cold. But if Ash was guilty then he was the cause of John Hill's assassination.

The next step was to talk to Lilla Paulus. Bob Bennett was willing to make a deal with her if that was the only way to get to Ash. Bob had Paulus brought in for questioning.

By this time Detectives Carpenter and Gamino had gathered a great deal of historical facts in the lives of Lilla and Ash Robinson. We could prove they had a long history and close friendship.

In spite of offering her a short prison sentence, Lilla Paulus would not talk. She would not cooperate. She remained loyal to Ash Robinson throughout all of the questioning and the trials to follow. In short, she was willing to serve the rest of her life in prison rather than deliver Ash to the criminal justice system.

Bobby Vandiver said Lilla told him that John Hill's former father-in-law, Ash Robinson, wanted Hill dead for killing his daughter. He dictated a detailed statement to that effect which was put in writing. Then Bobby signed his confession. Bennett secretly took the case to the Harris County grand jury.

Another good thing grand juries do is elicit sworn and secret testimony from a scared witness who doesn't want the world to know he is fingering someone.

Before Bennett went to the grand jury he had Bobby call Ash on the pretext he was looking for Lilla Paulus. Ash did not bite. He said he had not seen Lilla for six months and provided no other information. At least he admitted Lilla was his friend, but many in Houston already knew that.

Next, the police executed a search warrant at Lilla's home. They discovered several handwritten notes referring to Ash Robinson, enough for the necessary corroboration if Lilla agreed to testify.

Bob Bennett quickly secured a sealed indictment from the grand jury against Bobby Vandiver for murder. A sealed indictment stays sealed until ordered opened. A sealed indictment is not open to the press or anyone else. It prevents a defendant at large from getting wind he has been charged and then trying to flee.

In this case, the sealed indictment protected the State's star witness. If Ash paid for Hill's killing, he would have no trouble finding money to put an ex-con like Vandiver or his girlfriend away. Sealed indictments were also returned against Lilla Paulus and Marcia McKittrick for their part in the murder.

One night without notice Bob Bennett and the two detectives paid a surprise midnight visit on Ash Robinson at his River Oaks home. They told Ash they wanted to question him. Robinson was unflappable. He warned the three they had better not slander him.

Ash said, "I am not saying a word to you unless my lawyer is present."

A few weeks later, Ash, now realizing that he was under fire, flew to New York City to take a lie detector test. The examiner issued a written report saying Ash told the truth when he said he had nothing to do with the Hill assassination.

Lilla stood firm on her decision not to talk and denied knowing Ash.

When Marcia gave her sworn statement, she said she saw Ash the night he came to Lilla's house. He pulled out $7,000 in cash, counted out the bills, and handed the money to Lilla. The date of the exchange was shortly before John was assassinated. Marcia also said that on several previous occasions she saw Ash hand Lilla cash at Lilla's home. Who knows for what. Unfortunately, there was no independent corroboration outside these accomplice witnesses. Since, by law, one accomplice cannot corroborate another, we had no case against Ash Robinson.

Ash was playing it cool. He was getting the best of legal advice. He knew we only had accomplice testimony against him, and as long as Lilla stayed closed mouth, Ash was going to walk.

At this point, Percy Foreman entered the case to represent Lilla Paulus. We wondered if Ash had paid Foreman's fee. Ash was known to be a multimillionaire, even wealthy enough to afford Percy.

Bobby Vandiver remained free on bond. We kept it a secret that he was cooperating with us and would be one of our main witnesses. For some reason, Bobby Vandiver seemed desperate to get out of Houston and go back to Dallas. Bennett finally gave him permission and advised him to lay low. If he surfaced, his life might be short.

A hearing was set in Lilla Paulus' case. At 9:00 A.M. on the morning of the hearing, court was called to order but there was no Bobby Vandiver.

Bennett asked for a recess.

A quiet and cool guy, Bennet was burning inside. He had Carpenter and Gamino put out an "all points" all over Texas and L.A. for Bobby Vandiver.

Dallas police began combing Vandiver's old haunts. One running buddy of Bobby's said he left town a few days ago to go to Houston. This information prompted Houston homicide detectives to cover all possible routes between Dallas and Houston. Their plan was to stop in every café and gas station anywhere along the way. They would cover all trails like a blanket.

An HPD detective was checking out the town of Longview, a possible place where a motorist might stop on the way from Dallas to Houston. He spotted a roadside café and went in and introduced himself to the owner. He pulled out the picture of Bobby and said, "Have you possibly seen this guy come in to your place in the last few days?"

The manager was taken aback.

He said, "I certainly have. Let me tell you about him. This man came to town and would stop in here to grab a bite to eat and shoot pool. Four days ago, he came in and ordered lunch. While waiting to be served, he got into a pool game at that pool table over there. I had never seen the guy he was playing pool with. While this guy in your picture was cueing up, a Longview policeman I know walked in the door. He saw your guy look at him suspiciously, so he goes over to check the man out. I was standing right here. That officer had not accused him of anything. This guy goes for a pistol just stuck in his pants. The officer was faster on the draw. He killed him. The police here can tell you all about it. By the way, why are you looking for this guy?"

Bob and I discussed why Vandiver would draw on an armed cop. I said it did not make sense. Bob in his dry way said, "Who knows but Bobby might know Ash better than we do. If he testified against Lilla or Ash his life might be short."

With the case falling apart, a determined Bennett got ready for trial against Lilla Paulus. In the meantime Percy Foreman bowed out of the case in favor of his young law partner, Dick DeGuerin, a former assistant DA and quickly becoming one of Houston's best defense attorneys.

The judge in the case was one of my former assistants, Frank Price, a former state champion in handball. In fact he had played handball with both Bob Bennett and Dick DeGuerin in the past. In spite of news media accounts of wars between prosecutors and defense attorneys, most of the better lawyers on both sides are friends who enjoy exchanging war stories and then go after it tooth and nail in trial.

The question was, did the State have enough evidence to corroborate Marcia McKittrick and get a conviction against Lilla Paulus upheld on appeal? I thought this would be one tough climb, but Bennett went after it.

As Paulus' trial began, Bob told me Marcia McKittrick might back out. She would not tell him whether she would go through with testifying against Lilla Paulus. She told Bob, "You will have to put me on the stand to know what I have to say." At best she was being obstinate.

The trial began. He called Marcia to the stand. She came through and made a most believable witness.

After the State rested its case, Lilla Paulus took the stand and denied knowing Ash Robinson in the face of great evidence to the contrary.

Bennett found two willing witnesses who came forward and said they had both seen Ash and Lilla talking at various social events around town.

Lilla was an unusual personality, particularly for an ex-madam. By now she had a lovely daughter who attended the prestigious St. John's School. Lilla also ran with some well-connected and well-respected people. One witness, however, testified that Lilla always carried a pistol around with her. The jury also heard testimony Lilla had been engaged in prostitution some years before.

The jury did not buy Lilla's story.

In a dramatic turn of events, Lilla's daughter agreed to testify against her mother. She testified her mother forced her into acts of prostitution with older men when she was only a very young child, then did it again when she was only eleven years old. The jury had no problem finding Lilla guilty and assessing her punishment at thirty-five years in prison. Even after her sentencing she remained stubbornly loyal to Ash. We would have cut a sweet deal to get to Ash, but she remained mute.

In the end, we were never able to make a case on Ash Robinson. His handing over the money to Lilla Paulus was not enough. After Lilla's multiple appeals, her conviction was finally affirmed and she entered prison.

The case of John Hill vividly illustrates the crucial role of the grand jury in the investigation of crime as well as deciding whether to indict or not. I wish every citizen could serve three months on a grand jury and have their eyes opened about the other side of the law. I have not met one person who did not enjoy his or her grand jury experience.

CHAPTER FIFTEEN

The Payoff of a District Judge

*Do not accept a bribe for a bribe blinds the eyes of the wise
and twists the words of the righteous.*
—Deuteronomy 16:17

MOVING RIGHT ALONG, I tuned to KTRH once again. The newscaster said a robber had just been sentenced to fifty years for shooting a convenience store clerk during a hold up. This clerk had survived. I guess it was the sentence that caught my attention. On any given day some eighteen district judges would average sentencing a hundred defendants convicted of felonies. Roughly half would be sent to prison while the remaining half received probation.

The numbers of defendants going through our courts was staggering. Our judges earned their keep, and we were fortunate to have honest judges. A bedrock requirement for any city, state, or nation to prosper is honest government, including an honest judiciary. Bribes and payoffs are a way of life in many countries. The greatest single factor that keeps a Third World country a Third World country is corruption. Nothing brings a nation to its knees faster than corruption, whether it is in business, law enforcement, or the judiciary.

Until the Garth Bates case, there had not been a blight on any of our criminal judges in Harris County.

IN TEXAS AND IN Harris County we took pride in an honest judiciary. Most of our judges I knew were very competent and meted out rulings and punishments in a reasonably consistent manner.

Judge Ed Duggan bragged on how his court, Criminal District Court, was the oldest court in Texas. This court was so old it did not have a number, simply "Criminal District Court." I had been chief in that court when Judge Duggan swore me in as DA. Later the legislature came along and gave many of the Texas courts new numbers. This court became the 174th District Court, but it still had a special place in my heart.

When Duggan retired, Governor Preston Smith appointed Garth Bates as judge of the 174th District Court. Judge Bates hailed from a good family and had a strong track record of public service. Following military service in World War II, he became an assistant DA under Dan Jackson and then served under A.C. Winborn, two excellent district attorneys. Bates was then elected to the Texas legislature for two terms. In 1958 he was elected to the Houston City Council. After that, he practiced law and also served as a judge in one of the city's municipal courts.

After Judge Bates took the bench of the 174th District Court, he went out of his way to make friends with me. From the day he started, he projected a tough-on-crime image as he gave out heavier sentences than most judges. Defense attorneys dreaded having their clients' cases fall in his court. They couldn't fall back on the mercy of this judge if plea bargaining failed. Other than perhaps being too tough, he seemed conscientious and it appeared like he was trying to do a good job.

Judge Bates had served two years on the bench when a bomb was dropped on our office on a cold day in March. A vice squad sergeant walked into Special Crimes to see the chief, Assistant DA Bob Bennett. The sergeant said he was on a sensitive mission and could only talk to Bob.

Special Crimes had a good reputation for keeping confidential matters confidential and was relied on heavily by law enforcement officers throughout the county. More than once, officers who thought they were onto something sensitive would bypass their own chain of command and make their way to Special Crimes to pass on the information and get practical advice. Special Crimes and Organized Crime kept up with all kinds of criminal activity. Nothing took higher priority in our office than public corruption or organized crime.

The vice squad officer told Bob that a reliable informant of his had a friend by the name of Nukie Fontenot, better known as Frenchie. Frenchie was under indictment for armed robbery, and his case was pending in Judge Bates' court.

Frenchie had heard that Judge Bates threw the book at armed robbers so he was expecting a long sentence. Frenchie also knew our office was tough on armed robbers and had a policy against recommending probation for armed robbery. So he knew if he got convicted he was on his way to prison. Seldom did an armed robber—even a first offender—walk out of a courtroom in Harris County on probation. A guy driving the getaway car might get jail time and probation but not the man who stuck the gun in the clerk's face. And the man who masterminded an armed robbery was really in trouble.

Frenchie Fontenot was a businessman with a jewelry business; however, committing a crime on the side was not beneath him. One day a jewelry wholesaler walked into Fontenot's shop and showed him a large display of diamonds and other jewelry. Frenchie called on a couple of buddies to rob the salesman.

The buddies were caught, and the pair, along with Frenchie, were indicted for armed robbery. Henry Oncken was the chief prosecutor in the 174th District Court where the case fell. Henry tried the two robbers, who both received long prison sentences. Now Frenchie was the only defendant left, and he was the mastermind. Frenchie Fontenot had three choices: do a plea bargain, go to a jury, or take his chances with the judge. Each choice had "long prison sentence" written all over it.

By the strangest of coincidences, Frenchie had a friend by the name of Ed Riklin, who in turn just happened to be a close friend of Judge Bates, the judge of the court where Frenchie's case had randomly fallen. Ed Riklin played gin rummy with the judge almost daily and was also a daily visitor in Bates' courtroom. I have never known any other judge who had a friend who would come up to the courtroom for a daily visit. Riklin also seemed to have the run of the courtroom and spent considerable time chatting with Bates in the judge's chambers where the two were alone.

The vice officer informed Bob Bennett that Riklin had approached Fontenot and said, "I am a close friend of Judge Bates. If you can come up with sixty grand, I can assure you that Bates will give you probation."

Riklin went on to tell Frenchie about this special relationship he had with the judge. Riklin told Frenchie that he went down to Judge Bates' court almost every morning and knew everything that was going on.

After the vice squad officer received this information, he did his homework and learned that Riklin was a professional gambler. His only visible means of support was his ability to play cards.

Bennett was shocked of course. Judges in Harris County and Texas or almost anywhere in the U.S. just don't take bribes.

He also considered the thought that the whole thing could be a set up. Even if we bankrolled Frenchie to pay the $60,000 to Riklin, Riklin might simply take the money and leave town and never call the judge. Besides, if Bates was on the take and accepted bribes with any regularity, word would have been out on the street. At this point, no one had even heard a bad rumor about the judge.

Bob knew the last thing any of us wanted to do was to investigate a judge unless the judge was guilty and we could make a case; then we would want to rid the bench of that judge as quickly as possible.

Even if the information was true, putting together a case would be difficult. If we tried and failed, our office would look like grandstanders trying to unfairly take out a judge we did not like. These cases are hard to make, because the State can't make a case on accomplice testimony alone. We would need far more than Frenchie's testimony to corroborate the charge. Anyone participating in a scam is an accomplice, so Frenchie Fontenot would be an accomplice, even if he paid the judge money under our direction.

Special Crimes ran Frenchie on a lie detector test. When he passed, I said we should move forward. Bob and I understood any investigation could be a very slippery slope.

The next step was to quietly investigate Ed Riklin. He was forty-five years old and had a small police record, having pled guilty in the past to possessing gambling paraphernalia. He drove a new Cadillac and was known to carry a pistol. He was once arrested for toting a .38 revolver, but he was not convicted.

Riklin lived in an upscale apartment over on McCue Street in the shadows of the Galleria. He did not show any sign of employment of any kind. We could only surmise his gin rummy skills kept him afloat. But it did not make sense he was making a living off of playing gin when he was tied up most afternoons playing gin with the judge. Certainly the judge wasn't losing enough money every day to finance Riklin's lifestyle. Hopefully the judge was not stupid enough to keep on donating to a much better gin player. Maybe this bribery scheme could be a recent thing where Riklin had been developing this relationship with the judge in order to start setting up payoffs. One thing for sure is that gamblers never have enough money, so Riklin would always be trying to hustle a buck.

As far as we knew at that time, the judge did not have any financial troubles. We did make one error of omission. We did not go check the clerk's office to see if the judge had any civil judgments. Later on we were shocked at what we found.

Another insight into Riklin's character came unexpectedly from our Consumer Fraud Section, which was a part of the Special Crimes Bureau. A good number of complainants had come into our offices recently to complain to Assistant DA Wendell Odom, Jr., that Riklin has sold them insurance policies covering future repairs on their automobiles. Each of these complainants had his car break down after taking out a policy, but the policy never paid off. When these complainants tried to find Riklin or the business office of this insurance company, they came up blank. They wanted Consumer Fraud to investigate and prosecute Riklin. Those complaints confirmed again the judge was running in questionable company.

When Odom ran Riklin down to ask him about the matter and give him a chance to explain, Riklin ran to Judge Bates for help.

Incredibly, one morning Judge Bates called Wendell Odom on the telephone and ordered him to come to his courtroom. When Odom walked into the courtroom, the judge stopped his ongoing proceedings and said, "Mr. Odom, I vouch for Ed Riklin. I vouch for Ed Riklin." That was all the judge said. Wendell shook his head and walked away from this bizarre encounter.

The judge never spoke to Wendell again about the matter. Wendell got the message: The judge wanted him to lay off Riklin. So Wendell put his investigation in high gear, although he knew nothing about the secret investigation of Bates at this point. Bennett had to slow Wendell down as he did not want a consumer fraud case to mess up what could be a more important bribery charge against one of our sitting judges.

Bennett put a surveillance on Riklin's apartment. Most days after court adjourned, Judge Bates drove over to Riklin's place. The judge's Cadillac would be sitting on the street outside the apartment for several hours while, presumably, they played gin. Then Bates would head home around supper time.

Thus far, everything the informant had told the vice officer was true. What a judge does on his own time is up to him, but whiling away the afternoons with a professional gambler with a police record was not a prudent move.

Shortly thereafter, a coincidental circumstance got Assistant DA Henry Oncken's attention. Henry was the chief prosecutor in Judge Bates' court. He went down to First Assistant Sam Robertson's office to tell Sam that Bates put pressure on the Harris County Probation Department to hire a friend of his as his probation officer. The man, a Mr, Brown, did not have to go through the usual interviews the probation office required. It was also most apparent the man had no qualifications to be a probation officer. Past law

enforcement experience and/or a degree in Psychology or Criminal Justice
was usually called for.

After Judge Bates got Mr. Brown hired, the judge called a probation
supervisor to get Brown assigned to his court. Once in his court, Bates kept
the guy busy running personal errands and assisting the judge with paperwork on the judge's outside investments. Brown should have come to the
courtroom one or two mornings a week when the probations were handed
out; the rest of the time he should have been over in his probation office or
out in the field. He could not do his work because Judge Bates was ordering
him around and telling him how to spend his time; unfortunately, that time
was being spent on the judge's business. No one knew when Brown had time
to do real work like other probation officers.

We checked Brown's qualifications. As far as we could tell, he had none.
When First Assistant Robertson heard Henry Oncken's summary of
the probation situation, Sam sent him to talk to Bob Bennett. "Why Bob
Bennett?" Henry wondered as he headed up to Special Crimes.

Henry dropped into Bob's office and said "Sambo says I need to tell you
some stuff about Judge Bates."

Bennett quietly got up and shut his door.

From this visit on, Henry was part of the Bates investigation team. Henry
would keep tabs on the judge in the courtroom and look out for unusual
sentences and unusual characters hanging around court. Henry was to report
when the judge came and went.

Johnny Holmes, who was second in command of Special Crimes and
headed up our Organized Crime Section, was already working closely with
Bennett on the case. (Henry's part in the case eventually led to a transfer to
that bureau. Soon Henry headed up Major Frauds and later he was promoted
to chief of the Special Crimes Bureau. After Holmes became DA, Henry
served as First Assistant, then left the office to be a district judge and later
served as United States Attorney for the Southern District of Texas.)

During the Bates investigation, Henry reported the judge was now
trying to employ Riklin as one of his court personnel. This was confirmed
when Chief Deputy Sheriff Gus George told us Judge Bates had called him
requesting that Riklin be hired as bailiff in his court. Gus was mad as a wet
hen about that and thought it highly improper the judge would ask the
sheriff to hire a man with no law enforcement background for that position.
Gus was not just a little upset when he discovered that Riklin was a gambler
with a police record. When he called me I wanted to tell him what was going

on, but it was never a good idea to share this kind of information, even to one I trusted a hundred percent. Gus declined the judge's request with pleasure.

Taking a risk, Bennett asked for the two robbery detectives who had worked on the jewelry robbery to be assigned temporarily to Special Crimes to work on the Bates case. We knew them both, great guys and dedicated. Detectives Earl Musick and Sam Nuchia were added to the Special Crimes team. (Later Musick was permanently assigned to work with us in Special Crimes while Nuchia went on to get a law degree, became Chief of Police for the City of Houston and then served for years on the Texas Court of Appeals.)

Musick and Nuchia were instructed to talk to Frenchie about the bribe offer but not to talk about his robbery case. Frenchie had a lawyer in that case, and we did not want to mess up the robbery case.

When they confronted Frenchie with the story that he had been solicited to pay a large sum of money to obtain a probated sentence, Fontenot didn't argue. Without blinking he said it was true and he would do whatever the officers wanted. His only request was that his attorney be present when the ultimate plan was worked out. Frenchie Fontenot had plenty of street smarts.

He knew even without our telling him that we would not send him, a snitch, to prison, if he cooperated and we nailed a crooked judge. He knew he was making the deal of a lifetime, and that we would be delighted to sacrifice a robber for a district judge. Besides, when Fontenot received that ten years probation, he would have to tow the line.

The investigation moved fast. The plan was to have Frenchie meet with Riklin and record the conversation. Frenchie would be wired for sound. Fontenot was to say that $60,000 was all the money he had in the world and that he needed to make certain he had a deal if he were to make that kind of payoff. Frenchie would demand to know every detail and be present to see Riklin pass off the money to the judge. Of course, Special Crimes would be waiting in the wings in the surveillance van taking pictures and following the judge after the handoff.

And if it turned out to be just a scam by Riklin, then we would use the evidence to put him away for a long time based on the recordings and the forthcoming payoff.

Bob and team patiently waited for Riklin to make contact with Fontenot. Five days went by with no word. Was Riklin wise to Fontenot? Not likely. But Riklin might be scared of a bug on the phone; perhaps the judge would not be.

Bennett decided to gamble. He told Frenchie to call Judge Bates directly at his courthouse chambers. We would record every word. This is legal in Texas and most states so long as one party to the conversation consents to the recording. Frenchie was ready to roll.

Our Organized Crime Division had some fairly sophisticated equipment for that day, courtesy of the LEAA grant. The next morning, after the judge showed up for work, Frenchie made the call. The clerk answered and told Frenchie that court was in session, but he would buzz the judge out on the bench. Surprisingly, Judge Bates took the call, not having any idea that every word was being taped.

Fontenot began, "This is Frenchie Fontenot. I have been talking to Ed."

Judge Bates said, "I don't want any conversation with you. I just don't want to talk about your case. If you do, I'll have to send it to another judge."

After bantering around with Fontenot, Bates said, "You were indicted on one count and they changed it."

That was an unusual statement for the judge to make. He probably had five hundred cases pending in his court and would have no way to know the facts about any of these cases unless some motion or hearing was held in his presence. Frenchie had not been to court. The judge would have to go way out of his way to know about Frenchie's case.

After the call, Bob gave me a copy of the tape. I played it over and over. When I listened to the tape, I thought it not only unusual for the judge to know about the case, but the judge never asked, "Frenchie who?" He knew from that first sentence exactly who Fontenot was. We also concluded from those few words that he associated Frenchie with his friend Ed Riklin.

The biggest indicator of all that the judge was involved was the fact that he did not stop the conversation immediately and report it to the DA's office. Any honest judge would be shocked out of his boots for a defendant to call him directly.

But that was not the end. They went on.

Judge Bates told Frenchie, "Now I understand Ed (Riklin) has discussed your friendship with him and he is a man you can trust. Ed is a man that I trust. I would trust the fellow."

Why would the judge tell a defendant whom he is not even supposed to be talking to in the first place that he could trust the judge's friend? It was clear to all of us the judge was trying to communicate that whatever Riklin had to say about the matter was true so you can go ahead and deal with him. If there was a payoff to the judge later, I thought this conversation alone would probably be enough corroboration to uphold a conviction against Judge Bates.

Frenchie was cool. Before he hung up, he said to the judge, "He (Riklin) is trying to get $60,000 out of me."

Finally the judge said, "All right now, I'm not going to talk to you anymore. If you give me any indication of what the hell Ed's involvement is, I'm going to have to disqualify myself. I'm not going to say anymore."

In other words, the judge was saying, I know what this $60,000 is all about and you just do as Ed tells you; but if you talk to me about it anymore the deal is off.

At even the hint of a bribe, any honest judge would have gone into shock. He would have reported it to the chief judge and the DA. He would disqualify himself in the case and offer to appear before a grand jury. He would also have cited the individual for contempt and had another judge handle that. He would summon the guy's defense attorney of record to report to court so he could inform him of the situation and chew him out.

Further, why did the judge use the words "Ed's involvement" unless the judge knew his friend Ed was up to his neck in this? A judge doesn't talk to a defendant about his case any time other than in open court, in the presence of the defendant's lawyer.

But still the judge let this conversation continue.

Fontenot: "Why don't you get with Ed and let Ed handle it?"

Bates: "Well, all right."

Fontenot: "I want insurance if I am going to put out anything. That's all I'm asking for. I don't want to go to the pen for something like that."

Bates: "Well, I know it."

Later Bates said, "You have received very fair treatment so far, haven't you? If Ed wants to talk to me, I will talk to him anytime."

What more could Judge Bates have said to confirm to Fontenot that he was not only aware of the bribery but standing behind it? By the time I heard this much of the conversation, I knew that, even if we could not make a case due to lack of corroboration, we could turn the tape over to the Texas Judicial Commission, make Frenchie available as a witness, and Judge Bates would be defrocked and disbarred. They would have no choice except to remove Bates once this tape went public. Even so, we proceeded forth as this was a serious crime deserving more than removal.

The conversation closed on a high note.

Fontenot: "I have got the damn money."

Bates: "Well."

Fontenot: "I met with my man this morning."

Bates: "I don't know what you are talking about. Now listen, I'm not going to talk to you anymore. Otherwise I would have to disqualify myself. Do you understand that?"

Fontenot: "I understand."

Bates: "Thank you."

Fontenot: "Thank you, sir."

After the phone call, we doubled the watch on the apartment. When Bates got through with court at noon that day, he drove up to Riklin's apartment some twenty minutes later.

Quite frankly, I thought that Bates would jump all over Riklin for letting Frenchie call him like that. I also thought the judge would be spooked by Fontenot's call and call the deal off. He could still cover his tracks by making a report, turning it over to our office and claiming he just played along to catch a guy in a bribery attempt.

We also expected Riklin to call Fontenot and chew him out for calling the judge. If so, Fontenot stood ready to record that conversation as well.

Riklin did make that call, but it came days and not hours later. Riklin told Fontenot to have no further contact with Judge Bates.

My surprise on that tape was to hear Riklin tell Frenchie everything was still a "go." Bates was obviously a risk taker. Maybe he was desperate for money. Clearly Bates could see by now that Frenchie was not only a hijacker but a loose cannon who could bring him down.

Riklin ended the conversation by telling Frenchie he was not ever to use the telephone to call the judge again, saying, "I am afraid of wiretaps." Before Riklin hung up, he and Fontenot scheduled a face-to-face meeting.

Before that meeting, Fontenot had to appear before Judge Bates for the purpose of posting a new bond of $20,000. Fontenot's attorney requested the court enter an order reducing the bond to a lesser amount. Judge Bates agreed. This was not something the judge normally did for an accused armed robber. Immediately after the bond reduction was ordered, Riklin called Fontenot to take full credit for the judge's ruling. Riklin wanted to make certain Fontenot knew that he had close ties with the judge.

Before the meeting between Frenchie and Riklin, Bennett and team wired Fontenot. Bennett sent Fontenot to a friendly doctor who put a cast on Fontenot's arm. Frenchie's arm was not broken, but it was a good place to bury a mike.

The doctor, wanting to help the DA's office, not only provided the free service but wrote out a one-page "diagnosis" so Frenchie could prove to Riklin he really did have a broken arm from "unloading hay from his pick up." Bennett and Holmes left nothing to chance.

The meeting took place at the El Chico's Restaurant in the Northwest Mall. Riklin was on time. When he drove up, our guys noticed he was sporting a new two-tone blue Cadillac.

Riklin and Fontenot sat down. After a minute of small talk, Riklin told Frenchie it was going to take $30,000 up front to make sure that Fontenot would get his probated sentence. He told Fontenot this was a good deal because this judge comes down hard on armed robbers. Riklin advised Fontenot to sell his business and get the money; otherwise, he was on his way to prison.

After hearing this tape, Special Crimes decided to bring the investigation to closure and make the case against the judge.

Frenchie, following Bennett's instruction, told Riklin that he could come up with the money—all $60,000—but with conditions. "First," Fontenot informed the go-between, "I am going to put the cash in my safety deposit box in the Northwest Bank, the one over there," he said, pointing to the bank in the corner of the shopping center.

"Next, I am going to have to see you hand the money over to the judge. So if you and the judge don't show up in this parking lot where I can see all of that, we don't have a deal. I have to know the judge is in on this. I'll stay out of sight on the parking lot while this all takes place. I can't afford to pay all this money unless I make sure the judge gets his so he will actually give me probation."

Bennett and group figured that if Judge Bates would talk so boldly on the phone, he would make that trip to the shopping center. Then our guys would be close at hand inside Special Crime's unmarked van taking pictures. We would also tape everything Fontenot said to Riklin. Maybe we could catch the judge on tape if he came up and said something to Riklin or Fontenot. The tape, coupled with catching a payoff on film, should cement the case.

A week later, Fontenot met Riklin at El Chico's again to finalize the details. As they ate Mexican food, Fontenot kept asking Riklin how he could be sure Bates would give him a probated sentence.

Riklin repeatedly reassured Fontenot of his close relationship with the judge. During this meeting Riklin went to a pay phone and called Judge Bates. Riklin had Fontenot listen in to hear the judge's voice.

After that we had one last summit meeting of all the players. Sam Robertson, Bennett, Holmes, Oncken, Sam Nuchia, Earl Musick, Ken Rodgers of Special Crimes, and I all went over the plan.

We had to come up with $60,000 cash to give to Frenchie to hand over to Riklin. Riklin said the money had to be in hundred dollar bills, and all of the cash would be handed over from Frenchie to Riklin at one time.

One problem: We did not have $60,000 in cash lying around our office to front the deal.

We had to find someone willing to lend us $60,000. We wanted to get the money right away so Fontenot could show it to Riklin. We knew when he told the judge that he had seen Frenchie with $60,000 and ready to roll, the judge's mouth would water. Hopefully this would move the judge to agree to show up at the scene the day the bribe took place.

Obtaining $60,000 in hundreds was a serious issue. Holmes went to our county judge, Jon Lindsay, who was a friend of our office. (Judge Lindsay helped chaired the Commissioners Court which ran the county. He did not sit as a judge in the normal sense of the word.) Lindsay had contacts in the financial world including banks the county parked money in. With one phone call six hundred crisp $100 bills were on their way.

Our plan may have been brilliant, but our office having responsibility for all those hundreds made me nervous. I could see the judge or his confederates making off with the money and it never being recovered. It would take years of fund-raisers to pay off the bank.

Bennett had even more reason to worry. When he went to the bank, he had to sign for the money. "Aw, Chief, don't worry. This is just pocket change," he said good-naturedly. "It would only take all of my salary for three years to pay it back."

Pursuant to the plan, Frenchie rented a safety deposit box at the Northwest National Bank in the shopping center close to El Chico's. The Northwest Mall was a good place for us. We could park the van along with other vehicles and do surveillance without looking suspicious. Several of our unmarked cars would be there ready to give chase.

Fontenot was to meet Riklin at the bank and then walk Riklin to the safety deposit box. Before the actual handoff of the cash to Riklin, Fontenot was going to demand that Riklin speak with Bates one last time. In this conversation Bates was to confirm that as soon as he got the money, the probated sentence was a done deal. During this proposed call Fontenot would demand that he be permitted to stand close to the phone to hear the judge's confirmation. Fontenot's wire would hopefully pick up the judge's voice.

If Bates did not agree to show up in the parking lot, the plan would be slightly altered. Fontenot would go to the safety deposit box, get the sixty grand and turn the money over to Riklin in the parking lot. The handoff and the conversation with Fontenot would be filmed and recorded. Then we would arrest Riklin. We would then make a deal with Riklin. He could have a probated sentence if the judge went through with the deal and accepted the money from Riklin. We would wire Riklin when he went to his apartment and handed the money to the judge. We would arrest the judge with the money. All conversations between Riklin and Bates would be recorded as well. Of course we wanted Riklin, but we would have traded ten Riklins to get one bad judge out of office. The plan seemed foolproof, but we knew that the best laid plans of mice and men often go awry.

Things were set in place. Early the morning of the big day, a Special Crimes investigator made a photocopy of each of the $100 bills. Any money recovered from Riklin or the judge could then be identified by serial numbers. As he photocopied the bills, the investigator put the last ten $100 bills face down on the copy machine (all he could get on one sheet of paper). He pushed the button and made the copy but left the ten bills lying on the copy machine. That morning Special Crimes Assistant DA Ross Rommel arrived at work early, as was his practice. He went into the copy room to use the copier. When he pulled up the cover of the copier, he saw ten green pictures of Ben Franklin staring in his face. Later that morning when I heard the story, I told Sam Robertson, "Well, at least that is one thousand we don't have to worry about."

When Rommel told Holmes of the foul up, Holmes was pleased. Holmes said, "Why didn't I think of this? Giving the guy the cash a thousand short gives a reason for Frenchie to call the judge again to apologize for being a thousand short. We can tape the judge's response."

Except for the night of the TSU riot, the next several hours were my wildest day in the DA's office.

Surveillance teams moved out early to the Northwest National Bank location and to the Riklin apartment some ten miles away. Investigator Ken Rodgers reported first at 7:30 A.M. Ed Riklin, Judge Bates, and an unknown third party walked out of the Riklin apartment. They climbed into two separate vehicles and drove away.

Incredibly, Judge Bates was wearing the world's brightest blue jumpsuit and a red baseball hat. These baby blue, effervescent coverall jump suits were popular then. Such a get-up would make a person stand out in the crowd, and that must have been the judge's purpose. We surmised Bates did that so

Riklin could point him out on the parking lot. Obviously, the judge was going to miss court that morning.

Before anyone was supposed to show up at the Northwest Mall, Bob Bennett met Fontenot at 8:20 outside the bank. Bennett did not tell Fontenot about the one grand shortfall. When the bank opened its doors at 8:30, the two men entered the bank. Bob Bennett handed Fontenot the money and kept a watchful eye as Fontenot put stacks of hundreds in his new safety deposit box. Then the wait began.

At 9:00—right on time—Riklin drove his new Caddy into the shopping center. He was alone. Fontenot gave him a signal and went inside the bank to retrieve the cash from the box, which he handed off to Riklin.

Fontenot had been instructed to get Riklin into conversation, and he did. Riklin did not seem apprehensive.

As the two talked, Riklin opened up on what the money was going to be used for. He volunteered that he and the judge were to share the proceeds. That gave us more than we needed to show Riklin was involved in a felony conspiracy to bribe a judge.

Then came the shocker.

Before they finished talking, Judge Bates himself pulled up in his Cadillac. Driving merrily along in his bright blue jumpsuit and red cap, the judge nearly ran over Bennett and Nuchia as he came around the corner. Then he maneuvered his car to a parking spot some distance from the bank. Bob Bennett was well-known to all the judges in the courthouse, but his face must not have registered with the judge that morning. With a clear view to observe Riklin and Fontenot, the judge saw Fontenot hand the money to Riklin. Our video camera caught the judge looking right at Riklin and Fontenot during the exchange.

The judge's showing up was a surprise, but we were ready. We speculated that if Bates came on to the scene, Riklin would hand Bates his half in the parking lot. Then we would swoop down on both of them and arrest them with the money in their hands. The Special Crimes team was not going to arrest Bates unless he had the money on him—and we desperately needed to get the money back!

Then came another shocker.

Riklin did not hand off the money to the judge. In fact, he made no contact with him, whatsoever. Riklin got into his car and drove off with the $60,000. Bates waited a few seconds and then he took off.

At this point, we had lost the money. Our cars took chase, but their attempt to follow was unsuccessful. They lost both Riklin and Bates.

I was back in my office getting a blow-by-blow from one of the car phones out on the scene. The worst possible scenario had occurred. No arrest and no money. We knew that Judge Bates had a ranch outside of LaGrange, some hundred miles northwest of Houston. We also knew where Bates lived, and we knew the most likely meeting spot would be the Riklin apartment. But they could have pre-arranged a meeting anywhere. We did not have a clue.

Sam Nuchia called HPD headquarters and requested helicopters. HPD refused to help unless they were told why we needed the helicopters to look for two cars. This was not an unreasonable position for HPD to take, but I knew their leadership was highly embarrassed the next morning. When HPD refused us, we immediately contacted the Texas Department of Public Safety (DPS).

DPS had two choppers in the air in a minute, no questions asked. They also posted patrol cars to report on any cars coming and going at Bates' ranch. The McCue Street apartment and the Bates home were covered, as well.

Minutes became hours. It seemed like forever. I looked down at my watch and it was only 10:30 A.M. Then out of the blue, Judge Bates arrived at his home. A few minutes later he left the house. He had changed clothes and had on a suit. Our tail at the house lost the judge in traffic. Real-life car pursuits are far different than the movies.

The clock moved, but slowly. The guys were doing all the work; I was only sitting by the phone feeling helpless. With each passing hour our chances of recovering the money or making a solid case was going from slim to none.

Looking at my watch, I noticed it was 2:00 P.M., a full five hours since Riklin had met Frenchie. Some of our guys were set up on Interstate 10, since we knew that was the route Bates would have to take to get to his ranch outside LaGrange. Meanwhile, Johnny Holmes, Henry Oncken, and a state highway patrolman were set up on Interstate 45. The judge also had property up north of Houston in Trinity County and could possibly pass by there. Holmes and Oncken were hoping against hope that something good would happen.

While seated on the side of I-45, a radio call came in to their vehicle: Riklin had just driven up to his apartment.

Holmes and Oncken headed there as fast as they could. After they arrived, they waited on the street, just one block from the Galleria shopping center.

Holmes said, "Wouldn't it be funny if the judge showed up?"

Then immediately he added, "There he is!"

Just before the judge drove up, Riklin had been caught red-handed. At 2:15 Riklin had pulled up to his apartment. Our guys were watching as he got out of his car carrying a sawed-off shotgun by his side. The weapon appeared to have a short enough barrel to be illegal. That gave our crew probable cause for a legal arrest and also good reason to obtain a search warrant. One of the team drove off to get the warrant.

HPD officer Bob Reese, who was on special assignment to the Special Crimes Bureau, was standing close by. He ordered Riklin to drop the gun. When Riklin raised the weapon, Reese pulled the trigger. There was a misfire; otherwise Riklin would have been dead on the spot. Riklin dropped the shotgun when he heard the click of Reese's gun. The DA's men took Riklin into custody. He was asked if we could search his apartment. He consented. Now we didn't even need a search warrant.

The team started going through everything in the four room apartment. Certainly some of the hundreds had to be hidden somewhere. Every drawer and cabinet had been opened and the bed taken apart. Nothing. Then one of our guys eyes the couch. He sticks his hand deep down into the side of the plush sofa. Bingo. Buried in the pocket was a large number of hundreds. Three hundred hundreds. Thirty grand. All of Riklin's share of the bribe.

It was at this time, before they could cart Riklin off to jail, that Judge Bates pulled up in front of Riklin's place. Detective Earl Musick approached Bates' car first. He looked in and saw that the judge had a loaded pistol lying in plain sight in his front seat.

"You are under arrest, Your Honor," Musick said.

The detective saw the judge trying to stuff his key ring into his coat pocket. Musick ran his arm inside the car and grabbed the keys from the judge's hand. Inside that same coat pocket were twenty-nine $100 bills.

Of course the bills' serial numbers matched up with the ones we'd photo-copied, as did the Riklin stash recovered from the couch. The case was made.

A significant chunk of change was missing, $26,100, to be exact. The $60,000 minus Riklin's $30,000, minus the $2,900 Judge Bates had on him, and of course the $1,000 left on the copy machine. I was still concerned about the missing money, but it was not the end of the world. Finding the money on the judge would show he was on the take. Somewhere and somehow we would come up with the missing money and pay back the bank. I wasn't above holding a barbecue and begging for contributions. Today, DAs have all kinds of confiscated crime funds where this whole thing would not have been an issue.

Later that day and the next the remaining pieces fell together. After the payoff at the bank, Bates and Riklin went to an office kept by the judge's probation officer, Mr. Brown. Brown said Bates and Riklin handed him $10,000 in hundred dollar bills to be applied toward Riklin's purchase of an apartment in a place called the Beaconsfield Apartments. At that time the judge had the property tied up under his contract of sale. Bates told Brown he was selling one of the apartments to Riklin, who would get credit for the $10,000 down payment. Brown was probably just a middleman in the apartment transaction.

Brown said that he was to purchase a cashier's check with the money and deliver the cashier's check to the title company to hold in escrow as part of Bates' down payment for the Beaconsfield. After getting this money back, our shortfall was only $16,100.

We took the case to the grand jury within record time. They heard the evidence and were outraged. Following the indictment, Joe Reynolds, an old friend and excellent lawyer, called to tell me he was representing Bates.

Joe made it clear a plea bargain was out. With Joe, I knew we had to prepare for war. He was a hard charger and ethical, but you had to sit up in your seat when he was on the other side.

After the case was set for trial, Judge Bates voluntarily stepped down from the bench. He made it clear this was temporary pending the outcome. With an acquittal he would be sitting again unless removed by the State Judicial Commission in some long and arduous procedure.

In the meantime, we were still missing a good amount of cash.

One day my good friend Clyde Wilson, the famous private eye, called me to have lunch at Maxim's.

He said he wanted to talk to me about a possible criminal investigation involving a corporate client taken for a bundle. Clyde always represented the prosecution side and was normally hired by lawyers representing large corporations who suffered high losses from some fraudulent scheme.

Clyde got to the restaurant fifteen minutes late. After lunch, I understood why. Clyde wanted to make sure I was not in when he stopped by my office. He asked my secretary if he could use my phone. While supposedly making a phone call, he was sticking an envelope with the missing hundreds in my top desk drawer. When I returned and opened my desk for something else, I saw the money.

I knew exactly what had happened, as the serial numbers on the bills confirmed. Reynolds, a close friend of Clyde's, wanted to get the money back to us, but in a way where we could not prove it came from either him or his client. Joe and Clyde knew I had enough evidence without this cash and would not bring the matter up and embarrass either one of them for doing a good deed. I tossed my Rolaids in the trash can and got ready for trial.

Right after the judicial qualifications hearing, the jury trial began. I was trying the case with Johnny Holmes riding shotgun. Johnny had done the hard work of getting the evidence and witnesses organized.

The judge's defense was there was no bribe; the money found in Bates' coat pocket came from Riklin and was to be applied on Riklin's purchase of apartments that the judge owned. The judge would admit to high stakes gin games with Riklin and would claim at trial that the $2,900 taken out of his pocket came off of some rich guy that Riklin had just cleaned out during a friendly gin game.

After we put on all of the tapes and testimony about the $60,000, Joe Reynolds had Bates tell the jury he had no reason to take a bribe as he was well off. Joe tried to convince the jury the judge married into money, made a good salary, and had no reason to jeopardize his illustrious career by taking a bribe. The problem with this defense was that, following the judge's indictment, an enterprising *Chronicle* reporter, Jan Sanders, wrote an article that Garth Bates had $192,000 worth of civil judgments against him. Most of the indebtedness came as a result of the judge's bad land deals. Special Crimes had done its own analysis about the judge's history of indebtedness.

At this point in the trial we had not introduced any of that evidence as it was not admissible until the judge put these facts in issue. We had some witnesses on call and ready to testify. One of our witnesses was a partner with one of Houston's major law firms. He represented the bank and testified that Bates owed a small fortune to the bank. The lawyer testified that the bank, after checking out the judge's financial situation, believed he was so broke that they gladly settled with Bates for ten cents on the dollar, I knew the jury would resent a judge getting off so lightly when they had to pay their bills in full. We also introduced the unpaid civil judgments, proving again the judge's dire financial world.

Near the end of the trial I had Bates on cross-examination for several hours. Bates got so flustered on the stand that his lawyer asked the judge for an early lunch break. Holmes reached over and said, "You got him going good. He's going to break. Don't let the judge recess."

I said, "Johnny, I can't believe we have done this good. I'm quitting while we're ahead."

Before the case went to the jury, we called a Mr. Howard to the stand. Howard previously had been indicted for theft, and his case fell in Judge Bates' court. He said Ed Riklin approached him one day in the courtroom to say that for $10,000 his case could be taken care of. Howard said he stepped up to the bench to tell the judge about this bizarre offer. The judge's off-the-wall comment was, "Myself and Mr. Riklin are looking into the matter and Mr. Riklin will be handling it from now on. Don't worry about it." Howard went on to receive a probated sentence, which was a normal sentence for his particular case; however, his testimony illustrated the sad state of affairs in Judge Bates' court.

After closing arguments the jury deliberated and came back shortly with guilty.

Under Texas law, the defendant gets to choose whether the judge or the jury assesses the penalty if he is convicted. Bates chose the judge. Judge John Barron assessed Bates' punishment at eight years in the pen. The maximum sentence was ten years. The punishment sent out the message that accepting a bribe was serious. The judge went to prison where he was a model inmate and was released early. Before he went to prison he appealed his conviction, but the Texas Court of Criminal Appeals said there were no errors at the trial.

Later on, Riklin was tried and convicted. Before the trial his lawyer, Mike Ramsey, filed a motion to have the originals of the tapes examined. The judge consented and selected an expert in Salt Lake City. Ramsey and Oncken flew to Salt Lake and spent three days there while the expert concluded the tapes were authentic. Turns out the expert performed the same chore in the Watergate scandal examining the Nixon tapes.

Judge Bates paid a high price as he gave up his freedom, his district judgeship, and his good name. Our system of justice depends on honest cops, prosecutors, and judges. Thank goodness the Bates saga was a rare occurrence. Our state is fortunate to have so many honest and capable judges serving the public. Dedicated judges normally work for less than they could make in private practice. Along with the public prosecutors, they are the backbone of our justice system. I took no pleasure in the Bates conviction, a sad day indeed. At the same time, Special Crimes, led by Bennett and Holmes, had done their duty and had taken substantial risks to get the job done. Without our Special Crimes Bureau, I doubt we would have made this case. Certainly the Special Crimes crew, who at times felt like the whole case was unraveling, had to enjoy the moment the judge pulled up with the money in his pocket, only to be greeted by two assistant DAs.

On a note of irony, just before the trial started, the Texas Judicial Qualifications Commission began a hearing to remove Bates from office.

Our office provided the evidence and the prosecutor, Henry Oncken. The proceedings were public. Between this hearing and the start-up of the trial, everyone in Harris County should have been familiar with Garth Bates, whose bizarre conduct had caused so many headlines. Yet when the election of our judges took place—right in the middle of the Bates trial—Judge Bates was re-elected by a huge margin. Little do voters know about judicial races.

CHAPTER SIXTEEN

The Other Side of the Bar

The way of a fool is right in his own eyes, but he who heeds counsel is wise.
—Proverbs 12:15

FINALLY GETTING CLOSE ENOUGH to use my car phone to report in, faithful secretary Judy noted that members of the staff were dropping by to take her on cross about the afternoon staff meeting. "Why is he doing a staff meeting with all of us?" (160 assistant DAs, plus investigators). "Why on a Friday afternoon?" "And after his long Henley trial. What's up?"

"I'll tell them when I get there." I got to thinking how I was going to miss the office, the excitement and the constant mix of sarcasm and humor from my irreverent staff. Going to practice law in lower downtown I was going to have to change my dress. Dark blue suits, black shoes, and starched white shirts were in at Bracewell, while my double-knit sport coats were headed for Goodwill—that is, if they would take them. And I would have to go to Norton Ditto and pay a fortune for silk ties with the little patterns. At least my narrow dollar ties from the Tie Rack store had been dropped on Ted Busch three or four at a time each year to honor his birthday. Instead of being insulted, Ted wore the darn things. I would miss those scenes, even those non-conformist characters from the defense bar.

On the civil side of the law the atmosphere was more civil. Civil trial lawyers were generally more reserved and soft-spoken, not taken to outrageous statements, wild stories, spontaneous reactions, and the like. The average criminal defense attorney handled a large number of cases each year, and prosecutors often tried cases with only a short interview of the victim the day of trial. On the civil side, everyone knew in advance every answer to every significant question and then some. Depositions, interrogatories, and document production drained the suspense from an otherwise good drama. Additionally, those civil cases usually settled. The civil court judges seemed to have more vacant courtrooms during the week than across the street.

SOME OF THE MOST unforgettable characters I ever knew were defense attorneys.

The legendary Percy Foreman, one of the nation's top criminal lawyers, had to top the list. With his immense head full of shaggy hair flopping to the side, Percy's strolling into the courtroom was an event. His massive, six foot four frame announced his presence, followed with a deep jolly laugh and flowing sarcasm. Then Percy would flop back his long blonde-grey hair with his hand while the clerk, judge, and prosecutor waited to be entertained.

Percy did not like to lose a case to you, but please don't ignore him. He wallowed in the limelight wherever he moved. Even judges who were intent on moving the proceedings along paused in reverence when Foreman addressed the court.

Percy was gifted with a photographic memory. Total recall for every word uttered by every witness, even in a long trial. Unlike today's criminal lawyers in a high profile case, he went to trial without a single lawyer by his side. He might have his regular entourage of divorce clients and other hangers-on following him around, though. For the trial the only equipment or papers Percy brought to court were a blank yellow legal pad and a dozen highly sharpened No. 2 pencils. And if he wrote down more than a handful of words, that was rare.

My first trial with Percy was a murder case in Judge Langston King's court. I was the number two man at that time. My good friend Tommy Dunn was my chief prosecutor. Tommy carried the lead in the case but let me question some witnesses and make our final closing argument.

Tommy and I faced off against Percy with what we considered an open-and-shut murder case. Our poor victim had been unarmed. The defendant had killed him with multiple shots from an army .45, seemingly without reason. Tommy and I speculated how Percy would try to walk this client.

Foreman was representing a mild-mannered, middle-aged black man who had been a postman for thirty years. He had no criminal record, not so much as a traffic ticket.

The deceased was a younger black man and very large. He had a long criminal record with about a dozen arrests and two assault convictions, one ending up with a short stint in prison.

Naturally we took the position the deceased's past record had nothing to do with the killing and should not mentioned to the jury. We prevailed on Judge King to instruct Percy not to refer to those arrests or convictions without first approaching the bench.

Two witnesses in the apartment where the event took place testified they overheard a loud argument between the postman and the deceased over some money the dead man supposedly owed the postman; but neither witness heard any threats nor saw any acts of aggression by either man.

As the trial began, our first two witnesses were police officers who painted the scene and discussed their findings. With each officer Percy picked up the rap sheet of the deceased and walked up and down in front of the jury carrying it in his hand. The jurors all stared to see what it was. The criminal record was two pages long, stapled together and on legal size sheets, fourteen inches long. Percy would grip the end of the first page making the second page drag the floor.

"Judge, Mr. Foreman is exhibiting inadmissible evidence to the jury and we asked you to tell him to stop," Tommy protested.

"What do you have in your hand, Mr. Foreman?" Judge King asked.

"Just the deceased's criminal record, Your Honor. I assure this court I am not going to read anything about the deceased's long history of criminal violence to this jury. And judge, the jury is too far away to read about all of these arrests and convictions, anyway."

"Mr. Foreman, now don't do anything improper and let's move on, gentlemen."

"Judge, would you instruct him not to do that?" Tommy asked again.

"Mr. Foreman, put those papers away and don't refer to that criminal record anymore."

"Certainly, Judge. I will be more than pleased not to have to ever go into this man's sordid past again."

"That is enough, Mr. Foreman. Put the record away and don't refer to it anymore."

"Yes, Your Honor."

"Detective Barclay," Percy said. "You heard the court's ruling so don't you refer to the deceased's criminal record while I am questioning you. Understand?"

"Yes, I understand."

And on it went. Judge King was one of our best judges. No one but Percy could have gotten away with that exchange without risking contempt. Percy got away with things no other lawyer could. One reason is he kept the court and jury laughing and waiting on the edge of their seats to see what he would to do next.

The jury convicted the defendant of murder without malice. They assessed his punishment at five years but suspended the sentence. Percy and the client walked out of the courtroom together with big smiles on their faces.

When I went back to Judge Jimmie Duncan's court, I faced off against Percy when he was representing our city's most notorious pimp. The charge was carrying a pistol in the parking lot of the defendant's apartment complex. In this pistol possession case I could not bring up either the defendant's criminal record nor his occupation, unless somehow it became relevant. To do so would have caused a mistrial. Also the jury could not be told of the beautiful girls—barely of legal age—who were in his stable. Limited to the circumstances of proving only that he carried a pistol in his own parking lot, the jury had no reason to think Mike Said was anything but your ordinary law-abiding citizen trying to protect himself as he walked from his car to his apartment on a dark night.

The trial was over in short order with only one witness, the radio patrol officer making the arrest. Since the man was caught with the pistol next to where he lived, the judge instructed the jury that if they found he had the pistol on his own premises they should acquit him. I was expecting either a not guilty or a small fine. Surprisingly, the jury unloaded on this character with a ninety day jail sentence. The verdict surprised Percy and the court-room observers who had flocked to the courtroom to see him in action.

After the trial Michael Said's verdict drew a classic letter from the master.

"Dear Mr. Vance," the letter began. "I demand that you dismiss Mr. Said's case immediately and deliver a public apology on behalf of the District Attorney Office. Mr. Said is one of Houston's finest citizens and a man of exemplary character. Furthermore, for many years he has for years provided an excellent public service of making delightful entertainment available for some of our town's leading citizens even including a few esteemed public officials. Therefore I expect you to do your duty and issue a public apology before the media on the steps of the Harris County Courthouse at high noon of Friday next. Yours very truly, Percy Foreman, Esquire." Needless to say, I did no such thing, but the letter became a prized possession of mine.

Percy and I shared the podium at numerous criminal law seminars in Houston and around the state. Whoever introduced Percy would invariably describe him as the world's best and most famous criminal lawyer. Percy usually began his remarks with, "I would like to thank the gentleman for his most generous introduction. And I appreciated his learned opinion that I am one of—if not *the*—most famous and outstanding lawyers who ever lived. In all humility, who am I to disagree with the many learned and distinguished people who make this claim?"

Foreman began his career on the prosecution side. He had to have been a good prosecutor because he liked nothing better than to cross-examine and destroy any and all witnesses called by his opponent.

Percy knew his cases, particularly when to try them and when to plead them. When I was a chief prosecutor in Judge Duggan's court, I was itching to try a very aggravated rape case against Percy. The victim was going to make an excellent witness. Percy's client was a sadistic brute who beat the poor lady severely while raping her. I had made blowups of her bruised face and black eyes and interviewed the woman in advance of trial. I was ready.

The day of trial came. Percy strolled casually into the courtroom as the judge was calling his case. "The State is ready for trial, Your Honor," I said in a deep voice.

"Give me two minutes to confer with Mr. Vance, Your Honor," Percy said.

Percy and I walked out the side door of the courtroom and stood in the privacy of the hallway adjacent the judge's chambers. "Carol, how much time do you want in this case?"

"Percy, this is an aggravated case. I am not going to recommend one day less than fifty years."

"He'll take it. Get the court reporter. I need to get this over with because Judge King is waiting for me upstairs."

Ten minutes later he was on his way to Judge King's court and his client was on his way to prison. Percy knew when to hold 'em and when to fold 'em.

He was in hog heaven if he had a case where he could make the State's key witness a villain. But he also had a keen eye for a loser.

Foreman claimed to have one fee. In his own words, the fee was "all they have." When he spoke at seminars he said his clients should be acquitted because paying his fee was enough punishment for anybody.

He accepted diamonds, luxury cars (or any other kind), homes, antiques, shopping centers, what have you. County Tax Assessor Carl Smith told me Percy was the third largest land owner in Harris County, just behind Exxon and legendary oil man, R. E. "Bob" Smith. I doubt Percy even knew what he owned. He had scores of houses and there were rumors about warehouses filled with stuff.

Once he took in a small shopping center on a fee. The run-down property did not have any tenants so people parked there to shop across the street. To stop the trespassing Percy installed tank cement barriers and told me our office ought to prosecute those trespassers. Jokingly, I think.

One day another assistant and I got on the elevator to go to court. Percy and a sweet looking elderly black lady were already on the elevator. After Percy and I exchanged our usual sarcastic greetings, he exited at his floor. I turned to my friend and said, "I wonder whose house he got today?"

The little lady looked up at me and said, "Well, sir, he got mine. Isn't he just wonderful? That Mr. Foreman is my personal lawyer. My, oh my, that's wonderful!'"

As Percy got older, Richard "Racehorse" Haynes made his way into prominence. We tried a few of cases with each other.

Like Percy, Racehorse always entertained the judge, his opposing counsel, the spectators, and the jury. Richard was not a loner like Percy. He socialized with prosecutors, fellow defense attorneys, and judges.

Richard and I started practicing law about the same time. In his early days Richard cut his teeth on DWI cases. Haynes represented many a well-to-do businessman, the ones who could afford a large fee and were arrested after a few Scotch-and-waters at some fancy watering hole.

Racehorse's strategy was to get the jury to like his client so they would want to find him not guilty. Then his strategy was to cross-examine the witnesses until they made enough inconsistent statements to give the jury an excuse to find in favor of his client.

Richard would cross-examine police officers for hours on end. Instead of the usual ten or fifteen minute questioning, he could keep an officer on the stand for four hours to describe a ten-minute arrest. Building on minor contradictions, he hammered on reasonable doubt and the vagueness of intoxication as a science. Juries are usually hard on lawyers who waste their time with repetitive questions, but Richard simultaneously entertained the jury to the point they delighted in watching him work. Also he could ask the same question, but in ten slightly different ways, so as to get a favorable ruling when the prosecutor said, "Objection, repetitious."

Haynes reminded me of Johnny Carson. He was a favorite emcee and speaker around town. In fact, I called on him to handle the mike at my only fund-raiser when I first ran for office. At criminal law seminars and bar meetings, when I looked down at the program and saw I had to follow either Percy or Racehorse, I always wished I had called in sick.

Most of the better criminal lawyers in town started in the DA's office. Dick DeGuerin, Bob Bennett, Mike Hinton, Rusty Hardin, Ron Woods, Don Lambright, and many others went through this school of hard knocks. Assistant DAs might try more cases their first year of practice than many trial lawyers do in a lifetime.

Some top-notch lawyers did not start in the DA's office. Racehorse, Mike Ramsey, Craig Washington, and Mike DeGuerin all come to mind. Back in the sixties the Houston Bar Association, in conjunction with the judges, had a campaign to get every big time civil trial lawyer in Houston to represent indigent defendants over on the criminal side. This initiative followed the historic U.S. Supreme Court decision of *Gideon v. Wainwright*, which mandated that any poor person who might receive jail time had a right to have a free lawyer appointed by the court to defend him. As a result, the legendary civil lawyers of Houston were called to the criminal courts. Judges appointed lawyers like Leon Jaworski, John Hill, Jim Kronzer, and Curtiss Brown. For some of these lawyers it would be their first criminal trial.

Colonel Jaworski got his first opportunity to defend an indigent in Judge Ed Duggan's court. I was the chief in that court at the time. The defendant had earlier received fifty years for his armed robbery, but the Texas Court of Criminal Appeals had reversed the case. This trial would be a rerun of the first trial, except now the defendant would have for his lawyer the former president of the American Bar Association and the American College of Trial Lawyers, who had also been a chief prosecutor in the war crimes trials of World War II (he was later the Special Prosecutor of the Watergate scandal that caused President Nixon to resign). Out of respect, most of us referred to Leon Jaworski by his military rank.

The Colonel asked for a jury and we got on with it. What I believed would be a one-day trial turned into three, thanks to Leon's skillful and articulate cross-examination. The jury returned a guilty verdict. But, due no doubt to Colonel Jaworski's skillful work, they gave him the minimum punishment. The net result was this defendant now had five years to do, not fifty.

Seeing the Colonel in action taught me that trying a lawsuit, whether criminal or civil, involved the same set of skills. It gave me confidence I could end up on the civil side and try those lawsuits as well. The Colonel and I became closer friends as a result of the trial. In fact, he supported me in my quest for the DA's appointment.

I also had the privilege of trying a major case as district attorney with Curtiss Brown, one of the best plaintiff's lawyers in town. Curtiss later had a second career as chief judge of our Appellate Court. The bar always gave Curtiss its highest rating as an appellate judge.

Not long after I became DA, Curtiss was appointed to represent a defendant accused of the murder of a Houston police officer. Juries often give the death penalty for the murder of an officer.

Our evidence was strong. The jury convicted. The punishment was the main issue. In my opinion and that of everyone else watching, in making his final argument that day, Curtiss Brown saved that man's life.

Brown was permanently crippled and walked painfully slow on crutches. When he rose to address the jury he spent what seemed like forever to get out of his chair and hobble up in front of them.

As he tried to balance himself on the two crutches, he shuffled his notes in two shaking hands, holding tight to the crutch and the notes alike.

Curtiss apologized to the jury for reading his typewritten speech. He told the jury he was extremely nervous as this was his first criminal trial and this man's life was at stake. Then he read his argument slowly, word for word. His voice was so soft I could hardly make out the words. The jury leaned forward to take it in.

Curtiss attacked the logic of the death penalty. He quoted from philosophers, mainline church denomination position papers, the Bible, and a bevy of intellectual sources.

He closed with, "And some night you will be sitting around your kitchen table and you will see the light flicker and, as it does, you will know it is the voltage from that chair that is ending this man's life."

The jury gave the defendant life.

I think every criminal lawyer in Houston ended up with a copy of Curtiss' final argument.

SOME CRIMINAL DEFENSE ATTORNEYS made money off the volume of cases they handled rather than the wealth of individual clients. These lawyers showed up every day in multiple courts.

Two lawyers who specialized in the highest volume in the courthouse were C.C. Devine and Gabe Nahas.

C.C. Devine was an ex-policeman who weighed well over three hundred pounds. He wore custom-made suits of pure silk that were imported from

China. Even so, C.C. looked rumpled, like he slept in his suit the night before. C.C. looked straight out of central casting and could have been a double for Sidney Greenstreet. He resembled Hollywood's role model for a mob lawyer.

C.C. would arrive in court red in the face, out of breath, and sweating. He looked like a candidate for a coronary. He liked to go to trial and tried more cases than any prosecutor in the courthouse. If we had twenty cases on the docket, odds were that C.C. would represent two of the defendants.

Devine probably tried a hundred jury cases a year. Most were of the one-day variety. Shoplifters, a burglar caught inside a building, a ten-marijuana cigarette bust in a traffic arrest. He employed one simple strategy: He did not care what the jury or the judge thought; his every move was designed to make his client happy. Many a client of his had a big smile when C.C. relentlessly cross-examined a police officer with an affidavit face. Devine put on a great drama to impress his client. The strategy was disastrous. His clients got hammered day in and day out with heavy penalties. Few were acquitted. But all went off to prison happy.

C.C.'s caustic sarcasm and uninhibited vilification angered the jurors. Afterward, they would say things to me like, "That big fat lawyer made my blood boil." Many a juror said, "I wish the law allowed us to put that fat guy away." We all called C.C. "Andy" after the large and jovial movie star, Andy Devine.

Whenever a prosecutor made the mistake of boasting about winning a case, a fellow prosecutor would put him in his place with something like, "Against who? C.C. Devine?" But, as I said, C.C.'s clients were bussed off to prison happy campers. They went in such droves that a wing in our largest prison was jokingly called "The C.C. Devine Wing."

The great Erwin Goree Ernst was the only person I ever knew to lose a case to C.C. He never lived that one down. In the meantime, happy defendants serving maximum sentences were recommending "Andy" to their friends.

Only Gabe Nahas had anything close to that number of clients and trials. Gabe always had a couple of lawyers, true character types, standing by his side, nodding in agreement at every utterance he made.

Gabe Nahas was cut from a different cloth. He often did obnoxious things in court, but the love of his life was to create drama in the courtroom. He was an actor first. In a trial for manslaughter Gabe scooted across the floor in his chair and rammed our counsel table with a cloud crash. He was demonstrating how fast the other car, the one owned by the deceased, was going.

Judge Langston King came unglued and yelled for his bailiff.

"Mr. Spradley, Mr. Spradley! Mr. Spradley, I can't see down there. What is he doing, Mr. Spradley?"

"He's drivin' his car, Jedge," came the reply.

Gabe just looked up and smiled at Judge King.

Judge King sighed, "Let's move on, gentlemen."

In another trial in Judge King's court, Gabe got down on his knees and led the jury in the Lord's Prayer during his closing argument. Gabe was talking in almost a whisper. Again Judge King couldn't see over his high bench or hear Gabe.

"Mr. Spradley, Mr. Spradley! What in the world is Mr. Nahas doing with that jury?"

Mr. Spradley, who was old but looked young with his slicked down, dyed black hair, replied, "He's leading 'em in some kind of prayer, Jedge."

"Get him off the floor, Mr. Spradley! We'll have none of that in this court."

Gabe's clients were often convicted, but not at the rate of C.C. Devine's. Gabe was a short little man of Arab descent with a powerful voice. Even though Nahas hammed it up in most of his trials, he could try an excellent case.

Once, he did a masterful job in a highly publicized case where he must have received a large fee. Changing his approach, he was gentle and professional and polite. He walked his client.

Unlike C.C., who never smiled, Gabe was always smiling. He loved people. He would attack a police officer with a vengeance, but at the break he and the officer would be outside chatting like long lost buddies.

Gabe took Erwin Ernst, Fred Hooey, and me for a wonderful meal at his favorite Arab restaurant. He had an unlimited supply of human interest stories, most of which did not involve the law. In my eight years as an assistant, I don't recall a day Gabe did not bounce into court wearing some awful looking wide tie with a flower on it and a shaggy sport coat.

When I went into private practice I was taken in as a partner so I could handle the firm's white collar work. I did some of this in my first few years, primarily in the oil and gas area as well as some anti-trust cases. However, I just couldn't resist taking on a few criminal cases along the way. Usually I ended up with a good set of facts, a most unusual thing since the evidence is usually weighted in favor of the prosecution.

I actually represented three different defendants in three separate murder trials. The first was found not guilty by the jury by reason of insanity. The second murder case, after being reduced to negligent homicide by the grand jury, ended in an acquittal.

The third case was a highly publicized murder case where I was hired to assist another Houston attorney in the defense of a woman who shot and killed her doctor husband five times with a .357 magnum. She was found guilty of murder, but the jury gave her probation.

I did have one client go the pen after a six-week trial in federal court in Dallas during the savings and loan crisis days in the late 1980s. I represented the head of a large savings and loan chain who was hounded day and night for years by the federal task force, which was created to prosecute the S&L industry in Dallas.

Although I had excellent results as a defense attorney, I did not enjoy that role as much as prosecuting. It had nothing to do with representing someone who might be guilty. Everyone is entitled to a lawyer, and every lawyer should, within the confines of the law, of course, do his very best to represent his client.

The reason I preferred being a prosecutor was my realization of just how difficult it is to defend a case. As a prosecutor, I took the offensive from the start. I was the first to speak in the jury selection, the first to put on my case, and the first and last in making the final arguments. I could decide exactly how I would put on my case. That's a nice position to be in.

On the defense side, I found myself in an entirely reactive and defensive mode. In civil cases I much preferred the plaintiff's side for the same reason. I could put on my case the way I wanted to as opposed to reacting. It was sort of like football: more fun to be on the offense.

PERHAPS THE MOST SKILLFUL lawyer I ever came up against was Sam Hoover. Sam was skinny, short, and ugly. He weighed a little over a hundred pounds. He had a huge bald head atop that frame. He was brilliant. Give Sam a little hole during the trial, and he would drive a tank through it. After Sam would get a not guilty under impossible circumstances, we would tell the poor assistant he had just been "Hooverized."

Anytime Sam tried a case, lawyers would line the courtroom to see the surgeon at work. His words cut through the air like a scalpel. He never wasted a syllable. He did not entertain the jury or get them to laugh. His talent lay in his mastery of words.

Sam never carried a file or a note or even a single piece of paper to court. Even so, he could have read the record back verbatim just as well as the court reporter.

Hoover never avoided difficult cases. His clients were likely to be the professional burglar or robber who had committed some well-planned crime. The greater the challenge, the more Hoover flourished. Sam drove the old-time Burglary and Theft detectives up a wall. They were convinced he often engineered some of the town's biggest heists.

Sam came to Pasadena from Oklahoma where he had some issues with the law. After several years, he had built up a following in Pasadena and was elected mayor. Later he ran a good race for Harris County Judge but lost. He got out of politics to practice law full-time.

I recall my first burglary trial against Sam. He gave a unique final summation to the jury that only he could get away with.

We had a strong set of facts. My case had gone smoothly. The defendant did not testify. I thought a conviction was a done deal until Sam told the jury, "Members of the jury, you see my client sitting over there? He is no good. In fact he is downright sorry. You release him today and he will be burglarizing you or someone else tomorrow.

"The State showed he is a two-time loser. The truth is, they just told you part of the story. He is not just a two-time ex-con, but he has been arrested and convicted for burglary many times. His arrest record is as long as my arm. He deserves to be locked up. You will be safer if he goes to prison.

"But even so, this man has rights. One of his rights is that the State must prove him guilty beyond a reasonable doubt. You have to believe there is no reasonable doubt at all in this case before you can convict him.

"Yes, they showed he sold the stolen tea service and the three guns belonging to Mr. Hamilton to the pawn dealer. But no one could put him at the scene of the crime. We don't know what happened that night of the burglary, so you are duty-bound to acquit him if you have any kind of reasonable doubt."

The jury did just that.

One day Sam's luck ran out. Three men pulled an armed robbery in the home of a wealthy Houston couple. The multi-millionaire Meyer Shultze and his wife lived in an expensive home in Houston's prestigious Braeswood subdivision. The robbers had been told Meyer kept huge amounts of cash—at least $300,000—in his home to use for gambling on his vacations in Hot Springs.

The three masked men, who went by the names of Young, Sellars, and Spivey, armed with a sawed-off shotgun and two pistols, went to the home in early March of 1964. As a caretaker nurse was leaving the house, one of the men knocked her unconscious. The torture in the robbery was as bad as any courthouse old-timer could remember. The wife had her jaw broken and a good number of teeth knocked out. One of the men took out a butcher knife, heated it, and held it against her naked abdomen. She was repeatedly burned across the body and face with cigarettes and shocked with a cattle prod on her private parts. A fireplace poker and pistol were shoved up the same place. For the coup de grâce one of the men took his .44 magnum and shot her in the thigh.

Meyer was tortured in equal measure but remained unconscious through most of the long attack.

A shot was fired into the baby bed where their little child was sleeping. Most of the house's furnishings were severely damaged or destroyed as the men violently looked for the cash. Even the nurse spent several days in the hospital.

The men were arrested. Spivey said Sam Hoover set the whole deal up and planned the robbery. Spivey was promised immunity for his testimony. He reported that Hoover gave instructions to him and the other robbers over the phone when the cash could not be found.

The robbers were able to make off with $3,900, which Spivey said they all split up. Spivey laid out in detail how Hoover knew about the cash being hidden in the Meyer home and then gave the orders how to carry the robbery out.

The police ran a search warrant on Hoover's house which turned up two of the Shultzes' diamonds. Hoover's wife testified at trial and claimed the diamonds were hers.

Sam did not take the witness stand.

The police located a witness who was the son of the lady who operated a group of apartments Hoover owned. This witness put one of the robbers, the man called Young, in Sam Hoover's office shortly after the robbery. Hoover, it turned out, had told this witness—who had nothing to do with the robbery—"This diamond came from the Shultze robbery."

I admired my boss, District Attorney Frank Briscoe, for his bold move in granting Spivey immunity. Without Spivey or one of the other accomplices, there would have been no case against Hoover. I learned the value of having to step up to the plate and make a fast decision and taking the heat if things went wrong. The jury gave Hoover sixty years in prison.

Last I heard, Sam was still in prison. When I was chairman of the Texas Board of Criminal Justice in the nineties I would ask about Sam from time to time. What a wasted talent. Even though Texas now housed 160,000 inmates, Sam was a legend in prison. He was always polite, helpful, and admired by the wardens for the multiple tasks he did at their request. I will always believe Sam engineered that crime simply because he liked to live on the edge. He could have played it straight and made a fortune. He was as talented as any.

Representing a guilty party is an honorable thing to do. All lawyers are called to play by the rules, but within those rules they have a duty to represent their client—even a guilty one—to the best of their ability. I believe able and ethical lawyers on both sides make our system work best. It is an adversarial system.

With all of my criticism of the U.S. Supreme Court writing new words into our wonderful Constitution, that Court decision giving indigents a lawyer was long overdue. My personal experience was, the better the defense attorney was, the more I enjoyed the trial. The courtroom is no fun when you are up against a bad lawyer.

CHAPTER SEVENTEEN

Changing the Law in Texas

A just law is a man-made code that squares with the law of God.
—Martin Luther King

CHARLES DICKENS ONCE SAID, "The law is an ass." He must have been riding his donkey through Texas when he said that. During my years as an assistant, we were constantly frustrated by laws that were not just. Texas had its paramour statute permitting a legal execution by one man upon another and many other laws without logic or fairness.

I recalled one summer day back in Judge Sam Davis' court, when I was an assistant, I was excited to announce ready in a burglary case. Three guys had burglarized sixty homes over the course of a year. Their operation was simple. One would back his "delivery" truck up the driveway of a corner lot residence. As he kept lookout, his two colleagues broke open the back door and loaded large sacks full of guns, jewelry, china, paintings, and whatever else looked pretty. One day two smart detectives cruising an upscale neighborhood walked in on them. The driver ran his truck across the yard and escaped as the police got out of their unmarked car. One burglar dropped a TV and scooted over the fence while the detectives arrested the man inside.

The inside guy turned out to be out on bond for several other old burglary cases. Since he was a no show in court on previous cases, his bonds had been forfeited, and he had remained at large to ply his trade. He gave an oral confession which was tape recorded down at the station explaining all of the crimes he committed. The oral confession was not going to be admissible in evidence, however. Texas was and still is the only state in the union that, absent unusual circumstances, did not allow an oral confession into evidence. Even though he committed an offense while out on bail, after this new arrest the law demanded he have a reasonable bail set again so he could go free and burglarize some more.

This guy went in and out of the justice system like somebody buying a ticket to see a movie. The hockshops where this fellow and his cohorts were selling the stolen goods knew those tea services and mink stoles did not belong to the thieves walking in the door. But they could buy stolen goods without fear of prosecution. Even though this man had committed multiple burglaries, he could only be tried for burglary one case at a time. The jury was not allowed to know he committed other crimes unless he testified, which he was not about to do.

After I become district attorney I made up my mind to try to change some of our state's ridiculous laws. This became a high priority. Although the law reform did not occur overnight, after about eight years of lobbying, four sessions of the legislature, and with the fine efforts of the newly staffed Texas District and County Attorneys Association (TDCAA), we started seeing some dramatic results.

The leadership of the state got behind most of the changes that took place. We had strong support from Governor Connally, Speaker of the House Ben Barnes (and later when he was lieutenant governor), Lieutenant Governor Bill Hobby, and a host of senators and representatives who helped push our bills through the Texas legislature.

I started at this process as an impatient rookie, but session by session I learned the ropes. Enlisting support from other groups of businesspeople and law enforcement was a key ingredient. After our first legislative session was a complete bust, I was ready to throw in the towel, but we hung in there and gradually things started happening.

By the second session we were organized and had our priorities straight. Several of our former assistant DAs were serving in the legislature, namely Lee Duggan, Willis Whatley, and Cowboy Davis. They were joined by others around the state (like Bob Armstrong, the future land commissioner) so we had plenty of authors for bills and committee support needed to push the bills onto the floor of the House and Senate for a vote.

The first step was to identify the major concerns and concentrate on those. In the burglary case just mentioned, that burglar would not be able to keep on making bond today. Back then he had a state constitutional right to continue making bail. We pushed a bill to amend the Texas Constitution so that bail would be denied to a person who committed a felony while out on bail for another felony. The legislature finally passed a law allowing the people to vote on this amendment to our Texas Constitution. The change was overwhelmingly voted in.

After the constitutional amendment was voted on and approved, we took administrative steps within our office to identify career criminal types and prioritize their prosecution. We did this through our radically new Intake Division and a new Career Criminal Prosecution Unit that gave these kinds of defendants special treatment to see they were brought to trial rapidly and received appropriately long sentences. Keeping them off the street kept them from committing more crimes.

Our biggest failure was that we were never able to get the oral confession law changed. Also, I failed to convince anyone that judge sentencing— as practiced in our federal courts and most states—was better than jury sentencing. Texas still gives the accused an unheard-of advantage: He gets to choose whether the judge or jury will mete out his sentence.

Neither side should have the right to choose. Judges are far from perfect, but at least they have the advantage of years of experience along with pre-sentence reports prepared by the probation office to give them the information needed to determine an appropriate sentence.

Twelve jurors, who have never sentenced anyone for anything, and who are instructed they cannot discuss the actual amount of time the defendant might actually serve and are limited on what they can hear about the defendant's past simply do not have enough information to decide a fair and just sentence. I believe death penalty decisions should be reserved for the jury, but other sentencing should be left to the court.

Another change in the law helped us to nail professional burglars and thieves. Here the law was aimed at cracking down on the pawnshop operators who bought most of the stolen goods. The new law made it a *prima facie* case of theft for any pawnshop operator or dealer in goods to pay substantially less than the market value for those particular goods. The presumption was that the dealer should assume the property was stolen if the seller was willing to sell for a fraction of the value. Also, pawn and hockshop operators were made to keep records of sales, including who sold them the goods and for what price. The police finally had some teeth in the law to hold these businesses accountable. After all, the typical burglar only received ten cents on the dollar for his dangerous work while the hockshop owner bought at ten cents on the dollar and sold at fifty cents. The hockshop profited four times as much from the stolen goods as the thief did.

After my miserable start in the 1967 legislative session, we had a real breakthrough in the 1969 session (the Texas legislature meets in odd years, from roughly mid-January through Memorial Day). By 1969 I had pamphlets printed up and had garnered support from businesses, newspapers, and many organizations throughout the state. I had made a good number of talks around Texas and we were finally garnering support.

Near the start of the 1969 session, I was invited to speak at the Texas Law Enforcement Legislative Council (TLELC), which consisted of the Texas Sheriffs Association and all the various Texas police associations. These associations existed for the primary purpose of obtaining increased benefits for their members. They did not have a history of supporting reformation of the criminal law. After I gave my speech to those assembled in Austin, the presiding officer asked if I would step outside the room and wait while they discussed some important business. This seemed strange. I was with friends sympathetic to my ideas. Why was I asked to leave the room?

After about fifteen minutes, I was summoned back into the meeting room. The chairman of the group called me up to the podium. He said, "Carol, we have been needing to pass these laws you have been advocating for a long time. Finally you have done something about all of this. We are not lawyers, but we want to help you all we can. A few minutes ago we elected you as the new Executive Director of the Texas Law Enforcement Legislative Council. We also unanimously adopted your entire legislative program. Now whenever you go before any committee in the House or Senate, you can tell them that you have the backing of all the police chiefs, all the police departments, all the sheriffs, and all the constables and justices of the peace in Texas. You are our guy in Austin. You will be speaking for us as well as the DAs. We are also committed to having our members contact key representatives all over this state. We will be printing up tens of thousands of your legislative pamphlets with our endorsement on the cover. Our chiefs and sheriffs will be talking to civic groups all over the state."

The TLELC took my legislative handbook and did just what they said they would do. It also gave sheriffs and police chiefs something to talk about at all those Rotary meetings. The chiefs and sheriffs and others also did something I could not do. They used their long associations and friendships with the House and Senate members to urge passage. For the first time, I was encouraged we were going to bring some of these needed changes in the law into reality.

Our office had been running the law enforcement legislative agenda for the TDCAA for the first two sessions. By my third session we had a real boost

This group of people worked mighty hard to bring the National College of District Attorneys into existence. The NCDA added greatly to the professionalization of prosecutors in America. (L to R): John Neibel, Leon Jaworski, John M. Price, and me.

DIST. ATTY. CAROL VANCE, REP. GEORGE BUSH
Agree on Approach to Law Enforcement

DA Vance Awarded Jaycee Civic Honor

I met George Bush on the campaign trail. We later played tennis together a good number of times. Who would have known that I was sitting next to a future President of the United States.

I said enough about my visit with this icon already. In his early years, FBI Director J. Edgar Hoover was one heck of a crime fighter.

This award for being the outstanding district attorney in the U.S. is an excellent example of what a great staff we had. They did the work while I got the credit.

(Top) My wonderful mother (far left) could not have had a prouder moment than when I became DA. Here she is with dear friend Annie Mae McDaniel, the mother of Suzanne McDaniel, who started our Victim Witness Division. On the far right is Mike McKevitt, DA of Denver who was later elected to Congress.

(Middle) Sir Norman Skelhorn, who was in charge of all of the English prosecutors, John Samson, president of the Canadian prosecutors, and I started the International Association of Prosecutors.

(Bottom) Group picture taken at NDAA Meeting in 1973 at Mackinac Island, Michigan, where I was elected president of the NDAA. Colonel Leon Jaworski, past president of the ABA, was the speaker. He is at bottom left and wife Jeanette is third from left. In the very back row are Asst. DA Roland Dahlin, Dain Whitworth, Executive Director of the TDACA Association, Texas DA Oliver Kitzman and Assistant DA Ted Busch. Standing below Carolyn and me, bottom right, is youngest daughter Cheryl Ann.

(Left) Mike McSpadden and I won the State Bar tourney in tennis many times. We still play as doubles partners often. A great guy and friend and judge. (Right) When I became Chair of the Texas Department of Criminal Justice—a heck of a job for no pay—he swore me in.

Former Houston Mayor Welch and me. This is a later picture when Louie and I served on the Park Plaza Hospital Board together. He was a great mayor and held office during the time of the riots and civil unrest. We stayed up all night together in Police Chief Herman Short's office about all of that.

Pat Leahy (left) was a good friend. He was a DA in Vermont when elected to the Senate. The other guy is Harry Connick, a prince of a fellow and the DA of New Orleans, a welcome replacement for Jim Garrison. Harry's son is a pretty good actor and singer, by the way.

Holmes and me. I am not sure why I have to wear some stupid flower and Johnny does not, but between the two of us we served thirty-four years as DA. Johnny did twenty of that.

The old guys. In later years Clyde Wilson liked to get this group together to tell war stories. Clyde lived for the action. To my right are Sheriff Tommy Thomas (a former investigator for us), Clyde, Frank Briscoe, and Holmes.

A few years ago DA Chuck Rosenthal summoned me down to the Commissioners Court so those of us who started our Victim Witness Division could be recognized. Suzanne McDaniel was our first chief of that unit. From right to left are me, Suzanne, Amy Smith (the current head), and Chuck.

COLLEAGUES. Top row: Sam Robertson and Warren White; Bert Graham and Jim Larkin. Second row: my secretary Carolyn Hinton; my secretary Judy Wayt and Neil McKay. Third row: Tom Henderson, Lloyd Frazier, and Don Lambright. Bottom row: Ted Poe; Mike Hinton, Stu Stewart, and Sam Robertson.

PARTNERS IN MINISTRY

(Top) The genesis for the idea of a Christian prison was down in Brazil at a similar facility. Here are Chuck Colson and I outside that prison just one hour out of São Paulo.

(Middle) Here I am with friends Jim Rath, Tony Campolo, and John Tolson. Tolson started our first Bible study in the DA's office.

(Bottom) I have been on a mission trip here and there on occasion. This was the best place I could find to take a stand over in Malawi with my evangelist friend Shad Williams.

INTO PRISON
(Top) Governor Bush, soon to be president, and Chuck Colson had a great deal to do with starting the first faith-based prison in America. I was chairman of the prison system when this was all put together. Shown here are me, Carol, Tommy Dorsett (who directs the program now), the associate director at the time, and Governor Bush. After over ten years now the recidivism rate holds at an unbelievably low 8%.

(Middle) After I left the board they named the prison after me. Alan Polunsky who was chairman at the time presides at the ceremony.

FAMILY. What a difference time makes! The top photo is Carolyn and I and all of our grandchildren at the time. (Middle) Several years later, to celebrate our fifty-fifth wedding anniversay, the whole family enjoyed a vacation in Angel Fire, New Mexico. (Bottom) Carolyn and I enjoying a cruise for our fiftieth anniversary. We have certainly been blessed.

in our legislative efforts. Through a federal grant I helped obtain, the modern day staffing of the TDCAA took place. With our new executive director, Dain Whitworth, assisted by Mike McCormick, who would later serve as the chief judge of the Texas Court of Criminal Appeals, the association took over the tasks of keeping up with all the bills and getting the right prosecutors to come in and testify at the many committee hearings. Dain and Mike were next door to the capitol and could run over and talk to lawmakers and their staffs every day.

In addition to the various law enforcement groups, lobbyists representing several Texas industries got behind our reforms. Convenience store clerks were often killed in hijackings. Cleaners were being hit. Business burglaries escalated with the rise of crime. Many of these businesses contributed heavily to legislators and had full-time lobbyists who lobbied on behalf of our efforts. The lobbyists were well-connected and a source of well-aimed support. Many chambers of commerce lent their endorsements as well. Every day I received blind carbon copies of strong letters being sent out to senators and representatives from all over the state of Texas. Things were finally falling into place. Governor Connally incorporated our very words into his State of the State address to the opening of the session.

The changes that occurred were thanks in large part to members of my staff like Sam Robertson and Johnny Holmes, as well as others who accompanied me to Austin like Dick DeGuerin, Warren White, Mike Hinton, and Marc Wiegand. Texas DAs from all over the state, including Dallas' Henry Wade, never failed to show up and testify.

One of our goals was to bring the bail bondsmen under regulation. Bail bondsmen came and went as they pleased. The state was getting cheated. Defendants were being freed on bail who were high risk, adding to the crime problem. Bail bondsmen often put up little or no security to back up the bonds posted for dangerous defendants who did not show up in court.

Our office drafted legislation regulating the industry. It passed. A state regulatory commission was formed. They required bondsmen to be solvent so the state could collect when a defendant failed to show. Bondsmen with criminal records would not be licensed. Before this act passed, a bondsman could buy a two-acre tract for $10,000, claim it was worth two million, and post bonds accordingly. No longer would the bail business be a fly-by-night business.

One of my top priorities was the Speedy Trial Act. Our criminal justice system moved slower than a snail when I took office. Most felonies took two years to come to trial. When I left office the volume was 18,000 felonies per year. By a simple change in the law we cut the time between arrest and trial from two years to approximately six months to a year. The amount of time known crooks stayed on the street determined to some measure our city's crime rate. Many offenses are committed by those out on bail. Every study showed quick justice was as important as the penalty itself in reducing crime.

Our office drafted a speedy trial act. The police loved it. Innocent defendants should have loved it too, particularly those who could not make bail. Senator Max Sherman from West Texas took a great interest in this bill, agreed to author it, and helped it through the Senate. He assigned his assistant, Mike Pate, who later became a longtime law partner of mine at Bracewell and Giuliani, to work with me on the committee hearings and lobbying strategy.

There were many DAs who opposed the bill because they thought a clerical error of forgetting to put the defendant on the docket could cause that case to be dismissed. I believed we could keep those blunders to a minimum. A much greater good would come from keeping criminals off the streets.

The law passed, and I don't know of any cases dismissed because of it. Unfortunately, a recent legislature repealed the law. No doubt with the growing crime rate, we will regress back to longer delays between arrest and trial, giving determined crooks more time to ply their trade.

We also lobbied to increase the amount of time it takes for an inmate to be eligible for parole. In those days an inmate was eligible for parole after serving only one-fourth of his sentence. And with credits of two days for one in some instances, it seemed like inmates were being released before they arrived. The legislature upped the formula to a third. This was no great achievement, but at least they were moving in the right direction.

As to the drunk driving problem, I was one of a handful of prosecutors who supported the controversial "Liquor by the Drink" legislation. At that point in history one could not go into a bar and buy a single drink, but one could bring in an entire bottle and drink as much as his heart desired. I believed people would drink less if they had to pay a couple of dollars or so for one drink of whiskey than if they brought the entire fifth into a bar or restaurant. No self-respecting alcoholic wants to walk away from the last three inches of good whiskey. This often was the reason someone left a bar not fit to drive a car. Liquor by the drink would also cut down on the beer joint killings which usually found both the defendant and the deceased drunk in that bar. Liquor by the Drink passed after a hard fight.

I also pushed to lower the alcohol rate for drunk drivers. We ultimately made some headway on that issue; Texas dropped the standard from .015 to .010, or from eight drinks to five in one's system.

I worked hard to pass a law requiring parole supervision for all convicted felons released from prison. Nearly all offenders were released early in those days, some very early. Those who were paroled—that is, the safest risks—reported to parole officers and had stringent conditions to follow. The ones who were bad risks and still released, though not paroled, had no conditions imposed. In other words, society kept close tabs on the good risks while the bad risks were not being held accountable. After some hard lobbying the legislature changed the law. Now *all* offenders would report to probation officers and be required to work and make restitution and all those other good things. Unfortunately, the legislature just recently regressed and changed the law back like it used to be. The basic reason was the state of Texas was out of money. I still think we need to ride herd on the riskier group more than the safer group, but what do I know?

In order to reduce so many beer joint killings, I got the idea that it should be a felony to carry a gun inside a beer joint. I expected a big fight, but this statute passed with ease. In fact, the legislature broadened the scope of our proposal. The final bill made it a felony to take a gun into any grocery store, convenience store, or filling station that sold alcoholic beverages.

Another major change in the law was in the field of juvenile justice. The old law provided that a person who was sixteen or under and who committed a serious crime like murder could only be tried as a juvenile. The major injustice under the previous juvenile law was that a sixteen-year-old could commit a heinous murder but only be committed to a juvenile home until his or her twenty-first birthday.

Fifteen- and sixteen-year-olds were now entering the violent crime arena at a much higher rate than ever before in our history. This was due, no doubt, to the fact that the traditional home was being replaced with more children being born out of wedlock and kids growing up without fathers. Now a growing number of young people were pulling off rapes, robberies, and murders. The legislature passed a law permitting the DA to file a petition in juvenile court to try a fifteen- or sixteen-year-old as an adult for the more serious felonies.

The legislature also finally got serious about passing laws preventing egregious acts of pollution such as those happening daily along our ship channel.

Generally speaking, corporations could pollute at will and be free of any criminal responsibility.

Dr. Walter Quibedeaux, the perennial watchdog and head of pollution enforcement for Harris County, pushed for this legislation. U.S. Congressman Bob Eckhart, State Representative Rex Braun, and State Senator Chet Brooks were pushing and authoring the bills. At this time in the late sixties, a water moccasin couldn't live in the Houston Ship Channel. Except for an occasional sick alligator gar, there were no fish living in Buffalo Bayou.

After many trips to Austin, with Walter and me appearing before numerous committees, the new pollution laws were passed. Industrial pollution was reduced to the point fish were beginning to come back to Buffalo Bayou. The air was much cleaner. The odors subsided substantially. Most refineries got with it along the ship channel and most of the illegal discharging ceased. It was a new day.

During most legislative sessions I worked to increase the number of our criminal courts to keep up with the growing population. While I was DA, we went from six criminal district courts to eighteen. And we needed every one of them.

From mid-January until Memorial Day every other year the Texas legislature was in session. In my trips to Austin I made many friends and enjoyed their company. I knew all of Texas' thirty-one senators fairly well, along with a good number of the representatives. Most worked hard for the public interest and wanted to see the state of Texas a safe place to live. Senators like Barbara Jordan, Charlie Wilson, Grady Hazlewood, Pete Snelson, Tati Santiastaban, Chet Brooks, Max Sherman, and Charlie Herring were Texas legends back then. My own Harris County delegation treated me far better than I deserved.

Liberals and conservatives alike lined up on the law enforcement side. In my early days of lobbying, Ben Barnes became a good friend. He often included me in functions at his apartment in the capital where I enjoyed being with his fascinating inner circle of Texas legends like Ralph Wayne, George Christian, Larry Temple, John Mobley, and the illustrious Frank Erwin. Frank also held court after work hours at the Headliners or the Forty Acres. I was privileged to be his guest on occasion and do a little light lobbying with the assembled senators.

Ralph Wayne, a representative from Plainview, was Barnes' right-hand man and he let me use his office whenever I was working the House and Senate. Wayne often said, "Vance, you would screw up a two-car funeral."

Ralph was right, as demonstrated on one Saturday morning. Waiting to see Ben Barnes, whose office was behind the huge House chamber, I was throwing the football to Greg Barnes, Ben's son, not yet a teenager. As I over-threw Greg on one very long pass, the ball hit an elderly gentleman in the shoulder as he proceeded to walk into Ben's office. I exited without being seen. After a few minutes I innocently walked into Ben's office.

"Oh, Carol" Ben said, "I want you to meet Congressman Wright Patman, one of our nation's most distinguished congressmen."

Wright Patman was a legend in Congress and had been there for decades.

"By the way Carol, did you see Greg out there down the long hall throwing a football?"

"No Ben, I didn't see Greg throwing a football."

THE MOST SIGNIFICANT REFORMATION of the law I took part in was the passage of the new Texas Penal Code of 1974. Before the new code Texas had the nation's most outdated penal code, a hodgepodge of laws, many of which made little sense.

Instead of having one general law for theft, Texas had sixty special stat-utes making stealing a crime. For example, it was a felony to steal edible meat. This not only included a live cow from a pasture, but any edible meat; so stealing a drumstick or a wing from a supermarket shelf was also a felony offense.

There were fifty-seven separate statutes describing "official misconduct."

Murder without malice carried two to five years under the old law, while stealing $50 worth of hubcaps could get a man two to ten in prison.

The Texas Penal Code had not been overhauled since 1856 and was out-of-date. A survey of every felon prisoner in Texas revealed that all had been sentenced under 132 felony statutes. That meant the remaining 532 felony laws had not been used to sentence a single man to prison.

A new penal code was long overdo, and one of my favorite legal scholars, Page Keeton, Dean of the UT Law School, was chosen by the State Bar of Texas to head the committee to rewrite the code. At first I was the only prosecutor on the committee, but later Henry Wade of Dallas was added. Dean Keeton, with a tough job before him, pulled the committee together to do a good work. Even so, some of the laws had language a little more vague than the Texas prosecutors liked, not to mention some of the criminal statutes needed some major adjustment. The TDCAA appointed a special committee to rewrite the sticky parts of the State Bar product. Strong and substantive improvements were made; nevertheless, the good work of the Keeton Committee was left intact to rewrite the code in part and resolve these issues.

Tom Hanna, a good friend and the DA in Beaumont, along with ten others, including Sam Robertson, Mike Hinton, and myself, did the rewrite. The legislature accepted the TDCAA final product with little change. The new penal code plugged a bunch of loopholes in Texas law. Now we could try a burglar who burglarized fifty homes for all the heists at one time rather than having to try only one burglary at a time where the jury never knew about the other forty-nine.

The new code did away with most all of Texas' crazy laws, including the infamous paramour statute. The new code brought changes in the law I had been supporting for years. I think most all who understand anything about criminal law in Texas would say the effort was fifty to a hundred years overdue.

After some thirty-five years now, I believe most prosecutors, judges, and defense attorneys would agree Texas has gone from one of the worst to one of the best penal codes in the nation.

CHAPTER EIGHTEEN

A Supreme Court Justice Goes Bad

A false witness will not go unpunished.
—Proverbs 19:9

As I made my way back, I thought about all of the wonderful judges I was privileged to know and work with. Hardly a bad apple in the barrel. Really only two. One was Judge Garth Bates. The other was Don Yarbrough, who was elected to the Supreme Court of Texas.

One thing for certain, there is nothing better than to have a good judge try your case. My first boss, Pete Moore, was a prime example during his many years on the bench. With quick wit and a pleasant smile he ran an excellent court. The lawyers felt welcome. He moved the case on expeditiously, but if a lawyer needed a short recess or a conference at the bench, Pete obliged. Integrity on the bench was a bedrock requirement. I was glad most all of our judges passed that test.

In arguably the greatest fluke election in the history of the Texas Supreme Court—and perhaps any high office in this state—Don Yarbrough became Justice Yarbrough in the election of 1976. Yarbrough chose to run against one of the Court's most popular and respected judges, Charles Barrow of San Antonio.

I knew Charlie, who was kind enough to call me to play doubles on several occasions during my long stay in San Antonio when I tried Elmer Wayne Henley the first time. Barrow was a career judge of intelligence, integrity, and good judicial temperament.

Why Don Yarbrough picked Charlie to run against, I don't know. Yarbrough was only thirty-five, and, though a lawyer, had no judicial experience, and not much legal experience. But he ran for office without campaigning and won by a good margin simply because of his last name. No question, voters confused his name with that of Don Yarborough, a three-time candidate for governor, as there was only a one-letter difference in the spelling of their last names. (Yarborough almost won the governorship in 1962.) Also, Ralph Yarborough (no relation to either Don) had been Texas' longtime senior United States senator and was a household name.

There are so many judicial races in Texas that most voters don't have a clue who they are voting for. Don Yarbrough was easily elected in the Democratic primary. Winning the Democratic primary was tantamount to winning the general election, since Republicans held few offices in those days.

Duly elected by the voters of Texas, Don Yarbrough was sworn in for a six-year term in January of 1977. His election to the state's highest court came in the face of adverse publicity stemming from a formal investigation by the State Bar of Texas. Yarbrough had been sued time and time again for fraud by his own clients. In the one case that had gone to trial the jury ruled that Yarbrough had acted fraudulently. Stories began to surface before the election, but Yarbrough was elected over a judge of impeccable reputation.

The State Bar filed a lawsuit to revoke Yarbrough's law license. The petition alleged eighty separate infractions of fraudulent or unethical conduct. Even so, Yarbrough put on his black robe, moved into his Supreme Court office and joined the eight other members of the Court.

Not long after he took office, one of the staff lawyers for the State Bar called me from Austin. He asked me for a favor. Could one of our investigators locate an individual by the name of John Rothkopf? He said the FBI had been looking for Rothkopf for some time but had drawn a blank.

I shared the information with Johnny Holmes. He assigned the task of finding Rothkopf to Ken Rogers. Ken was an affable little bulldog of an investigator, most resourceful and very tenacious.

A couple of days later an enterprising young Houston *Post* reporter, Tom Kennedy, knocked on my door. Tom used to be a daily visitor when he covered the criminal courts and we were friends. He explained he was now on a special assignment working on a series of stories about Justice Yarbrough. Too bad Tom had not started on this assignment earlier and exposed Yarbrough before the election.

Tom was thorough and wanted all the facts before he did his series on the judge. Much of his knowledge came from public files at the State Bar in Austin. Kennedy also followed up with interviews of several citizens who had previous business dealings with the justice. Kennedy knew a lot more than we did. I promised to keep his information confidential as long as possible. He would share what he had with us, and I would tell him what I could.

At this point we had no investigation of Yarbrough, but I figured we were getting ready to start. I put First Assistant Holmes in charge and dispatched him to Austin. He would be backed up by Henry Oncken, now boss of Special Crimes.

Going through the Bar files, one matter in particular got Holmes' attention. Some time back, Yarbrough wanted to purchase a bank in Victoria, Texas. This bank had fired its president due to internal problems and the bank was for sale. Yarbrough wanted to buy control of the bank but needed $200,000 in cash to put down. He did not have that sum. Fairly soon, Yarbrough found an investor who could put up all of the money; however, this investor was not going to part with his money unless Yarbrough put up a letter of credit in his favor for $200,000 to secure the loan. Yarbrough agreed. If he defaulted on the note, the letter would become due, enabling the investor to walk away whole.

Yarbrough had a small problem. He had no money or any resources to buy the letter. Being resourceful, he called on his old friend, the fired bank president. Yarbrough promised that when he got control of the bank he would rehire the man as president, but on one condition: The former bank president had to draw up and sign a $200,000 letter of credit as president of the bank, even though he was not even an officer with standing to create a letter of credit for the bank. He was not even an employee of the bank at the time. That did not seem to bother Don Yarbrough.

The former president signed the letter of credit on behalf of the bank, but he did not backdate the letter to the time he was president. The letter showed on its face that it was issued after he had been fired. The letter of credit would probably appear valid to an innocent bystander, but it was worthless on its face. Since the letter was legally worthless, I can only speculate that the banker and perhaps Yarbrough somehow believed they could avoid the possibility of being indicted for bank fraud.

The investor, unaware the letter was bogus, lent the $200,000 to Yarbrough to buy the bank. Yarbrough took control of the bank and hired his buddy as president. The earlier deal between Yarbrough and this investor included an agreement where this letter of credit would be put in a safety deposit box in the bank. There would be two keys required to open the box, one held by the investor and the other by Yarbrough.

Things rocked along without incident until the investor got nervous and insisted on the opening of the locked box to make sure the letter of credit was there. Yarbrough and the fellow met. Both keys were used to open the box. The contents were dumped on the table. There was no letter of credit.

The cleanest way to make the case was to get the bank president to testify about what he knew. Of course, when he sang he would be implicating himself. Yarbrough was the biggest fish to catch in this scheme, had the most to gain, and was the brains behind it. We would gladly have let the president go if he testified against Yarbrough. When we were directed to the bank president's lawyer, he disclosed the U.S. District Attorney was already investigating both Yarbrough and the president. The bank president's lawyer said his client would gladly agree to our deal but only if the Feds also gave him immunity; otherwise, the deal made no sense at all for him.

Holmes and Oncken called on the federal prosecutors. They wanted to make a bank fraud case against both men. They came away thinking the Feds were more interested in prosecuting the bank president than Yarbrough as their primary concern was honesty within the banking system.

We had different priorities. Even though the bank president was involved in a serious offense, there were plenty of bank presidents and plenty of bank offenses by bank employees all over Texas. Some get in trouble every year in this state. But a sitting Supreme Court justice, one who wields great authority and makes state law, should be squeaky clean. Yarbrough was the number one target for us; the bank president was medium-sized potatoes by comparison.

In the interim, Ken had been looking for John Rothkopf. He discovered Rothkopf had an ancient felony theft case pending in Harris County. He had never been arrested on the charge so he could not have been brought to trial. The criminal charge had been filed and the indictment returned, but the case sat there. This is not unusual. There are hundreds of outstanding warrants all over this state for defendants charged with felonies. Unless some hot lead comes up, police do not have the time or resources to keep on looking for a man accused of some property crime. Now if Ken Rogers could locate Rothkopf, he would bring him directly to jail with their first stop at Special Crimes. That would make Ken's day.

A few days later, Holmes and Oncken were in their car returning to the office when Ken's voice came in over the DA radio.

"Holmes, you and Oncken get back here quick. I have a surprise for you. Can't talk over the air."

When the two men reached Ken's office door, it was locked. Rogers, upon hearing Holmes' voice, opened the door.

"Mr. Rothkopf, I want you to meet Mr. Henry Oncken and Mr. Johnny Holmes. These gentlemen want to have a little talk with you."

Holmes warned Rothkopf he was a suspect in an ongoing investigation involving Judge Yarbrough but told Rothkopf that his cooperation would serve him well.

Rothkopf was relieved to have been arrested. "I am scared for my life. I will tell you everything. I want to get this off my chest. It's a wild story."

Being extra cautious, Johnny told Rothkopf he wanted to talk to him but first he wanted to put him under formal arrest, get him arraigned, get him a lawyer appointed by the court, and then arrange for a low bail so Rothkopf would not be in jail. Then they would talk.

The next morning Rothkopf quietly went before the court. His name was added to the docket and the lawyer was appointed. Since his name was not on that day's public docket, there was no way for anyone to know that Rothkopf has been arrested or gone to court. The lawyer who was appointed advised Rothkopf to cooperate.

The rest of the story was one of the wildest things any of us had ever heard.

Rothkopf said he had a greater fear of being killed than of going to prison. He understood his story would go public at some point. He said when it did he would be in a safer position to avoid a hired killer.

Rothkopf explained his extreme fear. Yarbrough had enlisted Rothkopf's assistance to have this same Victoria banker killed because the banker knew too much and could send Yarbrough to the federal pen. Yarbrough told him the banker might make a deal with the Feds just to nail him. Yarbrough also told Rothkopf, "I don't want anyone talking to you, either."

For now the important thing was that his arrest and his cooperation with our office remain secret until a case was made on Yarbrough. Special Crimes needed time, a plan, and opportunity before Yarbrough got wise.

The plan we worked out was simple. Rothkopf was to contact Yarbrough and begin to meet with him. He would wear a hidden microphone so every word would be recorded. Since the Feds were not cooperating with us, this was our best shot at making a case. What kind of case it would be, we did not know.

When Holmes heard of the threat on the banker's life, he informed the banker's lawyer. Our office helped arrange for the banker to stay hidden until the entire sordid mess broke in the media; once it broke, the banker and Rothkopf would be much safer. The banker accepted our offer of immunity; he would have to take his chances with the Feds.

As part of the deal, the banker agreed to testify before the Harris County grand jury. The day he appeared, he was so frightened he wore a bulletproof vest into the grand jury room, perhaps a first. Holmes got him past curious reporters by having him walk in with the other grand jurors just like he was one of them.

After he testified, his testimony alone could have had Yarbrough removed from office. But for criminal case purposes, the banker was an accomplice. Accomplice testimony alone is never enough to convict. We still needed to work Rothkopf—and a break: Rothkopf was also an accomplice. The law is clear that one accomplice cannot corroborate another accomplice. We needed something tangible, some part of a criminal act that was not due to actions by either of the accomplices, to corroborate the crime.

Holmes had Rothkopf place a telephone call to Yarbrough. The conversation, recorded of course, would be the first in a series of bizarre exchanges between the pair. The justice told Rothkopf he wanted to meet him at "the office." "The office" referred to a secret meeting place the two had set up previously.

Later, when I listened to the tape, the judge's remarks were so off-the-wall that they seemed unreal. A sitting Supreme Court justice was instructing a police character about the progress being made in his quest to murder a bank president. The tape was dynamite and explained why Yarbrough did not want Rothkopf to be found.

About the same time Tom Kennedy came out with the first of his series of front-page stories describing the State Bar's disbarment suit against Yarbrough. The State Bar of Texas had to have been confident in victory down the road. The State Bar does not take on a sitting judge on the Supreme Court unless the powers-that-be in that organization know they can prevail. Tom quoted liberally from interviews of former clients of Yarbrough's and wrote scathing accounts of Yarbrough's handling of their legal affairs. Once Kennedy published his scoop, the Texas press corps leaped in on all fours.

In the lawsuit filed by the State Bar, Rothkopf was named as a witness. Reporters called Judge Yarbrough to get his response to the accusations. When they asked about his relationship with Rothkopf, he said he had not seen or talked to Rothkopf in months. He further emphasized that if only he could find Rothkopf, his troubles could be cleared up.

Yarbrough assured the press he wasn't about to resign his seat on the court. It was hard to believe he would lie so flagrantly about not speaking with Rothkopf when we had a tape recording of their conversation the day before.

The Rothkopf-to-Yarbrough telephone call led to the two meeting at "the office." Yarbrough set the time shortly after noon in order to give himself time to drive from Austin to Houston. "The office" was simply a place on the parking lot of the Sage Department Store west of downtown Houston, out on 1-10. We had wired Rothkopf with a concealed mike to memorialize the conversation.

Yarbrough arrived on time and they talked. Rothkopf had told us earlier that when Yarbrough first approached him to have the banker killed, he did not want to do that, so he told a wild story to the judge in order to buy some time. Rothkopf said he could not have the banker killed until he ran down "Pete." Pete of course was a totally fictitious character. Rothkopf assured the judge Pete would kill someone for as little as $2,000 and that Pete was one of the best hit men in the business.

As the tape played on, it was obvious to all that Rothkopf had been telling us the truth.

I expected Yarbrough to talk in circles, if he talked at all. Not so. Yarbrough talked freely about the proposed hit on the banker. Yarbrough brought up the subject of having the banker killed even before he asked Rothkopf how he had been getting along since the last time they had seen each other.

If we could have simply called Rothkopf and the banker to the witness stand and played the tape to any Texas jury, we would have had a conviction. Our problem was not what a Texas jury would do. Our problem was gathering legally sufficient evidence to pass the accomplice test. Another legal hurdle is that a conspiracy to commit murder has to be of serious intention and requires some overt act other than just conversation. Rothkopf was not seriously engaged in setting up a murder. He was play-acting. George Stumberg, my brilliant Criminal Law professor, would have loved to have used this scenario on his final exam. The good news was that even if we couldn't make a case, the evidence we were gathering was enough for the State Bar and the Texas Judicial Commission to remove the judge.

In a few days Special Crimes had Rothkopf call Yarbrough again. In this conversation, Rothkopf said, "If I am going to put a hit on the banker, I need cash now. Can you come up with $2,000?"

Yarbrough said no problem. Then he told Rothkopf to drive to Austin where he would introduce Rothkopf to a new banker friend. He said the banker was prepared to lend Rothkopf not just $2,000 but $10,000. Incredulously, Yarbrough also told Rothkopf that he, Justice Yarbrough, was going to have to come up with a false identity in order to apply for a loan when he met with the Austin banker. A sitting justice of our Supreme Court was engineering a fictitious loan as casually as ordering a cup of coffee.

The third recorded conversation came on Memorial Day. Henry Oncken will never forget this one. Yarbrough and Rothkopf were once again parked at the Sage Department Store parking lot near a fence at the rear of the premises. The sun was shining brightly in the sky and a bird was singing.

Unbelievably, Yarbrough said, "Here we are on Memorial Day, listening to a bird sing on this beautiful day, and we are plotting capital murder."

Our time was growing short to bring this case to closure. Yarbrough was going to wise up any day now. Special Crimes devised a plan. Rothkopf would arrange to meet with the judge in person in Austin. Rothkopf was using a car the judge had provided him. At this meeting we anticipated Yarbrough would sign over the title of the car and commit the crime of forgery. That would be a felony and enough to get a conviction if we could put together a case.

Yarbrough agreed to meet Rothkopf at the Austin Motel on South Congress in the shadows of the state capitol dome. Yarbrough, who had his residence in Houston, lived at the Austin Motel during the week while he was on the Supreme Court.

Holmes took a crew of eight with the surveillance van to Austin the evening before. Typical of Johnny, who liked to save the taxpayers' money, he housed the entire group in his dad's lake home out on Lake Travis. The lake location also kept the van and participants out of sight. Holmes had a private meeting earlier in the day with Rothkopf and his attorney to prepare Rothkopf to get the most out of what was likely to be their last encounter.

The next morning as expected, Yarbrough drove to his office in the Supreme Court building. Yarbrough had instructed Rothkopf to meet him at his motel's little restaurant later that morning. Our van pulled into a parking area close to an abandoned beauty shop across from the motel. The van was inconspicuous, but it housed a battery of watchful eyes that included Holmes, Jim Beauchamp (Rothkopf's lawyer), Assistant DA Dennis Green, and five investigators out of Special Crimes. Investigator Bill Hubbell was close by in his car. All observed Rothkopf pull up in his car and go into the restaurant to wait on Yarbrough.

Arriving twenty-two minutes late, Yarbrough pulled up to his motel, entered the restaurant, and sat down with Rothkopf. Photos were taken of the two together. Then came yet another wild and woolly conversation. Yarbrough says the bank loan deal is off. The bank officer said he couldn't make the loan without "gunking up" some fictitious financial statements, and he was not quite up to putting his career on the line for that. Yarbrough tells Rothkopf that if the Victoria banker is killed right now in the face of recent headlines, that he will be a prime suspect. He suggests things cool down for a while, so the murder plot will be postponed until a later time.

Yarbrough next turns his attention to the car that Rothkopf is driving. Months ago, Yarbrough had "lent" Rothkopf a 1974 Chevrolet Monte Carlo. Then he instructed Rothkopf to go see his banker friend in Victoria to get a loan on the car. The loan proceeds were to fund Rothkopf's living expenses while he stayed hidden out.

At that time Yarbrough had told Rothkopf, "You can live any place you like, just not Houston. The cops will be looking for you there." From that time on Yarbrough believed Rothkopf had moved far from Houston. Truth was, Rothkopf remained in Houston all along.

Other than not leaving Houston, Rothkopf had done as Yarbrough told him; he got the loan on the car even though the title was in Yarbrough's name. Now Yarbrough wanted to distance himself from the car by making certain the title is transferred to Rothkopf.

To accomplish this goal Yarbrough came up with fictitious papers stating this car belonged to a Billy Ray Waller, who allegedly lived in Alabama. At that time, Alabama was the only state in the country that was a non-title state. Alabama had a bad reputation among law enforcement officers as its maverick law allowed any car thief in the country to steal a car, go to Alabama, falsify an affidavit of ownership, and register the car in Alabama. With the Alabama title the person in possession of the car could say he had moved to another state, say Texas, and file paperwork to get an authentic Texas title. Ever since Yarbrough gave Rothkopf the car, Rothkopf had been driving around with Alabama plates, something he did not like to do. He knew Alabama plates aroused suspicion with police everywhere.

In the meeting that morning in the Austin Motel, Rothkopf complained to Yarbrough that he did not like driving a car with Alabama plates around the city of Huntsville, Texas (which was where Yarbrough believed Rothkopf lived). Yarbrough agreed that was not a good thing and told Rothkopf in the café, "I've got to first drive over to my office (at the Supreme Court) and pick up the Alabama papers to give to you. You be back here at noon so we can take care of all this."

Rothkopf climbed in his car and drove off. Investigator Bill Hubbell followed. Hubbell observed that Yarbrough also followed Rothkopf for a few blocks before peeling off. Hubbell speculated that Yarbrough was making sure Rothkopf was not going somewhere to meet someone. Yarbrough then drove to his office. This gave the Special Crimes crew opportunity to meet with Rothkopf to plan the second meeting.

At noon, Rothkopf returns to the Austin Motel in the 1974 Monte Carlo. Yarbrough arrives late, parks in front of the motel, and goes over to Rothkopf's car. Then the two drive their separate cars to the rear of the motel and enter Room 58, Yarbrough's Austin residence. The meeting inside lasts nearly forty minutes. Photos and tape recordings are made in order to prove the two men saw each other and talked on this particular day, a fact of some significance as Yarbrough was still telling the press he had not seen Rothkopf in many moons.

As soon as Rothkopf followed Yarbrough into his room, Yarbrough immediately put on a pair of gloves. Rothkopf looks over at him and says, "What are you doing?"

Yarbrough said, "Making sure my fingerprints are not on this f---ing title."

Rothkopf said, "You think it's that bad?"

"Well, if they ever trace it ... they'll trace it all the way back. They'll look at every f---ing little instrument. Fingerprints come off on paper. This thing was issued December 10, 1976, to Billy Ray Waller. So what you want to do is you want to write in bad handwriting right there, 'Billy Ray Waller' just like it is up there."

Then he asks Rothkopf to practice his handwriting. Rothkopf does this. Then Yarbrough tells Rothkopf to sign the papers by forging Billy Ray's name. Rothkopf signs as told. Yarbrough takes out another fountain pen with different colored ink and hands it to Rothkopf. "Now sign the name 'Roger Conway' here." Roger Conway is an alias that Yarbrough gave to Rothkopf some time back. We later learn Roger Conway is a dead lawyer who fits the general description of Rothkopf.

Yarbrough then spends several minutes giving Rothkopf detailed instructions on how to get a Texas title for this car. He carefully instructs Rothkopf how to scrape the Texas sticker off of the windshield as the car is supposed to have been brought into Texas from Alabama.

Next the conversation turns to the Victoria banker. Yarbrough says, "I can make it look like Clint Manges is after his ass, then he gets killed. Makes it look like Clint Manges did it." Clint Manges was a high-rolling Texas businessman who was in the papers all the time. Yarbrough is trying to convince Rothkopf that somehow Clint would be the prime suspect. That was such a stretch it did not make any sense at all.

Spraying the room with profanities, Yarbrough tells Rothkopf he is going to overcome all of his recent bad publicity. "I'm going to be governor in five years!"

Then he tells him how he is going to beat the disbarment suit filed by the State Bar of Texas. The final minutes are spent talking about past deals the two men were involved in. When another man's name comes up, Yarbrough says "F--- him." Yarbrough ends with, "I've got so many people to f--- that I haven't got ..." At this point for some reason the tape does not pick up the next words.

Rothkopf says, "You've got to make a list."

"I'll make a list ... but I will get them."

As Rothkopf gets ready to walk out the door, Yarbrough gives him explicit instructions how to reach him by phone at the Supreme Court after hours when his secretary has left for the day. Then he promises Rothkopf that he will provide bail and a lawyer should Rothkopf get arrested. Concerned about what Rothkopf might say if the police get a hold of him, Yarbrough says, "If you do get arrested, we'll get you out of the house (jail) right quick, but for heaven's sake, don't let them interrogate you or put you in some room and start questioning you."

A few minutes just after 1:00 P.M., Justice Yarbrough drives off to the Supreme Court to work on some opinion that might have lasting impact upon Texas law for years to come. Like the United States Supreme Court, the Texas Court only hears a fraction of all of the cases lawyers want them to hear. They usually choose cases of real significance. Yarbrough is still a voting member of the court but his assignments to write opinions by the Chief Justice have been scarce.

After the Austin Motel meeting the two men continue to meet. Each meeting is recorded. At one planned meeting at the "office," Yarbrough forgets to come. When Rothkopf calls to ask what happened, Yarbrough sets up another meeting and drives to Houston. All the while the State Bar lawsuit is brewing and stories are being written across the state about Justice Yarbrough. In answering questions by the press, Yarbrough continues to repeat he has not seen Rothkopf for months. "If I could just find this guy Rothkopf, all of these issues could be cleared up," the state's press corps reports him saying.

Finally, Special Crimes runs out of things for Rothkopf to talk about that might produce fruit. We need to bring matters to a close. I call my friend, Ronnie Earle, the district attorney of Travis County (where Austin is located and where the motel meetings took place).

Johnny Holmes, Henry Oncken, and I drive to Austin to meet with Ronnie and two of his assistants. We discuss the car title forgery which occurred in Room 58 of the Austin Motel. This appears to be our best case to pursue. Ronnie's office would have jurisdiction in the case. Therefore, his office would have to present the case to the Travis County grand jury.

Our plan calls for Rothkopf to testify before the Travis County grand jury where Holmes will question him. We will let the press know that we have found Rothkopf, but we will not tell them he has been cooperating with us nor that we found him some weeks ago.

The day comes. The press asks me what is going on with the Travis County grand jury. I tell them the grand jury is investigating Justice Yarbrough and that Rothkopf is in the grand jury room testifying. I purposely do not enter the grand jury room. I did not want to become a witness and be disqualified from trying the case.

Holmes briefs the grand jurors and then calls Rothkopf, who stays in the grand jury room for a long time. Grand jury proceedings are secret under Texas law and cannot be disclosed by anyone, so no one outside that room had any idea what Rothkopf said.

At the end of the day the press mobbed me when I walked from just outside the grand jury room into the public part of the hallway. After saying I was not at liberty to discuss grand jury testimony, I tell the press, "I believe this is a very serious matter, but keep in mind we just started. The grand jury has heard from only one witness and we don't want to jump to any conclusions."

Then I walk off.

That evening, Yarbrough's attorney, former Texas Attorney General Waggoner Carr, runs me down at my Austin hotel room. He must have called every hotel in town to find me after seeing the early evening news.

Waggoner and I were not close, but we were friends from back in the days he served as attorney general. He said he was representing Yarbrough. He demanded that the grand jury hear from Don Yarbrough. I told Waggoner that I agreed with him and that it was the only fair thing to do.

I said I would pass his request on to Ronnie Earle. Of course, Ronnie and I wanted the judge to testify before that grand jury. I couldn't believe our good fortune on that score. Yarbrough should not have wanted to go within a hundred miles of any grand jury room, particularly in light of his public statements saying he had not seen Rothkopf in many moons.

A little later that evening, Yarbrough himself, taking no chances, tracked down Johnny Holmes and demanded he let him testify before the grand jury. Holmes, who could hardly wait to get Yarbrough before the grand jury, said he would try to accommodate the judge and would see what he could do.

On June 28, 1977, Yarbrough entered the grand jury room in the Travis County Courthouse a few blocks from the State Capitol and his Supreme Court office. Three assistant district attorneys from Travis County were present along with Holmes, who did the questioning.

As customary, a court reporter made a transcript of everything Yarbrough said. Because Yarbrough's testimony had to be made public in the later indictment and resulting trial, the specifics are no longer secret.

To the grand jury Yarbrough described how he had been Rothkopf's lawyer in setting up a corporation so he and Rothkopf could get involved in the gold business. Yarbrough said he owned a substantial amount of stock in this company. The company's name was Gold and Silver Ltd. Yarbrough claimed the company had high profits from its gold sales.

Holmes let him ramble on about how there was a burglary on the safety deposit box in the Victoria bank and how he was innocent of the loss of a bunch of gold coins that belonged to someone else. Yarbrough admitted that he borrowed $25,000 and gave it to Rothkopf. He made it clear this was because of their partnership in the gold business.

Finally Holmes questioned Yarbrough about the car and the Alabama papers. Yarbrough had told the press once again the day before that if he could only find Rothkopf everything would be cleared up.

Yarbrough admitted to owning the Monte Carlo. He said he signed over the title to Rothkopf months before but claimed to know nothing about any Alabama title. Yarbrough said his final meeting with Rothkopf had taken place many months ago (this would have been long before any of the parking lot encounters we recorded). He denied meeting with Rothkopf at the Sage parking lot, the Austin restaurant, at the motel café, or in the motel room.

He told the grand jury he had not seen Rothkopf in a long time but he sure wanted to find him. Yarbrough denied putting on gloves and handling any car title, or participating in any forgery of any car title. He also denied having talked to Rothkopf by telephone in recent weeks. Of course, the grand jury already had our tapes and videos. Before Holmes was through with his questioning, Yarbrough had denied meeting with or talking to Rothkopf in thirteen separate lies that he told the grand jury.

When Yarbrough walked out of the grand jury room that day, we had a clear-cut crime of perjury. This perjury case could be made without the accomplice corroboration problems. We could forget about pursuing the theft of the car, the forgery of the car title that had not yet been acted on, the threat to kill the bank president, the trumped-up letter of credit, or anything else. We would keep it simple.

The grand jury indicted Justice Yarbrough for perjury.

Yarbrough had a right not to testify. He was a suspect and knew it. Nevertheless, both he and his attorney insisted he tell his side of the story. We encouraged the grand jury to accord him that privilege. He was not coerced into convicting himself.

About this same time, the Texas legislature took up the matter of impeachment. Impeachment would be a first for a Texas judge. An impeachment proceeding before the legislature is a trial. Each side calls witnesses, and there is cross-examination. The legislature wanted to subpoena our key witnesses to testify. They wanted to call Rothkopf to the stand.

I did not want to try our case in the legislature. It could turn out to be a circus.

I quickly contacted my friends, Lieutenant Governor Bill Hobby and House Speaker Bill Clayton, and told them of these concerns. I worked out a compromise with their committee people taking on this project. We would furnish the tapes of the Yarbrough-Rothkopf meetings but would not produce Rothkopf himself.

As Yarbrough faced impeachment, he made an unusual move. His strategy did not make sense to me. He called a press conference and before the assembled press corps he said, "I confess to you my wrong doings ... I did make a mistake ... I did sin against my God and the people ... Without reviewing the substance of my concerns, I never intended anyone be hurt."

I did notice that in his public repentance he did not confess to any specific trespass against the laws of the State of Texas. Perhaps he was trying to hold on to his Supreme Court seat even though he knew impeachment was imminent.

On the eve of the impeachment trial, Don Yarbrough resigned from the Supreme Court of Texas.

The forthcoming trial went as expected. Ronnie Earle, the Austin DA, was technically in charge of the case. Ronnie had asked me to try the case, to pick the jury, make the opening statement, and do the closing arguments. Henry Oncken sat next to me, and we took turns questioning the witnesses.

Waggoner Carr tried his best to get his client off, but he had no facts. Yarbrough had told the world and told the Travis County grand jury these meetings with Rothkopf did not take place. They did take place, were well-documented, and the jury, of course, found Yarbrough guilty.

The conviction came as a result of good work by Special Crimes, Holmes, Oncken, Kenny Rogers, and crew. In light of the fact the defendant was a Supreme Court justice, I felt compelled to try the case, but our greenest county court prosecutor could have obtained a guilty verdict.

There was one big glitch during the trial. We nearly lost our key witness, Bill Rothkopf.

Ken Rogers, our head investigator on the case, called to check in on Rothkopf one night and discovered he was very ill. Ken knew Rothkopf well by then and was used to holding his hand. When Ken stopped by to check on him, Rothkopf was hardly breathing. Ken rushed him to the hospital.

The doctor told Ken that Rothkopf had a collapsed lung and without treatment would have died. Rothkopf spent several days in the hospital. The State Bar promised to pay the medical bills. Ironically, we had all of this power and the resources to investigate the case but no money allotted to either care for or house a key witness. I was jealous of the Feds. They could house, protect a key witness under an assumed name, and feed him for years at a high cost. Not so with the State of Texas. Thank goodness confiscated drug money can now be used for necessary and legitimate purposes, like saving the life of a key witness. Rothkopf recovered before the trial started, thanks to the alertness of our investigator, Kenny Rogers.

Later the State Bar changed its mind and told us they would not pay the medical bill. I wrote their executive director, Tom Hannah, who was a good friend and the ex-DA from Jefferson County. I told him since the Bar had spent thousands of dollars in their litigation efforts to disbar Yarbrough, I was shocked they would not pay this measly bill for the guy who gave them Yarbrough on a stick. Tom got a check in the mail to us the next day. I could only imagine his conversation with those under him. Rothkopf's early demise would not have assisted our case. He was the main witness and the one the jury needed to hear from.

Judge Mace Thurmond presided over the trial. In March of 1978 Judge

Thurmond sentenced Yarbrough to seven years in prison.

Yarbrough appealed.

The judge released Yarbrough on his own personal recognizance, pending appeal. Our office was not notified of any hearing on the conditions of his release pending appeal. This was not unusual, as technically this was the Travis County DA's case, even though our office had put it together and tried it. The decision to cut Yarbrough loose on his personal recognizance would prove disastrous.

Three years later, Yarbrough's conviction was affirmed by the Texas Court of Criminal Appeals. That meant the Court of Criminal Appeals would send down a legal mandate ordering Yarbrough to report to prison as well as empowering the sheriff to take Yarbrough into custody.

When the mandate arrived, Don Yarbrough was not to be found. After all of this—his arrest, the jury trial, the resignation, the appeal, and the issuing of the mandate sentencing him to prison—Don Yarbrough had escaped his sentence, at least for the time being.

It was almost a year later before our office received word through law enforcement back channels that Yarbrough was living in Grenada, a little island in the Caribbean. He had enrolled in medical school there and word was he wished to become a doctor and begin a medical practice on the island.

When any convicted felon flees the U.S. to a foreign country, the United States has to begin extradition proceedings, usually a long and drawn out process. Grenada was known for harboring American criminals and chances of getting someone back from there were grim. Yarbrough had no intention of returning to Texas to do his sentence, so we were stymied.

Finally we got a break. Some enterprising policeman in Grenada learned that Yarbrough was scheduled to fly from Grenada to the island of Saint John. Saint John's is one of the Virgin Islands and under U.S. jurisdiction. When Yarbrough's airplane touched down, police were waiting. Not only would Yarbrough now have to serve his seven years, but DA Ronnie Earle had the Travis County grand jury indict him for bond jumping, a felony in Texas. This was a relatively new law and one I had lobbied long and hard for.

From Saint John's it was only the simple matter of flying him back to Texas where he finally entered prison. Now he had an additional seven years to serve for flight to avoid prosecution. He appealed this sentence as well.

Finally, finally, finally, on November 27, 1985, the Texas Court of Criminal

Appeals affirmed both sentences and laid the matter to rest. Don Yarbrough, former justice of the Supreme Court of Texas, heard the iron doors clink behind him as one of the most bizarre cases in the U.S. came to a close.

With two convictions, the last one for seven years, the Texas Board of Pardons and Paroles paroled Yarbrough after he had only served one year and four months on his sentence. I was not the DA at that time, but I know the parole board never checked with Johnny Holmes, who was by then the Harris County DA. When Yarbrough was released from the Texas prison, Governor Mark White said he was shocked. The governor said, "Yarbrough spent more time lying on the beach in Grenada than he did in prison." With all of the crazy cases I handled, this one was the most bizarre.

By the way, sometime after being released from the Texas prison, Yarbrough was indicted by the Feds and sent off to a federal prison on a federal bribery charge. That's the last I heard of him.

CHAPTER NINETEEN

Beyond Texas

I like for things to happen. And if they don't happen,
I like to make them happen.
—Winston Churchill

Next stop: Harris County. The mushrooming Houston skyline would soon come into view. Never would I dream that greater Houston would extend past Sugar Land and on down to Richmond, twenty-five miles from downtown. On my right was the last courthouse I would pass, the Fort Bend County Courthouse.

Fort Bend had elected and re-elected my friend Bob Bassett as DA for over forty years now. The journal for the National District Attorneys Association said Bob set a national record for a prosecutor holding office. I believe it is more difficult to be the DA in a small county than a big city. Everyone in the small towns thinks the DA should be available day or night to resolve any disputes over property lines or to stop a neighbor's dog from barking. At least in Boomtown the average citizen understands there are thousands of cases and a good number of assistant DAs who do the work.

Driving through Sugar Land that day I never dreamed the large field to my left would someday be a prison named "The Carol S. Vance Unit." More amazing still would be the fact I would be going out there on a weekly basis to teach Christian-based life skills to convicted felons. The Vance Unit blazed a trail as it was the first prison in the United States to feature all-Christian programming, thanks to a good friend and hero of mine by the name of Chuck Colson.

This all started as a result of my serving as chairman of the board of the Texas Department of Criminal Justice. TDCJ governs the Texas prison, probation, and parole systems. When I was on that board I went into prisons with Colson, Mike Barber, Bill Glass, and other Christian prison ministries. I got hooked. I saw men's lives change through their faith. My Christian ministries in various prisons would become a significant part of my life in "retirement."

While chairman of the Texas prison board, I went to Brazil with Chuck and a few others to study the only "Christian" prison in the world. What got my attention was that their repeat rate was less than 10 percent. Two years later, thanks to Governor George Bush's help and Chuck's leadership, we started such a thing in Texas. Now it has been copied around the nation with great results.

Next to the prison property was a rapidly expanding airport where a jet flew over my car to land. That recalled my jetting away to exciting places, particularly for the National District Attorneys Association (NDAA), an organization I was privileged to serve as president.

OF COURSE NOT ALL the trips to the NDAA were pleasant. One evening I touched down in a snowfall at the Milwaukee airport. As the darkening skies gave way to night, I registered in a downtown hotel, hung up my bag, and walked to a close-by restaurant. There I met my long lost army buddy, Lieutenant Willis Zick, now a district judge in Wisconsin. Fifteen years before, Willis and I became close friends going through officers' basic training at Camp Gordon, Georgia.

As new second lieutenants in the Military Police, we were fortunate to do our six month active duty during a break from law school. Our roughest duty was a one-week bivouac in the piney woods of Georgia in the heat of August. On Saturday mornings we stood at parade rest for hours because President Eisenhower might be flying into town. Who knew when the former Supreme Commander of the Allied Forces might want to hear the band playing and review the troops one more time while en route to a little golf course called Augusta National. So most Saturday mornings we stood in review just in case. One morning Ike drove by real fast in a jeep. From my platoon in the back row, I saw his face.

Willis and I were both maverick lieutenants who cut up a lot and looked for any excuse to shoot hoops or throw the football around when our company commanders were not around. Now, remarkably, we both had jobs of a more serious nature, something neither of us contemplated. Willis was springing for dinner at some famous German restaurant. I think Milwaukee only had German restaurants. I was choking down a Texas-sized chicken fried steak with a German name and a gigantic mug of Milwaukee's finest as I started to relax.

The week had gone fast. In three days I had been to Washington and met with the U.S. Attorney General, FBI Director J. Edgar Hoover, and testified before Congress. The next day I flew to Miami to testify before a congressional hearing about proposed drug trafficking laws. This event was mostly a photo op for the longtime Florida congressman who chaired the drug committee. Finishing in early afternoon, I barely made the flight for Milwaukee. Tomorrow morning I would kick off a National DA's training conference in Milwaukee and fly back to Houston in time for a banquet speech.

Gobbling away I became nauseated and dizzy. Willis saw I needed help. He guided me to his car and steered us through the snow-covered streets to the emergency room of the Milwaukee County Hospital.

"Your heart was beating too fast and your blood was acutely elevated," the nurse informed me.

At midnight the doctor came in and found nothing wrong. Willis drove me to my hotel at about 2:00 A.M. to finish the night. I made a low-energy talk the next morning and beat it home.

Most all of my activities on behalf of the National District Attorneys Association were downright fun as I made friendships with a bunch of characters who held the same office from all over the country. Through the NDAA I picked up great ideas on how to deal with unique problems in running a large prosecutors office. I volunteered for committees and special assignments and quickly went up through the officer ranks in record pace. Six years after being elected DA in Houston, I was elected president of the NDAA. I was still in my thirties and I think the youngest president they ever had.

The year I served as president-elect my job was to travel the country addressing state associations at their annual meetings. That year I traveled to twenty different states, often two on a weekend. Like a union leader I advised state boards of directors how to receive financial assistance for new projects under the new Law Enforcement Assistance Act. In 1973–74, during my time as president, I made multiple trips to testify before Congress and address national law enforcement organizations. I even spoke at the annual U.S. Appellate Judges Conference at the historic Del Coronado Hotel in San Diego. Heady stuff for a young guy.

My NDAA involvement started when we hosted the National District Attorneys Association meeting in Houston shortly after I took office. Four hundred visiting DAs hit Houston to enjoy an outpouring of hospitality. They toured NASA and climbed in moon launch simulators. At the new

Astrodome they had cocktails and dinner in the crooked shipwreck bar next to the bowling alley up in County Judge Roy Hofheinz's private suite overlooking the playing field. First Assistant Neil McKay showed up in kilts with his bagpipe band which marched through the crowd.

On our trip to the Space Center, Houston police turned on their sirens and pulled our tour buses over to the side of the road. Officers entered the bus saying they were looking for a fugitive disguised as a DA. Of course it was a joke. The pickup truck following the buses carried tubs of iced-down beer for the thirsty travelers. If such politically incorrect conduct happened in this day and time, we would be roasted. But the guys and gals loved it and would always remember Houston and its hospitality.

My friend Earl Morgan, the DA of Birmingham, Alabama, a state not exactly known for racial tolerance, ended up over in Third Ward after hours. He brought his guitar and liked to sing soul music. He quickly hitched up with a few of the southern jazz musicians. "White music just didn't get it," Earl said. Long after Earl left town, a guy came up to me at a black church one Sunday, where I was preaching. He asked when Earl was coming back. He said he wanted to put Earl under contract to play with his group.

Before I was elected president I served as treasurer of the NDAA. That year we met in New Orleans. This was during the middle of the hubbub over the Kennedy assassination. Big Jim Garrison, the New Orleans DA, was leading the charge to stir the pot. He had severely criticized the Warren Commission on their finding that the assassination had been one man acting alone, not a widespread conspiracy. Jim believed the assassination was part of a sinister plot. History proved him right, but Jim tried the wrong guy, Clay Shaw, who was acquitted and rightfully so. Recently released documents and evidence show that New Orleans' own mob boss, Carlos Marcello, had a great deal to do with not only the JFK assassination but Bobby Kennedy and Martin Luther King as well. Years later the movie *JFK* starred Kevin Costner playing Jim Garrison and turned him into a hero. At the time the NDAA convened in New Orleans Garrison was riding this horse for all it was worth onto the national stage.

After we showed up in New Orleans for our national meeting, several of us met with Jim and respectfully requested he not use the NDAA convention to push his assassination plot theories. Vice President Hubert Humphrey was to be our annual banquet speaker, and Jim had been critical of President Johnson and the Feds of late. Besides, Jim had nothing to do with the conference. He had not set it up or paid for it and had no voice in the program. His job was just to say, "Welcome to New Orleans."

To avoid the chance of embarrassment, our president, Bill Raggio of Reno, set up a meeting with Jim in Bill's suite at the hotel. About four of us were there when Garrison strolled in. Raggio delicately asked Jim not to talk about the Kennedy assassination during his welcoming remarks later that night at the annual banquet.

Jim said, "Don't worry about a thing, Bill. I won't offend a soul. All I am going to do is to tell the world what a sloppy job the Warren Commission did, what a big conspiracy the JFK assassination was, what really happened that day in Dallas, and how President Johnson and his cronies kept the whole thing quiet."

At that Raggio politely but firmly said, "Jim, if that is the way you feel, you are not going to speak tonight at the banquet."

Jim said, "What banquet?"

"The NDAA banquet. Tonight at this hotel. The one we've been talking about."

"Banquet? There isn't going to be any banquet." At that, Jim wheeled out the door. We stood there looking at each other.

Being the NDAA treasurer at the time, I knew we had paid a bundle to the Hotel Monteleone in advance for the dinner. Raggio dispatched me to find the manager to make certain the hotel would honor its contract and go forward as agreed. Four hundred DAs had paid hefty registration fees for this one fancy New Orleans gourmet experience. The hotel had already enjoyed good publicity from our nationally-known prominent figures coming in to speak.

I went downstairs and asked for the manager.

"He's unavailable. He won't be back until Monday," was the terse reply from a clerk behind the front desk,

"Tell me how I can reach him. I must talk to him," I said.

"I am sorry, sir. We don't give out that kind of information."

After some of my choice words, the clerk agreed to get the assistant manager. A young man came to the front and introduced himself.

"I'm with the NDAA," I told him. "You know, that large group of people staying with you. In fact, I am the treasurer, and I am checking on the banquet tonight to make sure it will go forward on schedule just like you promised in our contract."

"Sir, the banquet has been cancelled."

"Cancelled? The banquet has been cancelled? How? The NDAA has an agreement with you guys. We have paid for this. You can't cancel the banquet. No one has authority to cancel this event but the NDAA who made the deal with you. Besides we already paid you."

"Sorry, sir. Mr. Garrison, the district attorney, cancelled the banquet. If Mr. Garrison says the banquet is cancelled, then the banquet is cancelled."

"Mr. Garrison doesn't have a thing to do with this deal. This is a contract between the NDAA and the hotel. You have several hundred of our people filling up your hotel rooms. Mr. Garrison didn't contract with you. He is not part of this."

"Sir, you are in New Orleans. If Mr. Garrison says there will be no banquet, then there will be no banquet. Besides, we have no food. He ordered us to send the banquet food to an orphanage. The food is on its way out there now. We couldn't give a banquet if we wanted to."

"Do you mean that if the American Bar Association or the American Medical Association booked a convention and paid for a banquet for hundreds of your guests and Jim Garrison said, 'Cancel that banquet!' you would do it?"

"Sir, if Mr. Garrison says no banquet, then no banquet. I hope I have made myself clear."

"Well, I am treasurer of the NDAA and we want all of our money back. These guys have paid big bucks to dine off of you. Did Mr. Garrison get to keep the money, too."

"Sir, don't you forget the hotel paid for all that food and we are out a lot of money, sir. We did not decide to send it to the orphanage. Mr. Garrison did. Please tell your members the Monteleone is most regretful for any inconvenience."

Then the little wimp walked away through a door behind the counter. The clerk behind the desk followed him, leaving no one to fuss at.

The encounter demonstrated New Orleans had a different way of thinking about their government officials. In Houston I would have been laughed out of office and run out of town if I pulled a stunt like that. But to New Orleans, Garrison was a hero and dictator. Personalities trumped the law in this city where Carlos Marcello and organized crime wielded such great influence. As an aside, New Orleans built a domed stadium about the same size as Houston's a few years after the Astrodome was finished. The cost was four times as much. No one in New Orleans probably noticed. It was business as usual in the Big Easy.

That evening Carolyn and I and a few other of our officers stood outside the Hotel Monteleone ballroom telling disappointed prosecutors and wives the story. The Sunday morning *Tribune* carried a front-pager, "Garrison

Cancels Banquet, Orders Food to Orphanage." After that episode the NDAA avoided New Orleans until Garrison was out of office. Ultimately, a refreshing newcomer and solid DA, Harry Connick, Sr., took his place—yes, Harry Connick, Jr., is his son—and then we returned to New Orleans, still one of the prosecutors' favorite spots for meetings and conferences.

For years I served on the small NDAA Executive Committee, which annually gathered in Washington, D.C., to meet with the Attorney General, the Director of the FBI, and congressional leaders. In the earlier days we met with that famous crime fighter, J. Edgar Hoover.

Thousands of car theft cases were going unprosecuted because professional thieves stole cars and took them across state lines. The car thief knew the state where the offense occurred would not pay the high tariff to extradite the thief. Because it was a federal crime to take a stolen car across state lines, we wanted the Feds to get after these guys. But under J. Edgar, the Bureau had better things to do; so each year when our small NDAA Executive Committee paid a call on Mr. Hoover we tried to get him to change his policy. On arrival at the FBI headquarters we were escorted back into the inner chambers to Mr. Hoover's office to plead our case and discuss other matters. Mr. Hoover was always behind his huge desk which sat on a platform a foot or so off the ground. The short director looked down at the minions groveling at his feet.

Hoover had a bulldog face and looked more like his press caricatures than his actual photograph. Each year Hoover would say, "Thank you for coming and what can we do for you?"

No sooner would one of us attempt to explain the car theft dilemma before the Director would go off on a tirade about the hippies. This was the sixties and very early seventies, the years of the riots and the marches on the capitol. We were on his side on these issues as we had our problems with riots and civil unrest, too. Only when Hoover died was the policy changed and car thefts declined. As we exited Mr. Hoover's office, we were told to stand by a white line painted on the floor of his office. Mr. Hoover would step down for the photo op. Having said that, I was honored to meet the pug-faced lawman who brought down Al Capone and made inroads on organized crime in America.

While we were in Washington, we met with many dignitaries. DA Gary Byrne of Boston got us in to see Speaker John McCormack. Later Boston DA Newman Flanagan arranged for us to spend time with Speaker Tip O'Neil and Senator Ted Kennedy. Our small executive committee also met with six different attorneys general, President Ford, and others over the years.

One of our own, Mike McKevitt, the DA of Denver, was elected to Congress, so we would stop by to see him. Three DAs had been elected to the United States Senate: Pat Leahy of Vermont, a good friend and former vice president of the NDAA; Arlen Specter of Philadelphia; and Dennis DeConcini from Arizona.

William Rehnquist was an outstanding Chief Justice. I was on a program with him one night in Washington, D.C. With the liberal media and intellectuals trying to sell the idea that the Constitution is a living document, that it should be constantly changing to meet the needs of the day, I appreciated this Chief Justice who did his best to hold the line and say in his opinions that the Constitution is how it reads, not some fuzzy document that blows in every political wind.

Part of my many travels took me on a teaching-speaking circuit referred to as the "NDAA Road Shows." We put on courses on trial tactics all over the country. I usually spoke on how to make closing arguments. My friend Charlie Moylan, the district attorney of Baltimore, now on the Supreme Court of Maryland, gave delightful lectures on search and seizure. Pat Williams of Tulsa talked on homicide cases. Others joining us were John Price of Sacramento, Joe Carr of Los Angeles, Bill Cahn of Nassau County, New York, John Stamos of Chicago, Dick Gerstein of Miami, Preston Trimble of Norman, Oklahoma, and Bill Randall of St. Paul. In those days there was not the mandatory legal education that exists today. The DAs associations did not have staffed offices to do training so the NDAA had its own group of characters putting on the road shows.

There were some legendary DAs in the U.S. Two of the best were Frank Hogan and later Bob Morganthau, who together served Manhattan for well over fifty years when you added up their service. Bob just recently retired. Guys like Lew Slayton in Atlanta, Henry Wade in Dallas, Gary Byrne in Boston, John Price in Sacramento, and John Carrigan in Cleveland, were all good, honest, commonsense kind of guys.

Two of our longest serving district attorneys in Texas were Ronnie Earle of Austin and Tim Curry of Fort Worth. My own successor, Johnny Holmes, put in twenty years, a record for Harris County.

The NDAA took a leadership position putting on multi-disciplinary conferences for police, teachers, social workers, counselors, and all of those in disciplines that worked in that world of drug abuse, child abuse, battered wives, organized crime, consumer fraud, school dropouts, and you name it. Although I did too much traveling and accepted too many professional speaking invitations, Harris County benefited from the things I learned from other DAs.

The NDAA held conferences in many major cities. Not surprisingly, Boston, San Francisco, and Las Vegas seemed to draw the highest attendance.

At one of the conferences in Las Vegas, District Attorney George Franklin and I were having lunch in one of Howard Hughes' hotels on the Strip. A familiar face came over and joined us. It was the Brown Bomber, Joe Louis. Joe's tax problems had him on the ropes, so he worked at the hotel as the PR guy. I told Joe he did a great thing for America and freedom when he punched out that Nazi, Max Schmeling, in the Berlin Olympics to win the gold. Schmeling was Adolph Hitler's Exhibit No. 1 to prove the supremacy of the Aryan race and the Third Reich.

Back before the 1974 Penal Code passed, corporations could not be prosecuted under our Texas criminal laws. Since the meetings were productive I saw nothing wrong with saving county tax dollars by accepting Tenneco's invitation to fly a good number of our staff to attend the annual NDAA meeting in their company aircraft. Red Wells, a Tenneco VP in charge of governmental relations, enjoyed setting up these trips. He could do business with leaders and government officials wherever we traveled.

My friend Clyde Wilson was also a confidant of Tenneco's chairman of the board, Dick Freeman. Each year, Clyde and Red would compete to see who was going to line up the airplane to take us to an NDAA meeting.

Assistant District Attorney Ted Busch, one of my closest friends, was so active in the NDAA that he was the first assistant DA in the nation to be elected as one of its vice presidents. Ted, who headed our huge Trial Bureau, was popular and known by everyone. He was not shy in calling on DAs around the country to get something we needed out of another state.

After arranging our Tenneco flights for years, Red Wells only called me once to ask for a favor. He said, "Carol, my favorite nephew just graduated from Baylor Law School and wants to be a prosecutor. I am certainly not asking you to hire him, just interview him. He's a good kid."

I told Red I would be delighted to see the young man. Our office hired about twenty new prosecutors each year so we were always looking for good talent. I was hoping the nephew would either be a dud so Red would understand why we could not hire him, or else be an outstanding fellow we would want to hire. At the interview, the young man made a fine impression. He never met a stranger and obviously would do well in front of a jury. I would have hired him, but we had no vacancies. When several assistants left the office a few months later, I called Red to ask him where his nephew was. Red replied he was an assistant attorney general working in Austin. He was happy in his new job so Red said I shouldn't bother to call him.

Many years later I was attending a banquet up in Fort Worth. As it turned out this young man was the speaker. He looked down from the podium and said, "I am glad to see the former district attorney of Harris County in the audience. In fact, I applied for a job with him when I got out of law school. He was the only person to ever turn me down for a job." The crowd laughed. The speaker was Mark White, governor of Texas.

After the 1974 Texas Penal Code was enacted, corporations became subject to the criminal laws of Texas. Now there could be a conflict of interest, so that ended my Tenneco flights.

The NDAA had annual tennis and golf tournaments. I won the tennis tournament every year. John Van de Kamp, the Los Angeles DA, and I usually met in the finals until John was elected attorney general of California.

Many of my DA friends around the country enjoyed coming to Houston. One day my old tennis playing buddy, Brendan Byrne, the former DA of Newark, came to town. He was now governor of New Jersey. He picked me up in his limousine and we went out to the Astrodome to see his Phillies play. He took me into the locker room where the players all said, "Hi, Guv." When they strolled out to take batting practice, Brendan dragged me onto the field. As we stood behind home I kept my face down, fearful Houston Astros fans would see me consorting with the enemy.

One night, Bob Russell, the DA of Colorado Springs, and two of his assistants were in town and I took them out to the ballpark. About the second inning, the giant Astrodome scoreboard lit up like a Christmas tree, reading: "Welcome Robert Russell, District Attorney of Colorado Springs and guest of DA Carol Vance." No one in the stands applauded except Bob. He was so excited that he bought beer the rest of the evening for all those sitting around us.

The NDAA had its causes. One fight was against a new movement to legalize gambling in professional sports. Supporters were trying to get Congress to pass laws permitting gambling on football, baseball, basketball, and hockey games. As president of the NDAA I joined with the commissioners of the NFL, the NBA, and Major League Baseball, to oppose legalized gambling. I testified before a congressional committee on what gambling could do to sports in America. The next day we went to New York City to hold a press conference to air our viewpoint.

Bill Cahn, the immediate past president of the NDAA, and I, along with the commissioners, held a joint press conference at the Plaza Hotel in New York City. A couple of hundred reporters were in attendance.

The night before, Bill and I had a delightful dinner with Bowie Kuhn and Pete Rozelle, the commissioners of baseball and football, respectively. Those were two fine guys who appreciated our efforts to keep gambling out of their sports.

I believe our efforts kept this movement from taking hold. Months later, Bowie wrote me inviting me to sit in his box in the opening game of the World Series and, for that matter, any other games during the series. Oakland was trying for its third World Series title in a row and was going to play the Dodgers. I loved baseball since I was a kid and had a longing ambition to see a World Series game. Here I was, with this great invitation from the high commissioner himself, but declined due to a pending trial during Series week. I still have that letter.

AS I FINISHED MY term as president of the NDAA I was asked to make the banquet address for the Canadian Prosecutors' Association in Toronto. At the meeting was my host, John Samson of Canada, and Sir Norman Skelhorn, the director of all prosecutions carried on in the United Kingdom. The three of us decided to form an International Prosecutors Association. The NDAA would keep tabs on members. This association would make for better cooperation on international types of crimes and extraditions. We started off slowly, but now there is an effective international association in place.

Sir Norman and I became good friends. As Director of Public Prosecutions for all of England, he served for thirty years, under liberal and conservative prime ministers alike.

Once Sir Norman and Lady Skelhorn came to the U.S. and stayed with us in our home in Houston. Then we traveled to Austin where we stayed with Carolyn's parents out on Lake Travis. Sir Norman thought it was a blast when Carolyn's brother, Fred Kongabel, drove us in to a Longhorn game in his large motor home. Sir Norman, sitting on the couch with Scotch and soda in hand, observed such conduct as might be considered a bit outrageous in jolly old London. The Longhorns blew by Rice. Sir Norman enjoyed the game but asked why so many college-educated people would wear that dreadful orange.

There was always something extracurricular going on during my tenure

as DA. One year I was chairman of the Criminal Law Section of the State
Bar of Texas. I served several years as an elected representative on the ABA
Criminal Justice Section. I was also appointed to an ABA special committee
to develop the National Standards for Prosecutors. The prosecutors of
America, always a top notch group, were becoming even more professional in
the service of their communities.

One major project I was privileged to be involved in from the start was
the establishment of the National College of District Attorneys. Several of us
who were past presidents of the NDAA wanted a first-class national training
arm for the country's prosecutors. We wanted a well-funded and prestigious
school, something akin to the acclaimed FBI academy which trained state and
local law enforcement officers. We wanted a place where prosecutors could
receive basic and specialized training, like trial tactics, organized crime investigations, child abuse cases, cases of battered wives, drug cases, consumer
frauds, big time white collar crimes, pollution crimes, civil cases, in addition
to administrative training for newly elected district attorneys.

I was privileged to serve on a six-person task force which put the details
for the college together. Our chairman was John Price, the DA of Sacramento
and former president of the NDAA. Colonel Leon Jaworski not only played a
key role on the committee but lined up financing from several huge foundations on whose boards he served. The Colonel had been president of both the
ABA and the American College of Trial Lawyers, both of which organizations agreed to sponsor the college in conjunction with the NDAA. Dean John
Neibel of the University of Houston Law School served on our little task
force to get this college cranked up. The dean offered us a place to roost. The
National College of District Attorneys was given office space and the use of
classrooms and moot courtrooms by the UH Law School.

We had my friend Phil Hoffman's blessing as well. He was president of the
University of Houston. U of H has one of the finest schools of hotel management in the country, the Conrad Hilton College of Hotel and Restaurant
Management. The school even has a working hotel. With Phil's blessing we
had access to the hotel, which we used in the summer for our attendees. Our
prosecutors would come from around the nation and be housed in the new
high rise.

The National College of District Attorneys received support from the
Cullen, Moody, and Houston Endowment foundations. Even the J. Edgar
Hoover Foundation contributed. The college has been enormously successful
providing basic and advanced training of all kinds to the nation's prosecutors
for over thirty years now.

Well-known defense attorney Bill Walsh became the first temporary dean of the college, followed by Portland, Oregon's district attorney, George Van Hoomissen, our first permanent dean. Frank Coakley, the retired and popular longtime district attorney from Oakland, moved to Houston to be the assistant dean. After Van Hoomissen went back to Oregon to be a judge, Colonel John Douglass, the former head of the U.S. Army JAG School at Charlottesville took over. He was ultimately replaced by Bob Fertita, who had been on the NCDA staff from the start. Bob originally found his way to Houston when he and Houston Assistant DA Ted Busch exchanged places for a year. Bob was an assistant DA at the time in Baltimore.

Houston for years has played a great role in the progress of prosecutors around the nation. After John Price, I was the second chairman of the board of the college and served on that board for fifteen years. I still hold the title of board member emeritus.

One summer the NDAA put together a trip where we met with the attorneys general and members of the highest courts in London, Paris, Rome, Geneva, Austria, and Germany. We learned in detail how a good part of the civilized world approaches criminal justice. I learned that I like our system best, where the lawyers try the cases and not the judges. In continental Europe a panel of judges takes control of the case from start to finish. The lawyers ask question by permission of the court.

Crime knows no boundaries. It crosses state and international borders constantly. Knowing prosecutors from all over on a first name basis was a plus when our office needed help and gave me the chance to draw on stronger minds than my own for ideas of better serving the public.

CHAPTER TWENTY

The Transformation of Gerry Phelps

And we know that all things work together for good to those who love God, to those who are the called according to His purpose.
—Romans 8:28

TRUTH IS STRANGER THAN fiction. One of the strangest cases I ever tried was the Gerry Phelps case. If I had not been around to witness this lady before and after her encounters with the law, I would have been skeptical. This was one amazing transformation in the life of a human being. A miraculous turn around, so miraculous it could only have come from God.

When I encountered Gerry Charlotte Phelps, she was an associate professor. She taught economics at not one, but three universities: the University of Houston, South Texas College, and the University of Saint Thomas. She was popular, attractive, and soft-spoken. Gerry had her Master's degree and was about to obtain her PhD from the University of Texas. Her doctorate would be complete when she finished her dissertation on "Economics in Cuba." With Fidel Castro now in control, she had spent time working on her thesis in Cuba.

The Dean of the University of Houston's Behavioral Science College described her as "an excellent teacher with good credentials. She never expected her students to agree with her but encouraged them to attack her arguments with reasoning. She was very intelligent and knowledgeable in her field." Over at South Texas the student newspaper lead-in read, "Teacher enthralls students with intelligence, dedication." Besides her blue-ribbon credentials, the "quiet and sweet young lady" was a widow who was raising a young son.

One day I was sitting in my office when my friend Joe Singleton walked in. Joe was chief of the HPD Intelligence Division, and we shared a close history through the TSU riot. Bob Blaylock, who was shot in that same riot but now back in action, was at Joe's side. Joe ran one of the best intelligence outfits in the country. He kept me posted on all of the local political disturbances, namely the radicals or organized crime types who crossed the Harris County line. That was his job, and he did it well.

"Chief, you won't believe this," Joe said.

"Joe, with you it has to be wild and crazy. Is Stokely Carmichael stirring the pot again?"

"No, crazier than that. A woman professor is plotting a robbery to further her radical agenda. She has enlisted her own students to pull off the job."

"Robbery, armed robbery? Loaded guns? A professor and her students?" I asked, incredulous.

"This is real," Joe said. "We have a mole keeping us posted. They plan to hit a certain liquor store in the Memorial area and make off with a bundle of cash. After that we think they want to pull some more jobs. But this one is going down for certain.

"We know the plan. We know this professor is a radical. She has been spending time in Cuba, supposedly to do a thesis. We figure that is her cover for going down to Castro country. Our info is the hijacking will go down soon."

Joe continued. "I have a legal question for you. Can we let them go ahead and pull their robbery and then arrest them and make a case? Will the fact we let it happen when we could have stopped it ruin an otherwise good case? Also, the chief wants your personal signing off on this little project before we go forward. Just another day in the city, right?"

"Well, Joe, you know we can't prosecute a conspiracy case without an overt act. Also we would have to corroborate your accomplice's testimony to tie her in. So I say take a go at it. The robbery will be our corroborating overt act. Besides, we don't need to go on a conspiracy theory if we get her with the cash right after the robbery. Mark the bills and with even one on her we can make a robbery case. Even if she doesn't go in the store and pull the gun. But you need to catch her right after and as close to the vicinity as you can."

"Chief, she's supposed to be in on the robbery. We believe she'll be at the scene or close to it where she can take the money and run. Take it off the robbers' hands just in case someone gets their license number or takes after their car. They are to dump the guns and cash on her as soon after the robbery as they can." Joe said.

"Okay, catch them giving her the money and we can try her for the robbery."

"Yeah, got that covered. Also we'll blanket this thing with cameras and a mike in the store," Joe said. "Would you believe this? She is supposed to park her car only a couple of blocks from the liquor store so she can see the guys go in and come out."

"By the way, Joe, what are these students supposed to get out of all of this?" I asked.

"Nothing, I guess. Do college kids need a reason? Guess they are either in it for the thrill or she has them wanting to be part of whatever political stuff she is into."

This was the summer of 1968. Riots and demonstrations raged across the land. The TSU riot had just passed its first anniversary. Joe told me Gerry had made a recent trip to Cuba where she accompanied a group associated with a socialist newspaper. (Later on I learned that Gerry's main purpose for the robbery was to finance an underground press that would publish propaganda against the unpopular war in Vietnam. The war had been a primary cause for stirring up riots and trouble for some time.)

Plans were made as the big day approached. Police manned their stations around the Bigwick Liquor Store in a small shopping center in the upscale Memorial area. We found out later that one of the robbers, the one driving the getaway car, had worked for Bigwick and knew where the safe was located. The Houston Police Department had invited several dignitaries out to watch the bust; among them were the county judge, a Harris County commissioner, and a future sheriff. I was not happy with the Houston police letting uninvolved personnel have a ringside seat but did not veto the idea.

The day came. Police in unmarked cars waited a block away. Not a minute off schedule, three young men, Sam, age seventeen, Chris, twenty-one, and Bunker, twenty-seven, pulled up to the site. The younger two entered the liquor store while Bunker waited behind the wheel.

Even though the three wore masks, Bunker stayed in the car. He did not go in because he had worked in the store and was afraid that his voice would betray him. The other two rushed into the store with sawed-off shotguns. Wasting no time, they handcuffed the victims and threatened the cashier. The cashier quickly handed over the contents of the cash register, $1,200 in small bills.

Then, in what must have been record time, the two ran to the car and climbed in.

The car took off. Two blocks away they reached Gerry's car at the rendezvous point, where Gerry waited, alone. They handed her the money and dumped the guns inside her vehicle.

The young men quickly hit the road again with Gerry following close behind. Up ahead sat two patrol cars full of officers. The police cars wheeled out from the curb, blocking the street.

Gerry Phelps, like a professional driver, did a perfect spin around.

When she saw that her last exit route was blocked by two more patrol cars that had pulled in behind her, it was all over. The robbery and her arrest could not have taken over two minutes.

The police began a thorough search of her car. In her purse was a shopping list a little uncharacteristic of the suburban housewife: M1 carbines, sub-machine guns, shotguns, .357 magnum pistols with silencers, and fifty grenades. The sawed-off shotguns led to the filing of charges by the FBI, while Gerry and the young men were charged by the State of Texas with armed robbery.

The police took Gerry and the trio back to headquarters. Handcuffed, they entered the front door of the Houston Police Department headquarters before a crowd of media, flashbulbs exploding. The evening TV coverage and Houston dailies spoke of little else. The reporters were fascinated by Gerry Phelps' credentials. A respected professor as an armed robber was news indeed. The four were formally charged and high bonds were set.

Veteran lawyer Will Gray, one of Texas' best criminal appellate lawyers, ended up representing Gerry. There was so much publicity that Will filed a motion for a change of venue. He didn't think she could get a fair trial in Harris County. Will was probably right. Not ever wanting a politically sensitive trial that could trigger who knows what, I joined in his motion. There would be much less likelihood of a public demonstration in any other city than Houston. The judge ordered the trial to proceed in Fort Worth at the Tarrant County Courthouse. Veteran jurist, Judge Byron Matthews, would preside.

Getting ready to walk into court to try the case, I still did not have a clue what the defense strategy would be. Only Will Gray knew and he wasn't saying. Will had an impossible case to defend, but he had achieved some notable reversals in past cases in the face of strong evidence.

I had trouble understanding why an educated person with a respectable position would have gone this far off track. I read all the plaudits and praise of Gerry by her piers. The president of one university said, "Totally out of character. We never had a complaint. I found her to be a very personable young lady who liked to stay in shape by jogging. I knew she was interested in black student activities and civil rights, but so am I." Nevertheless, the robbery occurred and she was the mastermind.

Prior to the case going to trial, the judge called me to take me to see a Dallas Cowboys game. He was a big Cowboys fan. The jury was going to make the finding of guilt and do the sentencing. We didn't discuss the facts of the case, but we did discuss security. The judge was concerned with securing his courtroom and avoiding any trouble from demonstrators or nuts.

I told him things were quiet as far as the police knew, and that all of the intelligence agencies would be keeping their eyes and ears open. Plainclothes detectives, including a couple of Texas Rangers, would be in his courtroom. I told the judge that Will Gray was a heck of a good appellate lawyer and whenever Will made an objection the judge should take it seriously and take his time to rule. The worst thing the judge could do to me in this case would be to rule in my favor if Will was right.

We had the three young men cold on the armed robbery. Two agreed to cooperate and testify in detail about how Gerry planned the robbery and the things she said about why she wanted the money. Without the students' testimony Gerry could say she was waiting for three of her students to meet her at that intersection and they started dumping stuff from their car into her car. Gerry had no criminal record so a jury might believe her if she said she was innocent.

Gerry was our target. She was the teacher. These kids were not known to be involved in crime or radical causes. She got all the proceeds. In short, this was her deal, and she had our full attention.

The first day of the trial I looked across the counsel table and looked at Gerry. She did not look like any defendant I had ever tried. She was very calm and quiet. She spoke in a whisper to her lawyer. She had a pleasant smile and never frowned or put on that look of disgust when a witness was painting her into a corner. She looked mature and peaceful, not nervous like most female defendants. In her mid-thirties, she looked out of place as a defendant in an armed robbery case.

Rarely is a woman tried for armed robbery. Only one out of twenty inmates in prison are female. Most women defendants are charged with shoplifting, forged or hot checks, a drug charge, or shooting their husbands. Robbery by a female is rare. Also, few men or women with college degrees go to prison. You could probably count the number of women with a college degree in Texas prisons on one hand.

After the jury was seated, two of the co-defendants testified, starting with how they met Gerry through her classes at the University of Houston. Then they described the planning of the robbery. The arresting officers testified. Will offered little on cross-examination. There was nothing he could do. Lawyers can only play the hand they are dealt.

At the end of two days, our case was over. I said the State rests, and Will Gray immediately said the defendant rests. He wasn't about to call Gerry or any other fact witness to the stand. All he could hope for was a light sentence or a fluke reversal.

After the final arguments, the jury did not deliberate long. They found Gerry guilty and assessed her punishment at thirty-five years. One never knows what a jury will do, but I was shocked at the long length of the sentence. After all, she had no criminal history, not even a single arrest. On the other hand, she of all people should have known better. Had she plea bargained we would have insisted on a prison sentence, but probably in a five to ten year range, certainly not thirty-five years.

The two students who testified received ten years probation. Their records were clean and we owed them something for their cooperation. The third received a two-year sentence on a reduced charge.

I thought the case was over and I would never see Gerry Phelps again, but I was wrong. The real story here is not the crime or the trial but what Gerry later did with her life.

GERRY WAS TRANSFERRED BACK to the Harris County jail from Tarrant County. One who appeals his conviction has to remain in jail until the appellate court renders its opinion. Only after a conviction is upheld is the defendant shipped off to state prison. Sometimes a convicted felon had to wait in jail for up to two years before the Court of Criminal Appeals handed down its ruling.

While in jail Gerry continued to attract the attention of the press. She began to teach economics to inmates. Her teachings were not well-received by the sheriff or his jailers. They put her in solitary confinement.

In her cubbyhole of a cell she continued her exercise regimen by running in place daily. The jailers estimated she ran in place the equivalent of ten to fifteen miles a day. She was getting in great shape. Soon she departed this exercise routine to go on a hunger strike. The newspapers kept up with her rapid weight reduction. One day I read in the paper that she had gone from one hundred forty pounds down to only eighty. With doctors declaring her life in danger, she was transferred to Ben Taub, the Harris County charity hospital. There, she was force-fed to stay alive.

Gerry finally began to eat. Months later her case was heard by the appellate court. Ben Levy, as nice a person as one would ever meet and a regular lawyer for the ACLU, handled the appeal. The Texas Court of Criminal Appeals finally affirmed her conviction and Gerry was shipped off to the Goree Prison in Huntsville, the sole venue for women felons in Texas. There she dropped out of sight of the press.

I heard nothing else about Gerry until one day when I was accompanying the Harris County grand jury on a routine tour of the Texas prison system. As part of that tour we stopped off to visit the women's prison at Goree. While chatting with the warden, I asked him if he had ever met Gerry Phelps. The warden responded, "Have I ever!"

He immediately sent someone to round up the chaplain to join in our conversation. Both gentlemen could not say enough good things about Gerry Phelps. The warden said Gerry had done more to reform Goree than any other person.

Goree had a serious problem with women inmates fighting. Women were getting hurt. It was dangerous for the guards to try to break up a fight. This warden had been assigned to Goree to straighten things out. He said Gerry had a very rough beginning and had to be placed in solitary confinement on several occasions. But then one day she found Jesus. Her conversion was sudden. She gave up fighting the world and turned her life over to the Lord. Her life was never the same. From then on she had a passion to help the women, to convert them, to disciple them in the faith, to counsel with them about their hang-ups, and to teach them practical life skills so they could make it on the outside.

Gerry engaged in a serious study of the Bible led by the chaplain, a man by the name of Clifford Olsen. More and more women began to attend the Bible study after Gerry's conversion. Before long Gerry was teaching the women the Bible.

Chaplain Olsen described the change in prison as a revival. In his words, "Many, many were saved."

The women, instead of fighting daily, had gone to making friends. The garment factory, where most of the prisoners worked, had been a bloody place through the years. Most days there was at least one fight that broke out. Severe physical injuries occurred far too frequently, the reason for a new warden to take over. Now, after many women were seeing their lives changed, the garment factory was peaceful. There had not been a fight in the factory for nearly a year, the warden told me.

The women actually enjoyed going to work now, the warden said. The chaplain told me the whole thing was unbelievable. "Gerry's leadership is a major factor in the change of attitude."

The guards, who gave her a rough time at first, now gave her the run of the yard so she could counsel the other women. The chaplain said she spent a great deal of time praying with the inmates individually.

"Gerry really has a heart for these women. She is getting them ready to go back into the real world," the warden explained.

Chaplain Olsen said Gerry had begun to prepare for a future seminary enrollment; she wanted to be a pastor.

Finally, as I was leaving Goree that day, Olsen said, "Mr. Vance, this woman needs to get out. She just doesn't need to be here any longer. I pray you might see fit not to protest her parole when the time comes."

"Chaplain, based on yours and the warden's reports, I will heartily recommend parole. I wish all parole decisions were this easy."

Gerry was released after seven years' confinement. I did an unusual thing. I wrote the Parole Board a strong letter favoring parole. I could count on one hand the number of times I had written a letter *favoring* parole for someone. I was more likely to oppose it because we had too many situations where murderers with life sentences were getting out in eight years. In aggravated cases I usually opposed parole. In most cases, however, our office did not take a stand one way or another. I thought the parole people were in better position to make that call.

Upon release, Gerry hit the ground running to make up in the second half of her life what she missed out on in the first. In prison she had begun to prepare for the ministry. She taught herself Greek, the language of the New Testament.

As soon as she was permitted to leave the state, she settled in Bakersfield, California. Before much time passed she started a new homeless shelter in Bakersfield. A few years later Gerry moved north to San Jose to begin a second shelter. There she enrolled in a Reformed seminary to receive her ministerial training. She studied and went to class, all the while running the homeless shelter. Both shelters, each with a hundred and fifty beds, are still up and running. I still get letters to this good day to contribute to the San Jose shelter.

After her accomplishments in his town, the Mayor of Bakersfield declared a day in her honor, Gerry Phelps Day. Two thousand people showed up to celebrate her good works in feeding and housing the poor.

After some of her accomplishments, her lawyer, Ben Levy, and another friend of Gerry's who worked with the Harris County Commissioners Court, came to visit me. They brought a lot of proof and good stories about her accomplishments. They asked me to write a letter to the governor suggesting she receive a full pardon and restoration of citizenship. Governor Bill Clements, though a strong law-and-order guy, granted Gerry's request.

When I wrote my letter for Gerry's pardon, I wrote her a personal letter of encouragement. She passed my letter on to friends who were helping her. One sent a copy to the press. The letter ended, "Your friend in Christ, Carol Vance."

The press, always excitable when a Christian in public office mentions his faith, ran a page one story. The headline began, "Your Friend in Christ." I guess the press thought any mention of religion by a public official was newsworthy. I liked the story; it showed where I stood. Also, this case was the first time that I knew for sure God had done a good work on someone in prison. Now I do enough prison ministry to know this happens with some degree of frequency—but seldom such a radical change as with Gerry.

Gerry finished seminary and got her degree. She was ordained a Methodist minister. After several years in California, she left the West Coast and came back to Texas. She took a position as the pastor of a church in the town of Flatonia. The church grew under her leadership. From there she went to Austin and has been active in various Christian causes. She founded a ministry called CRISES (Christian Research Institute for Social and Economic Strategies). For a while I served on the board of CRISES.

Gerry is now an outspoken conservative who holds fast to biblical principles. Unlike some conservatives, however, she has a great passion for the least, the lost, and the left out. She is a friend of Marvin Olasky who wrote the classic book, *The Tragedy of American Compassion*. Marvin is editor of *World* magazine and a leading conservative Christian voice in America.

Gerry is a forceful writer and shares much wisdom on her web site gerry-charlottephelps.com. Her conversion experience and her outlook on life remind me greatly of my friend Chuck Colson, another person who went to prison and has not only done wonders for millions of prisoners but speaks with great wisdom about important issues our nation faces today.

From running with the troublemakers to feeding the poor, Gerry has

come full circle. Of her prison experience, she said, "Prison is one of the
kindest gifts of all. It turned me towards God and away from wasting my life.
Prison gave me the insights I need to minister to inmates, to the poor and
to the addicted and those who are down and out. Prison brought me face to
face with those big questions of life, is there a God, why am I here and what
does He want me to do?"

THESE DAYS I DO a lot of prison ministry. Usually I go to three prisons
a week in addition to preaching at the Harris County jail and a homeless
shelter. When I go, sometimes I think of Gerry's remarkable transformation
as well as that of many other inmates I have known. I was drawn into prison
ministry after having been appointed onto the Texas Board of Criminal
Justice and serving as its chairman for several years.

During that time, I helped open the prison doors wider to welcome volunteers, who were mostly all Christian. As mentioned earlier, with the leadership of Chuck Colson, founder of Prison Fellowship, and Governor George
W. Bush, a strong proponent of faith-based ministries, the first prison with
all-Christian programming was established in our nation. Today, other states
have followed suit. The Texas prison at Sugar Land was named after me after
I left the board. The incredibly low recidivism rate of 8 percent at the Carol
Vance Unit is living proof of what God can do. Gerry Phelps was my first
living example.

Today over 2,000,000 individuals are locked up in prisons in the
U.S. Over 90 percent are men. These prisoners are prolific and have over
5,000,000 children, most all of whom are at risk as they grow up in father-
less homes. Unless something is done, our crime rate will continue to climb
through the roof. A habitual offender costs the taxpayer over $1,000,000 on
average in the U.S. for being in and out of prison over a lifetime. And the far
greater cost to the victims of crime and their loved ones can't even begin to
be calculated.

When someone asks an old DA why I go out to those prisons and spend
time with these "convicts," I say, "To see God change lives. Come go with me."
I want to see those guys paying their bills, paying their taxes, and raising their
children instead of committing crimes at all of our expense.

Gerry, who was named to *Who's Who in America* some years ago, said it
best. "You know, the prisons have some good things going like their school
system and some vocational training. But in my experience, getting converted

is the most important thing. Until a woman gets converted she is not interested in school or learning a trade. Once converted she has a reason to live. Then she wants that education. Then she is happier. She now has learned to make it on the outside."

CHAPTER TWENTY-ONE

Deep Throat and the Supreme Court

I shall not attempt today to define (pornography) ... But I know it when I see it.
—Justice Potter Stewart in *Jacobellis v. Ohio*,
U.S. Supreme Court, 1984

MY FRIEND HENRY WADE was District Attorney of Dallas for a long time. He was an outstanding DA and nationally known for prosecuting Jack Ruby, the guy who shot Lee Harvey Oswald after Oswald had assassinated President Kennedy. But for all his public service and good works, Henry's name mainly goes down in history as the "Wade" in *Roe v. Wade*, the Supreme Court case that made abortion legal no matter what laws the states had passed.

I never had a *Roe v. Wade*, but I had my own little case out of the Supreme Court. It was called *Vance v. Universal Amusement Co., Inc.*, and was one of several leading cases which unfortunately made pornography cases almost impossible to prosecute.

Before *Vance v. Universal Amusement* (sometimes called *Vance v. Deep Throat*) surfaced, pornographic movies or lewd sex acts carried on in neighborhood settings could be shut down through civil injunctions. Public nuisances were fair game.

Backed by the appropriate ordinances, cities or counties could pounce on neighborhood blights where the girls took it all off and where lawless people hung out. The state or city could file a lawsuit in civil court, prove a nuisance existed, and usually get the judge to put a padlock on the place. Violations of the court's order subjected the perpetrators to heavy fines or jail sentences for contempt of court. Nuisance injunctions were most effective in cleaning up the dirt in the neighborhood.

Our office, working with our county attorney, had considerable success through the nuisance-injunctive route. File the suit, roll the projector, and hand the judge the order to sign.

Seldom did a judge turn us down.

In the *Vance* case, the defendant was an enterprise known as Universal Amusement, and the issue involved was the display of pornographic films like *Deep Throat*.

After we shut down their fun, Universal Amusement appealed the adverse ruling all the way to the U.S. Supreme Court. This is a feat in and of itself as few cases ever get to the Supreme Court.

In the *Vance v. Universal Amusement* opinion, the Court overturned the injunctions below and made the injunctive relief virtually useless. The Court ruled on constitutional grounds that we could only get an injunction one film at a time and we had to have a separate hearing—a mini trial, in other words—for each film we alleged was over the top.

Because the smut peddlers make hundreds of these movies each day and the films are inexpensive to make, having a trial on each film would be impossible.

Once again, five justices out of nine made a major change in what conduct would or would not be allowable in these United States. It did little good that Chief Justice Warren Berger, Justice Lewis Powell, and the two brightest guys on the court, Whizzer White and William Rehnquist, dissented.

Step by step and little by little the U.S. Supreme Court was changing the face of America. The practical result was that hard-core pornography was being legalized even though historically smut had never received protection under the Freedom of Speech Clause or any other clause of the Constitution.

When I started out as an assistant DA, juries convicted anyone caught with hard-core pornography. No one needed any legal definition of the stuff. To paraphrase Justice Potter Stewart, "I can't define it, but I know it when I see it." And in spite of the liberal rallying cry, no prosecutor I knew ever tried to prosecute the nudes painted in the Sistine Chapel or a replica of the mermaid's statue in Copenhagen.

Even so, avant-garde liberals flooded the public with dire warnings of prosecutors taking away our basic freedoms. Back in the old days we simply showed the objectionable movie to the jury and rested our case. The jury knew what pornography looked like and usually gave the maximum jail sentence to the defendant. Juries did not want these kinds of commercial ventures floating around their neighborhoods or anywhere else in their city.

As early as 1966, the year I took office, the Supreme Court in *Memoirs v. Massachusetts* (by a vote of 5–4, of course) adopted an impossible standard for prosecutors to convict someone on a pornography charge. In the majority opinion, three justices said obscene material could not be prosecuted unless the material had absolutely no redeeming social value of any kind. No prosecutor could get around that standard. One person's reaction to that question is as good as another. How, after ten psychologists testified for the defense that smut helped some poor guy with his sex problem, could any jury in good conscience return a guilty verdict?

In 1973's *Miller v. California* decision, the Supreme Court came up with the final say on the law. Led by Chief Justice Berger, the five-person majority specifically overturned the *Memoirs* rationale.

The *Miller* case, however, had its own test which was too high a hill to climb for prosecutors. The new test was that the prosecution had to prove that (1) the average person, applying contemporary community standards, would have to find the work taken as a whole appealed to the prurient interest; (2) that the work being prosecuted was not only patently offensive but was the kind of sexual conduct specifically prohibited by applicable state law; and (3) the work taken as a whole lacked any serious literary, artistic, political, or scientific value. Can the "average Joe" serving on the jury even understand those standards?

How does one prove any kind of obscene material lacks any serious literary, artistic, political, or scientific value? And what does that mean, anyway? It is not something a jury can get their heads around to make that judgment call.

Typically, in the cases that were being prosecuted across America, large numbers of experts with all kinds of degrees and credentials testified for both sides. How can a juror believe beyond a reasonable doubt something has no value when numerous educated experts testify it *does* have value?

Crimes need to have definite and exacting definitions, not vague general principles. And getting all twelve jurors to agree to convict was just not doable. A hung jury is as good as an acquittal in a pornography case.

Criminal laws are all based on plain and simple and definite concepts, except in pornography cases. What is a community? What is a standard? What is art? Who is to say a scientific purpose of some kind is not met? What is a social value? These terms mean different things to different people. What does political purpose have to do with smut?

Justice Berger may have meant well, but he laid an impossible burden on the prosecution.

Even the term "community standards" poses a great problem. What is a community? The Court did not say. We don't know in Harris County if the whole county is our community or whether it should be a city such as Pasadena or Tomball, or a neighborhood like Third Ward, the Montrose area, or River Oaks. And can the same movie be legal in my neighborhood but illegal across town? The bottom line was, the Supreme Court knew how to shut down pornography prosecution in America while making it appear they had still left that door open.

The movie *Deep Throat* was a prime example for us in Harris County of the difficulties of bringing a charge for showing a movie with explicit sex acts. How juries reacted to *Deep Throat* turned out to define pornography prosecution in America.

When *Deep Throat* first played in Houston the police raided the movie theatre, filed charges, and brought the film over for us to prosecute. I saw the first few minutes of this plot-barren, explicit sex movie and said prosecute. I honestly believed any jury in Harris County would convict and put the operator in jail for as long as they could.

I was dead wrong.

Sensing we were in for a legal battle and this was the test case, I assigned Assistant DA Mike Hinton to try the *Deep Throat* case. Mike was an excellent trial lawyer and could handle his own against any defense team, and I knew this movie would be well defended.

We presented the case to the grand jury. I personally asked each of these twelve fine men and women to watch the entire movie so the defense could not attack the indictment. A few grand jurors walked out in disgust. Another said she came close to throwing up. The grand jurors seemed to be representative of the law-abiding citizens you would expect. Every one of them were repulsed, wanted to get this movie off our streets, send the perpetrator to jail, and voted yes to the indictment.

In prosecuting *Deep Throat*—the same as many other prosecutors did around the country—we turned the movie's star Linda Lovelace into a celebrity and fed the coffers of organized crime through publicity that money could not have bought.

By the time Mike got the case to trial, *Deep Throat* was on its way to breaking attendance records across America. Mike, who now is one of the leading defense attorneys in our city, gave it his best shot, only to walk away with not one, but two hung juries.

The defense strategy was simple. *Deep Throat* was being watched across America by hundreds of thousands, if not millions, of people. Therefore, how could the longest running movie in many cities be an affront to any community? Attendance alone showed the movie was socially acceptable to a large segment of the population.

Professors, psychiatrists, psychologists, and social study experts eagerly took the stand to beat the drum to the same tune. These learned men and women said many people might not like this movie, but the movie does have social and/or psychological value to many others. Therefore, the movie passes both the redeeming social value and redeeming scientific value tests.

One expert even compared the artistic value of *Deep Throat* to *War and Peace*. (I won't say at which university he taught.)

The witnesses noted no movie could be an affront to anyone when the movie is that well-watched. Now, if we picked other films to prosecute, the defense would simply show *Deep Throat* and say that it passed the smell test, so what is this prosecutor trying to do by trying films that are no worse than *Deep Throat*?

Thinking that perhaps our first hung jury was a fluke, I told Mike to tee it up again.

He did. A second hung jury resulted. At that, we threw in the towel. We were chasing the wind.

It did not matter that organized crime was reaping the profits from *Deep Throat* and continuing to grind out porn flicks daily to distribute across America. I wondered where the women's rights activists had gone when we needed them most to stand up for the young women victims who were being forced into sexual slavery in these sexually-oriented businesses. I read where the average pay for the woman was $100 to make a film where the poor girl had to engage in multiple sex acts with multiple other men and women. (The guys mostly worked for free in this industry.)

Deep Throat cost $25,000 to make but grossed over $100,000,000 in the United States alone. In the history of the film industry, no movie has run so long in every major city in America—it played in Los Angeles for ten continuous years and was the city's highest grossing movie in both 1972 and 1973.

For her part, Linda Lovelace reportedly received a paltry $1,200. She became so famous she made a second movie, *Linda Lovelace for President*. (The film was not nominated for an Oscar.) Linda's life spiraled downward into an ocean of tragedy. According to some news reports this was as a direct result of her performance in *Deep Throat*.

There is no question in my mind but that the Supreme Court pulled a fast one. They seemingly upheld the right of the State to go after hard-core pornography but intentionally devised a formula where only a jury in Salt

Lake City would find an individual guilty. Today, because of this decision, organized crime has more money in its coffers to operate all kinds of criminal schemes. Much more important than that, there is little way to keep this stuff our of the public eye. What the media has cleverly called "soft porn" is really the hard-core porn of decades past, the kind of pictures, films, and the like that was kept from the public. Today anyone renting a hotel room is just one click away from viewing such material. And depending on what cable package one subscribes to, the same is true in millions of homes across America. Certainly the founders of our nation and writers of our Constitution meant for the states to determine these issues through their governing power. Porn has never been subject to any Constitutional "free speech" protection until recently.

Most historians believe a growing immorality brought down Rome. What is to keep it from happening here? In *Vance v. Deep Throat* we tried to enforce the law, but it was like fighting the wind.

CHAPTER TWENTY-TWO

The Last Case: Elmer Wayne Henley

To every thing there is a season, and a time to every purpose under the heaven: a time to be born, and a time to die; a time to plant, and a time to pluck up that which is planted.
—Ecclesiastes 3:1–2 (KJV)

ONE OF DARRELL ROYAL'S old quotes summarized my feelings: "I still enjoy coaching but I sure don't want to wear out my welcome." That was the way I felt as a long-term DA.

As I sailed towards town, the hour was getting close. I took Louisiana Street, going north. I purposely drove by the Pennzoil Building, the twin triangular towers of glass and steel in a pitch black mode. Bracewell and Patterson's plush offices occupied three floors in the building, designed by world-renowned architect Phillip Johnson.

Their offices were orderly and quiet. I would occupy one of two corner offices on the twenty-ninth floor which housed the litigation partners and associates. From my perch I could look out two sides of the all-glass building and see half of Harris County. I would be able to see a 747 making its final approach at Intercontinental Airport out one side and look down on my old office at the courthouse from the other side.

The quiet new quarters stood in contrast to the atmosphere in the DA's office. At Bracewell, lawyers and secretaries quietly pored over important-looking legal documents. Back at the DA's office, some assistant yelled across the hall to a secretary, "Go find me a legal pad—I've got a judge and jury waiting! And get that investigator of mine up to the courtroom right now!" In spite of the disorder, sparse quarters, and lower pay, no lawyers in town had more fun practicing law than assistant district attorneys.

In a few minutes I would face that moment of truth and say goodbye to dear friends, great guys and gals with whom I had spent up to twenty-two years of my life. My rough guess is that some five hundred different prosecutors had worked for me during my days as district attorney. I may have been their boss, but I saw them as friends. They treated me with a great respect, but a stranger standing close by would never know it listening to our conversations. The more experienced staff felt very comfortable poking at me in good-natured fun and making dry comments about my absentminded ways. We were all comfortable with each other, which made our work pleasant considering how often we dealt with the adversities of life. I never wanted a bunch of "yes men" around. The staff understood that.

Finally the moment had arrived as I snuck up the inner stairwell of the Criminal Courts Building to avoid seeing anyone. Will I miss the courthouse crowd, the action, the daily crises, the press, and the big cases? Probably, but one thing was certain. I wouldn't miss having to ever try the Henley case again.

My mind raced back to Elmer Wayne Henley and the Houston Mass Murders. How could that have ever happened?

THE HENLEY CASE CENTERED around one of America's saddest atrocities, the deliberate torture and killing of at least twenty-seven young teenage boys. The sordid tale began with a person by the name of Dean Corll. For a long time we did not know much about this man or what drove him to be the initiating force behind this American tragedy. Gradually Corll's background unfolded, but no one could ever come up with an answer as to why.

We did know that Corll enlisted two immature teenagers, Elmer Wayne Henley and David Brooks, and, using their creative energies, engaged in nights of terror, torture, and death.

Dean Corll was born in Indiana in 1939. He grew up in a combative home of conflict and loud arguments. His parents divorced when he was a young child but remarried each other a few years later. Corll's father dished out macabre beatings to young Dean for the smallest of trespasses.

The parents kept up their fights and harangues during the second marriage, the same as the first. Dean's mother, finally fed up, divorced Dean's father a second time and married another man. The new couple, along with Dean and his little brother, headed to Houston. Along the way Dean developed a heart condition due to rheumatic fever. His attendance at school suffered.

In 1964 Dean was drafted into the service, but because of homosexual leanings, he was administratively discharged and he returned to Houston. By the late sixties Dean had engaged in some sadistic homosexual encounters with young men.

Corll liked to befriend teenage boys. Along the way, in 1971, he ran across fifteen-year-old David Brooks. The two hit it off, and Corll talked Brooks into coming over to his place.

Brooks walked into Dean's home and was shocked to see a nude Dean Corll standing over two teenage boys who were strapped to a homemade torture rack.

Brooks left. He never knew if the boys lived or died.

Some weeks later, Corll met Elmer Wayne Henley, another fifteen-year-old, and invited him over. By then, David Brooks had gotten over his initial hesitation and had become a regular visitor. From that time on, the three hung out and the games accelerated.

Dean was older and clearly the leader. He had the money, he had the house, he had the vehicle. He also had the torture board and the lumber. He even had the handcuffs used to imprison the young victims.

Dean started paying Brooks and Henley to find young boys for him. The unsuspecting victims would be given a ride by Corll to his house in Pasadena. Although the circumstances varied in each case, the *modus operandi* usually followed the same pattern. Cruise around, find some young teenager or two hanging out and looking for excitement and alcohol or marijuana. And then talk those boys into the van to "go party" over at Dean's place.

The hook was usually the free marijuana. Sometimes they offered the teenagers money to come over. There were also promises of highs from sniffing glue; Corll promised an unlimited supply at his house. He even sometimes promised girls. Whatever it took.

It was time to party, the last party for all we came to know about. I can't say no youngster escaped this trio's clutches, but it defied logic for a kid to go through any part of this ordeal, escape, and then not tell parents, police, or somebody.

Once the one or two guys were drawn inside the house, Corll would bring out the glue and the brown paper bags. The alcohol and marijuana would flow. The object was to get the teenagers higher than a kite in order to be sitting ducks for the real game.

Then came Henley's favorite trick of "let's play how to get out of the handcuffs." Henley would put on a pair of handcuffs and then "miraculously" get free. The teenagers were fascinated and wanted to try that for themselves.

Corll obliged, trapping the guest in the handcuffs and rendering him helpless to be dragged over to the large eight-foot long torture board. The boy would then be spread-eagled with new handcuffs on wrists and ankles. Hopelessly bound, his doom was certain.

With the stoned teenager hanging cuffed on the torture board, the games would escalate. The victim would be stripped of his clothing and made to spend the rest of his short life attached to the board.

Sometimes the young victim would be kept alive over the weekend while Dean and his two buddies shot pellet guns into the young victim's body, including his scrotum. The naked youth, locked on the board, was the object of sordid games involving sadomasochistic sex.

Dean Corll was very strong. Sometimes strangling proved difficult so Corll would have to finish off the strangulation process himself. The young teenagers died in different ways as they cried out for their lives and begged to be released. Death came to nearly every victim who entered that house except Brooks and Henley, Dean's cohorts; Dean could not afford to leave a witness around.

After the victim was dead, the trio's challenge was to dispose of the body. Corll owned a van and had also constructed a homemade body box large enough to transport one or two dead boys to one of his favorite burial grounds.

The body would be covered with lime and wrapped in a plastic covering and loaded in the box. Then the three would drive to the "graveyard," dig a hole and drop in the body.

After the case broke, and following weeks and months of searches, a total of twenty-seven bodies were dug up from three locations. Some were buried at a spot deep in the piney woods of East Texas, not far from Lake Sam Rayburn. On one occasion Corll, Henley, and Brooks started out with two bodies to transport to this location. Upon arrival, the trio first fished the lake, then napped, and then had a picnic before commencing the burial.

The second burial spot was a boat stall in the Houston area. The stall had a dirt floor behind its locked door.

The third and last burial ground was a desolate beach on the Bolivar Peninsula a mile or so out of the town of High Island. The usual approach to High Island from Houston is to go to Galveston, cross over on the Bolivar ferry, and drive the thirty-mile isolated strip of peninsula to High Island.

Dean Corll seemed to be able to finance his perversions. He usually paid Henley and Brooks $100 each to land a kid in the van. Sexually perverse acts and a tortuous death was Dean's goal. The parents never knew who did what to whom, adding to their pain and suffering. I could not imagine what these moms and dads went through after hearing the news.

At the time this case broke, I had escaped the August Houston heat for Snowmass, Colorado, where the National District Attorneys Association was holding its annual meeting. Life was good. I had won the tennis singles and had been honored at the final banquet by a crazy comedian, who, armed with stories from my staff, roasted me unmercifully. More importantly, I was finishing up perhaps the busiest year of my life as I ended my term as president of the NDAA. Glad to have "been there and done that." Carolyn, the kids, and I were having a blast. Many prosecutors from our staff were there. It was a pleasant reprieve until the call came in. The date was August 8, 1973.

As I walked into my room the phone rang. It was Mike Hinton. Mike's excitable voice told me something dreadful had happened.

"Chief, I hate to bother you, but you have never seen anything like what we have on our hands back here in Houston. Two teenagers have been arrested. One killed an older guy named Corll. These three had a torture and killing factory out at this guy Corll's home in Pasadena. Corll was much older and induced his two teenager buddies to lure kids over to his house where they tortured these teens to death. The police are still digging up bodies. We don't know how many they killed. We probably don't know the half of it. You can't believe it, Chief.

"One teen led the police out to this boat storage yard where they are digging up bodies. They say the stench is unbearable. I'm down here at Homicide now. I had to run the press out of here. They were climbing all over us and we had work to do and couldn't even turn around."

Before I could express my concerns about evidence handling, he read my mind.

"Don't worry, Chief. We set up a method of preserving all of the evidence and clothes and stuff for each body. We have photographed everything and kept the evidence intact for each of these dead kids. Our big problem is we just don't know who the victims are."

I was reeling with the enormity of the case as he continued his report.

"We do know, at least, the main guys who did all this. This young seventeen-year-old, Elmer Wayne Henley, killed the ring leader, Corll, who owned the house where most of the murders took place. Looks like Henley and a kid named Brooks, who was in on the killings, too, will be the ones we will go after."

I told Mike I would leave Colorado immediately on the first flight I could find. Carolyn and the kids would have to drive back alone.

When I got back to Houston, the media was in a frenzy. I was used to dealing with reporters from our two papers, three TV stations, and two news radio stations. I knew all of them. They were polite and easy to talk to. I was accessible, and they did not hound me. But these murders had brought out the national press with every scandal sheet in the nation represented. I could not leave the office without being mobbed. Each reporter had to have a new series of stories each day. They were desperate for quotes from the head of Homicide, the key detectives, Mike Hinton, and me. We had reporters from Japan, Sweden, and the BBC, as well as the New York *Times*, Washington *Post*, *Time*, and *Newsweek*. Many brought along their own photographers. The networks came with their camera crews. Even the sensationalist rags you see at the grocery check out stands had their reporters in Houston.

Many of the out-of-state reporters centered their inquiries around Texans and their obsession with guns. For days the reporters swarmed. Whether it was the BBC or the *National Enquirer*, the question everyone from the press always posed to me was, "How could this happen?"

"I can't answer that one," was my only response, and I meant it.

They had other questions for me, of course. "When will the trial start?" "What about a grand jury investigation?" "How many will be charged?" "Have all of the bodies been recovered?"

For the first time I had trouble physically getting past the press to walk into the courthouse. The press resembled a mob yelling their questions in my face.

Homicide, the ME's office, and Hinton had been going at it day and night to try to get the facts straight and put the evidence in order. Fortunately Elmer Wayne Henley and David Owen Brooks had given detailed statements to the police telling at least some of their involvement. They had given Homicide the names of a few victims and led police to the three graveyards which, other than the boat stall, may have never been discovered. Without the bodies, we would have had no case nor idea of who had been murdered.

The whole case had broken under an unexpected and weird scenario. Henley, worried that Corll was going to kill him too, shot and killed Corll, called the police, and then related the sordid story, culminating with showing police the burial grounds. News cameras were rolling when he broke the news to his mother on the car phone of one of the reporters. The scene was played on national news over and over.

In his confession, Henley admitted to being in on ten killings and having choked some of those victims to death. Brooks, who gave two confessions, said he was present when most of the boys were put to death. Further, he said Henley killed one kid by putting a .25 automatic pistol to his head.

Shortly after I returned to Houston I let Mike Hinton off the hook so he could get back to some investigations he had going as head of Organized Crime. I assigned Don Lambright, the chief of our Felony Division, to head up the case. He dropped his plans to try a couple of upcoming cases and would live with the Henley-Brooks matter nearly day and night until our first trial ended.

Don did a great job as he interfaced with the brokenhearted family members, day after day and hour after hour. He lined up dental records from the victims' dentists and saw they were delivered properly to Dr. Jachimczyk, our medical examiner, who would match up the teeth with that of the discovered body from the grave.

The case was labor intensive. Calls about runaways came in every hour of the day. Don stayed on the phone talking to the parents and to local police from other jurisdictions. He had to drop most all of his other duties to handle the traffic.

The identification of each body was the most serious hurdle in order to get indictments and convictions against Henley and Brooks. Don also had to decide which cases we could make. Proving we had a dead body was not enough, not even with the confessions.

We had so many calls from the media around the world that I couldn't do my work. I routed the inquiries to Don. Of course he and I were always available to the local media, who were extremely helpful in writing stories about the young victims and showing the victims' clothing on television. That information led prospective parents to come in and volunteer dental records which led to some identifications. The entire process was arduous and heart-wrenching.

After several days of trying and intense work by veteran homicide lieutenant Breck Porter, we put the body count at twenty-seven. Seventeen bodies were dug up at the boat stall close to South Post Oak Road and Main Street, a long way from the last of several places where Corll had lived. With the help of a bulldozer, six bodies—mostly decayed—were found at the High Island beach, covered with the usual lime. The other four were found at Lake Sam Rayburn. Some enterprising reporter did some research and wrote that twenty-seven victims was a world record, breaking Juan Corona's record. Corona killed twenty-five farmhands in California in 1971. He got a life sentence two years later.

I don't know what we would have done without the cooperation of the two young defendants, Henley and Brooks. As bad as they were, the older Corll had led both of them into this episode and was the driving force behind it, even offering them financial incentives. That said, Brooks and Henley had plenty of blood on their hands and were deeply involved. They would be held accountable for a major role in the most sordid episode I had ever heard about in the history of United States.

The last night prior to Corll's death proves that truth is stranger than fiction. Perhaps Henley sensed his time might be getting short; Corll had already taken out so many young men. Why would he let the only two people who had the goods on him live? Without Henley or Brooks around no one might ever know anything about the murders.

THE FINAL NIGHT OF Dean Corll's life started out as usual. Henley cruised the city until he was able to pick up a twenty-year-old guy and a fifteen-year-old girl roaming the streets of Houston. With the promises of "party party" garnished with free marijuana and a glue sniffing experience, the pair succumbed and entered the Corll van.

Henley drove the two over to Corll's house in Pasadena. The only persons present that evening were Henley, Corll, and the two new partygoers. Brooks was not there. After getting real high from sniffing glue from brown paper bags, the four retired for the night.

Sometime after midnight Corll awoke. Henley and the other two had passed out or fallen asleep. He made his way into where the two guests were sleeping. He handcuffed both of them to the bed. Ordinarily, Corll would enlist Henley or Brooks to help handcuff the victims before moving them to the torture board. But this morning was different. After the handcuffing Corll decided to take Henley out. Probably he was thinking he needed to kill both Henley and Brooks and then there would be no one who could ever tie him in to the murders.

It was late at night. Henley was asleep on the bed in one of the bedrooms. Corll entered the room and reached down over the sleeping Henley to put the cuffs on.

Henley woke up, startled. Thinking fast, he told Corll that if he released him, he would help him kill the two guests.

Corll backed off, giving Henley a chance to wrest free. Henley knew where Corll kept a pistol, so he made a run for that room, grabbed the gun, and whirled around to see Corll coming at him with a large knife. Henley quickly raised the pistol and fired one shot. Dean Corll died instantly.

Henley called the police. When the Pasadena officers arrived, seventeen-year-old Elmer Wayne Henley was sitting on the curb, emotionally shaken and drained from the events. He gave a statement to the police describing much of the sordid history of the torture murders and disposal of bodies. This information led to the arrest of David Brooks. Brooks also confessed and recalled more details about the victims than did Henley.

Henley and Brooks were unemployed school dropouts at the time. Henley's mother was thirty-four years old and a friend of Dean Corll's. Dean was thirty-three, nearly twice the age of the two boys. Henley's mother told him she thought Corll was a nice man. She knew Henley visited with Corll over at the Corll house on a routine basis. Mrs. Henley approved of the friendship. After the case broke she told the press that Corll was just one of the boys. She seemed upset when a reporter asked her about the large disparity in Corll's age and that of her son.

The twenty-seven victims came from a variety of homes and neighborhoods. A few victims were dropouts hanging around the street looking for alcohol or marijuana. Others were good students who lived with both parents at home but were smooth-talked into going over to Corll's to party.

Finding out the names of each one of the victims was a formidable task. Indeed, some remains have still not been identified, decades later. The clothing saved from the gravesites helped in some cases but was not the absolute kind of identity we needed. The key was to come in the dental comparisons. With all of the murder cases I had tried and heard about, this was my first encounter with the use of dental records to determine the identity of the deceased. Most of the recovered bodies were decomposed. Faces were not recognizable. The boys were too young to have any fingerprints on file and besides, the skin deterioration on the fingertips made a positive ID through print comparisons impossible.

In a murder case, identification of the deceased is extremely important. Not only does the prosecutor need a body, but the body must to be identified. Our ME came through again.

Dr. Joe had the boys' teeth. He just needed to find the right dentist with matching patient X-rays. That would be proof positive. Each person's mouth, along with the size and shape of the teeth, is unique. No two fillings are going to be exactly the same. Most teenagers have fillings. There is no telling how many parents volunteered dental records that Dr. Joe and the many volunteer dentists examined. One by one over a period of many weeks a positive match was made on most of the bodies that were dug up. When Dr. Joe found X-rays that matched the mouth of a deceased teenager, he would bring that young man's dentist in to verify his findings. The individual dentists became as important to the case as our medical examiner.

With the identifications of some of the bodies we were ready to go forward with the prosecution. We obtained indictments from the Harris County grand jury, charging Henley with six murders. We picked cases with known victims where we had a parent or both parents available to testify. With most of the six boys, we had items of clothing found on the body that the parents could testify belonged to their son.

The defendants had an absolute right to separate trials so we knew we could not try Henley and Brooks together. I would have much preferred one trial so as not to put the parents through the same ordeal again. We decided to try Henley first. I would take the lead with Assistant DA Don Lambright riding shotgun. Don and I talked constantly but he did the hard work of preparing the case for trial.

Harris County kept several grand juries going at one time. Unfortunately, one was an activist grand jury that believed it was their duty to try to correct some of the ills of society. Instead of trying to make the decision on whether to true bill or no bill the Henley and Brooks cases, this grand jury began to call members of the police department before them and then leaked statements to the press, blaming the police for the murders. The grand jury asked key police officers and the police chief to brief them on the situation with runaway teenagers in Houston (some of the victims had been runaways). Instead of emphasizing the need for parental control, they held the police responsible for the problem. The grand jury did not point to a single material fact to support their conclusion, just vague opinions in a scathing report.

Police Chief Herman Short, never one to be shy, publicly condemned the report as "silly."

I never did understand what got into the grand jury to cause them to go down this path. I tried to point out that the case was solved, the right parties were charged, no evidence was lost, and all bodies we knew of were recovered. The report was goofy. Police can't stop runaways or take irresponsible kids off the streets. They can't even take the teenagers in custody or make sure they stay at home, even after returning a runaway to his house.

It is not uncommon for a parent to kick a rebellious or delinquent kid out of the house. There are some things in our city the police and the DA can't fix; raising kids and keeping up with every teenager in town are two of those things.

After the investigation subsided, Don got the case ready for trial. With the unprecedented publicity I knew it would be difficult for Henley to get a fair trial in Harris County. Emotions ran high. The public was saturated with the blow-by-blow accounts of the torture and body counts. I believed most prospective jurors in Harris County would have such strong feelings that picking a jury would be a near impossibility. Ordinarily, I liked to try Harris County cases in Harris County; a trial elsewhere was not easy on our budget. But if publicity alone was ever a reason for a change of venue, this one needed moving. Also, a refusal to move the case might be grounds for reversal.

Elmer Wayne Henley was represented by Will Gray and Ed Pegelow. I told Will up front that if he wanted a change of venue I would consent. Later, Will told me he was not going to go for a change of venue but was going to move for a continuance. The creative Will Gray filed a motion for continuance, asking the court to delay the trial until such time as an unbiased fair jury could be picked in Harris County. I wondered to myself how many years that would take. I knew the publicity was not going to die down anytime soon. I wanted to proceed to trial as quickly as possible. The public and parents needed to get this behind them. Justice needed to go forward.

Judge Bill Hatten drew the black bean, as the case fell in his court. He was a veteran jurist with good common sense and realized the impossibility of getting a jury in Harris County. He transferred the case to Bexar County in San Antonio to Judge Preston Dial, who agreed to take the case. Judge Hatten's decision to change venue over the objection of the defense was upheld on appeal. Judge Dial wasted no time in setting the case down for the pre-trial hearings.

When we appeared at pre-trial, Gray moved for a change of venue, claiming that Henley could not get a fair trial in San Antonio due to prejudice resulting from the massive statewide publicity. Instead of giving Will a hearing on his motion, Judge Dial ruled he was going forward with jury selection in San Antonio. He told Gray that if there was a problem getting a jury seated, he would then grant Will's motion for a change of venue.

I was glad we were going to a large and most pleasant city, probably the most popular tourist spot in Texas. Judge Dial set the trial less than three months away, July 1, 1974. On that day, I walked into a courtroom jam-packed with media people, shoulder to shoulder. A reporter from Sweden and another from Japan buttonholed me at the entrance of the Bexar County Courthouse. There were so many reporters and photographers they could not fit inside the courtroom. The judge found them another courtroom where the proceedings would be broadcast live via radio. Judges did not allow televised proceedings in those days, even with consent of the lawyers. A trial is a public event with a right for anyone to attend so long as there is room to sit. The clerk sent eighty-five reporters from all over the world to the other courtroom. Media artists were allowed to stay in Judge Dial's courtroom where the jury selection and trial were to take place.

I knew the trial would take about six weeks. I wanted some privacy from the press so I rented an apartment out from town with some tennis courts. Just being in a hotel room close to the courthouse would thrust me too close to the reporters. They wouldn't leave me alone in their quest for a new story each day. Besides, I knew some good tennis players in San Antonio. My friend Judge Barrow on the Court of Civil Appeals set up some nice double's games. It didn't get dark until 9:00 and we were out of court by 5:00. On a few occasions I had dinner with my old high school buddy, Bryan Strode. This case was going to go on for weeks. I would be a better lawyer if I could escape it just a little bit in the evenings.

We were able to pick a jury in less than a week. Surprisingly not many jurors, percentage-wise, had any predisposed opinion of guilt as to Henley.

Henley stood and pled "Not guilty." Those two words would be all the jury would hear from him for the duration. The judge looked over at me and said, "Mr. Vance, make your opening statement."

WE BEGAN OUR CASE with the maps, the blow ups, the confession, the long story of the search for bodies, the body box, the torture boards, diagrams of the Pasadena house, scenes at the boat stall, the lake, and the beach at High Island. And of course, the clothing the youngsters were wearing when killed. Picking up a tee shirt and handing it to a parent on the witness stand brought tears and emotions that overwhelmed some of the parents.

Don called the dentists and the medical examiner, Dr. Joe. He proved with clarity and certainty which teenagers had died at the hands of the trio.

Six weeks later we rested our case. Will Gray, who was not about to call Henley to the stand, rested behind us. One never knows what a jury will do, but I could not imagine a not guilty in this case.

After the final summations, the jury was not out long before returning six separate ninety-nine-year prison sentences, one for each of the six murders alleged in the indictments.

Judge Dial stacked the sentences. That meant that each sentence would begin when the former was complete. As a practical matter, Henley would not be getting out for a long time, perhaps the remainder of his life.

Close to a year later Don tried David Brooks and the jury gave him a life sentence.

Will Gray appealed the conviction of Elmer Wayne and, to my surprise, the Court of Criminal Appeals reversed the San Antonio conviction. The court said that Will Gray should have been afforded his right to pursue his change of venue motion. Judge Dial denied Gray's change of venue motion because there had been one change of venue already and where else in the state would the publicity have been any less? He knew the case had to be tried in Texas. Further, the judge made it clear that if it was difficult to get a jury he would transfer the case out of San Antonio.

On appeal Will had affidavits showing there were 240 stories written about this case in San Antonio newspapers and 85 local television broadcasts on the Henley case before the trial started. One radio station alone received over 600 wire stories to be aired. Will's exhibits showed many of the news stories took up a large part of the front page.

Also, back during the trial in July, Will claimed that some of the jurors had been contacted by the press. Our Houston press corps seldom ever contacted a juror unless it was to ask for comments from a juror after the trial was over. Will asked Judge Dial to hold a private hearing where only the judge and the jurors were present. Several jurors told the judge members of the media had contacted them. The jurors rightfully refused to talk to them. Six jurors had family members contacted by newsmen. Only four jurors were left alone by the media. The jurors of course said the contact made no difference to them and would not affect their verdict, so the judge proceeded with the trial.

To make matters worse, two newspapers put an artist's sketch with at least one or more of the juror's faces on the front page of the newspaper on several occasions. That was a rare move by a newspaper and perhaps shocked the appellate court.

Five years passed between the first trial and the second trial. The murder case broke on August 8, 1973. The San Antonio trial of Henley was in July 1974 (Brooks was tried separately in 1975). The Court of Criminal Appeals did not render its opinion until January 1979. Four-and-a-half years elapsed between the jury sentence and the appellate decision.

Now we were six years out from when the story broke and with a new trial in Corpus Christi, the place the case has been sent to. We would have to track down parents, police officers who had retired, and perhaps other witnesses. My main concern was putting the poor parents back through the ordeal of trial. I have to give Will Gray credit for his diligence in representing his client. I, too, was shocked that reporters contacted jurors while they were sitting on the case.

By the second trial, Don Lambright had left the office to pursue a most successful career defending people. Doug Shaver now was our chief trial counsel and handling trials of some of our major cases. This time we would take along a third lawyer, a young but capable legal scholar by the name of Lewis Dickson, Jr. His job was to watch the record and the court rulings and not let us flirt with any chance of a reversal. We had to watch Will like a hawk. (I should add that Lewis went on to be a law partner with Dick DeGuerin. I should also point out that not too long after this case ended, Doug Shaver became a district judge, was later selected as the chief administrative judge for Harris County, and most importantly, he married Judy, my wonderful secretary.)

The Corpus Christi trial would be tried in early summer of 1979 before the Honorable Noah Kennedy, an experienced and congenial judge with the perfect temperament for this case. As it turned out, all of the parents, dentists, and evidence was still available, along with the essential police officers.

Doug would streamline the case and take all of the technical witnesses. I would take most of the fact witnesses. The trial went for about five weeks. The jury was selected with relative ease as the passage of time dimmed memories and public interest. Some of the jurors had never even heard of Dean Corll or Elmer Wayne Henley.

The press corps had died down to a small Texas contingent. Reporters and cameramen from the major networks showed up but did not stay. There were so few press people present this time that Doug and I occasionally had dinner with those from Houston. Artists were still in the courtroom, drawing their hearts out, with the body box and torture board the main subject matter. The parents were more settled, but no question this was a second ordeal none wanted or expected.

Officer David Mullican of the Pasadena Police Department once again testified how he was the first officer to make the scene and talked to Henley. He was the officer who took the detailed confession from Henley and worked on the case until it was wrapped up. He later became the chief of police for the City of Pasadena, a sizable police department. Mullican, along with several Houston homicide officers, had done excellent work in every aspect of the case.

After the parents and other witnesses had to relive these experiences again, we rested our case. Will Gray rested behind us. This time the jury found Henley guilty in short order and assessed six separate life terms for the six murders, which, for all practical purposes, was the same as the six ninety-nine-year sentences the Bexar County jury dished out.

At last the case was over. It was appealed, of course, but the appeal went our way without any serious legal challenges.

Or was it over? Perhaps the Corll-Henley-Brooks case will never really end. As late as October 3, 2008, the Houston *Chronicle* headline announced that one of the last unidentified victims had been identified at last. The young man, Randall Harvey, was shot in the head and found at the boat stall. No one was able to make a positive ID until thirty-five years later. He had been missing since March 11, 1973. His remains were found back on August 8, 1973, with the many other young men, but his body could not be identified until science came up with DNA testing. The University of North Texas Center for Human Identification made the match using DNA samples from two of his siblings. The trials may have ended, but the heartache for the families never would. Such is the case whenever one person robs another of life itself. At least those of us in the District Attorney's office could help provide a measure of justice.

Strangely enough, those weeks in Corpus were relaxing. There were no glitches in the trial. The office was running like a clock under First Assistant Holmes' capable hands, not to mention the best senior staff members and chief prosecutors a DA could have. During those first tough years on this job I had felt indispensable. No longer, and thank goodness. And thank goodness the Henley case was history as well.

As I CLOSED DOWN this chapter of my life, I realized a certain symmetry in my career. My initial job with DA Dan Walton came about after Judge Lewis Dickson called to put in a good word. Now his son, Lewis Dickson, Jr., had been an assistant DA on our three-man trial team.

I had come to the end of my journey. I exited the stairwell on the fifth floor of the courthouse and entered the 174th District Court, Judge Duggan's old courtroom where I had been sworn in. As I opened the large mahogany door, I noticed our large staff had taken up every seat. I knew my secret was out. Someone spotted me, and the men and women of the DA's office arose with a warm applause.

I was going to miss these friends.

NOTES

ACKNOWLEDGMENTS

I AM INDEBTED TO the following people for helping me with some of the details of this book and helping ensure its accuracy. Bert Graham, the late Ted Busch, Johnny Holmes, Bob Bennett, Henry Oncken, Erwin Ernst, Don Lambright, Jim Larkin, Ron Woods, Mike Hinton, Roland Dahlin, Doug Shaver, Ron Kepple, and Tommy Dunn. Any errors that remain are solely my responsibility.

My deep appreciation goes to Kit Sublett, whose editing and publishing expertise was of great benefit. I met Kit through Young Life years ago and now he is a fine publisher. He took my manuscript and shaped it into a real book. *Boomtown DA* is definitely much better for all his hard work.

And of course, I will always owe a debt of gratitude to the many friends whose work on my behalf made it possible for me to become Harris County's DA. As I look back at this near-miraculous event—considering I was a youngster with no political experience, unknown in town, and who never had an eye on this office until a few months before—becoming district attorney was beyond my wildest dreams. Credit for both the appointment and running unopposed goes one hundred percent to lifelong friends, law school friends, and to some pretty stout new friends who joined together to make this possible. From the law firms, Hugh Patterson and Bill Barnett of Baker Botts; Leon Jaworski and Johnny Crooker, Jr., of Fulbright and Jaworski; Dan Arnold and Sam Davis from Vinson Elkins; Frank Davis and Seab Eastland from Andrews Kurth; Jack Binion, Bill Wright, and Louis Paine from Butler Binion; Walter Zivley and Charlie Sapp from Liddell Sapp; childhood friend Gus Schill and Ed Vickery from Royston Rayzor; and from Bracewell where I would end up some day, old friend Bill Wilde, Searcy Bracewell, Harry Patterson, Carlton Wilde, Hal DeMoss, and Joe Jaworski. I am grateful to many others as well, like Everett Collier, Bill Hobby, Lloyd Bentsen, old friend Virgil Cammack who took me all over the Pasadena area, the legendary Clyde Wilson who took me into many executive offices, and a host of others too numerous to mention.

APPENDIX A: WHERE ARE THEY NOW?

"As iron sharpens iron, so a man sharpens the countenance of his friend."
—Proverbs 27:17

BEING AN ASSISTANT DISTRICT attorney is the greatest job in the world.

I enjoyed my experience of being in court, day in and day out, trying cases, more than any other thing I did in the practice of law. Maybe it was because it was more carefree, even in spite of the serious cases we handled. Maybe it was because I loved to pick up a file and try a case. I loved to face a really good lawyer on the other side. I loved to exchange war stories over a beer or cup of coffee. I loved to see my old friends who I know shared these wild experiences of "pick up a file and run."

I think sometimes law schools push public service but do not appreciate the value of the role the prosecutor plays in the seeking of justice within our society.

I hope this book lands in some law libraries around the nation. I hope some would-be assistants get to read it and make a decision to join a district attorney's office somewhere and share the wonderful challenges and fun experiences. And I hope they get to work in an office like I did in Houston, Texas, for bosses like I had who let you try your case, who didn't fuss at you too much if you messed up, and who appreciated your presence. Okay, I know. I've rambled too long. But I was surrounded by an outstanding staff, by lawyers who were a lot smarter than me. By the gals and guys who did the hard work while I got the credit. Before you leave this book, let me tell you where a goodly number of my staff ended up.

It is exciting to think of where the job of assistant DA can lead. Exhibit One is, "Where are they now?"

BY ANYONE'S STANDARDS HARRIS County had—and has—one of the best offices in the country. Perhaps as many as five hundred assistant district attorneys worked in the office during my tenure as District Attorney. When I started we had thirty-two assistants, when I became DA the number was fifty-five, and when I left there were 160. Today the office has about 300 assistants.

Most assistants stayed in the office less than ten years. Some stayed only the three-year minimum which we asked. Others were there for a long time, even thirty to forty years like some of the assistants named below.

Most assistants left to go practice law, many as solo practitioners, some with small firms, while others joined large firms or started their own law firms. Many practiced criminal law. Others did plaintiff or defense work over in the civil trial area.

Some went with corporations. One, Richard Anderson, who was my administrative assistant and an assistant DA, is now chief executive officer for Delta Airlines. Wherever they went they took with them some great experiences and skills, including the ability to think on their feet when the unexpected happens, how to make important decisions (sometimes quickly), how to communicate clearly, to get along with colleagues, to be adversarial but hopefully civil, and to exercise leadership skills in tense situations. No question the DA's office trained some of the best lawyers in Houston.

DISTRICT ATTORNEYS OF HARRIS COUNTY
Johnny Holmes
Chuck Rosenthal
Ken Magidson

UNITED STATES ATTORNEY FOR THE SOUTHERN DISTRICT OF TEXAS
Ed McDonough
Ron Woods
Henry Oncken
Gaynelle Jones

ELECTED TO THE U.S. CONGRESS
Mike Andrews
Greg Laughlin
Ted Poe (still serving)

TEXAS SUPREME COURT
Mike Schneider

UNITED STATES DISTRICT JUDGE
Mike Schneider (went from the Supreme Court to the Federal
   Judiciary)

TEXAS COURT OF CRIMINAL APPEALS (THE HIGHEST TEXAS COURT FOR CRIMINAL CASES)
Carl Dally
Charles Campbell

UNITED STATES MAGISTRATES
Mary Milloy
Calvin Botley

TEXAS COURT OF APPEALS JUDGES
Sam Robertson
Jon Hughes
Lee Duggan
Allen Stilley
Mike Schneider
Jimmy James
Frank Price
Tim Taft
Ross Sears

DISTRICT COURT JUDGES
Dan Walton
Fred Hooey
Erwin Ernst
Ben Woodall
Pete Moore
Lee Duggan
Joe Guarino
Jimmy James
Frank Price
Allen Stilley
Wells Stewart
I. D. McMaster
Henry Oncken
Doug Shaver
Bob Burdette
Mike McSpadden
Gerald Goodwin

Bill Harmon
John Kyles
Brian Rains
George Godwin
Mike Wilkinson

COUNTY COURT AT LAW JUDGES
Conrad Castles
Pete Moore
Neil McKay
Joe Guarino
Lee Duggan
Bob Musslewhite
Wells Stewart
Shelly Hancock
Jim Muldrow
Nick Barrera

DISTRICT ATTORNEYS IN OTHER TEXAS COUNTIES
Erwin Ernst
Ray Montgomery
Gerald Goodwin
Sam Dick
John Bradley
John Holleman
Herb Hancock
Ken Sparks

TEXAS HOUSE OF REPRESENTATIVES
C.A. "Cowboy" Davis
Lee Duggan
Willis Whatley
Joe Crabb (still serving)

Former assistants make up many of Houston's top criminal lawyers such as Rusty Hardin, Bob Bennett, Dick DeGuerin, Bill Burge (now deceased), Don Lambight, and Mike Hinton. I took two good men with me to Bracewell and Patterson from the DA's office, Mike Kuhn and my tennis playing buddy, Marc Wiegand. Both became partners.

I certainly need to recognize those who spent their professional lives in the DA's office, like Johnny Holmes, Chuck Rosenthal, Ted Busch, Bert Graham, (who served as First Assistant for three DAs; a record, I might add), Jim Larkin, Jim Moseley, Ted Wilson, Keno Henderson, Rose Kennedy, Kris Moore, Calvin Hartman, Marie Munier, Elizabeth Godwin, Ted Wilson, Russell Turbeville, Allen McAshan, Bill Taylor, Jimmy Brough, Vic Pecorino, Ira Jones, Roland Elder, Gene Miles, Terry Wilson, and others.

It was an honor to have served with such men and women.

APPENDIX B: RUNNING THE OFFICE

SOME CLOSING THOUGHTS ABOUT running the DA's office. My assistants had the freedom to talk to me like a friend and not just tell me what I wanted to hear. I will repeat what I have said elsewhere in this book: They treated me with a great respect, but a stranger standing close by would never know it listening to our conversations. The more experienced staff felt very comfortable poking at me in good-natured fun and making dry comments about my absentminded ways. We were all comfortable with each other which made our serious work much more pleasant. I never wanted a bunch of "yes men" around. The staff understood that.

The general public had no real understanding about the DA's office. The general perception was that there was a district attorney with a few assistants handling all the cases and everyone in that office would be able to discuss any pending case. I could go to a reception and a stranger would walk up and say "I'm old Frank McMann, the one that had his Buick stolen. You remember the case, I'm sure. Remember the police said they caught that guy, and he was an ex-con. When is my case coming to trial?"

Many a citizen assumed the DA was on top of every crime in the county and every case in the office. Nothing was further from the truth. With 70,000 serious cases each year, the only cases I reviewed were those involving the death penalty, public corruption, and the unusually aggravated cases. Even the chiefs in each felony court or county court could not be expected to know the details of the thousand cases pending in their courts. Sometimes they read the file the first time when his or her assistant called in sick but the trial commenced that same morning. When you get down to it, the DA is like the head coach. He gets the publicity. He gets the criticism and the praise whether it is deserved or not. The top staff members are like the assistant coaches. The ones actually playing in the game are the assistants, manning the courts or working investigations or in some other specialized department. They are the team doing most of the lawyering and making the plays. They are the heart and soul of the office.

My most fun position was being the chief in district court. As such, I headed my own little firm of three lawyers, complete with investigator and secretary. I lived in the courtroom some days and other days had time to prepare for the murder and rape trials which occupied most of my time. I also sat second chair to the assistants assigned to me just to be a good mentor. My main mentor, the great Erwin Ernst, had done the same for me.

Win-loss records, by the way, are not all that important. Trying a tough case against a great lawyer and getting a guilty verdict might be an achievement, but outcomes usually depend on facts. Lawyers don't make facts. The real lawyers like the challenge of going up against the best. You learn a great deal more losing a case against a tough opponent than winning one by running over a lawyer who doesn't know what he's doing.

So I say, if you have a chance of being an assistant DA and feel it in your heart that that is the challenge for you, go for it. Even if you enjoy a few years and move on, that is not so bad, either.

Our office had many applications for assistant district attorney on hand at any given time. We should have been able to attract good potential lawyers, and we did. Conducting individual interviews, studying résumés, checking references, and deciding who to hire took an enormous amount of time. Mistakenly, I started out my journey as DA doing a lot of the interviewing and making all of the hiring decisions myself. I hired some wonderful talent, but it took a heavy toll, time-wise. Besides, many good minds are likely to reach a more thoughtful result. So after a few years I established a hiring committee. Most large offices will have a hiring committee or some formal process.

Before I instituted a hiring committee, I hired some outstanding lawyers such as Johnny Holmes, Mike McSpadden, Ted Poe, Mike Hinton, Stu Stewart, Bill Burge, Bert Graham, Don Lambright, Ron Woods, and a host of others. Even so, the hiring committee process was the way to go. Interviewing every applicant who walked in the door was more than a full-time job.

Copying the large law firms, I started a hiring committee of seven assistants to do the interviews, the background checks, to figure out the best ways to recruit, and of course to recommend to me the top candidates in their opinion. Like a good football team the success of our office revolved around the talent we acquired.

Training is an important component of any DA's office. When I joined the DA's office and even when I became DA, the only training was of the on-the-job variety. Eventually we started providing in-house training in particular areas of the law. Later on most of the formal training our prosecutors received was done through the Texas District and County Attorneys Association and the National College of District Attorneys. Both are still the primary training arms for Texas and the nation's prosecutors. I enrolled more people in the National College for District Attorneys than any other prosecutor in the country. As this book has made clear, I believed in training and in prosecutors from around the state and country getting together and exchanging ideas.

When it came to staff promotions I undertook that task myself during my early years. With a large staff and with turnover causing many promotional decisions, I started a promotion committee that consisted of the top staff. When they discussed and distilled the process, I would follow their recommendations. If a younger guy was jumping over an older guy, I wanted to know why. We wanted the best person for the job. Seniority played a role, but if one person was clearly better than another for a promotion, he or she got the job. Good and fair decisions in the promotions process builds staff morale perhaps more than any other factor.

By the way, before I close let me say we had some fun in the office too. I played left field on the DA's office softball team and quarterbacked our flag football team in city leagues. Mike McSpadden and I won every annual State Bar convention tennis tournament we entered. My friend Bill Bonham, a well-known Houston lawyer, and I won all of the annual Houston Bar tournaments we entered. Marc Wiegand, my administrative assistant and ex-UT player, and I also won some doubles tournaments. Sports and office social occasions were numerous with office picnics, an annual Christmas party, and a gathering at a local beer hall to honor those who were leaving the office. Over the years since my departure Bert Graham has organized a golf outing twice a year at Saledo for the former and current assistants. Some of the old veterans like Jim Larkin, Bert Graham, Doug Shaver, Keno Henderson, Jack Frels, and Warren White showed up, along with younger guys who were still in the office and who hit the ball a lot farther. The outing is now called the Ted Busch Open, in honor of that unforgettable character and close friend.

I have always believed the quality of life in any law office depends in good measure upon the relationships, the friendships, and good will for each other. I found that also to be true in private practice at Bracewell and Giuliani, where I am now a "Retired Senior Partner" enjoying the social benefits more than filling out time sheets.

All said and done, it is the assistant DAs that make this office. The least I can do is dedicate this book to them and tell lawyers and prospective lawyers what an exciting job this is. Grab a file, go try a case. Where else can you do that?

APPENDIX C: OFFICE ROSTERS

1961

ORGANIZATION DISTRICT ATTORNEY'S OFFICE
AS OF AUGUST 21, 1961

ADMINISTRATIVE DIVISION

Frank Briscoe, Rm. 7)
Wallace c. Moore,Rm.6) Sta.431
Judy Wayt, Rm. 7)
Vera B. Williams,Rm.19, Sta.455

FELONY DIVISION

CDCT EDMUND B. DUGGAN, JUDGE
      Lee P. Ward, Jr., Rm. 4)
      Gus J. Zgourides, Rm. 3)Sta.455
      Jim I.Smith, Jr., Rm. 3)
      C. F. Langston, Rm. 4)

CDCT LANGSTON G. KING, JUDGE
#2   Thomas C. Dunn)
      Edward N. Shaw,Jr.)Rm.14,Sta.816
      Theodore P. Busch)
      John S. Fox)

CDCT MIRON A. LOVE, JUDGE
#3   Neil McKay Rm.17)
      David Ball Rm.16) Sta.426
      J.R. Musslewhite Rm.16)
      Frank Wilson Rm.17)

CDCT A. H. KRICHAMER, JUDGE
#4   Jon N. Hughes, Rm. 9)
      Erwin G. Ernst, Rm.10) Sta.426
      Frank B. Davis, Rm.10)
      Virgil Hart, Rm. 9)

CDCT SAM W. DAVIS, JUDGE
#5   Howell E. Stone, Rm.11)
      Robert E. Delany,Rm.12) Sta.816
      Wells Stewart, Rm.12)
      Howard Gossage, Rm.11)

      Pat Cantrell) Rm.5, Sta. 455
      Lanelle Reese)
      Bernadine Watson, Rm.18, Sta.816
      Ione Critendon, Rm.18, Sta.426

MISDEMEANOR DIVISION

      Morgan W. Redd, Screening Asst.,
      Rm. 2, Sta. 436

CCCL GEORGE E. MILLER, JUDGE
#1   James M. Shatto)
      Clyde Bracken, Jr.)Rm.1,Sta.436
      Laurence Cottingham)

CCCL BILL RAGAN, JUDGE
#2   Dan Ryan)
      Paul Filer)Rm.1,Sta. 436
      I.D. McMaster)

CCCL JIMMIE DUNCAN, JUDGE
#3   Carol S. Vance)
      Jimmy James)Rm.1, Sta. 436
      Frank Puckett)

      Victor A. Dwyer,Sr.,Rm.2)Sta.436
      Hope Williams, Rm.1)

BRIEFING DIVISION

Sam H. Robertson, Rm.13)
Carl E.F. Dally, Rm15) Sta.451
Walter A. Carr, Rm.15)
Louise Shiver, Library)

COMMERCIAL FRAUD DIVISION

Willis J. Whatley, Rm.20,Sta.423
Allen Stilley)
Rita Marie Rekieta)
Sallie Kline)Rm.19,Sta.423
Sharon Maher)
Kay Jordan)

COMPLAINT DIVISION

Donald Keith) Lobby, Sta. 451
Eula Mae Bush)

GRAND JURY DIVISION

R. H. Gallier)
Joseph M. Guarino)
Rose Marie Kennedy)
E. C. Campbell) Suite 601
R. D. Langdon) Sta. 241
Frances Clewett)
Alicia V. Williams)
Marcia Heinsohn)

JUSTICE COURT DIVISION

James T. Garrett, Suite 601,Sta.241
Gene D. Miles, Suite 601,Sta.241
Ellen Tyner)
Abel Garcia) Rm. 704, Sta.808
Bobby J. Dodson)
Larry Carroll)

JUVENILE DIVISION

Ed Moorhead) Suite 601, Sta. 241
Ronald Blask) or Sta. 608

NON-SUPPORT DIVISION

Phyllis Bell)
Ada Cronfel)
Rosa Mae Florey)Suite 401,Sta.443
Eunice Johnson)
Katherine Kimball)
K. D. Wright)Suite 401,Sta.

316

1966

OFFICE OF THE DISTRICT ATTORNEY
CAROL S. VANCE-DISTRICT ATTORNEY
ORGANIZATION ROSTER-NOV. 1, 1966

ADMINISTRATIVE DIVISION

NEIL McKAY - First Asst.
John Gilleland- Adm.Asst.Ext.431
John S. Fox - Inv. Ext. 541
Judy Wayt - Sec'y, Ext. 431
Irene Harper - Sec'y, Ext. 431
Nancy Reichle - Sec'y, Ext. 451

GRAND JURY DIVISION, Ext. 241

CONRAD CASTLES, Asst. in Chg.
Rose Marie Kennedy, Asst.
Bob Floyd, Asst.
Bill White, Asst.
Ed McDonough, Asst.
Jim Moseley, Asst.
Ray Moses, Asst.
Al Thomas, Asst.
R.D. Langdon, Investigator
Mamie Koch, Sec'y
Marcia Heinsohn, Sec'y
Dee Bitner, Sec'y
Pat Cantrell, Sec'y

REPORTERS, Ext. 447

Robert G. Watts
Thomas McCracken
George A. York
Ronald E. Reeves
Joe Offield
Bill Duncan
Joe Fred Gregg

BAIL BOND DIVISION, Ext.491

JOE NARON, Asst. in Chg.
Eunice Johnston, Sec'y

TRIAL DIVISION (FELONY)

CD (DUGGAN,JUDGE)Ext.455
I.D. McMaster,Chief Pros.
Rick Stover, Asst.
Mac Dimmitt, Asst.
Jo Ann Henley, Sec'y
R.O. Biggs, Inv.

CD#2 (ODOM,JUDGE)Ext. 816
Thomas Dunn,Chief Pros.
Joe Maida, Asst.
Andy Horne, Asst.
Carolyn Rudd, Sec'y
Claude Langston, Inv.

CD#3 (LOVE,JUDGE)Ext.426
Frank Puckett,Chief Pros.
Ted Busch, Asst.
Jim Larkin, Asst.
Carolyn Limmer,Sec'y
Eddie Campbell,Inv.

CD#4 (WALTON,JUDGE)EXT.816
Erwin Ernst,Chief Pros.
Ruben Hope, Asst.
Wells Stewart, Asst.
Carolyn Rudd, Sec'y
T.C. Jones, Inv.

CD#5 (DAVIB,JUDGE)Ext.426
Don Keith,Chief Pros.
Allen Stilley,Asst.
Shelly Hancock,Asst.
Carolyn Limmer,Sec'y
Frank Wilson, Inv.

CD#6 (HOOEY,JUDGE)Ext.455
Bob Musslewhite,Chief Pros.
Ray Montgomery,Asst.
Joe Witherspoon,Asst.
Jo Ann Henley, Sec'y
Foy Melton, Inv.

TRIAL DIVISION (MISDEMEANOR)

CC#1 (MILLER,JUDGE)
Gene Miles,Chief Pros.
Ted Hirtz, Asst.
Jimmy Phillips,Asst.

CC#2 (MOORE,JUDGE)
Frank Price,Chief Pros.
Joe Doucette, Asst.
Phil Warner, Asst.

CC#3 (DUNCAN,JUDGE)
Jimmy James,Chief Pros.
Charles Bonney,Asst.
Fred Heacock,Asst.

CC#4 (GUARINO,JUDGE)
Tom Roberson,Chief Pros.
Bob Bennett,Asst.
Vic Pecorino, Asst.

MORGAN REDD,Screening Asst; Vic Dwyer, Inv.
Mary Hagerty, Martha Mathis, Nana Henry,
Secretaries

BRIEFING DIVISION, Ext. 866

JOE MOSS, Asst. in Chg.
James Brough, Asst.
Dick DeGuerin, Asst.
Phyllis Bell, Asst.
Louise Shiver, Sec'y

COMMERCIAL FRAUD,Ext. 423

ALLEN McASHAN, Asst. in Chg
Sallie Kline, Sec'y
Rita Rekieta, Sec'y
Lorraine Wynn, Sec'y

COMPLAINT DIVISION, Ext.451

ROBERT SCOTT, Asst. in Chg.
Sis Schallert, Receptionist

NON-SUPPORT DIV. Ext. 443

ROWLAND ELDER,Asst. in Chg.
Jim Muldrow, Asst.
Virgil Hart, Inv.
Rose Florey, Sec'y
Betty McGibeny, Sec'y
Gay Bugbee, Sec'y
Katherine Kimball, Sec'y

JUVENILE DIVISION, Ext.608

MAX CARLSON, Asst. in-Chg.
Dan McCairns, Asst.
Anita Clark, Sec'y
HPD Liaison - Sgt. Strebeck
- Ext. 470

1979

JUNE 6, 1979

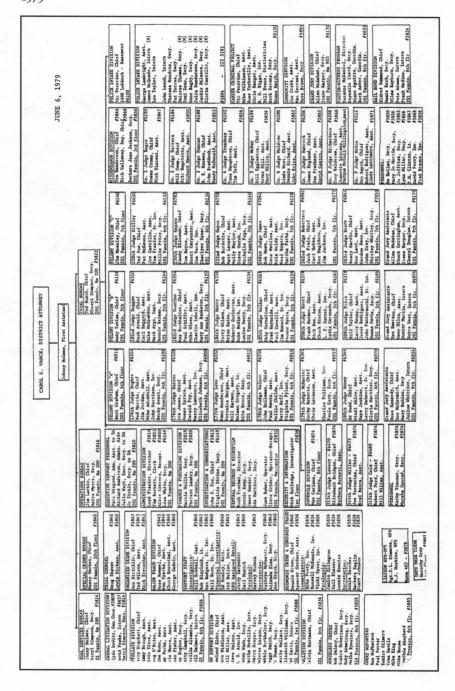

CAROL S. VANCE, DISTRICT ATTORNEY

APPENDIX D: 1976 OFFICE PORTRAIT

Attorney's
ice
County
xas
76

TRICT ATTORNEYS

SAM ROBERTSON
FIRST ASSISTANT

MACK ARNOLD   NICK BARRARA

BOB BURDETTE   BILL BURGE   K. BURKHALTER   TED BUSCH   NED C. BUTLER   DENNIS CAIN

JOHN DAVIS   DON DAWSON   BOB DELANY   CLYDE DeWITT   SAM DICK   GARY DiBELLA

J. FLATTEN   ROBERT FORD   JACK FRELS   B. GARDNER   BERT GRAHAM   J. GUERINOT

E. HAMMOND   CHRIS HANGER   RUSTY HARDIN   FRANK HARMON   K. HENDERSON   T. HENDERSON

DAVID JONES   IRA JONES   JIM JORDAN   ROSE KENNEDY   LARRY KNAPP   JIM LARKIN

D. McCORMICK   S. McINTOSH   PAUL MEWIS   D. MIDDLETON   GENE MILES   BILL MILLER

JIM MULDROW   V. MORGAN   GENE NETTLES   WENDELL ODOM   HENRY ONCKEN   VIC PECORINO

ROBERT ROSS   THOMAS ROYCE   LUPE SALINAS   P. SCHIFFER   ROBERT SHULTS   DOUG SHAVER

BILL TAYLOR   J. TERRACINA   ALVIN TITUS   ANDY TOBIAS   R. TURBEVILLE   L. URQUHART

MIKE HINTON   CARL HOBBS   J. HOLLEMAN   JOHN HOLMES   RAY HOWARD   GEO. JACOBS

MATT LEEPER   JIM LEITNER   KEN LEVI   C. LORENZEN   CHAS. MARTIN   A. McASLAN

BOB MOEN   WM.T. MOORE   NED MORRIS   STEVE MORRIS   JIM MOSELEY   JOE MOSS

F. PERRONE   TED POE   F. REYNOLDS   C. ROBERTS   ROSS ROMMEL   JIM ROSE

KEN SPARKS   STU STEWART   D. STRICKLIN   H. STRIPLING   ROBT SUSSMAN   A. STILLEY

M. WILKINSON   C. WILLIAMS   TED WILSON   TERRY WILSON   RON WOODS   M. ANDREWS

COLOPHON

DESIGN

Book designed by Whitecaps Media
Main body composed in Adobe Jenson Pro; titles composed in Hightower
Cover designed by Kit Sublett

IMAGE CREDITS

All photos courtesy of the author's private collection unless otherwise
noted. While effort has been made to determine the source of the
photos that has not always been possible.

Photos marked "Houston Chronicle" are courtesy of the newspaper; special
thanks to Alita Yu of the paper's Photo Library for her assistance

Back cover portrait courtesy of F. Carter Smith

Headlines and news articles used on the front and back covers are from the
Houston *Post*, the Houston *Press*, and the Houston *Chronicle*

About the Author

Carol Vance was elected district attorney of Harris County four times and never drew an opponent. He was honored by the National District Attorneys Association with their highest award and served as their president. During his time as DA, Carol tried twenty jury cases, perhaps an unmatched number for the nation's fourth largest city. Carol had a reputation as an excellent trial lawyer and was invited to be a fellow of the American College of Trial Lawyers.

Carol worked hard to reform the law in Texas, including his service on the committee that rewrote the Texas Penal Code. Due to his great interest in the training and professionalization of prosecutors, he was instrumental in helping start the first staff of the Texas District and County Attorneys Association and was a founder of the National College of District Attorneys.

After leaving the District Attorney's office, Carol went on to be a Senior Partner at the national law firm of Bracewell and Giuliani. He also served as Chairman of the Board of the Texas Department of Criminal Justice, which governs the Texas prison system.

Carol and his wife Carolyn have five children and fourteen grandchildren. Today Carol participates weekly in prison ministries, including teaching a course at the Carol S. Vance Prison, the nation's first prison with all-Christian programming. Occasionally he still runs into someone he prosecuted. The Vance Prison was named in his honor because he, along with Chuck Colson, Prison Fellowship, and Governor George Bush, worked to institute this faith-based prison. With its incredibly low recidivism rate the Vance unit has been the prototype for others like it around the country.